'Using a systematic comparative analytic framework, this book highlights the variation in labour movements in 13 Asian countries. The work lays bare the shortcomings of theories to adequately explain labour movements in this region. A must read for labour scholars!'

Sarosh Kuruvilla: Professor of Industrial Relations, Cornell University, USA, and Visiting Professor at the London School of Economics, UK

'This book highlights "varieties" of unions and labour movements in response to challenges in Asia, shaping the ways in which workers are organized, with fresh evidence and new theoretical perspectives. This is a must for all scholars of modern industrial relations'.

Dr Chang-Hee Lee, International Labour Organisation (ILO), Country Director for Vietnam

'This book provides a rich source of analysis of contemporary challenges and evolving perspectives on trade unions and labour movements in Asia. It represents an important and innovative contribution to the field of comparative industrial relations'.

Mia Ronnmar, Professor and Dean of Law at the University of Lund, Sweden, and President of the International Labour and Employment Relations Association (ILERA)

'The Asia-Pacific region is quite diverse in the make-up of its labour laws and labour institutions, despite geographical proximity. This book is essential reading for anyone interested in the near-term future of capitalism in the fastest growing region of the world'.

Anil Verma, Professor of Management and Former Director of the Centre for Industrial Relations and Human Resources, University of Toronto, Canada

'It is a rare edited volume that combines empirical sweep, methodological rigor and theoretical insight. This volume does that in ways that make it necessary reading for all those interested in comparative industrial relations and comparative political economy'.

Chris Howell, James Monroe Professor of Politics, Oberlin College, USA

'This book clearly shows that unions in emerging Asian economies create unique patterns of unionism distinct from Euro-American models. This book makes an important contribution to formulating a new theoretical framework that acknowledges these distinctive features'.

Dong-One Kim, Professor of Employment Relations at Korea University, South Korea

'This book provides detailed information about unions and their activities in Asia and Pacific countries using a systematic approach. It is essential reading for practitioners and scholars in order to obtain a dynamic picture of the contemporary and future developments in Asia'.

Michio Nitta, Emeritus Professor, Institute of Social Sciences, University of Tokyo, Japan

'Using a consistent framework, this book examines labor movements in thirteen Asia-Pacific countries. It provides great detail on labor market structures, labor politics and union strategies. It is a "must read" for employment relations scholars across the globe'.

Peter Berg, Professor of Employment Relations, Michigan State University, USA

Trade Unions and Labour Movements in the Asia-Pacific Region

Recent developments in the world economy, including deindustrialisation and the digital revolution, have led to an increasingly individualistic relationship between workers and employers, which in turn has weakened labour movements and worker representation. However, this process is not universal, including in some countries of Asia, where trade unions are closely aligned with the interests of the dominant political party and the state. This book considers the many challenges facing trade unions and worker representation in a wide range of Asian countries. For each country, full background is given on how trade unions and other forms of worker representation have arisen. Key questions then considered include the challenges facing trade unions and worker representation in each country, the extent to which these are a result of global or local developments and the actions being taken by trade unions and worker representative bodies to cope with the challenges.

Byoung-Hoon Lee is a professor at the Department of Sociology, Chung-Ang University. He received his Ph.D. at the Industrial and Labour Relations School, Cornell University. He previously worked as a research fellow at the Korea Labour Institute. He undertook presidential positions in various organisations, such as Korea Labour & Employment Relations Association, Labour Administration Reform Commission and Fair Labour Commission of People's Solidarity for Participatory Democracy. At present, he is the chairman of Public Workers Solidarity Foundation. He was a co-editor of a special volume of *Journal of Industrial Relations* concerning Varieties of Labour Movements in the Asia-Pacific region. He is recently working on labour and worker solidarity, precarious workers and labour market segmentation, informality of employment relations, the impact of digital revolution on working life and labour history in Korea.

Sek-Hong Ng graduated from the University of Hong Kong and undertook postgraduate studies in industrial sociology and industrial relations at the London School of Economics and Political Sciences, where he completed his doctoral thesis under the supervision of Professor Keith Thurley. He returned to Hong Kong and joined the University of Hong Kong in the Department of Management Studies, later the School of Business. He is currently an honorary professor with the Faculty of Business and Economics at the University of Hong Kong. He writes in the areas of employment and labour relations, trade unions and labour law. He is currently working on the study of labour law in the People's Republic of China as well as an occupational study on workers' expectations and alienation in Hong Kong.

Russell D. Lansbury is Emeritus Professor of Employment Relations at the University of Sydney Business School where he was also associate dean (research) and a head of department. He gained a PhD in Industrial Relations from the London School of Economics and has been awarded honorary doctorates by Lulea Technical University in Sweden and Macquarie University in Australia. He was a senior fulbright fellow at MIT and Harvard University as well as a visiting fellow at the Swedish National Institute for Worklife Research. He has been a Shaw Foundation Visiting Professor at Nanyang Technological University in Singapore. He is a joint editor of *International and Comparative Employment Relations* (Sage Books) now in its sixth edition. His research has focused on comparative employment relations in various industry sectors including auto manufacturing, banking and mining.

Routledge Studies in the Growth Economies of Asia

136 The Diffusion of Western Economic Ideas in East Asia
Edited by Malcolm Warner

137 Employers' Associations in Asia
Employer Collective Action
Edited by John Benson, Ying Zhu and Howard Gospel

138 Business Leaders and Leadership in Asia
Ying Zhu, Shuang Ren, Ngan Collins and Malcolm Warner

139 Innovation, Investment and Intellectual Property in South Korea
Park to Park
Ruth Taplin

140 A Microcredit Alternative in South Asia
Akhuwat's Experiment
Shahrukh Rafi Khan and Natasha Ansari

141 Development Agenda and Donor Influence in South Asia
Bangladesh's Experiences in the PRSP Regime
Mohammad Mizanur Rahman

142 How China's Silk Road Initiative is Changing the Global Economic Landscape
Edited by Yuan Li and Markus Taube

143 Trade Unions and Labour Movements in the Asia-Pacific Region
Edited by Byoung-Hoon Lee, Sek-Hong Ng and Russell D. Lansbury

For more information about this series, please visit: https://www.routledge.com

Trade Unions and Labour Movements in the Asia-Pacific Region

Edited by
Byoung-Hoon Lee, Sek-Hong Ng
and Russell D. Lansbury

Routledge
Taylor & Francis Group
LONDON AND NEW YORK

First published 2020
by Routledge
2 Park Square, Milton Park, Abingdon, Oxon OX14 4RN

and by Routledge
605 Third Avenue, New York, NY 10017

First issued in paperback 2021

Routledge is an imprint of the Taylor & Francis Group, an informa business

British Library Cataloguing-in-Publication Data
A catalogue record for this book is available from the British Library

Library of Congress Cataloging-in-Publication Data
A catalog record has been requested for this book

ISBN 13: 978-0-367-77713-5 (pbk)
ISBN 13: 978-0-367-19049-1 (hbk)

Typeset in Times New Roman
by codeMantra

Contents

Figures

Tables

Contributors

Chew Soon Beng is an Adjunct Professor of the Nanyang Centre for Public Administration and Senior Fellow at the Rajaratnam School of International Studies at the Nanyang Technological University, Singapore. He received his Ph.D. from the University of Western Ontario, Canada. He has authored *Small Firms in Singapore* (Oxford University Press), *Trade Unionism in Singapore* (McGraw Hill), *Employment-Driven Industrial Relations Regimes* (Avebury), *Values and Lifestyles of Young Singaporeans* (Prentice-Hall), *Foreign Enterprises in China: Operation and Management* (in Chinese) and *Public Policy in Labour Markets* (World Scientific). He has also published in multiple journals. His current research interests include union social responsibility and strategic collective bargaining.

Ngan Collins is an associate professor in the School of Management, RMIT University, Australia. She holds a Ph.D. from the University of Melbourne. She has researched and published widely on industrial relations and HRM in Asian emerging economies, focusing on Vietnam. Her book *Economic Reform and Employment Relations in Vietnam* (Routledge, 2009), was the first in-depth research on Vietnam's employment relations. It has been used as a key material for research and teaching on Vietnam's employment relations and human resource management in many universities and International Labour Organisation programmes. Her most recent co-authored book is *Business Leaders and Leadership in Asia* (Routledge, 2018).

Fang Lee Cooke, Professor of Human Resource Management (HRM) and Asia Studies at Monash Business School, Monash University, Australia. Previously, she was a full professor (since 2005) at Manchester Business School, University of Manchester, UK. Her research interests are in the area of employment relations, gender studies, diversity management, strategic HRM, knowledge management and innovation, outsourcing, international HRM, employment of Chinese migrants and HRM in the care sector.

Rae Cooper is a professor and associate dean (programmes) in the University of Sydney Business School. She is co-director of the School's Women, Work and Leadership Research Group and an associate editor of the *Journal of Industrial Relations*. She is co-author of the leading textbook,

Employment Relations: Theory and Practice. She is now working on three major research projects: the future of women's work; women's work in non-traditional occupations and pathways to non-executive directorships. In addition to her academic roles, she has been a non-executive director on public sector boards and has played a leadership role in several organisations in the women's policy area.

Bradon Ellem is a Professor of Employment Relations in the University of Sydney Business School. Since 2006, he has been a co-editor-in-chief of the *Journal of Industrial Relations*. He is a senior honorary research fellow in the University of Western Australia Business School. His research now mostly concentrates on the geography of employment relations in resources. His history of employment relations in the iron ore industry, *The Pilbara: From the Deserts Profits Come*, was published by UWA Publishing in 2017.

Michele Ford is Professor of Southeast Asian Studies and Director of the Sydney Southeast Asia Centre at the University of Sydney. Her research focuses Southeast Asian labour movements, labour relations in global production networks and trade union aid. She is the author of *Workers and Intellectuals: NGOs, Trade Unions and the Indonesian Labour Movement* (NUS/Hawaii/KITLV, 2009) and *From Migrant to Worker: Global Unions and Temporary Labor Migration in Asia* (Cornell ILR Press, 2019). She is also editor of *Social Activism in Southeast Asia* (Routledge, 2013) and the co-editor of several volumes including *Beyond Oligarchy: Wealth, Power, and Contemporary Indonesian Politics* (Cornell SEAP, 2014).

Katsuyuki Kubo is a Professor of Business Economics at Waseda University. He received his B.A. and M.A. from Keio University, and a Ph.D. from the London School of Economics. After serving as a lecturer at the Hitotsubashi University, he took up his present position, where he teaches and undertakes research in the areas of compensation, corporate governance, corporate finance and organisational economics. He has published articles on corporate governance in journals such as *Corporate Governance: An international Review*, *Japanese Economic Review* and *Journal of the Japanese and International Economies*.

Russell D. Lansbury is Emeritus Professor of Employment Relations at the University of Sydney Business School where he was associate dean (Research) and a head of department. He gained a Ph.D. in Industrial Relations from the London School of Economics. He was a senior fulbright fellow at MIT and Harvard University as well as a visiting fellow at the Swedish National Institute for Worklife Research. He is a joint editor of *International and Comparative Employment Relations* (Sage Books) now in its sixth edition. His research has focused on comparative employment relations in various industry sectors including auto manufacturing, banking and mining

Byoung-Hoon Lee is a professor at the Department of Sociology, Chung-Ang University. He received his Ph.D. at Industrial and Labour Relations

School, Cornell University and previously worked at the Korea Labour Institute. He was a co-editor of a special volume of *Journal of Industrial Relations* concerning Varieties of Labour Movements in the Asia-Pacific region. In recent years, he has published journal papers and book chapters on labour and worker solidarity, precarious workers and labour market segmentation, the impact of digital revolution on working life and labour union movements in South Korea.

Sek-Hong Ng graduated from the University of Hong Kong and undertook postgraduate studies in industrial sociology and industrial relations at the London School of Economics and Political Sciences, where he completed his doctoral thesis under the supervision of Professor Keith Thurley. He returned to Hong Kong and joined the University of Hong Kong in the Department of Management Studies, later the School of Business. He is now an honorary professor with the Faculty of Business and Economics of this University. He writes in the area of employment and labour relations, trade unions and labour law. He is now working on the study of labour law in the People's Republic of China as well as an occupational study on workers' expectations and alienation in Hong Kong.

Rene E. Ofreneo is Professor Emeritus of the University of the Philippines and served as Dean of the University's School of Labor and Industrial Relations three times. He served as DOLE Undersecretary for Labor Relations in 1997–1998, at the height of the Asian financial crisis. He helped settle major national strikes during this period and facilitated the registration of more than hundred unions. He has written extensively on agrarian and economic issues in the Philippines and Asia-Pacific. He is an advocate of green economy and social protection for all.

Shih-wei Pan is an associate professor at the Department of Labour Relations, Chinese Culture University in Taiwan. He received his Ph.D. at the Industrial and Labor Relations School, Cornell University. Earlier before his academic training, he held various union career in Taiwan's local, national unions and was involved in the activities of International Metalworkers' Federation and as the Executive Board Member of the ICFTU. His academic career in Chinese Culture University led to his involvement in labour policy and legislation-making and was consulted by government. In 2007, he was invited by Ma In-Jeou as the chief labour policymaker for his national presidential campaign. In 2008, Ma's new government appointed him as the Vice Minister of Labour and later in 2012 as the Labour Minister. He founded Ethical Management Consulting Inc. in 2018 and currently is providing his expertise on labour relations and sustainable development for the global footwear maker Pou Chen Group.

Rahul Suresh Sapkal is Assistant Professor of Economics at Maharashtra National Law University Mumbai. He holds a Ph.D. in Law and Economics from the European Doctorate Program in Law and Economics (conducted by Erasmus University Rotterdam, The Netherlands; University of Bologna, Italy; and University of Hamburg, Germany). He is a visiting research fellow at Rotterdam Institute of Law and Economics, The Netherlands, for the academic year 2018–2019. He has worked as a researcher with CORD-UNICEF; International Labor Organization, New Delhi; and Tata Institute of Social Sciences, Mumbai. He is a member of governing board of Workers Solidarity Network of Action Aid (India).

K.R. Shyam Sundar is a professor, Human Resources Management Area, at XLRI, Xavier School of Management, Jamshedpur, India. He holds a Ph.D. in Economics from Mumbai University. He has published over sixty research articles and book reviews in journals, authored ten books and edited three books in the fields of Industrial Relations and Labour Economics. He has undertaken projects for the ILO, the European Union and other international organisations. He is the member of several editorial boards of leading academic journals including the *Indian Journal of Labour Economics.*

Ryan Tan Hin Tuan is a research associate with the Economics Growth Centre, Nanyang Technological University, Singapore. He earned his M.Sc. (Applied Economics) from the Nanyang Technological University, Singapore, and his B.Sc. (Computer Science) from the University of British Columbia, Canada. He is a certified project manager (US, Singapore) with 20 years of professional experience in the public and private sectors in Singapore. Over the past few years, he has conducted training programmes on Public Policy in Singapore for senior officials from ASEAN countries.

Peter Wad is Associate Professor Emeritus at the Copenhagen Business School (CBS), Denmark. He graduated from Copenhagen University in 1979 with an M.Sc. (research) in Cultural Sociology and has been studying Malaysian trade unionism since 1983. He joined CBS as a full-time research associate professor in 1995 and was appointed associate professor in 2002. He has published extensively in anthologies on labour issues including Trade Unions and the New Industrialisation of the Third World (1988); Labour in Southeast Asia (2004); Global Unions (2007) and in international journals including *The Journal of Industrial Relations, Geoforum* and *The Nordic Journal of Working Life Studies.* His research has focused on trade unionism in East and Southeast Asia and more particularly on automotive workers' unions, including a chapter in *Cars, Automobility and Development in East Asia* (2017).

Thunyalak Weerasombat, is an assistant professor at the Department of Labour and Welfare Management, Faculty of Social Administration, Thammasat University in Bangkok. She received B.A. from Thammasat, an M.A. from National Institute of Development Administration (NIDA) and a Ph.D. from Australian School of Business, the University of New South Wales (UNSW) in 2011. Her areas of interest include labour management and skill development. Her recent research is on labour management in Thai automobile suppliers.

Foreword

Harry C. Katz, Jack Sheinkman Professor and Director of
the Scheinman Institute on Conflict Resolution,
ILR School, Cornell University

This volume provides an insightful examination of the recent evolution of employment relations in thirteen countries in the Asia-Pacific region. Its findings will be of interest to academics and practitioners alike. Using a consistent framework, the country chapters are broad in scope and include analysis of union revitalisation strategies and labour politics.

Developments in each of the thirteen countries are interesting in their own right. Together the chapters provide a welcome counterpart to previous employment relations research which has unduly focused on developments in Europe and North America. Employment relations in the thirteen countries are deserving of attention in part because of the economic vitality of the Asian-Pacific region. The co-editors remind us that this region has averaged annual economic growth of 7.6% from 2007 to 2017 and the region has the lowest unemployment rate in the world.

Employment relations in the Asia-Pacific region have several noteworthy characteristics. With a few country exceptions, independent unionism is rather weak and even where it was historically strong, as in Australia, union strength and membership has declined much in recent years. The country chapters show that this weakness, in part, derives as a consequence of the presence of dominating states. Union weakness is also propelled by the large share of the workforce in the region who work in the informal sector. Furthermore, the recent spread of both non-regular employment and the fragmented nature of work in the formal sector have further weakened unions. Yet, even in the face of historical union weakness, the country chapters highlight the variety of union revitalisation that is growing in the region.

An interesting aspect of union revitalisation is how it often links with, and draws strength from, the activities of non-governmental organisations (NGOs) and other civil society organisations. The importance of these links should come as no surprise as this trend is widespread in other regions of the world. This volume does suggest that these links may be particularly deep in the Asia-Pacific region, and in this way, developments in this region may be leading other regions. The strong ties that are emerging between unions and other forms of collective action may spring from the historical weaknesses within independent labour movements and state resistance to union activity which is common to many Asia-Pacific countries. Nonetheless, the growth in forms of collective action that are not based in unions and/or collective bargaining is not surprising, given the inherent desire within the workforce to use collective action of one sort or another to influence employment conditions, which has long been argued by the field of industrial relations.

I learned much from reading this volume and I bet you will too. Enjoy the read!

Acknowledgements

We wish to acknowledge the support from the Brain Korea 21 Team of Sociology Department, Chung Ang University, for hosting a workshop for contributing authors in Seoul in 2018. We thank Jimin Gim for her significant role in organising the workshop as well as preparation of the manuscript and liaison with the authors and publisher. Pham Thi Chung also provided valuable assistance with the process of obtaining reviews of the chapters for this book and liaising with authors.

We are grateful to the following academics and country experts who reviewed draft chapters and provided valuable feedback to the authors and the editors:

Janis Bailey, Griffith University, Australia
William Brown, Cambridge University, UK
Chaturong Napathorn, Thammasat University, Thailand
Cheng Chih-yu, National Chengchi University, Taiwan
Vicki Chrinis, University of Wollongong, Australia
Hyunji Kwon, Seoul National University, South Korea
Lae Dilokvidhyarat, Chulalongkorn University, Thailand
Lim Chong Yah, Nanyang Technological University, Singapore
Joseph Anthony Lim, University of the Philippines, Philippines
Mitsuharu Miyamoto, Senshu University, Japan
Praveen Jha, Center for Economic Studies and Planning, Jawaharlal Nehru University, India
Debi Saini, Human Resource Management Area, MDI, India
Martin Sirait, University of Malaysia, Malaysia
Pauline Stanton, RMIT University, Australia
Hiromasa Suzuki, Waseda University, Japan
Patricia Todd, University of Western Australia, Australia
Malcolm Warner, Cambridge University, UK
David Wan, Singapore University of Social Sciences
Chris F. Wright, University of Sydney, Australia
Wu Yu-jen, National Chung Cheng University, Taiwan
Xuebing Cao, Keele University, UK
Ying Zhu, University of South Australia, Australia

Abbreviations

1MDB	1 Malaysia Development Berhad
ACFTU	The All-China Federation of Trade Unions
ACTU	Australian Council of Trade Unions
ADB	Asian Development Back
AFL-CLO	American Federation of Labor and Congress of Industrial Organisations
AFTA ASEAN	Free Trade Area
ALP	Australian Labor Party
ALSOE	Administrative Law of State-Owned Enterprise
ANM	Action Network for Migrants
APEC	Asia-Pacific Economic Co-operation
APHEDA	International Union Aid Organization of the Australian Council of Trade Unions
APRO	Asia Pacific Regional Organisation
ASEAN	Association of Southeast Asian Nations
ATN	Anti-Human Trafficking Network in Thailand
AWAs	Australian Workplace Agreements
BATU	the Asian Brotherhood of Trade Unions
BEPEZ	EPZ in Bataan
BEST	Basic Education for Skills Training
BJP	Bharatiya Janata Party
BMS	Bhartiya Mazdoor Sangh
BN	National Front (Barisan Nasional)
BOP	Balance of Payments
BPS	Badan Pusat Statistik (Indonesian Statistics Bureau)
BTI	Bertelsmann Stiftung's Transformation Index
BTUC	The British Trade Union Congress
BWM	Bonded Warehousing Manufacturing
CA	Collective Agreement
CB	Central Bank
CBAs	Collective Bargaining and Agreements
CBOs	Community-Based Organisations
CBPOP	Centre for BPO Professionals

CC-BPO	Call Center – Business Process Outsourcing
CCP	Chinese Communist Party
CFE	Committee of Future Economy
CIR	Court of Industrial Relations
CITU	Centre for Indian Trade Unions
CMEs	Coordinated Market Economies
COEs	Cooperative Owned Enterprises
CPA	Communist Party of Australia
CPE	Comparative Political Economies
CPF	Central Provident Fund
CSC	Committee on Singapore's Competitiveness
CSOs	Civil Society Organisations
CSR	Corporate Social Responsibility
CTUOs	Central Trade Union Organisations
CWA	Collective Working Agreement
DOLISA	Department of Labour, Invalids and Social Affairs
DPEs	Domestic Private Enterprises
DPP	Democratic Progressive Party
EC	Economic Committee
ECOP	Employer Confederation of the Philippines
EIEUs	Electronic Industry Employees Unions
EIWU	Electrical Industry Workers' Union
EOI	Export-Oriented Industrial
EPZs	Export-Processing Zones
ER	Employee Relations
EU	European Union
FDI	Foreign Direct Investment
FGDs	Focus Group Discussions
FITE	Forum for IT Employees
FKTU	Federation of Korean Trade Unions
FOEs	Foreign-Owned Enterprises
FOF	Federacion Obrera de Filipinas
FSPMI	Federations of Indonesian Metalworkers Unions (Federasi Serikat Pekerja Metal Indonesia)
FTU	Hong Kong Federation of Trade Unions
FWS	Flexible Wage System
GCKTU	General Council of Korean Trade Unions
GDP	Gross Domestic Product
GFAs	Global Framework Agreements
GFKTU	General Federation of Korean Trade Unions
GLICs	Government-Linked Investment Companies
GLSs	Government-Linked Sector
GSO	General Statistic Office
GUFs	Global Union Federations
HCMC	Ho Chi Minh City

HMEs	Hierarchical Market Economies
HRM	Human Resource Management
HSU	Hope Solidarity Union
ICFTU	the International Confederation of Free Trade Unions
IHD	Institute for Human Development
ILC	Indian Labour Conference
ILERA	the International Labour and Employment Relations Association
ILMS	Institute of Labour and Manpower Studies
ILO	International Labour Organisation
INTUC	Indian National Congress and its labour wing Indian National Trade Union Congress
IR	Internal Relationships
IRS	Industrial Relations System
ISI	Import-Substituting Industrialisation
IT	Internet Technology
ITF	International Federation of Transport Workers' Unions
ITUC	International Trade Union Congress
IUF	International Union of Food, Agricultural, Hotel, Restaurant, Catering, Tobacco and Allied Workers' Associations
IWW	Industrial Workers of the World
JCCs	Joint Consultation Committees
JIT	Just-In-Time
JLMC	Joint Labor–Management Committee
JSPS	Japan Society for Promotion of Science
JTUC	Rengo (Japan Trade Union Confederation)
KCTU	Korea Confederation of Trade Unions
KCWU	Korea Construction Workers Union
KFIU	Korea Finance Industry Union
KHMWU	Korea Health and Medical Workers Union
KITU	Karnataka State IT/ITES Employees Union
KLI	Korea Labour Institute
KLUC	Korean Labour Union Confederation
KMT	Kuomintang
KMWU	Korea Metal Workers Union
KSBSI	Confederation of Indonesian Prosperous Labour Unions (Konfederasi Serikat Buruh Sejahtera Indonesia)
KSPI	Confederation of Indonesian Trade Unions (Konfederasi Serikat Pekerja Indonesia)
KSPSI	Confederation of All-Indonesian Workers Unions (Konfederasi Serikat Pekerja Seluruh Indonesia)
KTIWU	Korea Taxi Industry Workers Union
KTUC	Korean Trade Union Congress

KTWU	Korea Transport Workers Union
LAB	Labour Advisory Board
LDG	Liberalisation, Disinvestment and Globalisation
LIEO	Labour-Intensive Export-Oriented
LMCs	Labour-Management Committees
LMEs	Liberal Market Economies
LPN	Labour Rights Promotion Network Foundation
LTs	Lau Tuan (Labour Advocacy Groups)
LUA	Labour Union Act
MAOWW	Malaysian Association of Working Women
MCWIE	Magna Carta for Workers in the Informal Economy
MERALCO	Manila Electric Company
MHR RTU	Ministry of Human Resources Registrar of Trade Unions
MNCs	Multinational Corporations
MOL	Ministry of Labor
MOLISA	Ministry of Labour, Invalids and Social Affairs
MPBI	Indonesian Labour Council (Majelis Pekerja Buruh Indonesia)
MTUC	Malaysian Trades Union Congress
MWG	Migrant Working Group
MWP	Malaysian Workers' Party
NATO	North Atlantic Treaty Organization
NATU	National Association of Trade Unions
NBSC	National Bureau of Statistics of China
NCMB	National Conciliation and Mediation Board
NDA	National Democratic Alliance
NGOs	Non-Governmental Organisations
NIEs	Newly Industrialising Economies
NLRC	National Labor Relations Commission
NPMO	National Platform for Mass Organisations
NPTWU	National Public and Transport Workers Union
NTUC	National Trades Union Congress
NTUI	National Trade Union Initiative
NUBE	National Union of Bank Employees
NUMU	National Union of Media Workers
NUPW	National Union of Plantation Workers
NWC	The National Wages Council
OCWs	Overseas Contract Workers
OECD	Organisation for Economic Co-operation and Development
OFWs	Overseas Filipino Workers
OSHCs	Occupational Safety and Health Committees
OSHCs	Occupational Safety and Health
PAFLU	Philippine Association of Free Labor Unions

PAP	Peoples' Action Party
PCCI	Philippine Chamber of Commerce and Industry
PE	Private Equity
PH	Oppositional Political Alliance ('Alliance of Hope')
PKS	Prosperous Justice Party (Partai Keadilan Sejahtera)
PM	Peninsular Malaysia
PMEs	Professionals, Managers and Executives
POs	People's Organisations
PRC	People's Republic of China
PRK	People's Justice Party (PKR)
PRM	Malaysian People's Party
PSI	Public Services International
PTTI	Postal, Telegraph and Telecommunication International
PWM	Progressive Wage Model
QF	Qualification Framework
RENGO-RIALS	Rengo-Research Institute for Advancement of Living Standards
RM	Malaysian Ringgit (the currency of the country. Also known as MYR)
ROC	Republic of China
RTU	Registrar of Trade Unions
SALs	Structural Adjustment Loans
SAM	Friends of the Earth Malaysia
SAP	Structural Adjustment Program
SAR	Special Administrative Region
SATU	Singapore Association of Trade Unions
SDGs	Strategic Development Goals
SDGs	Sustainable Development Goals
SEWA	Self Employed Women's Association
SHGs	Self-help Groups
SMU	Social Movement Unionism
SOE	State-Owned Enterprises
SRP	Skills Redevelopment Programme
STUC	Singapore Trades Union Congress
TADM	Tripartite Alliance for Dispute Management
TAFEP	Tripartite Alliance for Fair and Progressive Employment Practices
TAL	Tripartite Alliance Limited
TFAU	Taoyuan Flight Attendants Union
TLSC	Thai Labour Solidarity Committee
TMFUG	Thai and Migrant Fisher Union Group
TPP	Trans-Pacific Partnership Agreement
TUC	Hong Kong and Kowloon Trades Union Council
TUCP	Trade Union Congress of the Philippines

UA ZENSEN	The Japanese Federation of Textile, Chemical, Food, Commercial, Service and General Workers' Unions
UAG	Unions Area Group
UIF	Union Impresores de Filipinas
UK	United Kingdom
UMNO	United Malays National Organization
UNI	Union Network International
UNITES	Union for Information Technology Enabled Services Professionals
UOD	Union Obrera Democratica
USA	United States of America
USSR	Union of Soviet Socialist Republics
UTF	Union del Trabajo de Filipinas
UWOs	Unorganised Workers' Organisations
VCA	Vietnam Cooperatives Alliance
VCCI	Vietnam Chamber of Commerce and Industry
VCP	Vietnam Communist Party
VGCL	Vietnamese General Confederation of Labour
VoC	Varieties of Capitalism
VoU	Varieties of Unionism
WB	World Bank
WBITSA	West Bengal Information Technology Services Association
WCL	World Congress of Labour
WIEGO	Women Informal Employment: Globalising and Organising
WTO	World Trade Organisation

Part 1

Introduction

1 Refining varieties of unions and labour movements

Perspectives from the Asia-Pacific region

Russell D. Lansbury, Byoung-Hoon Lee and Sek-Hong Ng

Trade unions and labour movements in many countries within the Asia-Pacific region are confronted with critical challenges, derived mainly from global socio-economic trends, including post-industrialisation and digital revolution which are transforming the world around us. Globalisation, which may be characterised as a process of increasing worldwide interconnectedness across national boundaries, has led to a significant shift in the power relations between employers and workers (Bamber et al. 2016, Buchholz et al. 2009). Within the globalising environment, employers have been able to impose greater market risks and labour flexibility on their employees, resulting in an asymmetric labour-management relationship (Baccaro and Howell 2011, Hyman 2007). Neoliberal policies have also weakened the collectivist identity of working people and have strengthened attempts by employers and governments to individualise the post-industrial employment relationship (Peetz 2010). These structural transformations have contributed to the growing social inequality and rendered working people's lives more vulnerable throughout the world (Applebaum et al. 2010). The weakening of labour movements, particularly trade unions, has been a consequence of these global trends.

Labour movements, which protected and enhanced working people's lives during the earlier era of industrialisation, have been exposed to a variety of internal problems in the era of globalising post-industrialisation. However, five phenomena that Rose (1993) identified as core problems facing labour unions more than two decades ago remain relevant to the current situation in many countries, including those in the Asia-Pacific region, namely:

- Contraction – as union membership continues to decline;
- Pacification – as unions' collective action, including strikes, has decreased;
- De-institutionalisation – as unions' legal rights have been further restricted;
- Exclusion – as unions increasingly are excluded from workplace governance and the state's policymaking processes;
- Demoralisation – as unions' societal credibility and public image have been eroded.

Unions have also suffered from 'institutional sclerosis', as their bureaucratised operations have not dealt effectively with radically changing environments (Pocock 1998). In addition, unions are criticised for narrowing their representational protection to 'insiders' (members) and excluding unorganised 'outsiders', thereby creating a crisis of solidarity in labour movements. As a consequence, some unions have metamorphised into a self-interested weapon of organised workers groups, rather than providing a democratic voice for the entire working class and being a 'sword of justice' (Lee 2011). However, while unionisation appears to be in retreat in its traditional heartland of Europe and the Americas, the number of union members has been growing in some regions of the world such as South Asia. Furthermore, unionisation has also been increasing in some industries such as professional football players' associations around the world, including Asia (Dabscheck 2017).

Varieties of unions and labour movements

The attenuation of labour movements is not uniform across the world. As the 'varieties of capitalism' (VoC) perspective indicates, the impact of globalisation on labour markets and working people's lives varies across countries, since it is filtered by different institutional foundations of national political economies (Hall and Soskice 2001). For instance, globalisation appears to have had a more damaging effect on unions in liberal market economies (e.g., the United States and the United Kingdom) than their counterparts in some coordinated market economies (e.g., Germany and the Nordic countries; Thelen 2001). The intensity and concrete forms of challenges, posed to labour movements by mega-trends, vary across countries and are influenced by both the context of national institutional foundations and the historical traditions of unionism and worker activism in each country. Hence, many unions have developed and implemented diverse strategies in order to cope with crises arising from various external challenges and internal problems, as they seek to revitalise labour movements. Frege and Kelly (2003) identify six strategies for the revitalisation of the labour movement in the current global economy, namely: organising, labour-management partnership, political action, reform of union structures, coalition-building and international solidarity. Comparing five Western countries, they argue that renewal strategies adopted by unions vary in accordance with the differing political economy models of institutional arrangements which exist (Frege and Kelly 2003).

The 'varieties of unionism' (VoU) perspective has both academic and practical relevance to the strategic choices regarding labour movement revitalisation. However, this perspective also has limitations. Like the 'VoC' typologies, which are largely focused on the advanced market economies, the 'VoU' perspective is primarily based on the situation and experiences of unions in Western developed countries. Thus, it is debatable whether either the 'VoU' or 'VoC' perspectives can be applied to the different contexts of developing countries and state-led economies. Wright et al. (2017) have noted the limitations of the 'varieties' approach when comparing either national systems or union movements and argued for the a novel multi-scaled analytical framework which would take into account the influence of the institutional dynamics of industrial sectors and global production networks as well as national systems. This approach would look beyond the VoC and VoU perspectives to embrace a more dynamic and diverse array of regulatory systems, including the gig economy and other developments in the world of work and employment relations.

Currently, the capitalist market economic system is dominant, with only a few exceptions. Globalisation accelerated after the fall of the Socialist Bloc in the late 1980s and fostered the integration of non-Western countries into the world market. However, there exist greater varieties of capitalist market economies than the VoC literature assumes. Although many non-Western countries embrace the common governing logic and institutional foundations of the capitalist market economy, the concrete forms and features of their market economies not only differ from the Western advanced countries but are also heterogeneous. They vary in accordance with their historical trajectory, their levels of industrialisation and economic development, the nature of their political regimes, the extent of democratisation, sociocultural traditions and ethnic composition. Hence, labour movements in non-Western countries have distinctive socio-economic status in their relationships with the state, labour-capital power balance and their labour market structures, which are different from most Western advanced countries. In many developing economies, labour movements are often a junior partner of the authoritarian state and are subject to exploitative anti-labour practices imposed by foreign capital or state-business coalitions. They also have to deal with pre-modern issues derived from the extensive presence of the informal labour market. Confronted with the common threats of globalisation, which can render working people's lives vulnerable, unions and collective workers groups in the non-Western countries have tried to revitalise their labour movements like their counterparts in the Western advanced countries However, labour movements take different approaches which reflect their distinctive national contexts.

This volume aims to broaden a research horizon of the 'VoU' perspective, by comparing labour movements of thirteen countries in the Asia-Pacific region. In geographical terms, six countries in our volume are located in Southeast Asia: Indonesia, Malaysia, the Philippines, Thailand, Vietnam and Singapore. Five countries are in East Asia: China, Hong Kong, Taiwan, Japan and South Korea. India represents South Asia and Australia the Pacific. The Asia-Pacific region has become an engine of global economic growth and includes very diverse ethnic, sociocultural and economic communities. The thirteen countries in this volume reflect the great diversity of the Asia-Pacific region in many respects: China and India are the two giant developing economies. Since the Deng Xiaoping era, China has been transformed from a socialist economy into a state-led market economy, still under government restrictions, but with a vigorous form of Chinese-style capitalism. By contrast, India has followed a long tradition of quasi-democratic socialism, particularly under the Congress Party when it was led by Indira Gandhi, but has changed to Bharatiya Janata Party (BJP)-led governments, in recent times, without experiencing major political unrest. Vietnam is one of the most populous countries in the region and is following a similar but different path to China in terms of a state-led market economy. Hong Kong and Taiwan are both in the shadow of China, each seeking to maintain or develop democratic institutions while being economically connected to China. South Korea was one of the first successful newly industrialising economies (NIEs) in Asia and is following a similar economic trajectory to Japan. Other countries in the region: Indonesia, Malaysia, Thailand and, to a certain extent, the Philippines, represent successful examples of the second generation of Asian NIEs. Japan, Singapore and Australia are the wealthiest and most advanced economies in the region. Japan was the first industrialised Asian country, Singapore is an affluent but small city state, while Australia is building a multicultural society and becoming more integrated with Asia, while maintaining strong historical ties to Europe. The trading relationship with China is a common feature of all the Asian economies covered in this book. All have a strong economic interaction with China which can be complicated by political considerations as China seeks to exert its influence in the region.

Given the diverse historical backgrounds and institutional foundations of their political economies, the thirteen country cases in this book provide a good opportunity to explore varieties of labour movements from a broader comparative perspective. In order to facilitate comparisons of the evolution of different labour movements, their priorities and causal factors of their success and failure, a common research framework was developed. The authors of each country chapter have addressed the following questions in various ways:

1. What has been the recent evolution of labour movement in each country?
2. What are core challenges confronting the labour movement both within and outside workers' organisations?
3. What strategic actions are being taken by the labour movement in response to the challenges in each country?
4. What has the labour movement achieved or failed to achieve, and what are major factors influencing these outcomes?
5. What theoretical implications can be drawn from case studies of labour movements in each country in order to further develop the VoU perspective?

Based upon this common framework, the country chapters in this book shed light on specific topics covered in the VoU in the Asia-Pacific region.

Faced with different challenges and distinctive national contexts, labour unions and workers groups have taken diverse strategic approaches towards the revitalisation of labour movements.

The Asia-Pacific context

Asia has become one of the most dynamic regions of the world as economic growth reached an average of 7.6% between 2007 and 2017, which was double the global rate during this period. Labour productivity (defined as output per worker) increased by an average of 5% annually, which was also double the global average. According to a recent International Labour Organisation (ILO) Report, the region has both the world's largest proportion of workers in the working-age population and lowest unemployment rate (ILO 2018).

Yet despite these impressive statistics, there is great variation between countries in the region. In 2017, more than one quarter of families lived in moderate to extreme poverty and nearly one in two workers remained in vulnerable employment (with little job security), while two in every three workers were in informal employment. Few countries in the region have a fully functioning social protection system which can help to stabilise household income levels and ease the impact of economic shocks, such as another global economic recession.

It is important to avoid over-generalising about the Asia-Pacific region which encompasses over forty countries, each of which has its own history, culture, social norms, natural resources and political institutions. This book covers thirteen countries in the region with an emphasis on those located in East and Southeast Asia, with India representing South Asia and Australia as the sole Pacific nation. Yet the countries in this book demonstrate the diversity of income levels, labour markets and worker representation through trade unions and other forms of organisation which seek to give workers a voice in determining their wages and conditions.

Some upper middle-income economies in the region, such as Australia, Japan, Singapore and South Korea, have made significant progress in export-led growth but still have workers in vulnerable jobs and underemployment. Middle-income economies, such as China, Hong Kong, Taiwan and Malaysia, have followed successful growth strategies which are based on macroeconomic policies but have paid relatively little attention to social welfare development and labour market governance. The industrialising, lower middle-income countries, such as India, Indonesia, Thailand, Vietnam and the Philippines, also have enjoyed high economic growth rates but still have many in their workforces in vulnerable employment and in moderate to extreme poverty. Even within countries which have experienced great economic progress in recent years, such as South Korea and Taiwan, there is a growing disconnect between growth and inclusiveness, measured by income inequality (ILO 2018)

The ILO Report on Asia-Pacific Employment and Social Outlook (2018) highlighted the barriers that exist to achieving the United Nation's Strategic Development Goals (SDGs) by 2030. This Report also argued that economic growth in the region is built on fragile foundations and needs to be refocussed on the four pillars of the ILO's Decent Work Agenda: promoting decent jobs, guaranteeing rights at work, extending social protection and promoting social dialogue. But there is scant attention paid in the ILO Report to the need to strengthen collective bargaining rights which can only be achieved if there are strong and effective trade unions or other forms of worker collectives which can bargain on their behalf. Labour market institutions and laws are necessary to provide workers with the ability to negotiate better wages and conditions as well as giving them a voice in managerial decisions which affect them in the workplace.

This book seeks to provide an assessment of unions and other forms of worker representation in the Asia-Pacific region by examining the situation in thirteen countries. The key issues raised in relation to the varieties of labour movements in each of the thirteen countries are briefly summarised below and then examined in greater depth in the chapters which follow.

Case studies from the Asia-Pacific region

In Australia, trade unions have experienced declining membership from a peak of 60% of all wage earners forty years ago to a current density of less than 15%. Various reasons have been advanced for this decline including structural change of the economy and the workforce as well as legal reforms introduced by conservative governments to curb union power. The union movement has employed a number of strategies seeking to arrest and reverse its membership decline, including union mergers and active organising drives, but these have achieved only limited success. Yet unions still exercise political influence through the Australian Labor Party, and continue to play an important role as an advocate for wage earners in industrial tribunals. Although there has been the growth of social movements which seek to advance workers' rights, there remain major challenges to revitalise and reform the union movement. Unions in Australia have sought greater engagement with their counterparts in Asia and the Pacific, as the region becomes more economically integrated.

Workers in China face a very different situation to most countries in the region, with the exception of Vietnam, as the government recognises only one trade union: The All-China Federation of Trade Unions (ACFTU) is effectively an organ of the state. However, with the decline of state-owned enterprises and the emergence of local and foreign-owned private companies, workers have engaged in unofficial strikes, particularly in manufacturing, in order to seek increased wages and improved working conditions. New forms of organisation and non-governmental organisations (NGOs) have been formed to support Chinese workers. Yet their future depends on whether the Chinese government continues to tolerate or decide to suppress alternatives to the official trade union movement and permit greater independence of the ACFTU from the state.

The unionisation rate in Hong Kong (known as a Special Administrative Region of the People's Republic of China (PRC)) is relatively stable but collective bargaining is weak. With the exception of major disputes in 2005 and 2013, there is little overt industrial conflict. The labour movement is divided along political lines between two major union centres. The larger Federation of Trade Unions (FTU) is similar to the ACFTU, with whom it is closely connected, and principally serves the interests of the Chinese government. The FTU operates as a quasi-political party but lacks an effective workplace delegate structure. The FTU also remains aloof from the international trade union movement. By contrast, the smaller Confederation of Trade Unions (CTU) is linked to the less influential Labour Party, has stronger international links and behaves more like a labour-oriented NGO. However, neither the FTU nor the CTU knew how to react to the 'Occupy/Yellow Umbrella' movement in 2014 and both have been wary of social movements, even though these may be of increasing influence in the future.

By contrast with China, India has a large but fragmented union movement. Worker representation has been dominated by conventional trade unions which are mostly affiliated with a variety of political parties. Trade unions are strongly represented in some sectors and regions, and the absolute number of union members has been increasing in recent years. However, unions represent only a small proportion of workers who are drawn predominantly from the formal sector of the economy. Many labour laws are in need of urgent reform. While some significant experiments are being undertaken to expand union coverage and to fight for new rights for workers, the current union leadership faces challenges by new NGOs and community organisations seeking to provide workers with a stronger voice in the workplace.

Indonesia's labour movement has undergone significant transformation since the end of President Suharto's 'New Order' regime twenty years ago. Although the unions have gained greater political and economic influence and have pursued new strategies, many of their gains are fragile in the context of institutional volatility. Neither the 'VoC' nor 'VoU' frameworks adequately capture or explain the dramatic shift in opportunity structures faced by unions in a rapidly changing Indonesia. Both unions and other forms of worker representation in Indonesia face an uncertain future.

Japan has experienced major changes in the labour market and employment relationships in recent decades. Two important employment practices in large Japanese firms, long-term employment and seniority wage systems, are changing in response to external pressures on the Japanese economy. Changes are also occurring in worker representation systems in large companies which were hitherto dominated by enterprise unions and joint labour-management committees. The globalisation of financial markets has affected labour markets and resulted in an increased proportion of non-regular workers. Firms are placing greater emphasis on shareholder value as foreign institutions increase their shareholding in Japanese companies.

In Malaysia, the trade union movement is facing internal and external challenges as well as new opportunities. The workforce is increasingly composed of migrant workers who are les inclined to join unions. Employers have adopted anti-union strategies and legislation by previous governments has resulted in narrow legal-administrative opportunities for unions. Although union strategies to counteract these developments have largely failed, the 2018 election victory by the former Oppostion parties in an 'Alliance of Hope' coalition has created new opportunities for revitalisation of the union movement. The current Malaysian government has promised legal and administrative reforms which could provide a wider institutional space for unions, although employers may continue to oppose union organising activities.

The Philippines traditionally had a fairly progressive legal framework which recognised the rights of workers to form unions and bargain collectively. However, unionised workers who enjoy collective bargaining rights represent less than 1% of the workforce. Yet despite their shrinking membership, unions continue to exercise an influential voice in society. Furthermore, various forms of alternative worker initiatives have emerged as social movements to promote the rights of neglected groups, such as home-based workers. A major challenge for unions is the increasing integration of the Philippines into the global economy in which Filipino workers are segmented and without adequate rights and representation.

In Singapore, the labour movement has been closely integrated with the Peoples' Action Party (PAP), founded by the late Lee Kuan Yew, a former Prime Minister, which has dominated government since the formation of the independent nation-state. The union leadership, which is closely aligned with the PAP, have supported the government's economic agenda through 'tripartite partnerships' with employers. However, Singapore is facing new challenges arising from economic volatility, technological disruptions and globalisation. The local Singaporean workforce has different lifestyle and career aspirations from the past. The 'new generation' of Singapore workers are more diverse and face greater uncertainty in a period of economic restructuring. The union movement may need to widen its worker representation and labour market policies in order to maintain its relevance to the Singaporean workforce of the future.

The union movement in South Korea faces two key challenges. First, there is increasing polarisation between regular workers in large firms and those in smaller firms, with non-regular employment, in terms of wages, fringe benefits and job training. Second, there has been a proliferation of the non-regular workforce since the financial crisis of 1997, who suffer discrimination in terms of compensation, employment, labour standards and access to social welfare. These developments have created a solidarity crisis within the union movement. The strategies adopted by the Korean labour movement to deal with these challenges include support for industry-wide unionisation and centralised collective bargaining. A new union model is also being developed to organise workers at the margin of the labour market, including: youth, the elderly and non-regular workers. It remains to be seen if these strategies will result in a resurgence of union membership.

In Taiwan, the state has withdrawn from its previous benevolent role towards unions and the rights of workers in favour of more flexible policies which emphasise economic competitiveness. Taiwan continues to be characterised by a strong state and a weak labour movement. Although unions campaign to improve workers' rights, their effectiveness is hampered by fragmentation and their lack of capacity for economic negotiation. Both labour and management are likely to continue to rely on the government to resolve problems rather than dealing directly with each other to settle matters of difference. Hence, unions remain underdeveloped in their role as workers' representatives in employment relations and labour market negotiations.

In Thailand, unions and other forms of worker representation remain weak. This is due to two main factors. First, the suppression of labour during the anti-Communist Cold War era coincided with the rapid industrialisation of Thailand which relied on low wages and lack of workers' rights. Second, unions were excluded from organising informal and migrant labour which was increasingly used in Thailand as the economy became more globalised. Recently, workers have resorted to new forms of organised labour, such as the Thai Labour Solidarity Committee, but these have to contend with the increased use of flexible forms of employment by employers and the unwillingness of Thai governments to improve the legal rights of workers and their unions.

In Vietnam, the official union movement has a high level of formal status but relatively little influence in the labour market and economy. Since the economic reforms (doi moi) which began in the late 1980s, there have been increasing tensions and conflict between workers and management, particularly in the growing private sector and foreign-owned firms. While the official trade unions have been attempting to influence employers, the government continues to exercise direct and dominant control over the union movement. It remains to be seen if the unions or other forms of worker representation will emerge as more independent actors become involved in labour-management relations in Vietnam.

Conclusions

As demonstrated by the country case studies in this book, labour movements in the Asia-Pacific are confronted by diverse challenges, which are both external, relating to the actions of employers or the state, or changes in the economy or polity and internal, relating to membership, resources or strategic capabilities, which sometimes interact. Some challenges to Asian labour movements are comparable with those in Europe and North America, such as declining density and weakening social leverage of unions under neoliberal labour market reforms (for example: in South Korea, Japan and Australia). Other challenges which are more characteristic of the situation in Asia include coercive management practices, insurgency among the rank-and-file membership, interventionist labour policies by the state and the massive presence of the informal employment sector (for example: in China and India). The repertoire of revitalising strategies adopted by labour movements in the Asia-Pacific countries is quite similar to that of the counterparts in the Western advanced economies, identified by Frege and Kelly (2003), but may take different forms. The revitalisation strategies include organising drives to recruit new members, organisational renewal, labour-management partnerships, transnational solidarity with other unions and various forms of political action. Some specific forms of strategies adopted by labour movements of the Asia-Pacific Region, however, differ from the Western counterparts. For example: the Malaysian unions' organising campaigns and Indian transnational activism have been aimed at gaining the active involvement of the state to embrace workers' interests in its labour policy; Korean unions have sought to move towards centralised bargaining arrangements as well as industry unionism, so far with mixed outcomes. Japanese unions have adopted labour-management partnerships in an effort to organise part-time workers within the established norms of cooperative industrial relations. Australian unions have combined various revitalisation strategies, yet have experienced growing distance in their relationship with the state, so that they find themselves 'dancing alone'. China provides an interesting case where bureaucratised unions are facing growing worker militancy under the state-led polity and the transition to a market economy. Hence, labour movements in Asia-Pacific region have revealed distinctive strategic approaches which are different from those in Western advanced economies in relation to their revitalisation. Asian labour movements are situated in different national contexts of political economy and industrial relations. Hence, they are dealing with challenges posed by the twenty-first century's globalising economy in their own ways. It is intended that this volume will contribute to a broader comparative perspective in order to further refine the 'VoU' concept in the context of the Asia-Pacific region.

References

Applebaum, E., Bosch, G., Gautie, J., Mason, G., Mayhew, K., Salverda, W., Schmitt, J., and Westergaard-Nielsen, N. (2010) "Introduction and Overview", in J. Gauitie and J. Schmitt (eds.), *Low Wage Work in the Wealthy World*. New York: Russell Sage, 1–32.

Baccaro, L., and Howell, C. (2011) "A Common Neo-liberalmTrajectory: The Transformation of Industrial Relations in Advanced Capitalism", *Politics and Society*, Vol. 44, 175–207.

Bamber, G.J., Lansbury, R.D., Wailes, N., and Wright, C. eds. (2016) *International and Comparative Employment Relations*. London: Sage.

Buchhol, S.D. Hofäcker, M., Mills, H., Blossfeld, K., and Hofmeister, H. (2009) "Life Course in the Globalization Process: The Development of Social Inequalities in Modern Societies", *European Sociological Review*, Vol. 25, No. 1, 53–71.

Dabscheck, B. (2017) "Forming Teams of their Own: The Dramatic Emergence of Player Associations Across the Globe", *Law In Sport*, January.

Frege, C. and Kelly, J. (2003) "Union Revitalization Strategy in Comparative Perspective", *European Journal of Industrial Relations*, Vol. 9, No. 1, 7–24.

Hall, P. and Soskice, D. (2001) *Varieties of Capitalism: The Institutional Foundations of Competitive Advantage*. Oxford: Oxford University Press.

Howell, C. (2003) "Varieties of Capitalism: And Then There was One?" *Comparative Politics*, Vol. 36, 103–124.

Hyman, R. (2007), "How Can Trade Unions Act Strategically?" *Transfer: European Review of Labour and Research*, Vol. 13, No. 2, 193–210.

ILO (2018) *Asia-Pacific Employment and Social Outlook*. Geneva: ILO.

Lee, B. (2011) "Labor Solidarity in the Era of Neoliberal Globalization", *Development and Society*, Vol. 40, No. 2, 319–334.

Peetz, D. (2010) "Are Individualistic Attitudes Killing Collectivism?" *Transfer*, Vol. 16, No. 3, 383–398.

Pocock, B. (1998) "Institutional Sclerosis: Prospects for Trade Union Transformation", *Labour & Industry*, Vol. 9, No. 1, 17–36.

Rose, M. (1993) "Trade Unions – Ruin, Retreat, or Rally?" *Work, Employment & Society*, Vol. 7, No. 2, 291–311.

Schneider, B. (2012) "Contrasting Capitalisms: Latin America in Comparative Perspective", in J. Santiso and J. Dayton-Johnson (eds.), *Latin American Political Economy*. Oxford: Oxford University Press, 381–402.

Thelen, K. (2001), "Varieties of Labor Politics in the Developed Democracies", in P. Hall and D. Soskice (eds.), *Varieties of Capitalism: the Institutional Foundations of Competitive Advantage*. Oxford: Oxford University Press, 71–103.

Wright, C.F., Wailes, N., Bamber, G.J., and Lansbury R.D. (2017) "Beyond National Systems, Towards a 'Gig Economy? A Research Agenda for International and Comparative Employment Relations", *Employee Rights and Responsibility Journal*, Vol. 29, No. 4. 247–257.

World Bank (2018) *World Development Report: The Changing Nature of Work*. Washington, DC: World Bank.

2 Perspectives on Asian unionism as a regional pattern

Sek-Hong Ng, Russell D. Lansbury, and Byoung-Hoon Lee

Introduction

This chapter presents some cursory ideas which, hopefully, can shed light on the subject-area of 'Asian Unionism'. Obviously, any constructive treatment of 'Asian unionism' should begin by exploring the extent to which commonalities are shared by the labour movements across societies in this region, Asia. Inspection of the country chapters in this volume reveals not only these common elements shared by the national labour movements but also, unsurprisingly, visible diversities of unionism which exist across nations. Within Asia, few national labour movements are well integrated, stable and solidaristic, while most are still haunted by internal fissuring, inter-union rivalry and fragmentation. Some are even obscure, volatile and effacing. In the present age of a 'global economy', which can add impetus to the socio-economic development of nation-states in the region, labour movements have to respond to the vicissitudes of industrialism and capitalism in ways and strategies which converge as well as diverge. This makes it interesting to attempt at generalising across nation-states to arrive at, even at best imperfect, a cursory image of what can be a coherent pattern of 'Asian unionism'.

This book owes its inspiration largely to Keith Thurley's writings on 'Asian unionism'. Those shared features distinctive of Asian labour movements, lucidly surveyed in Keith Thurley's essays about thirty years ago, might have now become anachronistic. Yet his central argument which postulated, by extrapolating from the contextual variables of culture, history and ideological creed, that unions in Asia might not subscribe, as is almost sacrosanct and doctrinal for Western unionism, to adversarial collective bargaining, has proved sustainable and highly accurate and relevant to the current situation. The 'impracticability' of collective bargaining, a highly unstable and truncated class system overladen by cross-cutting ethnic and social affiliations, a high propensity for militant sociopolitical conflicts and even armed duels as well as the exigencies of geopolitics within the Asian 'theatre', all create an Asian pattern of unionism distinctive from the Euro-America pattern. Of course, we may find even more similarities from Latin America in common with Asian unionism. By comparison, in terms of wholistic regionalism (vide the 'continent'), North America is dualistic, Australia is increasingly pluralistic, Europe (at least west of Russia) is now tenuously held together by the European Union (with the advents of 'Brexit'), Latin America is fragmented and yet shares a Latin culture in common. Does Asia, equally divided, owe a regional identity (or togetherness) to the so-called Asian values?

The coverage of this book is not exclusively Oriental as it includes a portrayal of an Occidental variant, which is the Australian sub-type, to serve as a comparative benchmark. By summarising across country patterns of unionism in Asia, this book attempts to make some tentative statements on the common challenges now faced by national labour movements within the region, leading on to the types of responses, whether strategic or 'stop-gap' and ad hoc, espoused by organised labour when confronted by these challenges. It is possible for these challenges and responses to resemble or digress, wholesale or fragmental, among nation-states. They denote 'convergence' or 'divergence' or both, which can be only partial on each count.

We concede that, by summarising across our country chapters on Asian trade unionism in this book, diversities revealed are so entrenched, while confusion and amorphousness of union policies and practices are so prevalent, that any generalisation at constructing a specifically Asian 'variant' of unionism in unison can be delusive. It may be less problematic for us to try to sketch, if only tentatively, an image of an 'Asian' hallmark or an 'Asian brand' of trade unionism. However, it will be uncritical and haphazard to do it just by lumping together a cross-section, by snapshot, of unionism in Asian societies into a hybrid type which is hardly more than a 'hotchpotch' mix. This is exactly what we sought to avoid when, embarking on this a comparative exercise of investigating the various faces of Asian unionism, we drew up a checklist of key issues for understanding the current landscape of Asian unionism and requested authors of individual chapters to write their country pieces within a common scheme. The countries and territories covered in this book are not exhaustive but hopefully illuminate both similarities and diversities among Asian societies in the domain of their labour movements.

This chapter examines the extent to which these Asian workers' movements which, save for a few, betray little eminence as social movements, share certain common themes and exhibit certain convergent patterns. It may be too hasty, if not overstretching, to envisage and approve the assertion that we can derive, by (empirical) generalisation and (theoretical) postulation, an 'Asian' format (called an 'Asian variant') on a global typing scale called 'variety of unionism' (VoU). Although the name of such a proposition can appeal eventually, much work still needs to be done to refine such a 'VoU' continuum to make it rational and legitimate. In its current form, for which we have proposed some refinements, the 'VoU' precept still looks preliminary. Much has still to be done before such a 'taxonomy' can crystallise into a viable and vindicated theoretical framework of full academic rigor to steer cross-cultural comparative works on labour unionism.

There is a historical perspective, not only for understanding labour movements but also when coming to grips with the existing literature on Asian unionism. In this connection, we can revert to the works of Thurley, Schregle, Dore, Turner et al. and England in the 1980s and earlier, of Abbeglen, Levine and Chesneuax in the 1950s and 1960s. These pioneering works each enumerated a (national) a pattern of unionism of an Asian tradition which differed substantially from Western unionism. Their insightful ideas, now traceable back to more than thirty years ago, provide pertinent cues to fashioning our vision on 'Asian unionism'.

A 'cultural' and 'institutional' perspective on Asian unionism?

Keith Thurley argued for an 'alternative' perspective to conventional Western literature when theorising on 'Asian unionism'. He derived his notion of 'Asian unionism' in part from the earlier works of Levine, Abbelglen and Hanami on Japanese unionism (Abbeglen, 1958; Levine, 1963; Hanami, 1979). His idea finds resonance also with his contemporaries, like Dore (1990) who explained and appraised Japanese industrial relations and enterprise unionism within the cultural milieu of Japanese ethno-centric traits and vestiges of Confucian values; and Schregle (1981) who argued for an International Labour Organisation (ILO) policy for the Asian region tailored to its disinterest in adversarial collective bargaining and yet a creed for national development. Furthermore, Ramos (1981) lamented the dearth of any comparative studies on Asian employment and labour unionism when collective bargaining in the Philippines, albeit rudimentary, was pioneering in the East Asian context.

Besides these works cited by Keith Thurley and his own works, Chesneaux's excursive treaty on the history of the Chinese labour movement since its inception through the collapse of the 1925–1926 Hong Kong Canton General Strike examined a highly effective urban social movement, allied with the students and the peasants, set in the context of China's political economy (Chesneaux, 1968). His works, shedding light on one of the world's most vibrant labour movements the 1920s, is instructional for our present comparative treatment of Asia's national labour movements in selected Asian societies (Chesneaux, 1968). Last but not the least, the empirical study by Turner et al. on Hong Kong labour and labour movement, commissioned by the British government and covering intensive interviews with labour unions and a territory-wide sampled survey of employee attitudes (Turner et al., 1980), was benchmarking for the study of unionism in Asia. This work was exemplary in illustrating how history, culture and geopolitics can fashion the structure and functions of labour unions as a social institution of in the Asian context.

Keith Thurley's approach was essentially Weberian, dealing first with the structure and institution of unions (and their associated functions) and subsequently with 'culture' as the contextual variable. Within his conceptual scheme of 'Asian unionism', he echoed Schregle in identifying four crucial factors for explaining and predicting Asian unions' structure and the kind of activities they perform. These are (i) the extent and methods of state's intervention in the national economy apart from the 'public household', (ii) the prevalence and configuration of 'dualism' (the primary versus the secondary sector) in the economy and labour market, (iii) unions' priority given to collective bargaining and other functions than union-management bargaining and (iv) their relationship with the polity and especially the political parties (Thurley, 1988: 26–27). Reminiscent of Dunlop's 'general system' model for comparative industrial relations studies, Keith Thurley postulated that the dual dimensions of the polity and socio-economic institutions were strategic in deciding the key interests and hence policy goals which Asian unions seek to serve. Yet these are often conditioned, if not constrained, by the wider cultural context, which could be 'Confucian' (ibid.: 26). Currently, it is fashionable to cap this contextual variable, instead, with the label of 'Asian values' or Oriental values (McGregor, 2018: chapter 6).

Construing from the above argument, Keith Thurley envisaged an 'ideal-type' or 'visionary' agenda of 'critical issues' for Asian unionism. The checklist included (i) regulation of the employment contract and employment protection; (ii) negotiation of framework agreements on payment systems or pay level (which was and are still practised by guild-like industrial unions jointly with employers' associations in the building and construction trades in Hong Kong); (iii) co-determination with management in the formulation of manpower deployment policies, supposedly to include defined promotion and transfer chances; (iv) skilling, skill obsolescence, re-skilling and vocational education, either jointly with management or outside the workplace; (v) productivity deals and projects; (vi) regulation and settlement of industrial conflicts, both individual and collective and either disputes of rights or of interests; (vii) in-house and workplace communication; and (viii) participation in enterprise development (Thurley, 1988: 27–30).

Such a checklist, compiled thirty years ago, was clearly normative and prescriptive. It was beyond attainment by any Asian unions at that time. Neither can they today. It is beyond the scope of this book to appraise its applicability in this new era. Yet, still the list can help educate contemporary labour movements in Asia when looking ahead and deliberating on how to proceed.

For mapping 'Asian unionism' by comparative studies of national patterns in this volume, we have been inspired by Keith Thurley. Instead of drawing up an ideal checklist for auditing union performance in the region, which Keith Thurley might have intended to do, we have designed a common and comparative framework to facilitate comparisons of national patterns of Asian unions. The comparative scheme is based also upon list of key issues on Asian unionism pertaining to their present shape, membership and organisational structure, policy goals and strategy design, relationship with the state and political economy, and overseas and domestic affiliations, etc. Perhaps, it is still beyond our reach to arrive at a consensual perspective on what would constitute 'Asian unionism', being universal to the Asian region, or to theorise conclusively on an 'Asian variant of union'. By canvassing refining the notion of 'Asian unionism' as a 'Variant of unionism', this volume at least represents a conscious attempt to systematise the comparative study of these national patterns across a significant space in Asia.

As our 'introductory' chapter suggests, there exists a legitimate case to refine first the 'variety of capitalism' (VoC) schema, so that it can be adopted and translated, upon adaptation, to building an analogous classificatory schema on types of unionism, labelled hence as VoU. The implications are the legitimate validity of subscribing (perhaps ideological and Euro-centric to the cynical) to 'Asian unionism' to an universal classificatory typology, the VoU schema. In terms of such a global-wide typology writ large, we can subsequently denominate 'Asian unionism' as an 'Asian variant of unionism'. The advents of optimistic 'universalism' connoted by the 'convergence' thesis are evident from the above statement. Nonetheless, its vein is in line with Keith Thurley's Weberian embrace, when he contended:

> ... there is a universal case for unions in work organizations, although there are special characteristics in Asian society and culture which do reinforce this case. The differences for Asian unions lie in the way that their interests are perceived, the basis of such interests in the economic and industrial structures involved in the countries concerned ....
>
> (ibid.: 27)

Of course, no single typology or classificatory framework can claim perfection, for obvious reasons. There are evident limitations and gaps in the validity of such a conceptual apparatus as VoC being tailored for the project of typing trade unionism. Classifying unionism is not entirely analogous to the VoC. But at least, it provides a starting point for comparative works by raising the 'Asian' issue.

Towards 'Asian unionism'? From 'culture' to 'institutions'

It is legitimate to advance the concept of 'Asian unionism' and also to define its landscape either by equating it spatially with a 'regional' pattern (if Asia is geographically wholistic) or by conceiving it as a 'cultural pattern' (if it is holistic ethnographically or in terms of shared values). We argue that it is perfunctory to invoke the concept 'Asian pattern' without considering it in terms of its constituent culture, be it pluralistic or unified. Falling short of a cultural perspective on unionism for a vast continent such as Asia will almost preclude the postulation of an 'Asian variant of unionism', if this is to be authentic and not 'synthetic'. Why an 'Asian variant' needs to be distinguished from its Western counterpart?

Such clues come from historians like Hobsbawm and Ferguson who observe that Asia is so diversified that spatially it represents a 'residual hotchpotch category' (see Ferguson (2012) on 'civilization'). Instead, the fall-back position is to argue for a possible form of 'Asia togetherness' or of an 'Asian entity' by citing a 'trendy' term when we are caught in the currency of a debate on 'Westernization versus Easternization'. This term we call 'Asian values' (Patten, 1999: chapter 5; Jacques, 2012: chapters 12 and 13). The rider to add, as to be argued later, is that it is still legitimate to say something about 'Asian values' even if it is recognised that an identity of an Asian entity may not be justifiable ethnologically, insofar as the ethnography of Asia is easily glutted, with several thousand ethnic groups, large or small discernible (Vatikiotis, 2018: chapters 1 and 9, especially p. 36). Conversely, worker collectivities and fraternities in many Asian societies are embedded in Asian values. While there exists some comparability between South America and Asia, it can be deceptive to equate simplistically Latin America with Confucian Asia. Asian values cannot be categorised as a unitary culture embraced by the umbrella of Confucian legacies. This will also be discussed later in the context of its implications for Asian labour movements.

Instead, 'Asian values' are paradoxically a mix of anachronism and innovations. Besides, Asian values are also to a certain extent a 'refugee' culture to make it extremely adaptable. The 'VoC' framework and, by extension, the 'VoU' schema are limited for dealing with and classifying Asian unions also partly for this reason. Highly developed Western societies are pervaded by an overt managerial concern with 'control and predictability', so that both their management and unionism, as the agent of capital, are devoted to a variety of 'regimes of law and rules' from which various integrative and regulatory institutions for market and enterprise governance emanate. However, it entails overtly an 'institutional' approach in generalising and classifying 'market economies', so that every one of their properties, including trade unionism, is predicated and premised upon sociopolitical stability in Euro-America. But this is not the case, either Asia or Latin America. It is hence too sophisticated and cumbersome, in terms of the details of the governance/regulatory regime entailed, for these institutions to mature as they have in the Occidental context, when most of these Asian societies are still caught in turmoil every now and then.

Daniel Bell conceives the make-up of society in terms of a hierarchy of three realms: descending from culture, polity, to techno-economic structure (Bell, 1978: 10). This view is mirrored by Keith Thurley when he propounded, together with Wirdenius, the notion of 'European management' when they addressed the domain of culture and the domain of institutions within a successful and causally related system. Hence, they invoked the 'cultural' perspective, also of the Weberian tradition, which links Protestant ethics with the secular success of Western capitalism and the Mandarin quest for Confucian aestheticism with stagnation and 'armchair' excellence in China and the Far East. Thurley and Wirdenius advanced the notion of 'European management', by drawing upon empirical data on British, Nordic and Continental experiences. According to their thesis, the study of 'European management' as a regional or cultural pattern is concerned with not only deciphering cultural traits alone but also understanding as how culture shapes, as its functions, the institutions which coordinate and regulate. The locus of interest of investigating European pattern of management theory-cum-practices hence shifts away from the 'problem of demonstrating that cultural differences are important for managers to understand, ... as self-evident', to 'the much more interesting question of how different cultural assumptions may influence management practice and lead to competing models of excellence' (Thurely and Wirdenius, 1989: 4). To say, 'European management' is hence boundary demarcation, in search for an alternative pattern which is distinctive from others, like the American or the Japanese. Such a message applies to our present project, which says 'Asian unionism' as an alternative to other cultural patterns and not merely a 'variant' of some universal else.

Where are Asian unions heading and what lies ahead?

We have observed that relations between the state and the unions in Asia, embracing an age of enlightenment and emancipation, are intricate and complex. Asian unions need to be vigilant about opportunities and risks and, in order to embrace and accommodate with these secular tendencies, to be malleable and versatile in dealing with the changing nature of their role (and functions) as an institution of 'industrialism' which can evolve supposedly with an Asian flavour. The dilemma is that the adapted institution can be recast so much and so deep that it no longer attests to its Western root, as echoed notably, by the chronic Sino-Euro-American debate on the relativity of the realm of 'human rights', in part paralleled by the two-side debate on what constitutes 'bona-fide unionism' (a label which the British colonial government was always reluctant to bestow upon China-rooted unionism in Hong Kong, as attested by its union history). There were and are ample examples in Asia of unions being assimilated into the establishment and the established order. This often refers now to the entire institutional arrangement which is not only pivoted around the state but as the 'civilized' jacket to wear to testify to these Asian nations as 'civil societies' as the admission ticket to participation in the international community of trade and exchange of capital and people, the human capital. As alerted by Hobsbawm, institutions have an innate drift towards complacency and inertia in 'flirting with the status quo' even when catching 'fatigue' (Hobsbawm, 1990: 14–20). As one of the oldest institutional off-shoots from industrialisation and industrialism, unions served and can still serve the societal functions of helping stabilise and integrate the workplace/industrial order, let alone committing the workforce to patriotic goals and the nation's productivity. This pattern of state-union alliance happened, of course, in China but also in Indonesia, Malaysia, as well as in South Korea and Taiwan (the latter two polities were, however, de-cased from Japanese and not Western 'colonialism') in the earlier decades of the post-war epoch and before the 'democratization' of the polity in these Asian countries (Maeda et al., 1996).

Worldwide, such a 'state-cum-union' power relationship, with the latter performing either as a collateral stake-holding partner (in Western developed democracies) or dedicatedly as an entrusted state organ (as in most Asian cases) has been for a time popularised as the 'corporatist' model. This reflects the optimism of convergent pluralism as epitomised by the 'welfare state' and the 'social contract' in the developed West in the post-industrial advents, as in the vein of Lester's 'As Union Mature' and Galbraith's 'Ministerial Union' theses (Lester, 1958; Galbraith, 1972). Yet, the term began to lose its flavour after scepticism cast by Goldthorpe for its deceptive simplification (Goldthorpe, 1984: 323–42). Its 'capitalist' connotation has also been greeted by resentment from union leaders. In the West, a substitute for the notion now advocated is 'participation', alongside 'activation' (Dorre et al., 2009: 'Conclusion'). Yet the label of 'corporatist unionism' is still used today for denoting the 'state integrated' monolithic labour movement system, practised not only in the socialist states of China and Vietnam (Westad, 2013: 405–09) but also in the capitalist city state of Singapore (Ng and Warner, 1998: 150–52). The Singapore model is probably the closest approximate to 'corporatism' in the absence of any conspicuous programmes of nationalising private industry. However, the ACFTU is unequivocally socialist as it professes; it obviously resists a capitalist label, as 'corporatist'.

The so-called rights movement can be extrapolated to embrace another major challenge to Asian unionism today. This is the basic question of the legitimate and workable span of its organisational jurisdiction. Specifically, what types of stake-holders or sectional and secular interests which it can claim to represent? Can and does its boundary exceed the constituency of just the urban working class? And the reciprocal question also comes afront: can the waged and salaried employees be represented by alternative way other than that of workers' combinations as trade unions? The task of attempting at such boundary demarcation can be fluid and malleable in the Asian context, since nothing is yet definite in charting the structure and function of Asian unionism even now it is now thirty years after Keith Thurley about an alternative union model in 'Asian trade unionism'.

Again, it is illuminating to cite the case of Latin America for comparison. In the latter situation, the development of embracing and non-exclusive unionism has been constrained strongly by the factor of ethnic plurality. Latin American unionism often cannot jump such a tribal hurdle. Asian societies in many nations and cities are multi-racial and a culture of inclusivity seems to have prevailed. Yet ethnic homogeneity tends to denominate the structural fabrics of unionism in such metropolitan cities as Hong Kong.

In this highly urbanised and cosmopolitan society, non-Chinese employees in the civil service need to organise their expatriate staff unions, while the mainstream labour movement shows little initiative to assimilate imported foreign guest workers and is still adamant in excluding any guest foreign workers, except household domestic maids. Such a parochial perspective of protectionist unionism, which draws a 'we-they' divide along ethnic cleavages (rather than along the 'class' divide, as it has been the typical consciousness of orthodox Western unionism), is yet changing evidently among many Asian nations, now that the issue of 'precarity' at employment and the secular ethics of accommodating and embracing diversities have captured the imagination of their labour movements. Under such a mission of accentuated importance, the challenge to be faced by these Asian labour movements is hence how to penetrate and absorb these ethnic 'enclaves' in the working population, rather than leaving them unattended in the 'they' external sector, as in the past.

Unsurprisingly, creeping growth of union pluralism made possible by democratic political reforms tends to fragment the labour movement. These mushrooming 'alternative labour movements', sometimes sponsored by the Church but often backed by pro-democratic pressure groups in the United States and Europe, are now flanked on the periphery by a ring of these 'voluntary and "social work"' agencies, which coalesce into the 'third sector' of the non-government organisations (NGOs), labelled by Giddens as the 'civil societies' writ small (Giddens, 2000: 78–84). The latter, often appearing as secular missionaries to help ameliorate social injustices of a generic or specific nature, easily spill over to the 'turf' of the labour unions. Although Giddens draws a boundary between the labour unions (external to 'third sector') and the NGOs (located within the 'third sector' of 'civil societies'), such a boundary is swiftly withering in Asia. Whether conventional unions proper and the NGOs are complementary with each other to share, or will be mutually competitive with each other to bid for, jurisdiction of governance and actions in the labour and employment arena is to be tested in the region. By contrast, Latin America is still relatively immune from the aggrandisement of the NGO movement, probably because of the continent's highly dissected and truncated political terrain glutted by radical political and worker parties, the city worker movements and the agrarian peasant movements and most notorious, feuding ethnic cliques (Hobsbawm, 2016: chapters 3 and 30; Andrews, 2017: chapter 5).

In East Asia and Southeast Asia, de-regulation of formerly coercive state control on trade union organisations and their ability to associate, to bargain collectively and to strike has created a 'service market of worker combinations'. This provides the contested arena for rival and sectarian labour organisations in nation-states such as South Korea, Malaysia, Indonesia and Taiwan. Inter-union competition due to 'multi-unionism', now compounded by the NGO movements which tend to usurp unionism, still engulfs organised labour in many Asian nation-states and, in turn, fragments the labour movement and weakens its solidarity. The 'playing field' of social-cum-labour movement is now glutted by influences from various sources. First are the 'popularist movements', which can be parochial albeit emancipatory in articulating and exposing deep-rooted antipathies or even hostilities (if not hatred). The second are the secular and non-partisan NGO establishment. The third is the Church (especially after the secularisation of the Catholic Church and other Christian denominations in the wake of Western economic affluence after the birth of the European Union). The fourth source of challenges may now come from the new knowledge occupations with middle-class sympathies and aspirations. The NGOs may edge out the labour movement proper, since they seem to enjoy the comparative advantage by behaving like the community unions: that they are mostly adhocracies, lacking bureaucratic institutional form. It suggests structural fluidity which can make these NGOs malleable and versatile and can be generic or indifferent in any basic sociopolitical objectives. From a functional-institutional perspective, the NGOs are perilous for trade unionism with a potential of displacing the latter, which was unequivocally the standard-bearer of social movements in the sixties, seventies and eighties, as defunct. Thus, in an endeavour to articulate and champion for the rights of the working class in such a 'competitive service market', the NGOs are now ready to protest, strike and picket with unprecedented vigour. The effects are hence socially disruptive, as their actions, agitation and unrest, often staged at or external to the workplace, pervert and upset the stability of the former industrial order under the old regime, resulting in a bizarre and volatile state of industrial order punctuated even by occasional social unrest. Contrary to what Giddens predicts on the eve of the turn of the millennium (Giddens, 1991: chapter 5), the arena of social movements in Asia has not consolidated into a sustainability ecological quest to protect the environment. The field has been become instead more fragmented and divided.

Of course, it is still the momentum of new and emancipatory labour enactments which has been almost deterministic in shaping Asian unionism since the tide of 'democratisation' of Asian polities in the late 1980s and early 1990s. Labour enactments are contingent upon several factors which mirror the institutional relationship between the state and the labour movement in many Asian societies. In these societies, the tacit trade-off is between a legal regime which protects individual employment, albeit circumscribing freedom of workers combination, on the one hand, while, on the other hand, the 'novel' alternative of state abstention for collective laissez-faire (a British tradition of 'voluntarism') is obvious (Ng and Warner, 1998: chapter 7). Almost invariably, the choice of the state and organised labour in every Asian economy is for the first and former matrix, especially at the peril of a growing army of precarious employment seemingly attributable to an exploitative and non-equitable 'international division of labour' within a globalised economy. However, it is still uncertain and problematic as whether such a proficient technocracy of labour administration exists in most parts of Asia

(Thurley, 1983: 117–19). Hence, there is an evident case, as an agenda for the future, for both the state and the labour movement to work together in order to make the first option 'practicable', given the limits of 'practicable democracy' and 'practicable authority' of the three parties, the state, capital and organised labour (Fletcher, 1973:139–46). This again prompts another issue: which is the stability or even, the longevity of social institutions for industrial societies. Are Asian unions so tenuous that they may start to wither away before they are able to mature?

Some concluding remarks

This collection of essays on trade unionism across a spectrum of Asian economies is a concerted attempt of the contributors to generalise across nations in Asia in order to construct a so-called Asian VoU. Unavoidably, there are some reservations cast on the notion of VoC and, by implication, that of VoU. In this volume, we explore as whether it is 'practicable' to chart a pattern of Asian trade unionism by identifying some of the common challenges faced by unions in different Asian societies, in the advent of a 'global economy', compounded by 're-casualization' which breeds an 'urban proletariat'. Atypical employment has been intensified in scale and complexity due to the rise of the shared economy of the 'gig' or 'cyber' constellation. Its creeping effects are being felt in most parts of Asia. In China, the All-China Federation of Trade Unions (ACFTU) anticipates that the development of the cyber network and the cellular phones may touch off a virtual 'revolution' of unions' mode of communication and organisation within its membership (ACFTU, 2018: 11–20). However, the most important impetus for changes and reforms has been the imperative, for the developing Asian economies, to move towards closer convergence with the regulatory regimes of rules promulgated by such international governance bodies as the World Trade Organisation (WTO), ILO and the EU. This is the protocol governing entry to and sustaining participation in the international arena of free trade. Summarising across these country chapters which each charts Asian unions in the relevant nation-state, we postulate that we can construct an Asian pattern, or an Asian VoU by starting from these challenges and exploring the responses and strategies of Asian unions shaping their work agendas, both at present and in future. In this definition and typing exercise, 'culture' and 'history' are cited as the contextual perimeters, which are yet malleable rather than constant. As observed by Giddens, when we talk about renewal, rejuvenation or 'renaissance', there is always a connotation of 'circularity' which underline the twin realm of both culture and history, so that a reversal, in fragments and not entirety, from the modern present to the traditional past is plausible.

Given the cultural and historical context, it is hence 'practicable' for us to invoke our most accustomed and conventional way, which is an 'institutional' perspective of comparative treatment of unionism in different

Asian societies. While aware of a commonplace criticism on the 'institutional' approach for being static, as constrained by the structural-functional exposition on core institutions like the nation-state and the labour movement, we suggest that it is always essential to complement it with the 'historical' dimension, in order to incorporate a longitudinal (across time) profile on unionism in Asian societies. Every country chapter in this volume has hence acquired, by varying degree, such a temporal portrayal of unionism in each jurisdiction.

While the union institutions of worker combinations in most emergent national economies seem to be able to participate, to varying degree, in 'inclusive democracy' purportedly sustained by the state, often bailed upon the unions' promise to help support the state's altruistic mission of national economic growth. A 'social contract' exists, albeit apparent and less than 'explicit', in many of these new Asian nation-states. It is possible to recognise an analogy, even partial, between Asian and Latin American unionism, as the dialectic institutional products of industrial (post-industrial) and agrarian capitalism. Yet, such convergence is at best partial. At a high level of generality, such convergence also embraces, from a wider comparative perspective, emulation of their counterparts in Western societies.

However, by the thesis of 'union exhaustion', Western labour unions have not yet uplifted themselves from their 'stagnation' doldrums, which has beset them since the rise of neoliberalism (as epitomised by Reagan's and Thatcher's competitive free market capitalism; see Atkinson, 2018:128–32; Ferguson, 2014: 116–24). Apart from hostile union legislation, the relative expansion of white-collar employment, the hegemony of trans-national corporations, a pertinent reason for 'union exhaustion' is the union's decay due to 'institutional fatigue' or 'over-maturity' or ageing as manifest in the bureaucratic inertia of their organisation, governance structure and leadership, not to mention the burdensome chain of procedural and substantive routinisation of their 'life-blood', collective bargaining. Will Asian unionism court similar fate? The answer can be twofold.

First, from an evolutionary and institutional perspective, the universalism of unionism as endemic to industrialisation and 'industrialism/post-industrialism' is frequently taken for granted. The labour movement has been the 'avant-garde' of social movements for almost a century in the West since the heyday of the 'Industrial Revolution' and it has hence matured upon 'institutionalization' and 'routinization'. It is suspected that it is still in the 'avant-garde' stage in Latin America, being one allied with or aloof from the peasant and student movements. Similarly, the contention is that unionism in most Asian nations has neither matured, due to earlier social and political instability in the region, to which the triple movements of urban workers, agrarian labour (peasants) and students contributed significantly. The prospect for unionism within some new Asian economies to take root is a priori condition, as echoed in Latin America but lacking consonance with Europe, that the polity and society have become stabilised, with a possibility for the state and organised labour to evolve some form of standing 'corporatist partnership'. Singapore is often cited as a classic example. It is not likely, by comparison, that any type of either ageing or developed 'unionism' canvassed for the 'liberal market economy' (LME) or the 'coordinated market economy' (CME) ideal types within the Euro-(Northern) American league can offer a 'practicable' model for their new Asian counterparts.

Alternatively, a more pessimistic viewpoint suggests that political and industrial stability is always fragile for many Asian nation-states, as in the situation of Latin America. If this should happen to some Asian societies, unionism may never been able to find 'space' in time to 'mature' institutionally but always remain, even only cyclically, 'evangelistic' and 'chiliastic'. To the radical socialists (Marxists), the labour movement remains as 'the vanguard of history', so long as they resist or are denied 'institutionalization' (Giddens, 1991: 158–59). The historical context, as in Latin America, is the prolonged and sustained volatility and fluidity of the political economy. This syndrome can still happen to some parts of Asia, engendering a high ('re-flexibility') risk due to insurgencies, revolutions, coups and factional feuds.

Yet, the long-term prospect of Asian unionism is novel, if not conjectural. The locus of such extrapolation is less evolutionary and institutional in overtone than the previous one. It is instructed by Giddens' prophecy on 'post-modernity', which is disruptive. What he conjures for the 'post-modern' future is still remote, even in the West. First, it is fictional for the market to lose its pre-eminence in arbitrating on resource allocation; the market will be no longer a market any more if its function degenerates into that of serving only as a signal in a 'post-scarcity' economy. Second, such a post-scarcity society will have sublimated into the ideal realm of 'socialism' if the governing authority maintains continuing and high vigilance in responding to the preferences of all sections of its citizenry, entailing a high level of 'inclusive and equal participation of diversity' labelled as 'polyarchy' (Giddens, 1991: 167–68).

The improbability of such visionary 'utopian realism' is almost certain, unlikely for the future 'Occidental' world and 'realistically' too distant away in the Oriental East, even still lesser in Latin America (Giddens calls it 'utopian realism' which is, he concedes, more notional than with reach). However, a fraction of his prophecy may apply to unionism in Asia. He is pessimistic about labour movements, which once embraced all causes of social movements from every social entity in the West (in China, the worker movement which nurtured the birth of the Chinese Communist Party (CCP) in 1921 eventually absorbed the student and the peasant movements to succeed in the 1949 Liberation of China) have lost their 'transformational impact and impetus' when they began to mature as established institutions. The cage of 'technocratic' or 'ministerial' captivity has literally reduced the autonomy of organised labour, which waived their evangelism and militancy in exchange for the trilateral political partnership, which it can share jointly with the state and capital under the 'social contract'. To Giddens, the labour movement can hence be just transient and specific to the age of 'industrialism', after which they begin 'ageing', often degenerating into simply 'interest group among others' (Giddens, 1991:158–59). The labour movement, descending from its zenith, will be overtaken and assimilated into a wider generic social movement. Labelled by Giddens as the 'emancipatory' sites of sociopolitical actions such as 'civil disobedience', this movement will no longer be pivoted around the workplace (now that a 'platform' shared economy is brewing) but can embrace peace, ecology, democracy and freedom, as well as the search for civil rights and justice (Giddens, ibid., 160–72). Interestingly, such a generic social movement, sustained on the students and intellectuals' recalcitrance, did show a brief appearance in the Orient, as the Umbrella Movement which almost paralysed the banking centre of the city of Hong Kong in 2014–2015, and about which organised labour was yet almost indifferent.

Do these Western experiences hence suggest that unionism, like other social institutions, has its 'life-cycle'? As pointed out by Ferguson, unless rejuvenated with determined or even disruptive overhauls, they are likely to decay to become more dysfunctional than functional in performing their 'social mission'. The perils are fatigue and complacency and the parochialism of vested interests due to the process of 'domestication'. This problem is especially noticeable with unions which are born out of recalcitrant sentiments against alien forces (which are capitalism in the West and colonial imperialism in the Orient). They come of age when they mature and become civilised by waiving their evangelistic character and, instead, harmonising their objectives and actions with the established polity and its 'rules of the game' so as to gain recognition and participation. Both Eric Hobsbawm and Daniel Bell warned sternly against the ascendency and degeneration of Western unionism as the dialectic institutional product of Western capitalism (Hobsbawm, 1990: 283–85; Bell: 2000: chapter10). Besides, the paradox of institutional structuration is the well-rehearsed pathos of over-bureaucratisation, even later rationalised by the institutionalists as either 'technocracy' and 'meritocracy'. To a large extent, when Western unionism excels as 'business unionism' (in Hong Kong, the colonial government propagated such economic unionism as 'responsible unionism' in the 1950s and 1960s of the last century, in counterpoise to radical unionism with Bolshevik sympathies for being subversive), they court the fate of 'union exhaustion' by making not only the union structure and governance but also the game of collective bargaining too 'bureaucratic' and cumbersome, a process of self-captivation reminiscent of the bureaucratic cage and Michel's 'Iron Law of Oligarchy' (Michels, 1927).

By comparison, Asian unions are not yet hence beset. In China and Hong Kong, for instance, union density has not receded but has been slightly on the rise. In a sense, unionism in Asia is still a long way from maturity in the Western sense, and the same in Latin America. Unions in many Asian societies are still relatively malleable, in terms of structure and functions. They are still incapable of organising effectively and systematically the workplace, even now when the lesser workplace has become once again virtual or irrelevant. Many of them cannot charge an expensive union due and hence still operate by lay leadership, the amateur and non-professional nature of which is still a besetting source of bizarre and confused union organisation. Yet the strategic advantage has been their 'adhocratic' character, which makes these Asian unions more adaptable and malleable. They can be almost as flexible and fluid as the NGOs. Sometimes the boundary can be so vague or elusive that it may not be impossible to shuttle between the two domains, subject to the constraints of the trade union law. By comparison, Oriental unions, less caged in tedious 'institutional encasement', is theoretically more amenable than Western unions to the type of 'transformation' hinted by Giddens, in order to attain a new estate of the realm in 'self-reflexive emancipation'. Asia as a region, despite its diversity, is still politically more stable than Latin America. In many Asian societies, the nationalistic creed for economic self-strengthening and advance still appeals to the working class and is shared by the professional/intellectual middle class. We have argued that class consciousness may have grown less relevant in Britain and other Western societies (Hobsbawm, 1990: 311–322) and has never been that relevant in the Asian context. There is a potential for Asian unions to extend their turf to go upstream as well in embracing also new occupational groups of the 'knowledge and service workers'. To echo Keith Thurley, the mission is worth canvassing for Asian unions to partner with the state in promoting human capital, a labour market of 'fairer deal' and hence the nation's economic growth and affluence for its citizenry.

In Giddens' social project for the macro future, the drive for 'collective emancipation' among the refractory masses will be so potent that the other social movements like those for peace, ecology and 'extreme inclusion' all need to take on an evangelistic overtone to appeal. He suspects that Western labour movements, unable to correct their 'institutional fatigue' decisively, will continue as a lukewarm social force. There is little of the VoC or VoU model to offer any viable solution to this malaise of secular institutional decay for developed Western unionism.

Conversely, still in a global context of relative 'late-development', Asian unions may not be as vulnerable to the dilemma as narrated above. Strictly speaking, however, it is difficult to allude that the labour movements in China, Japan, Singapore and Hong Kong have not yet matured, as each against its history. They may be at cross-roads too, but not as thorny as in the developed West. Their hitherto limitation may hence be the source of latent blessing, which lies with the relative paucity of a collective bargaining culture as a highly institutionalised arrangement. In Hong Kong, for example, unions do not lack their historic experiences in collective bargaining but were malleable in waiving conveniently its practice, when demanded by the shifting political economy. Collective bargaining has never been upheld as sacrosanct and definitive for the labour movements of China and of Hong Kong, both of which extended historically from the Chinese guilds for which indentures and collective deals were no stranger. Collectivism has always been a cultural feature of the Orient, but in the past, it combined with either occupational trades or ethnic affiliations to form a tradition of ethnic guilds (clan associations), trade guilds or a mix of both.

For most Asian unions, 'union adhocracy' seems to be the rule than exception: the leadership is often lay while full-time salaried union executives are sparse; whereas few workplaces are organised by locals which may superimpose an elaborate and yet expensive shop-steward system on the shop-floor. An implication for democratic governance is that the grass roots always have access to and not insulated from the leadership, especially where the union is small. It appears as a union weakness that most unions (with the probable exception of Japanese and Singapore unions) are not co-opted by management to serve on the in-house grievance/disciplinary review system, not to mention as worker directors on the company boards of governance. Again, structural weakness can suggest functional resilience for Asian unions: they are able to dissociate, even so involuntarily, from managerial decision-making and hence can better avert sharing any managerial responsibilities by not so 'designated' for a junior 'ministerial role'.

Asian unions are yet ambivalent about the inroad made by the NGOs into the labour arena. It is beyond the scope of this book to examine as to details how NGOs operate in Asia and the extent to which they have contributed to the 'de-institutionalization' of industrial and other forms of social conflict. Yet, in the Hong Kong context of a capitalist economy within a socialist motherland, organised labour has been up to now held the NGOs 'at bay' but as demonstrated by the social protest of 'Occupation Central' in which the NGOs played a formidable role, social strike can eclipse and even displace labour strife and industrial protests by unions. Elsewhere in Asia, NGOs have attracted a larger clientele in the market of rights campaigns and protests, in both the extra work and work spheres. This seems to be the case of China, Taiwan, South Korea, the Philippines and most nations on the Indo-China Peninsula. To many of these Asian labour movements, the NGOs are either church-sponsored or secularised allies equally missionary in their zeal. However, there can be two problems posed by the NGOs to the labour movement proper. First is the lack of clear boundary demarcation, especially since NGOs do not organise for membership but often organise on an ad hoc basis for social issues and labour protests. They are likely to usurp the function of unions by removing issues from the workplace to the site of the neighbourhood community to combine with other non-workplace issues. Second, there is still a problem of proper disclosure of information on the internal governance and funding resources of NGOs. In a way, the NGOs are still a 'hiatus' or 'masked masquerades' in Asia. Whether or not they warrant branding as the civil society (writ small) and the 'third sector' organisations still need critical inquisition.

To conclude, both C. Wright Mills (1970) and Daniel Bell (1978) alerted us to the importance of charting and understanding the cultural-historical dimension of the political economy and socio-economic phenomena before coming to grips with the structure and functions of institutions of industrial societies. For Asian unionism, we suggest that the notion of Asian unions as a regional pattern based upon certain shared cultural traits and the meeting of certain common challenges as late-developing societies in an era of globalisation of the market, technology and electronic communication, on the one hand and, on the other hand, the notion of an 'Asian variant of unionism' as an extension of the institutional exposition on VoC can meet. We start to explore as how the notion of VoC and VoU can be refined as typing frameworks for classification. In the concluding chapters, we chart how Asian unions may converge and differ among the Asian polities we investigate in this comparative volume. Such similarities and variations lend a further empirical basis for us to vindicate and improve upon the VoU precept. Of course, as Keith Thurley and Han Wirdenius talked about 'European Management', we reiterate, hopefully with more vindicating evidence and elucidating argument which may need painstaking future research to materialise, that it is legitimate and an legitimate aspiration for us, as Keith Thurley propounded thirty years ago, to suggest and expect 'Asian unionism' as a fathomable regional entity which has been crystallising and will crystallise.

The above notwithstanding, a contextual variable which has proved almost beyond fathom and yet can be overwhelming is the 'geopolitics' of the region. Western colonialism was, paradoxically, a stabilising force for the region yet, unwittingly, post-war de-colonisation dis-stabilised the region's order, compounded by almost thirty years of China's self-seclusion after the 1949 Liberation. Today, the region is pervaded by the tussle for influence between the United States and China, which is 'testing the waters' of the 'First World' while still standard-bearing among its fellow nation-states in the 'Third World'. In a sense, China's initiative on 'One Belt, One Road' emanates seemingly from its import, from the developed West, of 'multilateralism' (an icon for 'globalization'), the 'rule of law', the 'welfare state' (a tradition which socialist China has never lacked given its pre-reform experience with 'enterprise welfarism') and 'civil society' which cherishes not only civil liberties (of which China's performance is still subject to international scrutiny) but also 'community-like commonwealth'. Such a 'One Belt, One Road' project, being engineered in the effacing shadow of the 'British commonwealth', has both a capital-cum-technology and human capital/labour market connotation. It will be interesting to observe as how the All-China Federation of China, the national union centre in China, and the labour movements elsewhere in Asia where the 'Belt/Road' carriage visits, are going to respond to such an element and also the extent to which they can work together on the human side to make the best and reduce best the risks of such a trans-national project.

References

Abegglen, J. (1958) *The Japanese Factory*, Glencoe, Illinois: The Free Press.

Andrews, J. (2017) *The World in Conflict: Understanding the World's Troublespots.* Updated edition, London: The Economist in association with Profile Books.

Atkinson, A. (2018) *Inequality: What Can be Done?* Cambridge, MA: Harvard University Press.

Bell, D. (1978) *The Cultural Contradictions of Capitalism*, New York: Basic Books.

Bell, D. (2000) *The End of Ideology: On the Exhaustion of Political Ideas in the Fifties*, Cambridge, MA: Harvard University Press.

Chesneaux, J. (1968) *The Chinese Labour Movement 1919–1927*, Stanford, CA: Stanford University Press.

Dore, R. (1990) *British Factory-Japanese Factory: The Origins of National Diversity in Industrial Relations*, revised edition with a New Afterword by the Author, Berkeley: University of California Press.

Dorre, K. Lessenich, S. and Rosa, H. translated by J. Herrmann and L. Balhorn (2009) *Sociology, Capitalism, Critique*, London: Verso.

Ferguson, N. (2012) *Civilization*, London: Penguin Books.

Ferguson, N. (2014) *The Great Degeneration: How Institutions Decay and Economies Die*, London: Penguin Books.

Fletcher, C. (1973) "The End of Management", in J. Child (ed.), *Man and Organization*, London: George Allen and Unwin, pp. 135–157.

Galbraith, J. (1972) *The New Industrial State*, 2nd edition, Harmondsworth: Penguin Books.

Giddens, A. (1991) *The Consequences of Modernity*, Cambridge: Polity Press.

Giddens, A. (2000) *The Third Way and Its Critics*, Cambridge: Polity Press.

Goldthorpe, J. (1984) "The End of Convergence: Corporatist and Dualist Tendencies in Modern Western Societies", in J. Goldthorpe (ed.), *Order and Conflict in Contemporary Capitalism: Studies in the Political Economy of Western European Nations*, Oxford: Clarendon Press, pp. 315–341.

Hanami, T. (1979) *Labour Law and Industrial Relations in Japan, Devanter*, The Netherlands: Kluwer.

Hobsbawm, E. (1990) *Industry and Empire: From 1750 to the Present Day*, London: Penguin Books.

Hobsbawm, E. and edited by L. Bethell (2016) *Villa Revolucion on Latin America*, London: Little, Brown and Abascus.

Jacques, M. (2012) *When China Rules the World*, 2nd edition, London: Penguin Books.

Lester, R. (1958) *As Unions Mature*, Princeton, NJ: Princeton University Press.

Levine, S. (1963) "Japanese Trade-Unionism as a Model in Economic Development", in E.M. Kassalow (ed.), *National Labor Movements in the Postwar World*, North Western University Press.

Maeda, M., Ng, S.H., Hong, J.C. and Lin, J.Y. (1996) "The Role of the State and Labour's Response to Industrial Development: An Asian 'Drama' of Three New Industrial Economies", in I. Nish, G. Redding and S.H. Ng (eds.), *Work and Society: Labour and Hunan Resources in East Asia*, Hong Kong: Hong Kong University Press, pp. 167–197.

McGregor, R. (2018) *Asia's Reckoning: The Struggle for Global Dominance*, London: Penguin Books.

Michels, R. (November, 1927) "Some Reflections on the Sociological Character of Political Parties", *The American Political Science Review*, vol. 21, no. 4, 753–772.

Ng, S.H. and Warner, M. (1998) *China's Trade Unions and Management*, London: Macmillan Press.

Ramos, E. (1981) "Industrial Relations Strategies of Trade Unions in South East Asia: A Comparative Analysis", in The Japan Institute of Labour (ed.), *Agenda for Industrial Relations in Asia Development*, Tokyo: The Japan Institute of Labour.

Patten, C. (1999) *East and West*, 2nd edition, London: Pan Books.

Schregle, J. (1981) "In Search of Alternative Models for Asian Industrial Relations: A Discussion Paper" in The Japan Institute of Labour (ed.), *Agenda for Industrial Relations in Asian Development*, Tokyo: The Japan Institute of Labour.

The All-China Federation of Trade Unions (2018) *2017 Zhong Guo Hui Nan Jan (The Almanac of the Chinese Labour Movement 2017)*, Beijing: Chinese Workers Press.

Thurley, K. (1983) "The Role of Labour Administration in Industrial Society", in S.H. Ng and D. Levin (eds.), *Contemporary Issues in Hong Kong Labour Relations*, Hong Kong: Centre of Asian Studies, University of Hong Kong, pp. 106–120.

Thurley, K. (1988) "Trade Unionism in Asian Countries", in Y.C. Yao, D. Levin, S.H. Ng and E. Sinn (eds.), *Labour Movement in a Changing Society: The Experience of Hong Kong*, Hong Kong: Centre of Asian Studies, University of Hong Kong pp. 24–31.

Thurley, K. and Wirdenius, H. (1989) *Towards European Management*, London: Pitman Publishing.

Turner, A., Gardner, M., Hart, K., Morris, R., Ng, S.H., Quinlan, M., and Yerbury, D. (1980) *The Last Colony: But Whose? A Study of the Labour Movement, Labour Market and Labour Relations in Hong Kong*, Cambridge: Cambridge University Press.

Vatikiotis, M. (2018) *Blood and Silk: Power and Conflict in Modern Southeast Asia*, London: Weidenfeld and Nicolson.

Westad, O. (2013) *Restless Empire: China and the World Since 1750*, London: Vintage Books.

Wright Mills, C. (1970) *The Sociological Imagination*, Harmondsworth: Penguin Books.

Part 2

Country chapters

3 Australian unions

Crisis, strategy, survival

Rae Cooper and Bradon Ellem

Introduction

We begin this chapter by asking what it means to write about Australia in a book on Asian unions. Just where Australia sits in relation to Asia is no simple matter. Australia's relationship with Asia has been fraught since Australia was colonised by the British at the end of the eighteenth century. Australians have tended to see their country as, at best, in but not of Asia (Walker, 1999). For much of the twentieth century, policymakers and institutions (including unions) actively excluded Asian peoples and their goods from the country. Today, however, the connections between Australia and Asia are critically important. Australia's three major export sectors – iron ore, coal, education – are Asia-focused. Another, tourism, is increasingly so. These Asia-reliant sectors have different patterns of employment and industrial relations from each other. Some are unionised, some are not; where unions operate, they are markedly diverse from one sector to another.

If Australian industrial relations and unions are, as we shall see, different from the (admittedly heterogeneous) forms across Asia, many sectors of the economy are shaped by, and even dependent upon, Asian economies. We need to take account of this while also explaining that the core of the union movement lies not so much in these export sectors but firmly within the confines of the national economy. It lies among employees of the state; it is increasingly feminised; and among those women workers we find almost the only areas of union growth this century. The overall decline in union membership has been dramatic: from over 60% in the mid-1950s (Bain and Price, 1980: 121–25) to 15% today.

Notwithstanding Australia's credentials as a 'liberal market economy' (LME), we will show that the state is critical to the shape of work, regulation and unionism. This is so not only in terms of 'the state as employer', but in other and just as fundamental ways. These facts invite some reflection and international comparison. The role of the state in Australia may be different from its role in other Asian economies and industrial relations (Ford and Gillan, 2016; Moore, 2018), but we cannot understand Australian unions without understanding that the state is a vital actor. Australia's place as a postcolonial society in Asia, the uneven nature of the its economy – at once trade-dependent, service-based and relatively affluent – and the link between unions and state all pose puzzles for theorising 'varieties of capitalism' and varieties of unionism in Australia, matters to which we return in concluding.

As in the other chapters, we address five issues: how unions developed; the main problems they now face; their responses; their successes; and theorising the implications for comparison, context and 'variety'. In dealing with these matters, we set out in some detail the history of unions in Australia, arguing that this is critical to understanding the present and to locating the forms of Australian unionism in a comparative context. We not only think about how to compare countries in terms of variety (Hall and Soskice, 2001) but examine how different capitalisms (and 'their' unions) are interconnected (Peck and Theodore, 2007). This approach allows us to explain the nature of unionism and the crisis in membership in Australia. We can then address the current state of the union movement before drawing out some wider lessons for comparative study. A central feature of our argument is that contemporary Australian unionism must be put in the context of a crisis that stretches back forty years, a crisis in which the changing role of the state has been a central factor.

The making of unionism in Australia

Many overviews of unions in Australia begin with, or concentrate on, the immediate context or, at the most, twentieth-century developments, but here we show how union origins in the previous century were important, shaped in part by Australia's very different relationships with Britain and Asia. In one sense, trade unionism in Australia is older than white society in the country because, for example, one union, an Australasian branch, was set up on a ship bound for the colonies. Unions developed among skilled workers, almost all of whom were men and of British birth. To them, unionism was the norm and while it may seem to trite to say that they established unions 'because they could', it is not an unreasonable claim. Craftsmen and semi-skilled workers laboured in relatively strong colonial economies, and they had unusual labour market power because additional supplies of labour were months away in Britain (Quinlan, 1987; Hagan, 1989).

These unions were localised, reflecting the scale of product markets and labour markets; they were not colonial bodies at all, far less national ones. They were as keen to restrict as to organise, recruiting (and excluding) based on skill, gender and race and, to some extent, social class and 'respectability'. Like the colonies themselves, the unions were marked by race and racism from the beginning. Australia's First Peoples were mostly excluded from the growing capitalist economy, their 60,000 years of experience on the land swept aside as surely as many of the people were themselves, especially with the massive expansion of the wool industry which underpinned colonial growth and demanded sole use of what had been Indigenous people's land (see among many Reynolds, 1981).

With changes to capital, production and labour markets, craft unions came to sit uneasily alongside unions which organised the unskilled and, more hesitantly, women workers. By 1890, over 20% of the workforce was unionised in some of the Australian colonies, a higher rate than 'at home' in Britain or in Asian countries to the north. Some of these newer unions, notably among coal-miners and shearers became national (or more accurately inter-colonial) organisations before there was a nation-state (Buckley, 1970; Markey, 1985; Buckley and Wheelwright, 1988).

Unionism that reached beyond skilled workers lay in sectors of the economy that were from the beginning 'globalised' and masculinised, namely, shearing, mining and transport. The urban building industry and an increasing array of mostly small-scale manufacturing plants with only limited application of mass, Taylorist, techniques also soon developed (Buckley and Wheelwright, 1988; Markey, 1988). Like craft unions elsewhere, these bodies were, as Hyman (2001) puts it, market-focused: they aimed to secure immediate, material gains for their members and typically avoided formal political engagement. As in small-scale capitalist economies elsewhere, unionism was but one way for these men to advance themselves: becoming 'masters' was a more typical aspiration than overthrowing them (Hagan, 1989).

Australian unions came under attack in most of the colonies in the 1890s in ways not dissimilar to the contemporary world as global economic pressure played out locally: the seemingly powerful unions in export and transport sectors were attacked by employers insisting on 'freedom of contract', that is, individual agreements. Employer hostility and state repression were in part shaped by economic pressures as global industries collapsed with falling commodity prices in a generalised depression, in some places at least as bad as that of the 1930s (Hagan, 1989).

Australian unions, economy and state

The state was critical to how these changing structures affected unions then and for most of the twentieth century. In the 1890s, the state sided with rural and mining capital but as workers regrouped through political action and as manufacturing became stronger, policymakers in the new Commonwealth of Australia set about controlling the more militant employers (and unions) after 1901 through a tightly integrated set of policies around trade protection which brought manufacturers 'into the tent' and provided minimum conditions for employees and, in effect, union recognition. This alliance between sections of capital and labour underpinned a system of conciliation and arbitration set up nationally in 1904. Arbitration was part of a set of policies that ranged beyond industrial relations. It was a markedly exclusivist arrangement: deeply racialised, through the 'White Australia Policy', and explicitly gendered, through state-sanctioned gender divisions of labour and discriminatory wages policy around a male breadwinner model (Ryan and Conlon, 1975). Among other things, this policy framework was intended to wholly isolate the new country of Australia from Asia. Immigration policy excluded those from non-English-speaking backgrounds. Non-Europeans, whom most saw as a wage threat, were regarded with a visceral racism.

Compulsory conciliation and arbitration meant that the state would provide support for unions. This was a major reversal of policy from the 1890s. In the lock-outs and strikes of 1890s depression, the state's intervention had been wholly on the side of employers, breaking unions and using armed force against them (Markey, 1988: chapter 5). However, most unionists believed that the state could provide redress – almost all white males could vote – and they established social democratic labour parties which quickly won parliamentary success in some of the colonies. As Macintyre puts it: 'forms of political representation made it possible for an electoral majority to intervene in industrial relations and impede capital from taking full rewards for its [industrial] victory' (Macintyre, 1983: 105).

The new labour law encouraged the formation of unions and employer associations to promote industrial peace and it was observed that: 'The system of arbitration ... is based on unionism. Indeed, without unions, it is hard to conceive how arbitration could be worked' (Higgins, 1920: 15). 'Awards', delivered by tribunals to settle disputes between employers and unions, required employers to abide by rulings in relation to substantive conditions of employment and to recognise unions. These awards applied to all employees, whether they were unionists or not. Over time, the tribunal delivered what in effect was a national wages policy. Women were restricted to low-paid work or confined to the role of 'mother to the nation' (Ryan and Conlon, 1975; Lake, 1986). In short, unions were embedded within specific racial, gender and class arrangements and, in turn, located in clearly articulated ways with the global economy.

A wartime Australian Labor Party (ALP) government (in office overall from 1941 to 1949) provided policies designed to deliver full employment for men, a by-product of which was enhanced bargaining power for better-organised unions. Union density (the percentage of the workforce belonging to a union) reached 60% in the 1950s. Through the arbitration system and via the concept of 'comparative wage justice', the gains won by these unions flowed to less well-placed workers. Minimum conditions for practically all non-managerial employees were set by union-bargained agreements. State laws allowed 'closed shop' arrangements or 'preference in employment' for unionists and sanctioned such agreements which had been negotiated directly between employers and unions. On one estimate, 70% of all union members were covered by compulsory unionism arrangements by the 1960s (Peetz, 1998: 87). Furthermore, the state effectively shielded unions from common law threats around restraint of trade, ringfencing them within the labour law regime.

Unions were also circumscribed by these arrangements. They had no lawful right to strike and had to be nationally 'registered' (as opposed to being organised on a State-basis) to secure national awards. For many (but not all) unions, arbitral processes became the default method of defending members' interests. 'Preference' became a substitute for organising. Unions might not have been the 'industrial cosmetics' that one critic called them (Howard, 1977), but they were shaped by the state and in some sectors reliant upon it. Even their national peak body, the Australian Council of Trade Unions (ACTU), established in 1927, was, for much of its history, chiefly a lobbyist and a coordinator of wage campaigns in the tribunal despite the hopes of radicals for something like the syndicalism of a 'one big union' (Hagan, 1981).

These arbitration-based and exclusivist class compromises were not, however, unchallenged. Unions were not homogeneous and uniformly arbitration-oriented. Indeed, in the very year that the national tribunal handed down its first wage decision, 1907, syndicalism came to Australia with the Industrial Workers of the World (IWW). For the IWW, tribunals were 'bosses' courts', tying workers to an inherently malevolent state. They eschewed politics for 'direct action'. The IWW had some influence in mining and other areas of (mostly) male employment but of more enduring importance as a challenge from the left was the Communist Party of Australia (CPA). The CPA's membership peaked when the Second World War ended by which time the party had won the leadership of unions in mining, transport, some manufacturing sectors and among schoolteachers and clerks. Communist-led unions pushed arbitration tribunals and Labor governments for major improvements in wages and hours after the war (Sheridan, 1989).

Other unionists (and of course employers and governments) were deeply alarmed by the CPA's rise. From 1945, ALP-based 'Industrial Groups' supported by sections of the Catholic Church and others opposed to communist influence in unions fought for control of the movement. Bitter factional struggles divided unions and the party itself for the best part of twenty years. Communist influence was reduced – they lost control of several key unions – but thereafter in most States, they established a loose alliance with the ALP's left factions (Murray, 1970). It was chiefly from here that that challenges came to the class compromise that had led to arbitration and to the race and gender orders woven through it. These militant unions supported class-conscious solidarity with Asian workers, the most notable being in actions in support of struggles against colonialism for independence in Asia and later in opposition to the US-initiated war in Vietnam (Saunders, 1982).

Unions were slow to challenge other structures and inequalities, most notably the gender order, even around so basic an issue as 'equal pay for the sexes', but in the 1930s, there were some such campaigns in the clothing industry (Ellem, 1989) and from the late 1960s, when women's liberation activists took up the cause. When fundamental changes to wage-fixing principles for women finally took place in 1972, the gender wage gap began to close, a process that continued until the mid-1990s after which the gap grew once more (Whitehouse, 2004).

Regardless of their hue, almost all Australian unions were tied to politics. Most were affiliated to the ALP and saw political involvement as essential to defending the arbitration system. This version of 'labourism' built not only around the arbitration system but, for most, White Australia, trade protection and support for the ALP, shaped the union movement for most of the twentieth century. Long periods of Labor Party success in the States, if not nationally, and legislative measures around leave, safety and workers' compensation evidenced the success of this strategy (Hagan, 1989). Arguably, the crisis unions have faced over the last forty years is because they have been unable to build new power bases in a much-changed national economy and institutional context.

Remaking work and unions

The decline in union membership and of the coverage and scope of collective bargaining is a familiar phenomenon across other English-speaking countries and even Western Europe (Baccaro and Howell, 2017). Common explanations apply: the changing nature of work, declining employment in union strongholds, changes to management practices and unions' difficulties in adapting. In Australia, there is a national peculiarity in that many of these factors reshaped the landscape before conservative parties won national office and pursued an anti-union agenda. This turn, a fundamental reorientation of the state, was most marked from 1996, well after similar changes in other Anglophone countries. By that time, membership had already fallen from an all-time high of 2.659 million in 1990 to 2.194 million. Union density has fallen in every year since 1976. It stood at 31.1% in 1996, down on the 61% of the mid-1950s (Bain and Price, 1980: 121–25; Peetz, 1998: chapter 1).

The prosperity of the post-war boom obscured emergent trends, notably related to employment growth in areas of union weakness, that became more obvious in the 1990s. From the 1970s, as membership density fell, unions were affected numerically and also strategically: they lost members as the number of jobs fell in manufacturing, mining and transport. The most militant unions, once the leaders in wage campaigns and, often, in political agitation, were the hardest hit. We now examine these changes in more detail.

Unions in the both the archetypal LME, the USA, and the coordinated market economies (CMEs) of Europe provided lessons for Australian unions. Government and employer attacks on unions in Britain and the USA shaped the mindset of Australian union leaders as they contemplated strategies which turned on redefining their relationships with the ALP to respond to economic change. These changes were also shaped by readings of industrial relations in countries such as Sweden and Austria where it appeared that high union membership sat side by side with productive workplaces and social harmony (ACTU, 1987; Scott, 2009).

The most important of these responses was a kind of national partnership with the state, the signing of a Prices and Incomes Accord between the ALP and the ACTU. This agreement, signed just before an election brought the party to office in 1983, reflected the growing power of the ACTU over its affiliates (Briggs, 2004). Unions committed themselves to wage restraint in return for the maintenance of the 'social wage' through changes to superannuation, healthcare, education and other social measures. Later Accord agreements in the 1990s shifted to more micro concerns, re-gearing both industry and award regulation as a century of trade protection came to an end (Ewer et al., 1987; Briggs, 2004). The decisive change was the introduction of enterprise-based bargaining to replace the system of multi-employer bargaining that had developed over the twentieth century.

The union movement also set out to restructure itself, with the initial goal of workplace efficiencies and cost efficiencies in unions themselves. The strategy was also driven by the alliance of government and the ACTU. Under the banner of 'strategic unionism', unions merged, with dramatic results to the shape of the union movement. Between 1989 and 1994, the number of federally registered (roughly meaning national unions) fell from 299 to 52 (ABS6323.0, 1995). By the mid-1990s, 98% of the members of ACTU affiliates were members of the largest 20 unions (ACTU, 1995).

Despite – or, in some critics' minds, because of – these changes, membership fell (Costa and Duffy, 1990). The clear break in union membership came in 1993 when, after years of falling density, the raw number of union members began to drop. This decline in aggregate numbers made the density decline even more stark because the number of people in work was growing and more alarming because it affected the financial base of unions. Drawn from the besieged union movement in the USA, the 'organising model' came to Australia. The proponents of this strategy argued that unionism was based on a 'transactional' relationship between union members and union organisation that was not sustainable (ACTU, 1999).

The ACTU, therefore, exhorted unions to adopt organising with its 'transformational' vision for union activity centred on growing membership, building workplace activism and enhancing internal democracy (Cooper, 2003). The ACTU adopted organising as a formal strategy in 1999 and sought to resource and drive it through its affiliates. The ACTU's policies in *Future Strategies: Unions Working for a Fairer Australia* (ACTU, 2003) evoked memories of a similar document from 1987, *Australia Reconstructed*, but they were very different. As we have seen in examining the merger strategy, the early focus was on restructuring and improved service delivery, but by 2003, in line with the organising model, the focus was on an activist membership base driving renewal with delegates as the critical component in union effectiveness (ACTU, 2003: 22; Cooper, 2003). The ACTU argued that new sources of power in 'the community' and in coalition with other political groups were essential because of changes among employers and in the state (ACTU, 1999).

Notwithstanding these apparent changes, it remained the case that in many sectors there was a persistent 'institutional sclerosis' (Pocock, 1998) as leaderships, typically older and male, were reluctant to drive meaningful cultural change in their organisations. And where structural change did take place, it was often the case that leaders were still different from their younger, female memberships.

Employer hostility and state anti-unionism

As unions tried to remake themselves, employers, chiefly in export sectors, were influenced by state hostility to unions in Britain and the USA. They began to argue against state support for the award system, arbitration and even unionism itself (Dabscheck, 1995; Sheldon and Thornthwaite, 1999). Major employers argued that with product and finance markets having been globalised, the labour market could no longer be regulated as it had been (see Dabscheck, 1989, for an overview). The Labor government responded to these threats – and to global economic change and local economic weakness – by using the Accord to introduce 'managed decentralism' under which the national wage-fixing tribunal and the ACTU attempted to drive workplace change (Buchanan and Callus, 1993). When 'enterprise bargaining', that is, collective bargaining at the workplace level, was introduced in 1992 as the next step in 'decentralism', the ACTU and major blue-collar unions supported it – indeed drove it (Briggs, 2001; Hancock, 2016).

Many of these changes, and all the tripartite structures which accompanied them, were swept away by an anti-union government after 1996, but one important one survived: the introduction of a compulsory superannuation scheme to improve upon the pension for retirees. Unions have a formal governance role in these now lucrative 'industry super funds'. At the time for writing, this role is under threat from finance interests, wary of the scale of coverage of these funds (and their superior rates of return compared to commercial retail funds). For our purposes, the point is that, despite falling membership, these arrangements could provide alternative forms of voice and power (Mees, 2018). In this respect, Australian unions are not only distinct from those in Asia but also from those in Anglophone countries where such arrangements are unknown.

Neither the fall in strikes through the 1980s and 1990s nor the generally cooperative approach of unions mollified the opponents of unions. Well in advance of national change, they enjoyed success in several Australian States which amended labour law to undermine arbitration and union power. Two significant States led the charge: Victoria, the manufacturing heartland of the country, and Western Australia, the increasingly important mining centre (Nolan, 1998).

In 1996, a conservative national government was elected, sharing the view with its State-based counterparts that union power had to be reduced. The *Workplace Relations Act 1996* reduced the scope of collective bargaining and arbitration: awards could only contain twenty matters (many had previously had over a hundred) and the power of the national tribunal to settle industrial disputes was scaled back. Unions faced fines for industrial action and limits on access to workplaces. For the first time in national labour law, there were individual contracts, Australian Workplace Agreements (AWAs). AWAs allowed employers to bypass unions and undermine collectively bargained standards. They over-rode awards and other collective agreements (Cooper and Ellem, 2008). AWAs did not reach much beyond the 3% of the workforce (Peetz, 2007), but they threatened unions because they precluded union representation. Employers could use the threat of AWAs to drive 'concession bargaining' (Cooper et al., 2009).

The conservatives won four successive elections, but only the last of these, in 2004, gave them control of both Houses of Parliament and, therefore, an untrammelled capacity to make change. These changes were badged as 'Work Choices', a prescriptive set of rules to constrain union power, with new institutions and practices to *re*-regulate industrial relations (Ellem et al., 2005). Work Choices recast agreement making and undermined union rights and collective bargaining, entrenching AWAs and expanding the scope of non-union collective agreements (Stewart, 2006). No new awards would be made except as part of an 'award review' process designed to rationalise the remaining awards. New employees could be compelled to sign AWAs as a precondition of employment; 'employer greenfields agreements' meant in effect employers making agreements with themselves. Employers were not required to negotiate with unions even if a majority of employees wanted a union collective agreement (Cooper and Ellem, 2011).

The laws alarmed not only unions but a broader constituency. By 2007, an election year, they had become the number one political issue. Unions led a fightback with their *Your Rights at Work* strategy based on big-budget media, local campaigns and a consistent message about the government's attack on *individual* rights. The strategy was designed to sidestep any community antipathy to unions with this focus on rights. The ALP won the election in November 2007 with one of the largest ever swings against a government. Industrial relations policy was the vote-changing issue (Muir, 2008; Wilson and Spies-Butcher, 2011; Ellem, 2013).

Unions under the fair work regime

If the state had been the driving force and enabler of de-unionisation, might political and legislative change provide redress? The *Fair Work Act 2009* was implemented by the Labor government after the election landslide in November 2007. It introduced a new collective bargaining framework and reworked the minimum standards framework (Cooper, 2010). A 'Better Off Overall Test' was designed to ensure that employees were not disadvantaged in the negotiation of workplace arrangements. Notably, while there was capacity for employees and employers to negotiate individual arrangements, no new AWAs could be made (Cooper and Ellem, 2009).

The Act remade the relationship between the state and unions, undoing many of the changes made after 1996 but *not* restoring the arbitration system. Collective bargaining was understood as an *individual* right – as it had been in the Your Rights at Work campaign – and as a means to enhance productivity and build higher earnings. It was based on 'good faith bargaining', underpinned with a novel element, 'majority support determinations', through which union claims that a workforce wanted collective bargaining could be tested.

From the time the *Fair Work Act* was introduced until writing this chapter in 2018, there were criticisms of the framework from unions. Rather than opening up collective bargaining to those who had been excluded under the previous regime, it ringfenced the process. Union bargaining could still be stymied if employers were determined to avoid engagement, and it was difficult for unions to force them to the table or to defend existing conditions. A Low Paid Bargaining Stream and Equal Remuneration Orders represented an attempt by the framers of the legislation to provide mechanisms to improve the wages of employees with low levels of bargaining power, who were mostly women (Cooper, 2009 2014) but the union consensus was that these mechanisms were inadequate (Korseen, 2016; ACTU, 2018; Irvine et al., 2018). Union leaders argued that low wages growth was caused by the 'smothering' effects of the 'restrictive, excessively regulated' bargaining framework (McManus quoted in Karp, 2018). It was not only unions who expressed concern about low national wages growth, with similar arguments about the impact of declining union power emerging among key regulators and policymakers (Nicholson et al., 2017; Iggulden, 2018).

Notwithstanding the limits of the Act from a union perspective, most employer groups have pushed for further controls on unions and for more individual flexibilities. Back in government since 2013, the conservative parties were resistant to much of this pressure, not least because *Work Choices*, or anything like it, remained politically toxic. What the government did do, aided, it must be said, by some troubling behaviour by some union leaders, was paint unions as merely another interest group and a selfish and outmoded one at that. This approach took the particular form of commissions of inquiry into corruption, revitalised bodies to police the building industry and new legislation to govern 'registered organisations' (Pekarek and Gahan, 2016).

Whatever the argument about the Fair Work framework's impact on wages, it is clear, as shown in Table 3.1 and Figure 3.1, that the new system did not bolster union membership. In 2016, just 14.5% of the workforce was unionised, with public sector density sitting at 38.5% and in the private sector slipping to one in ten workers (see Table 3.1). Areas that were once union heartlands have been effectively de-unionised (see Table 3.2).

At the same time, a gendered realignment of union membership has occurred. In 2010, women became more highly unionised than men for the first time. Male union density declined from 20.1% in 2009 to 17.9% in 2010. Female union density fell too but now stood at 18.7% (ABS6310.0, 2012). Almost

Table 3.1 Union Membership and Density 1996–2016

Year	*Total Members*	*Union Density (%)*
1996	2,194,300	31.1
1997	2,110,300	30.3
1998	2,037,500	28.1
1999	1,878,200	25.7
2000	1,901,800	24.7
2001	1,902,700	24.5
2002	1,833,700	23.1
2003	1,866,700	23.0
2004	1,842,200	22.7
2005	1,911,900	22.4
2006	1,786,000	20.3
2007	1,696,400	18.9
2008	1,752,900	18.9
2009	1,835,100	19.7
2010	1,787,800	18.3
2011	1,834,700	18.4
2012	1,840,400	18.2
2013	1,747,600	17.0
2014	1,570,400	15.1
2015	N/A	N/A
2016	1,547,200	14.5

Sources: ABS 6310.0 *Employee Earnings, Benefits and Trade Union Membership*. Canberra: Australian Bureau of Statistics (2013), ABS 6330.0 *Characteristics of Employment*. Canberra: Australian Bureau of Statistics (2016a). The figures are for August each year.

Note: Since 2015, the ABS discontinued the annual collection of union membership data, which is now reported on a biannual basis.

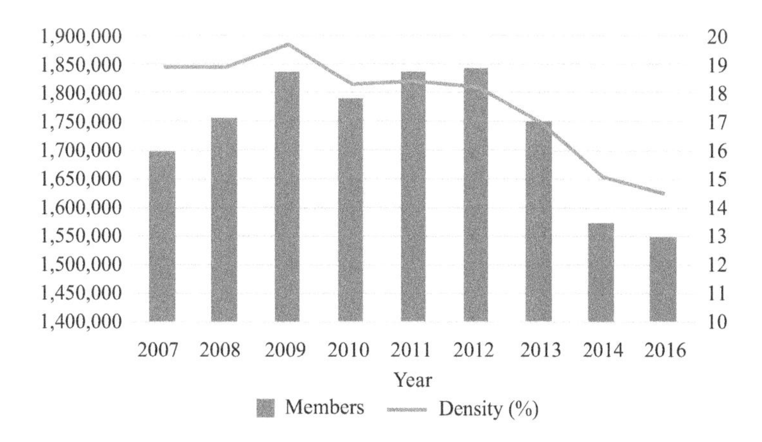

Figure 3.1 Union Membership and Density 2007–2016.

all the jobs growth in the country in the period since the 1990s has been provided by the health and human services sectors. On Australian government projections (Department of Employment, 2017), this will continue as major policy change (such as the roll-out of a new national disability scheme)

Table 3.2 Trade Union Membership by Industry Sector, 2016

Industry of Main Job	*Trade Union Member in Connection with Main Job*	*Not a Trade Union Member in Main Job*	*Total*	*Proportion of Employed Persons Who Were Trade Union Members in Main Job (%)*
Agriculture, forestry and fishing	5.3	267.2	279.6	1.9
Mining	35.8	169.9	214.5	16.7
Manufacturing	108.6	708.3	858.2	12.7
Electricity, gas, water and waste services	34.3	96.9	134.8	25.4
Construction	98.6	886.0	1,049.1	9.4
Wholesale trade	18.2	350.3	380.1	4.8
Retail trade	128.7	999.9	1,195.7	10.8
Accommodation and food services	19.4	793.1	847.4	2.3
Transport, postal and warehousing	115.7	447.0	589.5	19.6
Information media and telecommunications	18.4	179.1	208.4	8.8
Financial and insurance services	40.6	357.5	416.5	9.7
Rental, hiring and real estate services	2.8	201.6	209.6	1.3
Professional, scientific and technical services	20.9	979.2	1,036.4	2.0
Administrative and support services	18.6	418.1	449.1	4.1
Public administration and safety	232.2	498.4	758.5	30.6
Education and training	308.7	654.3	989.2	31.2
Healthcare and social assistance	317.5	1,133.9	1,503.5	21.1
Arts and recreation services	17.9	194.0	224.5	8.0
Other services	21.6	443.8	488.2	4.4
Total	1561.8	9773.1	11831.7	13.2

Sources: ABS 6310.0 *Employee Earnings, Benefits and Trade Union Membership*. Canberra: Australian Bureau of Statistics (2013), ABS 6330.0 *Characteristics of Employment*. Canberra: Australian Bureau of Statistics (2016a).

continues and as the share of Australians with disability and who are frail/aged continues to grow each year (National Disability Services, 2016).

One of the reasons for the limited impact of legislative change may be that even if those changes had been more robust, they might still have little impact because of organisational and workplace change. The problems arising have been acute: underpayment of workers in franchises, hyper-exploitation of international students in general and of casual labour in horticulture and the rise of the 'platform economy' (Clibborn, 2015; Pekarek and Gahan,

2016; Clibborn and Wright, 2018). Alternative forms of worker representation and mobilisation have not emerged as they have in other countries (including some Asian ones). There has been, though, signs of union innovation to address at least some of these threats (Minter, 2017; Nicholson et al., 2017), but membership levels remain low.

Varieties of unionism

As noted in the introduction to this volume, most studies of comparative employment relations have been shaped by the work of Hall and Soskice (2001), while Frege and Kelly (2003) have been influential in comparative studies of trade unionism. Here we cannot rehearse the criticisms of these approaches. Suffice to say that in our chapter, we have shown the utility of several of those critiques in pointing to: within-country variation and the importance of connection between countries as well as comparison between them (Peck and Theodore, 2007), the need for historical analysis in making and remaking of employment relations (Howell, 2003) and how global flows of capital and labour affect national economies (Coe and Yeung, 2015).

We suggest that liberalisation in Australia has been so marked that the country has 'changed type'. While much debate has focused on assessing whether 'national systems' are characterised by 'convergence' to an LME norm or continued 'divergence', the implication of our analysis is that in the last thirty years or so an Australian 'variety of liberalisation' has emerged (see Baccaro and Howell, 2017, on Western Europe) in which the state has facilitated the demands of key employer groups for more 'flexible' employment relations.

In their much-cited comparative overview of union strategy, Frege and Kelly (2003) set out six strategies which unions have pursued amid the crisis of membership and power: organising, changes to structure, coalition-building, social partnership, political action and international networking. The critical starting point for their analysis is, however, not unions as such but the different national settings in which union movements are situated. They argue that in Anglo-Saxon countries, the context faced by unions has changed markedly and been more hostile than in (European) CMEs. They suggest that this setting impelled change in unions. In Frege and Kelly's work, unions (or national union movements) choose between these six strategies – assuming unions do change at all, of course – depending upon how leaders assess the contexts they face. Specifically, they argue that unions in Anglo-Saxon countries had to develop new strategies because the national settings had changed so much (Frege and Kelly, 2003: 9).

For us, the intriguing element of this framework is that practically all these strategies have been deployed by the ACTU and national unions since the membership crisis we have identified in this chapter. From a union perspective, this is an alarming thought because none of them have enhanced union power. Things might have been still worse of course absent those strategies, but we cannot know that for sure.

Furthermore, most of these strategies had been deployed before the state turned against unions from 1996 and well before newer threats through subcontracting, gig platforms and of automation. As Table 3.3 summarises, social partnership and political action had combined through the Accord from 1983, structural change through mergers had taken place from the late 1980s, organising was an official policy from 1999 and coalition-building was a core component of the *Your Rights at Work* campaign between 2004 and 2007. International networking has a lower profile, but several unions have

Table 3.3 Australian Union Strategy: Adapting Frege and Kelly (2003)

Strategy	*Applicability*	*Potential Benefits*	*Potential Risks and Limitations*
Reform of union structures	Union mergers *pre*-crisis: ACTU-driven and state-enabled in the 1980s Mergers continue on a case-by-case basis, still typically in terms of political alignments and cultural fit	Stronger financial base; originally envisaged in terms of workplace efficient as well as benefits to members; enhanced power and resources to achieve other goals, be they partnership or traditional militancy	Perception of lost occupational identity or members' control Risk of failure and opportunity cost if reforms do not deliver
International solidarity	Affiliation to global unions a long-standing phenomenon albeit not always closely engaged Some Australians in leadership positions in GUFs recently	Knowledge of, and networks in, global corporations and their supply chains Use of power base in Australia to support campaigns elsewhere as well as vice versa	Few risks but potential benefits not always clear or material
Labour–management partnerships	Mostly national, ACTU-led, although there have been some sector or regional examples at times	'Social wage' improvements: the Prices and Incomes Accord 1983–1996 was the prime example of such a national strategy Sector-level or regional attempts typically about jobs	Co-option by state or management; disempowerment of members' capacity
Organising	From 1999, ACTU policy of 'Organising' Adopted at least in form by most major unions with some defining themselves as organising unions	Improved membership and financial base and member engagement Enhanced capacity to achieve other goals and improved wages and conditions	Resource-intensive; members may still prefer 'servicing'; failure can be demoralising

Strategy	*Applicability*	*Potential Benefits*	*Potential Risks and Limitations*
Political action	A central strategy since 1891 in most colonies/states and then nationally; partly because of links with the state through the arbitration system in most of twentieth century Occasional alliances with other left-wing parties	Use of state power to provide union recognition and minimum conditions	Over-reliance on the state hampers strategic adjustments when the government changes State minima may obscure apparent need for unionism and incentive to join unions
Coalition-building	Historically, not a strong element of Australian union strategy Ad hoc, time/place specific instances arguably increasing at the time of writing	Local campaigns around specific issues from time to time have succeeded *Your Rights at Work* campaign 2005–2007 the most sustained and successful national campaign	Sustainability over the longer term

used it with some success in campaigns against particular firms; Australian union officials play leading roles in the International Transport Workers' Federation and the International Trade Union Confederation; and unionists in the state of Western Australia attempted to create linkages across the Indian Ocean. Nonetheless, partly for historical reasons, Australian unions' roles in global union federations are limited (on these bodies in general, see Ford and Gillan, 2015). For all the changes we have described, there are also consistencies. Unlike many of the other countries in this volume (and in some sites in the global north), Australia did not see the wholesale emergence of new forms of unionism, or even new unions, or of the rise of NGOs, worker centres or community groups as alternative forms of voice or mobilisation. Unions have remained, in however attenuated a way, the dominant form of collective representation for workers. The task in this chapter, therefore, has been to explain how a long-established union movement, older than the nation itself, has changed and has sought to adapt itself to external threats and uncertainties.

Looking ahead, unions need either to reinvigorate traditional sources of power or, as they have been seeking to, create new relationships to build legitimacy. Unions are perhaps better placed to do this than are those in other countries. Surveys show that unions are viewed more favourably than big business by Australian citizens and that the trend has been shifting their way for a generation (Cameron and McAllister, 2016: 84), although it might be noted that favourable views of unionism shift in parallel to the falling rates of strikes, that is, their apparent capacity to inflict pain on employers.

Conclusion

We have shown how unions arose in Australia and how, among other things, much of this history was shaped by the geography of Australia – in, but not of, Asia. We note that, unlike in many other places, unions in Australia were and remain the key form of worker representation. Neither works councils nor community-based organisations have been as important. We have also shown how we position this account in terms of thinking through 'variety' in the present era. To conclude, we draw out the key findings in relation to the three other questions with which this book is concerned: the core challenges confronting unions, strategic actions that are being adopted and the achievements of unions and the factors influencing these outcomes. We begin with the last of these because it was precisely these achievements which in part inspired the counter-attack on the union movement.

Through their own efforts and through arbitration and the ALP, unions delivered minimum conditions which extended beyond their own membership. Awards were central to this set of achievements, as were 'national wage cases' and 'test cases' run by the ACTU. Among the latter were protections around termination and change and a series of cases around parental leave. More generally, safety procedures and workers' compensation laws were superior to Asian states if lagging some European countries.

With the critical caveat that the majority of these changes were won when the Australian economy was sheltered by trade protection, we note that these efforts delivered relatively egalitarian earnings outcomes both between and within classes and, from the 1970s until the 1990s, even in terms of gender. As we have seen, there were striking omissions and exclusions involved but we also stress that, formally at least, unions and 'the old system' delivered a wage system which meant that native-born workers were not threatened by a low-wage immigrant sector nor were those immigrant workers excluded from the system. That system was, therefore, important in underpinning Australia's transition to a multi-cultural society. As in other countries, the same can no longer be said as racial tensions rise.

There were limits to the power unions exercised and to the ambitions they had. With only rare exceptions did unions threaten the power of employers at the point of production. Managerial prerogative was protected by arbitration; unions were typically as keen as employers to contain workers' challenges to it. We have also shown how a particular alignment of class and institutional arrangements lay behind unionism's achievements. As those arrangements changed, so did the fortunes of Australian unions. The sources of power which unions had drawn upon were much altered and, in some cases, removed. The relationship between unions and the state was perhaps the most important of these changes. Unions had once been central to how the state managed industrial relations – too much so for the liking of many on the left as well as the right. By the beginning of this century, unions instead had become 'outsiders' (Cooper et al., 2017), with governments either antagonistic towards, or at best merely tolerant of, them. These changes took place as work itself was transformed under post-Fordism and as the Australian economy became more integrated with, and reliant upon, Asia.

The strategic actions which unions have taken since decline began have had a marked geography to them: the 1980s push for restructuring and co-operation was explicitly modelled on the CMEs of Europe; in the changed climate of the 1990s, adoption of organising was shaped by the experience of unions in the LME heartland, the USA. The former lived and died with an ALP government; the latter may have ameliorated decline but did not reverse it. Unions are now committed to changing, as they must, the laws governing the regulation of work and seeking innovative ways to deal with the changing nature of that work. Unions appear to have retained a degree of legitimacy amid growing inequality and the heightened power of major corporations. This setting may provide the basis for unions once again to speak for a constituency beyond their own members and indeed beyond Australia.

References

ABS (1995) 6323.0. *Trade Union Statistics, Australia.* Canberra: Australian Bureau of Statistics.

ABS (various years) ABS6310.0. *Employee Earnings, Benefits and Trade Union Membership, Australia.* Canberra: Australian Bureau of Statistics.

ABS (various years) ABS6330.0. *Characteristics of Employment.* Canberra: Australian Bureau of Statistics.

ACTU (1987) *Australia Reconstructed.* Canberra: Australian Government Publishing Service.

ACTU (1995) 'Finance Committee Report', Report to ACTU Congress, ACTU Congress 1995.

ACTU (1999) *unions@work.* Melbourne: Australian Council of Trade Unions.

ACTU (2003) *Future Strategies: Unions Working for a Fairer Australia.* Melbourne: Australian Council of Trade Unions.

ACTU (2018) 'Gender Equality'.https://cdn.workplaceexpress.com.au/files/2018/ACTUgenderreportsummaryA4_ctr_workingwomen_genderequality_p4wm.pdf

Baccaro L and Howell C (2017) *Trajectories of Neoliberal Transformation: European Industrial Relations Since the 1970s.* Cambridge: Cambridge University Press.

Bain G S and Price R (1980) *Profiles of Union Growth: A Comparative Statistical Portrait of Eight Countries.* Oxford: Basil Blackwell.

Briggs C (2004) The end of a cycle? The Australian Council of Trade Unions in historical perspective. In Ellem B, Markey, R and Shields J (eds) *Peak Unions in Australia: Origins, Purpose, Power, Agency.* Leichhardt: Federation Press, pp. 236–60.

Briggs C (2001) Australian exceptionalism: the role of trade unions in the emergence of enterprise bargaining. *Journal of Industrial Relations* 43(1): 27–43.

Buchanan J and Callus R (1993) Efficiency and equity at work: the need for labour market reform in Australia. *Journal of Industrial Relations* 35(4): 515–37.

Buckley K (1970) *The Amalgamated Engineers in Australia 1852–1920.* Canberra: ANU Press.

Buckley K and Wheelwright T (1988) *No Paradise for Workers: Capitalism and the Common People in Australia*. Melbourne: Oxford University Press.

Cameron S and McAllister I (2016) *Trends in Australian Political Opinion: Results from the Australian Election Study 1987– 2016*. Canberra: Australian National University.

Clibborn S (2015) Why undocumented immigrant workers should have workplace rights. *Economic and Labour Relations Review* 26(3): 465–73.

Clibborn S and Wright C (2018) Employer theft of temporary migrant workers' wages in Australia: why has the state failed to act? *Economic and Labour Relations Review* 29(2): 207–27.

Coe N and Yeung H-W (2015) *Global Production Networks: Theorizing Economic Development in an Interconnected World*. Oxford: Oxford University Press.

Cooper R (2003) Peak council organising at work: ACTU strategy 1994–2000. *Labour & Industry* 14(1): 1–21.

Cooper R (2009) Forward with fairness? Industrial relations under labor in 2008. *Journal of Industrial Relations* 51(3): 285–96.

Cooper R (2010) The 'new' industrial relations and international economic crisis: Australia in 2009. *Journal of Industrial Relations* 52(3): 261–74.

Cooper R (2014) Low paid care work bargaining and employee voice in Australia. In: Bogg A and Novitz T (eds) *Voices at Work: Continuity and Change in the Common Law World*. Oxford: Oxford University Press, pp. 55–66.

Cooper R and Ellem B (2009) Fair work and the re-regulation of collective bargaining. *Australian Journal of Labour Law* 22(3): 284–305.

Cooper R and Ellem B (2011) 'Less than zero': union recognition and bargaining rights in Australia. *Labor History* 52(1): 49–69.

Cooper R, Ellem B, Briggs C and van den Broek D (2009), Anti-unionism, employer strategy and the Australian state, 1996–2005. *Labor Studies Journal* 34(3): 339–362.

Cooper R, Ellem B and Wright C (2015) Policy and the labour movement. In Head B and Crowley K (eds) *Policy Analysis in Australia*. Bristol: Policy Press, pp. 231–44.

Costa M and Duffy M (1990) Trade union strategy in the 1990s. *The Economic and Labour Relations Review* 1(1): 145–64.

Dabscheck B (1989) *Australian Industrial Relations in the 1980s*. Melbourne: Oxford University Press.

Dabscheck B (1995) *The Struggle for Australian Industrial Relations*. Melbourne: Oxford University Press.

Department of Employment (2017) *Employment Outlook to May 2022*. Canberra: Australian Bureau of Statistics.

Ellem B (1989) *In Women's Hands? A History of Clothing Trades Unionism in Australia* Kensington: UNSW Press.

Ellem B (2013) Peak union campaigning: Fighting for rights at work in Australia. *British Journal of Industrial Relations* 51(2): 264–87.

Ellem B Baird M, Cooper R and Lansbury R (2005) Work Choices: Myth-Making at Work. *Journal of Australian Political Economy*, 56: 13–31.

Ewer P, Higgins W and Stevens A (1987) *Unions and the Future of Australian Manufacturing*. North Sydney: Allen & Unwin.

Ford M and Gillan M (2015) Employment relations and the state in Southeast Asia. *Journal of Industrial Relations* 58(2): 167–82.

Ford M and Gillan M (2016) The global union federations in international industrial relations: A critical review. *Journal of Industrial Relations* 57(3): 456–75.

Frege C and Kelly J (2003) Union revitalization strategies in comparative perspective. *European Journal of Industrial Relations* 9(1): 7–24.

Hagan J (1989) The Australian union movement: context and perspective. In Ford B and Plowman D (eds) *Australian Unions: An Industrial Relations Perspective*. South Melbourne: Macmillan, pp. 18–48.

Hall P and Soskice D (2001) *Varieties of Capitalism: The Institutional Foundations of Comparative Advantage*. Oxford: Oxford University Press.

Hancock K (2016) Reforming industrial relations: revisiting the 1980s and 1990s. In Hancock K and Lansbury R (eds) *Industrial Relations Reform: Looking to the Future*. Leichhardt: Federation Press, pp. 1–15.

Higgins H (1920) *A New Province for Law and Order*. Sydney: Constable and Company.

Howard W (1977) Australian trade unions in the context of union theory. *Journal of Industrial Relations* 19(3): 255–73.

Howell C (2003) Varieties of capitalism: And then there was one? *Comparative Politics* 36(1): 103–24.

Hyman R (2001) *Understanding European Trade Unionism: Between Market Class and Society*. London: SAGE.

Iggulden T (2018) Low wage growth undercutting government's positive economic message. *ABC*. www.abc.net.au/news/2018-02-02/low-wage-growth-undercuts-governments-message/9391778. Accessed 2 February.

Irvine S, Thorpe K and McDonald P (2018) Low-paid 'women's work': why early childhood educators are walking out. *The Conversation*. http://theconversation.com/low-paid-womens-work-why-early-childhood-educators-are-walking-out-91402. Accessed 25 March.

Karp P (2018) Sally McManus says enterprise bargaining is smothering wage growth. *The Guardian*. www.theguardian.com/australia-news/2018/mar/21/sally-mcmanus-says-enterprise-bargaining-is-smothering-wage-growth. Accessed 21 March.

Korseen T (2016) Childcare workers walk off the job for the first time in 30 years to campaign for better pay. *Herald Sun*. www.heraldsun.com.au/news/victoria/childcare-workers-walk-off-the-job-for-first-time-in-30-years-to-campaign-for-better-pay/news-story/06b23683e87ae592c0d27537c33b2ff3. Accessed 25 March.

Lake M (1986) The politics of respectability: identifying the masculinist context. *Historical Studies* 22(86): 116–31.

Macintyre S (1983) Labour, capital and arbitration. In Head B (ed.) *State and Economy in Australia*. Melbourne: Oxford University Press, pp. 98–114.

Markey R (1985) New Unionism in Australia, 1880–1900. *Labour History* 48: 15–28.

Markey R (1988) *The Making of the Labor Party in NSW 1880–1900*. Kensington: UNSW Press.

Mees B (2018) Employee representation and pension fund governance in Australia. *Economic and Industrial Democracy*. Online first, March. doi:10.1177/0143831X17752265

Minter K (2017) Negotiating labour standards in the gig economy: Airtasker and Unions New South Wales. *The Economic and Labour Relations Review* 28(3): 438–54.

Muir K (2008) *Worth Fighting For: Inside the Your Rights at Work Campaign*. Sydney: UNSW Press.

Murray R (1970) *The Split: Australian Labor in the Fifties*. Melbourne: Cheshire.

Moore J (2018) *Varieties of Capitalism in Southeast Asia*/ Cham: Springer International Publishing.

National Disability Services (2016) *State of the Disability Sector Report 2016*. Centre for Applied Disability Research available at www.nds.org.au/images/news/sods2016/State_of_the_Disability_Sector_report_2016.pdf

Nicholson D, Pekarek A and Gahan P (2017) Unions and collective bargaining in Australia in 2016. *Journal of Industrial Relations* 59(3): 305–22.

Nolan D ed (1998) *The Australasian Labour Law Reforms: Australia and New Zealand at the End of the Twentieth Century*. Annandale: The Federation Press.

Peck J and Theodore N (2007) Variegated capitalism. *Progress in Human Geography* 31(6): 731–72.

Peetz D (1998) *Unions in a Contrary World: The Future of the Australian Trade Union Movement*. Cambridge: Cambridge University Press.

Peetz D (2007) *Assessing the Impact of 'WorkChoices' – One Year On*. Melbourne: Report to the Department of Innovation Industry and Regional Development Victoria.

Pekarek A and Gahan P (2016) Unions and collective bargaining in Australia in 2015. *Journal of Industrial Relations* 58(3): 356–71.

Pocock B (1998) Institutional sclerosis: prospects for trade union transformation. *Labour and Industry* 9(1): 17–36.

Quinlan M (1987) Early trade union organisation in Australia: Three Australian colonies 1829–1850. *Labour & Industry* 1(1): 61–95.

Reynolds H (1981) *The Other Side of the Frontier: Aboriginal Resistance to the Invasion of Australia*. Ringwood: Penguin.

Ryan E and Conlon A (1975) *Gentle Invaders: Australian Women at Work*. Ringwood: Penguin.

Saunders M (1982) The trade unions in Australia and opposition to Vietnam and conscription: 1965–73. *Labour History* 43: 64–82.

Scott A (2009) Looking to Sweden in order to reconstruct Australia. *Scandinavian Journal of History* 34(3): 330–52.

Sheldon P and Thornthwaite L eds (1999) *Employer Associations and Industrial Relations Change: Catalysts or Captives?* Sydney: Allen & Unwin.

Sheridan T (1989) *Division of Labour: Industrial Relations in the Chifley Years 1945–1949*. South Melbourne: Oxford University Press.

Stewart A (2006) *Stewart's Guide to Employment Law*. Leichhardt: The Federation Press.

Walker D (1999) *Anxious Nation: Australia and the Rise of Asia 1850–1939*. St Lucia: University of Queensland Press.

Whitehouse G (2004) Justice and equity: women and indigenous workers. In Isaac J and Macintyre S (eds) *The New Province for Law and Order: 100 Years of Australian Industrial Conciliation and Arbitration*. Cambridge: Cambridge University Press, pp. 207–40.

Wilson S and Spies-Butchers B (2011) When labour makes a difference: union mobilization and the 2007 federal election in Australia. *British Journal of Industrial Relations* 49(2): 306–31.

4 Unions and alternative forms of worker representation in China in an era of privatisation and globalisation

Fang Lee Cooke

Introduction

Research on Chinese trade unions has primarily focused on their functions, strategies and challenges since the beginning of the economic reform in the late 1970s that has led to the rapid growth of the private manufacturing sector and the decline of the state sector. Lack of independence and inefficacy in representing workers' rights and interests have been familiar critiques levelled against the All-China Federation of Trade Unions (ACFTU), the only official union recognised by the Chinese government, due to the lack of organisational capacity and political will. This chapter provides an evaluation of the evolving role of the ACFTU organisations at various levels and the emerging role of alternative agents of workers' representation, notably non-government organisations (NGOs). This chapter highlights different attitudes, coverages and functions of ACFTU organisations across different levels, industrial sectors and ownership forms. It argues that research on Chinese unionism should adopt a more nuanced approach and a variety of perspectives to uncover varieties of unionism in terms of strategic and operational priorities, constraints, capabilities and effects.

Unions and Workers' Congress: institutional structure and functional challenges

Chinese trade unions

The ACFTU is the only trade union officially recognised by the Chinese government for workers' representation. Established in 1925, the ACFTU has been operating under the leadership of the Chinese Communist Party (CCP). It is essentially part of the state political, institutional and mass organising apparatus controlled by the CCP and largely funded by the state (Chen, 2009; Cooke, 2011b; Howell, 2008; Taylor and Li, 2007; Zhu et al., 2011). Existing research on the ACFTU has revealed its tension with the CCP at several junctures since the founding of socialist China, mainly with the former attempting to gain more independence from the political structure constrained by the CCP and to adopt a more assertive stance in representing workers' rights and interests (e.g., Harper, 1968; Jiang, 1996; Pringle, 2011). For example, Sheehan's (1998) examination of internal communication documents of the ACFTU revealed complaints that they were treated as a work department of the CCP and were unable to do anything else for the workers other than being sympathetic to their problems (see also Bai, 2011).

The functions of the ACFTU are typical of those defined for the trade unions in socialist countries (e.g., Clarke, 2005). According to Ross Martin's (1989) typologies, the Chinese trade unions fall within 'the authoritarians' category as the 'state instruments', carrying out a 'decisively subordinate role' (p. 70) that is 'concerned with *both* production and protection' (p. 78, original emphasis). The trade unions' primary responsibility is the state (Martin, 1989) whose interest is not necessarily aligned with that of the grass roots. In other words, trade unions assume a dual function of organising workers in ways to facilitate productivity improvement (e.g., through suggestion schemes, problem-solving teams, skill contests and welfare activities) of the enterprise, on the one hand, and to represent the workers and defend their rights and interests, on the other hand. During the state-planned economy period, the ACFTU's role was largely confined to the former. The deficiency of the ACFTU's role in representing workers became more and more evident following the economic reform that started in 1978.

As the state sector's share in employment shrank from over 78% of the urban workforce in 1978 to less than 15% in 2016 (National Bureau of Statistics of China (NBSC), 2017), the rapid expansion of the private sector has brought with it not only dramatic economic growth but also a sharp rise in labour disputes. The tension between the two functions of the trade unions, i.e., production facilitator and rights defender, has intensified. The lack of autonomy of the ACFTU and its perceived inefficacy in protecting and advancing workers' rights and interests has attracted much criticism (e.g., Chan, 1993, 1998, 2000; Clarke, 2005; Howell, 2003, 2008; Pringle, 2011; Taylor and Li, 2007). As Chen (2009, p. 662) observed, 'their [ACFTU's] governmental status prevents them from operating through the mobilising of grassroots or exerting their influence by empowering their grassroots branches'. Trade unions are seen as the mouthpiece of the state and their legitimacy in representing the workers has been questioned. The fact that ACFTU officials are mostly appointed by the government authority (for union organisations above the enterprise level) and the enterprise (for enterprise union organisations) rather than elected by the workers (e.g., Taylor and Li, 2007) exacerbates the scepticism.

Attempts in direct elections of grass-roots trade union officials as part of the union reform in several eastern coastal provinces, such as Guangdong, Zhejiang and Shandong, since the mid-1990s has not taken roots or rolled out to other provinces nationally (Howell, 2008). Political, structural and institutional constraints, resistance from the ACFTU itself, and the lack of organising capacities as well as willingness of grass-roots workers to take on union cadre positions for fear of employer retaliation are contributing factors that have undermined the opportunity of the grass-roots union organisations to become a 'more effective, worker-oriented organisation' (Budd et al., 2014; Howell, 2008, p. 845; Liu, 2010; Meng, 2017). Nevertheless, the emphasis on building a 'harmonious society' and the increase of workers' self-organising has pressurised the ACFTU organisations to be more proactive in supporting grass-roots unions (e.g., Brown and Chang, 2017; Chang and Cooke, 2018; Liu, 2010).

In November 2015, the Chinese government called for another wave of union reform through the 'ACFTU Reform Pilot Program' (《全国总工会改革试点方案》hereafter 'Programme'). The Programme demands ACFTU organisations to strengthen three dimensions (*zengsanxing*增三性) and remove four dimensions (*qusihua*去四化). *Zengsanxing* refers to enhancing the politicalness, advanceness and mass nature of trade union work, whereas *qusihua* refers to de-bureaucratise, de-aristocratise, de-entertainment-oriented and de-administratise of the union mode of functioning and activities (ACFTU Reform Pilot Work Leading Group, 2017). In the last two years, ACFTU organisations at the provincial and municipal level have responded to the request of the Programme by implementing a number of initiatives, which then cascaded down to the lower levels of ACFTU organisations. Some of the initiatives have been promoted/extended to unionised enterprises. Initiatives have taken various forms and substance, reflecting local situations and conditions. Reports from official websites of provincial and municipal ACFTU organisations indicate that simplifying union organisational structure through merger and downsizing, becoming more connected with the gross roots, competence building, digitalising union services to/communication with workers, and, most importantly, alignment with the CCP ideology and the strategic development plan of the state (e.g., 'fulfilling the China Dream' and 'China Manufacturing 2025') are the key foci. In other words, CCP control may be sustained and tightened, and the productivity enhancement function of the ACFTU will be emphasised. It is unclear how effective these institutional and service innovations have been in terms of improving grass-roots workers' welfare and well-being.

At the enterprise level, union coverage is more extensive in the state sector than the private sector, and once the union is recognised in the enterprise, union membership level is usually high, typically covering over 90% of the workforce in the enterprise (c.f., NBSC, 2017). However, a high level of union membership does not imply union strength in collective bargaining or wage negotiation. This is because the ACFTU is mainly concerned with establishing its presence in the enterprise rather than the interests of workers or mobilising them (Bai, 2011). Research on trade unions at the enterprise level, especially with regard to the setup of the trade unions in private and foreign-funded factories, further revealed the monopoly of enterprise management over the union and questioned the legality of union chairpersons who are often senior managers at the same time (e.g., Chan, 2001; Chang and Cooke, 2018). For example, Yu's (2008) study of the establishment and operation of a worker-elected trade union in a Taiwanese-funded shoe factory in southern China showed that the union was controlled by management and used as a gimmick to enhance the company's corporate social responsibility reputation instead of a genuine instrument to promote workplace democracy. In particular, the union had no wage bargaining power, had to side with the management or step aside when labour–management disputes occurred and was mainly playing a welfare role, a role which was traditionally played by unions in the state-owned enterprises (Yu, 2008). Chan et al.'s (2017, p. 602) study of foreign-funded enterprises in southeast China revealed that management strategy 'was critical in shaping the union's role' and 'this was influenced by factors such as home-country policies, the expectations of overseas customers, management ideology and pressures from the ACFTU and the party-state to comply with the requirement for a union'.

Existing research of workplace unions commonly revealed the welfare role, rather than the rights defending role, of the unions (Bai, 2011; Cooke, 2011a; Warner, 2008; Yu, 2008). Worker-led workplace unions and workers-elected union representatives may be suppressed by the enterprise, such has been the case of Walmart stores in China (e.g., Li and Liu, 2016). Nevertheless, Lee et al.'s (2016, p. 229) study of the evolution of collective bargaining observed that while the local federation of trade unions 'carefully controls labour relations at the workplace', 'the new election practices for enterprise union committees and wage bargaining create an institutional space for rank-and-file workers to articulate their views and to negotiate with management at the workplace'. Chang and Cooke's (2018) study echoed this finding.

Emerging studies on the relationship between unionism and wage increase revealed different findings. For example, Liu's (2010) case study of four local union organisations in the period of 2005–2007 showed considerable differences in organising strategies and effect on workers' collective wage bargaining. Using 'provincial-level data from the period of 1994–2008', Budd et al.'s (2014, p. 185) study of 'the relationship between union density and wages, employment, productivity, and economic output in China' suggests that 'union density does not affect average wage levels, but is positively associated with aggregate productivity and output'. These findings support the argument that ACFTU organisations act mainly 'as agents of the enterprise and the state in delivering productivity enhancements at the expense of, rather than through the cooperation of, workers' (Budd et al., 2014, p. 203). In contrast, Yao and Zhong's (2013) smaller scale study single-year data revealed the positive relationship between union presence and wage increase. It is also worth noting that data used in Budd et al.'s (2014) study was over ten years old, and more studies need to be conducted with more up-to-date data and on a larger scale to capture current situation.

Workers' Congress

According to the Labour Law of the People's Republic of China enacted in 1995 (hereafter Labour Law), the 'representative function' of the unions is supplemented by the Staff and Workers' Representatives Congress (hereafter Workers' Congress) within the enterprise. Guided by the trade union as the executive organ, the Workers' Congress is an official mechanism of workers' direct participation, through representatives elected by the workers, in the enterprise's decision-making and management. Initially introduced in the state-owned enterprises in the late 1940s following the establishment of socialist China, the Workers' Congress has been given an enhanced role since the 1980s in response to the marketisation of the economy (e.g., Huang et al., 2016). Existing research indicates that, similar to the trade unions, Workers' Congress has largely not been an effective actor in voicing workers' needs and interests, despite its role as a democratic socialist workplace institution for workers to exercise their power of democratic management (e.g., Zhu and Chan, 2005). It was reported that Workers' Congress tend to lean towards the management side in joint decision-making (Ding et al., 1997).

The majority of the private firms have not set up a Workers' Congress. For those that have, and it seems that an increasing number have done so under the pressure of the local authorities as evidence of regulatory compliance, Workers Congress serves mainly as an extended human resource management (HRM) function in practice instead of playing an industrial democracy role on behalf of the workers (Cooke, 2012). Nevertheless, Huang et al.'s (2016) study of the role of democratic management in improving labour relations in coal mining firms suggests that the democratic management can improve labour relations of the firm, but it requires the commitment of the senior management.

Labour disputes and representational legitimacy of the trade unions

The rapid growth of the Chinese economy following the open-door policy of 1978 has drawn millions of surplus rural workers into the urban sector, who are primarily employed in dirty, high-risk and laborious work in informal employment mode with poor terms and conditions (e.g., Cooke and Brown, 2015). According to Yu (2012), urban wage remuneration peaked at 56.5% of gross domestic product (GDP) in 1983 and then steadily declined to 36.7% in 2005. In 2009, the minimum wage level was about 30% of the average wage. According to a survey conducted by ACFTU in 2010, 23.4% of the workers surveyed had not received a pay rise in the previous five years. The same survey also revealed that 75.2% of the workers surveyed believed that the income distribution was unfair, with 61% of those surveyed believing that the biggest unfairness to be the unduly low wage level of ordinary workers (cited in Yu, 2012). The erosion of real wage (basic wages, bonuses and welfare benefits) growth compared to the growth of national GDP and company profit and poor labour standards have been the main sources of workers' grievance that has led to the rising level of labour disputes since the 1990s (e.g., Cooke, 2008; Lee, 2007; Lin, 2017; see also NBSC, 2017). Other sources also indicated the growth of self-organising industrial actions that have not been officially recorded in the labour dispute resolution system (e.g., Elfstrom and Kuruvilla, 2014; Meng, 2017).

The summer of 2010 witnessed another wave of strikes, ignited by the Honda (Nanhai) strike in southern China (c.f., Chan and Hui, 2017; Elfstrom and Kuruvilla, 2014; Gray and Jang, 2015; Lyddon et al., 2015). These industrial actions were wildcat in the absence of a clear articulation in the labour legislation of the right to strike. In particular, the trade unions have no legal right to organise strikes but have the right to be involved in the settlement of labour disputes, including strikes (Chang and Cooke, 2015). According to union officials interviewed, in handling strike actions, the most important function of the ACFTU branch organisations is to maintain stability of the society, protecting workers' rights and interests comes second (e.g., Chang and Cooke, 2018; Cooke, 2011a). Chen (2010) also pointed out the double role, i.e., the political and legal role, of the trade unions in handling collective actions: mediating disputes and pre-empting/preventing independent organising. Existing evidence suggests that most workers do not turn to the trade unions as their agents for grievance redressal (Cooke et al., 2016) or dispute resolution (Cooke, 2013). As a significant proportion of the workers involved in labour disputes are rural migrant workers, their lack of identification with the trade unions, in part due to their temporary attachment to their urban jobs, is a contributing factor to the workers' indifference to the union (Lee, 2007).

The 2010 summer strike wave sparked another wave of research interest in labour disputes in China (e.g., Chan and Hui, 2012; Chang, 2013; Chin and Liu, 2015; Elfstrom and Kuruvilla, 2014; Lüthje, 2014; Lyddon et al., 2015; Meng, 2017). Extant studies have assessed the implications of the strikes for trade union reforms (e.g., Chan and Hui, 2014; Hui and Chan, 2015; Lüthje, 2014). In particular, it is believed that strikes have led to the democratic election of grass-roots union representatives at workplaces, i.e., strike-driven direct election (e.g., Hui and Chan, 2015) in contrast to the previous top-down-driven direct election initiated by the party-state or its apparatus (e.g., Pringle, 2011). Lüthje (2014, 558) has also revealed how the strikes in Guangdong province have created (renewed) momentum for trade union reforms and 'opened the door for collectively bargained labour standards in the automobile industry at the regional level, which could also provide a model for other regions and industries in China' in spite of 'setbacks and political uncertainties'.

What has been less examined in extant strike studies is the role of the trade unions during the strike beyond the simplistic stereotype and broad-brush depiction of union officials' role as the state apparatus in suppressing workers' actions in order to maintain social stability. As Chang and Cooke's (2018) study revealed, union cadres and representatives at various levels play different roles in the strike event and its aftermath. A more in-depth approach is required to develop an informed understanding of union cadres' and representatives' respective agency role underpinned by their personal ideology, organisational resources and the broader political environment. These complexities and nuances shape the strike outcomes and the ensuing changes in the labour relations of the case company (Chang and Cooke, 2018).

Emerging research evidence suggests that how union leaders are elected or appointed may also affect their role and impact. For example, Fan et al.'s (2018) matched employer-employee survey study of 1,208 firms and 10,087 workers in 2016 revealed that union presence at the firm level does not seem to have a significant impact on mitigating labour conflicts. By contrast, active unions which are led by leaders appointed by the company management seem to be associated with a higher probability of labour conflicts. This finding may be explained by the fact that the unions fail to voice employees' grievances and are (perceived to be) acting on behalf of the management. While this relatively large-scale matched study has revealed important findings, it also raised many empirical questions for future research that may have theoretical implications in conceptualising Chinese unionism. For example, can company-appointed union leaders be differentiated into different categories contingent upon the motives of the company in setting up the union and appointing the leaders? Which types of union leaders (e.g., government appointed vs. company appointed) are beneficial or harmful to workers' representation and conflict resolution, and if so, under what circumstances? In-depth qualitative studies may be helpful in uncovering these nuances to complement large-scale national surveys.

Alternative workers' organising bodies

Given the suppression of independent trade unions and the close sanction by the Chinese government of NGOs, the presence, strength and effect of alternative workers' organising bodies, such as labour NGOs, have been limited, episodic and localised (see Froissart, 2011; Fu, 2017; Howard, 1995, 2015; Lee and Shen, 2011; Chan, 2018, for more detailed discussion). They are mainly present in the south-east China (Guangdong province) and largely organise workers outside the workplace. A small number of law firms also acted as labour dispute advisers and representing workers in labour disputes in a semi-charity manner. Political precariousness means that they have limited autonomy and resources to represent and organise the workers. According to the government regulations, civil organisations are required to have a supervising body within the government which oversees their decision-making and has the authority to close down the organisation. This high level of intervention makes it difficult for NGOs, some of whom are criticised by the ACFTU officials as the representatives of foreign interests, to register as a non-profit organisation. To overcome the legal and political constraints, many NGOs register as a commercial undertaking (Wang, 2008).

Despite these constraints, international NGOs and domestic ones under the international patronage have been playing an important role in monitoring the compliance of labour standards and regulations, particularly in the export-oriented manufacturing sector in southeast China. They also provide financial, medical, legal, educational and emotional support to the workers in sweatshop plants through some forms of organising primarily outside the workplaces (Cooke, 2011c).[1] They fill the gaps where union organisations have failed to reach. The existence of labour NGOs indicates a new form of activism based on their pragmatic positioning and technical competence to provide voice and support to those most needed (Chan, 2018; Froissart, 2011; Lee and Shen, 2011).

Strategies, initiatives and achievements of the ACFTU

Trade unions in China operate outside as well as inside employing organisations. In general, union organisations above the enterprise level have more resources and are much more active, compared with unions at the enterprise level. The latter report to the former but are often controlled by the enterprise management. Above the enterprise level, ACFTU organisations have been charged with promoting employees participation in technological innovation at workplaces, establishing trade union units in private enterprises, facilitating enterprise unions in collective bargaining and resolving labour disputes, poverty relief, monitoring and facilitating the setting up of social insurance schemes, skills training and provision of services and organising social activities.

Hyman (2001) advanced three models of trade unionism in the Western economies:

- Market-orientation, for example, by seeking to improve members' well-being through collective bargaining,
- Class-orientation, for example, by promoting working class' interest in the society in a more radical approach, and
- Society-orientation, for example, by strengthening 'the voice of workers in the broader society' and acting 'as a force for social, moral and political integration' (cited in Gospel, 2008, pp. 14–15).

Small traces of each of these three models can be found in the ACFTU's historical trajectory. For example, a radical class-oriented approach was adopted during the two decades of the revolutionary period that had led to the seizing power by the CCP against the national party and the founding of socialist China in 1949. This class-oriented approach continued to be influential during the state-planned economy period when the working class was hailed as 'the master of the country'. During this period, the ACFTU also assumed the social actor role by engaging in the education and moral teaching of workers in the state sector and providing welfare services. As China's economic transformation deepened from the 1980s, the market-oriented goal ascended in the ACFTU agenda. ACFTU grass-roots organisations become an active labour market broker, providing training and employment services to displaced workers from the state-owned enterprise as well as migrant workers. Meanwhile, the ACFTU was made more aware of its responsibility to the state in maintaining 'social harmony' by containing labour unrest.

Under pressure from the government to become more proactive in organising and representing the workforce, particularly the rural migrant workers against a backdrop of rising levels of labour disputes and stagnation of wage increase in spite of the rapid economic growth, the ACFTU launched a national recruitment drive in 2003 that led to the recruitment of over 70 million rural migrant workers into the union by the end of 2008 (see Table 4.1). In 2008, backed by the government, the ACFTU launched

Table 4.1 ACFTU Organising Strategy and Effects

Strategy	Methods of Recruitment and Activities	Outcomes/Effects
Workplace organising	***Recruitment methods*** • Mobilising labour regulations and local government authorities to seek employer's recognition • Once employer's recognition is secured, then recruit members at the workplace *en mass* through employer's support and peer pressure ***Activities:*** • HR function (e.g., organising productivity enhancement initiatives, such as skill competition, problem-solving task force) • Welfare role (e.g., employee care programmes) • Representation function • Assisting employers and workers to develop a partnership approach for consultation	• Less costly as cost mostly absorbed by employers • Integration of recruitment and organising • Easier to organise workers once access is allowed by employers • Easier to maintain communication • Easier to represent collectively • Easier to identify key supporters to establish a core team to strengthen union presence and function • Shared problems and shared solutions to maximise the impact of the trade union • Members more likely to identify themselves with the trade union • Benefits of joining the trade union firm specific • Less competition from other functional organisations • May circumvent to management control • May act as an extended management function and lose credibility with workers

(Continued)

Strategy	Methods of Recruitment and Activities	Outcomes/Effects
Distant organisation	***Recruitment methods*** • Public campaign to raise trade union profile and awareness • Offering free or low-cost services and advice as attraction • Collaboration with local government authorities, community bodies and enterprises • Grievance-based recruitment • Social media ***Activities:*** • Service provision (e.g., training, employment information, legal advice, health and safety advice and other information) • Representing function (e.g., negotiation with employers, representation in tribunal and court)	• More costly • Recruitment and organising not integrated • Possibility of recruiting a large number efficiently, e.g., in job fairs and employment and training centres • Possibility of disseminating the benefits of joining trade union through word of mouth across the country • More difficult to organise, retain and represent migrant workers collectively • Individuals less likely to identify themselves with the trade union and only turn to trade union for benefits rather than unionism • Dependence of full-time union officials to undertake activities • Results more individual-oriented rather than collective • Need to coordinate with other functional organisations (e.g., local labour authority, employment and training centres) • Potential competition with other functional organisations service providers

an intensive three-month campaign to 'unionise the Fortune 500' whose unionisation rate in China was significantly lower (less than 50%) than the average unionisation rate (73%) in overseas-invested companies as a whole. This led to a rapid increase of unionisation rate to over 80% by September 2008 (cited in *China Labour Bulletin* 2009). It should be noted that some high-profile foreign-invested firms recognised the trade unions in order to silence critics (e.g., Wang, 2008).

In addition to 'workplace organisation', ACFTU local organisations also deployed the 'distance expansion' strategy, as classified by Kelly and Heery (1989), to recruit rural migrant workers as members through job fairs and with service packages (e.g., training) as inducement. While the latter approach can help recruit union members quickly, this is largely a servicing approach rather than organising in a strict sense, since it has limited, if any, organising power to represent the workers in collective bargaining with particular employers. Without recognition by the employers, the unions can only represent workers outside the workplace and provide services to them in an individual capacity (e.g., through legal representation). At the national level, however, the ACFTU has played an important role in pressing for legislative reform to provide more protection to the workers, such was the case in the drafting of the Labour Contract Law enacted in 2008 (Cooke, 2011c). Under the direction of the government, ACFTU organisations have also been instrumental in assisting workers to collect wages owed to them by domestic employers, such as manufacturing plants, mining firms and construction sites where the wage arrears phenomenon is endemic (e.g., ACFTU, 2015).

In 2015, the State Council of China issued a document: 'Opinions on Building Harmonious Labour Relations', which emphasises its intention to strengthen workers' basic rights, including tighter enforcement of on-time wage payment, rest days and further regulating the use of hourly work, dispatched labour, human resource outsourcing and subcontracting (*Jilin Workers' Newspaper*, 2015). This high-profile policy document provided renewed momentum/pressure for ACFTU organisations to develop local initiatives to help enterprises improve labour relations. In response, ACFTU organisations have targeted economic development zones and industrial parks, which have concentrations of manufacturing firms, to introduce locally developed initiatives. These initiatives include both hard and soft programmes, such as 'harmonious labour relations' measurement indices with 'Model Company' prizes as some of the incentives for participation, unionisation drive, training and development courses for enterprise union officials and representatives, skill contests, service provisions. ACFTU organisations from these zones and parks model each other's initiatives as well as developing their own programmes and implementation strategies.

For example, according to the ACFTU officials from one of the nationally leading economic development zones interviewed by the author in early 2018, they use a two-pronged strategy to package their programmes and initiatives to the enterprises within their zone. At the surface are the service-oriented programmes with financial (e.g., fund for enterprise to develop initiatives) and reputational (awards and prizes) incentives to build relationships and win cooperation with the enterprise unions. Below this soft package is the hard requirement, such as reducing the level of labour disputes and industrial accidents. More and more new initiatives are being launched, often with the involvement of enterprises and workers themselves. In some cases, the enterprise not only implemented the initiative but also improvised and diffused it to other enterprises via the ACFTU organisation as good practices.

At the national level, it is unclear how effective these initiatives have been in developing harmonious labour relations. However, it is evident that union strengths, capability and resources vary across the country, industry and ownership forms. For example, union activities in the traditional state sector remain largely welfare oriented, productivity enhancement driven and stability sensitive. By contrast, union activities associated with the private sector may be more associated with health and safety training, rights awareness education and dispute resolution. The emerging diversities and varieties of unionism and union activities within China are an area where future research efforts can be placed.

Theoretical approaches to unionism research in the Chinese context

Trade unions and labour relations in the Chinese context have been largely examined from the political economy, and more precisely, Marxist perspective and institutional perspective. ACFTU organisations have been portrayed in a rather critical light, often in a broad-brush manner. A small number of in-depth case studies, nevertheless, have provided a more balanced and differentiated account which revealed the varying strategies of trade union organisations and the positive role of union officials and representatives, for example, in promoting workplace democracy (e.g., Yu, 2008), collective bargaining (e.g., Liu, 2010) and resolving strikes (e.g., Chang and Cooke, 2018) in ways that have been gainful for the workers. In particular, union officials' political will and political resources prove to be crucial to successful grass-roots union organising (e.g., Chang and Cooke, 2018; Liu, 2010). Xu et al.'s (2014) study also observed that, with their rising political and professional strength, the trade unions have become more capable and effective in advancing workers' interests through labour relations mediation channels, and that the union-led wage collective bargaining appears to have some positive outcomes.

It is clear that there is plenty of scope for enlarging and enriching union studies, in terms of approaches and methods to adopt and issues to examine, in order to provide a more balanced and comprehensive assessment about the trade unions. In terms of approaches, future research may study different groups of workers across different sectors and ownership forms, including those who are involved in strikes/labour disputes and those who may not have grievances, to develop a more precise understanding of what do workers want in their specific stages of working life. It is important to recognise that Chinese workers are not a homogeneous group, nor do they all have the same demands. Similarly, union officials and representatives may have different aspirations, ideologies, skill sets and political and social resources. Future research may explore, for example, the career aspirations and competence development of union officials and representatives. Such a focus may shed light on the capacity and strategy of individual union officials and representatives in advancing the cause of unionism and workers' benefits and well-being. In other words, we need to develop a deeper understanding of the agency role of the union officials and representatives by investigating how these agents create institutional and organisational space within the constraints of the formal institutional and organisational system to advance the workers' interest. As Coe and Jordhus-Lier (2010, p. 221) pointed out, agency 'is always relational, and never completely autonomous'.

Future research may be conducted by adopting a behavioural approach, given the limited research of behavioural industrial relations in the Chinese context compared to the behavioural research in the HRM field. In addition, how trade unions may play a preventative role of workplace grievances as well as a remedial role when workplace relationships break down may be examined from HRM perspective, informed by cultural awareness, both organisational and societal. The Chinese culture emphasises harmony in social relations and a preventative approach to conflict detection and resolution. This does not suggest that labour conflicts should be glossed over in the name of social harmony. Rather, studies of unionism need to reflect such a cultural sensitivity and nuances to understand how Confucianism, paternalism and conservatism inform union activities in day-to-day operations.

Given the insufficient human resource capacity in many Chinese firms and the limitation of social security provisions at the society level, the welfare role of the ACFTU organisations should not be dismissed so readily. Instead, their likely impact can be assessed based on the types of roles and recipients at different levels. For example, adopting the conservation of resources theory, Hu et al.'s (2018) survey study of 585 employees from enterprises in five provinces in China showed that in enterprises where unions are well-built, unions are seen by employees as a dependable, albeit moderate, source of support when employees' resources are perceived to be at risk. The same study also found that 'the level of union commitment and participation increases when the labour relations climate is adverse and the level of job satisfaction decreases' (Hu et al., 2018, p. 13). More broadly, studies may assess the relationships between the presence of unions and productivity, productivity improvement, profit, skill development and employability, employee satisfaction, workers' well-being and other intangible benefits/outcomes. This requires an interdisciplinary approach (e.g., organisational behaviour, labour economics) with both micro- and macro-level orientations.

In short, research on Chinese trade unions need to adopt a more inclusive approach to capture the diversity and divergence across sectors and ownership forms (e.g., Budd et al., 2014; Cooke, 2013), the fragmentation and segmentation of labour relation practices even within the same industrial sector in a large country (Lüthje, 2014) and differences in grass-roots ACFTU organisations in their organising strategies (Liu, 2010). Research in these directions will contribute to the broader understanding of varieties of capitalism/societies and varieties of unionism.

Conclusions

This chapter reviewed existing studies on the trade unions in China in terms of its structure, functions, challenges and effects as the only official workers' organising body. The transformation of Chinese industrial relations since the 1980s have not brought fundamental changes to the trade unions, despite calls, and expectations, to do so by scholars (e.g., Chang and Brown, 2013; Lüthje, 2014). However, there are signs of union effects in organising and representing workers. ACFTU organisations have implemented a number of initiatives through hard and soft approaches with varying effects at different levels. This chapter suggests a number of themes on which future research can focus, as well as approaches through which these areas can be studied. It calls for a pluralistic, in addition to the radical pluralistic, approach to assessing the role and effect of trade unions at various levels and from the lenses of different categories of workers and other stakeholders.

Future research should also go beyond assessing the unions related to specific workplace issues, but their broader role in, and likely effect on, the society. Equally, future research should be more sensitive to union strategy and choices, for example, to what extent and in what ways do ACFTU organisations shape grass-roots union agendas and consequently the variety of unionism despite various constraints? At a higher level, the role of the autocratic state can be examined with more nuances than it has been portrayed. It is clear that one union representing all the workers is a function of control rather than representation or a controlled form of representation. However, control or representation are processes, the outcome is aimed to improve workers' employment conditions and well-being. The value of state-led/involvement may be given more recognition than it has been granted in the Chinese internal relationships (IR)/unionism literature – in fact, the problems of the IR and labour disputes have largely stemmed from the lack of (effective) state intervention. Given the dynamic development of its economic and industrial relations landscape and the large gaps that exist in current research, China remains a fertile context for research on unionism and industrial relations more broadly.

Acknowledgement

A small part of this chapter draws from: Chang, C. and Cooke, F. L. (2018), 'Layers of union organisation and representation: A case study of a strike in a Japanese-funded auto plant in China', *Asia Pacific Journal of Human Resources.*

Note

1 See Froissart (2011) for a more detailed account of NGOs' role in organising rural migrant workers in China.

References

All-China Federation of Trade Unions Reform Pilot Work Leading Group (2017) *A Summary Report on the Trial Work of the National Trade Union Reform*. 28th March 2017, http://acftu.people.com.cn/n1/2017/0328/c67560-29174319.html, accessed on 17 April 2018.

ACFTU (2015) Unions, Government Join Efforts in Curbing Wage Arrears. http://en.acftu.org/28605/201503/27/150327112348420.shtml, accessed on 9 July 2018.

Bai RX (2011) The role of the All China Federation of Trade Unions: Implications for Chinese workers today. *The Journal of Labor and Society* 14: 19–39.

Brown W and Chang K (eds) *The Emerging Industrial Relations of China*. Cambridge: Cambridge University press.

Budd JW, Chi W, Wang YJ and Xie QY (2014) What do unions in China do? Provincial-level evidence on wages, employment, productivity, and economic output. *Journal of Labor Research* 35: 185–204.

Chan A (1993) Revolution or corporatism? Workers and trade unions in Post-Mao China. *The Australian Journal of Chinese Affairs* 29: 31–61.

Chan A (1998) Labour regulations in foreign-funded ventures, Chinese trade unions, and the prospects for collective bargaining. In O'Leary G, (ed.), *Adjusting to Capitalism: Chinese Workers and the State*. New York: M. E. Sharpe, pp. 122–149.

Chan A (2000) Globalization, China's free (read bonded) labour market, and the Chinese trade unions. *Asia Pacific Business Review* 6(3–4): 260–281.

Chan A (2001) *China's Workers under Assault: The Exploitation of Labour in a Globalising Economy*. New York: M. E. Sharpe.

Chan A (2018) The relationship between labour NGOs and Chinese workers in an authoritarian regime. *Global Labour Journal* 9(1): 1–18.

Chang, C. and Cooke, F. L. (2018), 'Layers of union organisation and representation: A case study of a strike in a Japanese-funded auto plant in China', *Asia Pacific Journal of Human Resources*, 56:4, 492–517.

Chan C and Hui E (2012) The dynamics and dilemma of workplace trade union reform in China: the case of the Honda workers' strike. *Journal of Industrial Relations* 54(5): 653–668.

Chan C and Hui E (2014) The development of collective bargaining in China: from "Collective bargaining by riot" to "Party state-led wage bargaining". *China Quarterly* 217: 221–242.

Chan C and Hui E (2017) Bringing class struggles back: a Marxian analysis of the state and class relations in China. *Globalizations* 14(2): 232–244.

Chan A, Snape E, Luo M and Zhai YZ (2017) The developing role of unions in China's foreign-Invested enterprises. *British Journal of Industrial Relations* 55(3): 602–625.

Chang K (2013) Legitimacy and the legal regulation of strikes in China: a case study of the Nanhai Honda Strike. *The International Journal of Comparative Labour Law and Industrial Relations* 29: 133–144.

Chang K and Brown W (2013) The transition from individual to collective labor relations in China. *Industrial Relations Journal* 44(2): 102–121.

Chang K and Cooke FL (2015) Legislating the right to strike in China: Historical development and prospects. *Journal of Industrial Relations* 57(3): 440–455.

Chang C and Cooke FL (2018) Layers of union organisation and representation: a case study of a strike in a Japanese-funded auto plant in China. *Asia Pacific Journal of Human Resources* 56(4), 492–517.

Chen J (1999) *The Trade Unions in Reforms and the Reforms of the Trade Unions*. Beijing: Chinese Workers Press.

Chen F (2009) Union power in China: source, operation, and constraints. *Modern China* 35(6): 662–689.

Chen F (2010) Trade unions and the quadripartite interactions in strike settlement in China. *The China Quarterly* 201: 104–124.

Chin T and Liu RH (2015) Understanding labor conflicts in Chinese manufacturing: a Yin-Yang harmony perspective. *International Journal of Conflict Management* 26(3): 288–315.

China Labour Bulletin (2009) *Protecting Workers' Rights or Serving the Party: The Way Forward for China's Trade Unions.* www.clb.org.hk/en/files/share/File/research_reports/acftu_report.pdf (assessed 18 August 2014).

Clarke S (2005) Post-socialist trade unions: China and Russia. *Industrial Relations Journal* 36(1): 2–18.

Coe N and D Jordhus-Lier (2010) Constrained agency? Re-evaluating the geographies of labour. *Progress in Human Geography* 35(2): 211–233.

Cooke FL (2008) China: Labour organisations representing women. In Broadbent K and Ford M (eds) *Women and Labour Organising in Asia: Diversity, Autonomy and Activism.* London: Routledge, pp. 34–49.

Cooke FL (2011a) Gender organising in China: A study of female workers' representation needs and their perceptions of union efficacy. *International Journal of Human Resource Management* 22(12): 2558–2574.

Cooke FL (2011b) Unions in China in a period of marketisation. In Gall G, Wilkinson A and Hurd R (eds) *International Handbook on Labour Unions: Responses to Neo-Liberalism.* Cheltenham: Edward Elgar, pp. 105–124.

Cooke FL (2011c) The enactment of three new labour laws in China: Unintended consequences and the emergence of "new" actors in employment relations. In Lee S and McCann D (eds) *Regulating for Decent Work: New Directions in Labour Market Regulation.* Basingstoke: Palgrave Macmillan and Geneva: International Labour Organisation, pp. 180–205.

Cooke FL (2012) *Human Resource Management in China: New Trends and Practices.* London: Routledge.

Cooke FL (2013) New dynamics of industrial conflicts in China: causes, expressions and resolution alternatives. In Gall G (ed) *New Forms and Expressions of Conflict at Work.* Basingstoke: Palgrave Macmillan, pp. 108–129.

Cooke FL and Brown R (2015) The regulation of non-standard forms of work in China, Japan and Republic of Korea. International Labour Organisation Working Paper, Conditions or Work and Employment Series No. 64, Geneva, Switzerland.

Cooke FL, Xie YH and Duan WM (2016) Workers' grievances and resolution mechanisms in Chinese manufacturing firms: key characteristics and the influence of contextual factors. *The International Journal of Human Resource Management* 27(18): 2119–2141.

Ding D, Fields D and Akhtar S (1997) An empirical study of human resource management policies and practices in foreign-invested enterprises in China: The case of Shenzhen special economic zone. *The International Journal of Human Resource Management* 8(5): 595–613.

Elfstrom M and S Kuruvilla (2014) The changing nature of labor unrest in China. *Industrial and Labor Relations Review* 67(2): 453–480.

Fan, HB, Dong, YM, Hu, D Z and Luo, LF (2018) Do labour unions mitigate labour conflicts in China's manufacturing firms? Evidence from the China employer-employee survey. *International Journal of Conflict Management* doi:10.1108/IJCMA-09-2017-0116.

Froissart C (2011) "NGOs" defending migrant workers' rights: semi-union organisations contribute to the regime's dynamic stability. *China Perspectives* 2: 18–25.

Fu D (2017) Fragmented control: governing contentious labor organisations in China. *Governance* 30(3): 445–462.

Gospel H (2008) Trade unions in theory and practice: Perspectives from advanced industrial countries. In Benson J and Zhu Y (eds) *Trade Unions in Asia: An Economic and Sociological Analysis*. London: Routledge, pp. 11–23.

Gray K and Jang Y (2015) Labour unrest in the global political economy: the case of China's 2010 strike wave. *New Political Economy* 20(4): 594–613.

Harper P (1968) The party and the unions in communist China. *The China Quarterly* 37, 84–119.

Howell J (1995) Prospects for NGOs in China. *Development in Practice* 5(1): 5–15.

Howell J (2003) Trade unionism in China: sinking or swimming? *The Journal of Communist Studies and Transition Politics* 19(1): 102–122.

Howell J (2008) All-China federation of trades unions beyond reform? the slow march of direct elections. *The China Quarterly* 196: 845–863.

Howard J (2015) Shall we dance? Welfarist incorporation and the politics of state–labour NGO relations. *The China Quarterly* 223: 702–723.

Hu EH, Zhang, ML, Shan, HM, Zhang, L and Yue YQ (2018) Job satisfaction and union participation in China: developing and testing a mediated moderation model. *Employee Relations* doi:10.1108/ER-10-2017-0245.

Huang W, Li YH, Wang S and Weng JJ (2016) Can "democratic management" improve labour relations in market-driven China? *Asia Pacific Journal of Human Resources* 54(2): 230–257.

Hui E and Chan C (2015) Beyond the union-centred approach: a critical evaluation of recent trade union elections in China. *British Journal of Industrial Relations* 53(3): 601–627.

Jiang KW (1996) The conflict between trade unions and the party-state –the reform of Chinese trade unions in the 80s. *Hong Kong Journal of Social Sciences* 8: 121–158. In Chinese.

Jilin Workers' Newspaper (2015) Opinions on building harmonious labour relations. 2nd April: p. 3.

Kelly J and Heery E (1989) Full-time officers and trade union recruitment. *British Journal of Industrial Relations* 27(2): 196–213.

Lee CK (2007) *Against the Law: Labor Protests in China's Rustbelt and Sunbelt.* Berkeley: University of California.

Lee CH, Brown W and Wen XY (2016) What sort of collective bargaining is emerging in China? *British Journal of Industrial Relations* 54(1): 214–236.

Lee CK and Shen Y (2011) The anti-solidarity machine? Labor nongovernmental organisations in China. In Kuruvilla S, Gallagher, M and Lee CK (eds) *From Iron Rice Bowl to Informalization: Markets, State and Workers in a Changing China.* Ithaca, NY: ILR Press, pp. 173–187.

Li CY and Liu MW (2016) A pathway to a vital labour movement in China? A case study of a union-led protest against Walmart. In Liu MW and Smith C (eds) *China at Work: A Labour Process Perspective on the Transformation of Work and Employment in China.* Basingstoke: Palgrave Macmillan, pp. 281–311.

Lin J (2017) Do more strikes mean a stronger working class's agency: a comparative study in post-socialist China. *Journal of Labor and Society* 20: 85–106.

Liu M (2010) Union organising in China: Still a monolithic labor movement? *Industrial & Labor Relations Review* 64(1): 30–52.

Lüthje B (2014) Labour relations, production regimes and labour conflicts in the Chinese automotive industry. *International Labour Review* 153(4): 535–560.

Lyddon D, Cao, XB, Meng Q and Lu J (2015) A strike of "unorganised" workers in a Chinese car factory: the Nanhai Honda events of 2010. *Industrial Relations Journal* 46(2): 134–152.

Martin R (1989) *Trade Unionism: Purposes and Forms*. Oxford: Clarendon Press.

Meng Q (2017) Strikes: rights and resolution. In Brown W and Chang K (eds) *The Emerging Industrial Relations of China*. Cambridge: Cambridge University press, pp. 184–209.

National Bureau of Statistics of China (2017) *China Labour Statistical Yearbook 2017*. Beijing: China Statistics Press.

Pringle T (2011) *Trade Unions in China: The Challenge of Labour Unrest*. London: Routledge.

Sheehan J (1998) *Chinese Workers: A New History*. London: Routledge.

Taylor B and Li Q (2007) Is the ACFTU a union and does it matter? *Journal of Industrial Relations* 49(5): 701–715.

Wang K (2008) A changing arena of industrial relations in China: what is happening after 1978. *Employee Relations* 30(2): 190–216.

Warner M (2008) Trade unions in China: in search of a new role in the "Harmonious Society". In Benson J and Zhu Y (eds) *Trade Unions in Asia: An Economic and Sociological Analysis*. London: Routledge: pp. 140–156.

Xu SY, Huang XY, Zhang LH, Xu CY and Verma A (2014) A quadripartite layered resolution mechanisms of Chinese workers' strike – A new interpretation based on a case study. *Management World*: 60–80.

Yao Y and Zhong N (2013) Unions and workers' welfare in Chinese firms. *Journal of Labor Economics* 31(3): 633–667.

Yu XM (2008) Workplace democracy in China's foreign-funded enterprises: a multilevel case study of employee representation. *Economic and Industrial Democracy* 29(2): 274–300.

Yu BQ (2012) Decent work and the path for achieving it. *Jianghan Forum* 2: 43–46. In Chinese.

Zhu XY and Chan A (2005) Staff and workers' representative congress: an institutionalized channel for expression of employees' interests? *Chinese Sociology and Anthropology* 37(4): 6–33.

Zhu Y, Warner M and Feng T (2011) Employment relations "with Chinese characteristics": the role of trade unions in China. *International Labour Review* 150(1–2): 127–143.

5 Compatibles or incompatibles

Hong Kong unions as one brand of 'Asian unionism'

Sek-Hong Ng

Introduction

The industrial relations system in Hong Kong entails a brand of 'voluntarism' of the British tradition, evidenced by the 1968 Donovan Commission but emasculated by the Industrial Relations Act of 1971 (Rogin, 1962; Lewis, 1976; Flanders, 1975; Clegg, 1983: 15–17). Emerged as the world's 'freest economy' for 'neo-classic capitalism', Hong Kong lacks constitution-structural compatibility with its socialist and sovereign mother country, the People's Republic of China (PRC). In 1997, the former British colony reverted back to China as its Special Administrative Region (SAR). The Sino-British diplomatic deal was to conserve Hong Kong as 'the other system' under China's unification formula of 'one country, two systems'.

Hong Kong unions enjoy ample freedom in employee representation vis-à-vis the employers and the state. However, collective bargaining has never taken root as a workplace culture. This chapter notes such apparent contradiction, which underscores these unions as a brand of 'Asian unionism' and leaves the question of 'how much this character is shared elsewhere by other brands of Asian unions' to be answered towards the conclusion of this book.

Some basic concepts

The thesis of 'capitalism diversity' and of 'varieties of capitalism' (VoC) (Hall and Soskice, 2001) argues that in spite of the unifying effects of 'industrialism' and 'globalisation', diversities exist among capitalist market economies in their normative superstructure and institutional structure, hence yielding VoC (Hamann and Kelly, 2008).The thesis argues that the effects of 'globalisation' are not always even, due to historical, normative, institutional and environmental factors which affect the polity, economy, social structure and culture. The locus of comparison is the variable: degree of 'institutional regulation and coordination', both public and private. A bi-polar typology hence identifies 'liberal market economies' (LME), vis-à-vis 'coordinated market economies' (CME). The thesis has been applied widely to various cross-cultural studies on employment.

Such a thesis postulates 'partial convergence', with elements of both 'convergence' and 'divergence' co-existing. However, to argue for 'convergence' due to 'globalisation', premised upon the diffusion of Western institutions, hints upon an ethnocentric bias of 'western hegemony/superiority' which can be superstitious. Symmetrically, to subscribe to so-called better Asian values can be blind-folded. Yet the debate continues unabated (Patten, 1999: 146–160, 2018: 198–203; Ferguson, 2012; Jacques, 2012: 537–546; Fenby, 2017: chapter 5; Rachman, 2017).

'Market economy' is a now a commonplace label especially since adopted by China for labelling generically her innovative reforms to decentralise its economy. The label of 'market economy' has since been of common usage, and yet Daniel Bell expressed scepticism that any economy has an endemic nature of the 'market'; it is fallacious to personify the 'market' which is man-made (Bell, 1978: 276–80). Besides, is 'capitalism' universalistic? China always resents being classified by Western commentators as 'capitalist'. The recent plead by its leadership to 'furthering socialism with Chinese characteristics' testifies to the nation's loyalty to its socialist discourse under the dictatorship of the Chinese Communist Party (CCP). The 'China Dream' is fashioned by the CCP: 'China 0: Building a Modern, Harmonious and Creative Society' (Brown, 2017: 215–6). North Korea and Vietnam are also still communist.

To accommodate exceptions, the 'VoC' thesis is restated to allow for an 'Asian market economy variety' to embrace those nations which are not capitalist. Yet such refinement and the indeterminacy of a 'multi-variate' treatment betray its conceptual weakness. In this connection, this chapter will examine Hong Kong unions as a 'brand' of 'Asian unionism', rather than forcing them into a fictitious category as a variety of 'Asian unionism'.

The evolution of Hong Kong unionism is a politico-industrial drama shaped by geopolitics. It emerged as the cradle of Chinese unionism in the early twentieth century and proved its sustainability after re-integration with China. Built on Hong Kong's experiences and drawing upon examples of other Asian societies, Professor Thurley proposed a thesis of 'Asian unionism' in its right. It echoes his earlier work on 'European management', which points to 'the gap between theory and practice for management in Europe' (Thurley and Wirdenius, 1989: 97–102). To understand the distinctiveness of Asian unionism, it is hence important to start theory-building, not by forcing it into Western-made categories but by observing how these unions operate to infer their functions within a theoretical scheme. Asian unions are 'parochial' with vestiges of 'traditionalism', yet easily affected by the vicissitudes of colonialism-cum-decolonisation. They are malleable, like an 'adhocracy' often run by lay officials (England and Rear, 1975: 99–100; Turner et al., 1980; Mintzberg, 1983). Between class and national consciousness, Asian unions elect for patriotic sentiments, often collaborating with 'home capital' to advance the national economy (Thurley, 1983: 108–13, 117–9, 1988).

Thurley's thesis has resonance with Dore's exposition on 'Japanese enterprise unionism'. The house union in Hitachi investigated by Dore consults with management to which it defers yet yearning for 'anti-capitalism' in its politico-ideological 'vision' for the distant future (Dore, 1990: 163–185). However, Thurley's Asian unions are not necessarily collective bargaining but cater to other industrial functions consistent with workers' needs and economic growth (Thurley, 1988: 26–30).

Thurley's thesis on 'Asian unionism', which cites a four-factor explanatory scheme, is conjunctional with his earlier works on the role of the state in industrial relations (Thurley, 1983: 111–9). The role of the state, to which Asian unions have to respond, refers not only to the scope of the 'visible hand' but also to the more chiliastic embrace of patriotism (the first and fourth factors in the Thurley model). The more complex variable is the relative autonomy/dependency of the individual employee. Asian workers were perceived as relatively dependent upon the collectivity, private or public. Japanese workers depended upon the paternalistic corporation, while in Hong Kong, Chinese workers were linked closely with their family, clan and neighbourhood community when facing the agonies of a glutted employment market in the 1950s. The union fraternities played a role too. However, later, in the 1980s, unions modernised their agendas when their providential role was eclipsed by a rudimentary 'welfare state' which provided social wages and public housing on a world's pioneering scale.

Unions proliferate and contribute to social pluralism in Hong Kong, where people are linked with each other by webs of cross-cutting and shifting social networks, both primary and secondary. It prevents society from 'crystallising' along embedded class lines (Turner et al., 1980: 9). Less affected by a 'we-they' class consciousness, unions are not consistently hostile towards capital. Their relationship with the state is ambivalent yet intricate. Trade union laws are permissive, giving ample scope for unions as an institution of 'industrial relations voluntarism'. Paradoxically, there exists a heavy dosage of 'legalism', where labour laws are painstakingly enforced by a technocratic labour administration and often observed faithfully by employers and employees as 'the standard and moral' (Ng, 1982: 275). In Hong Kong, coercive labour law has largely disappeared, following the reform era of the 1970s and 1980s.

The following text has two parts. The first is a historical overview. The second will be the discussions dealing with unionism in the economy, polity, globalisation, late development and late capitalism, culture and institutions.

Pre-war unionism

Modern unionism first appeared in the colony in the late 1910s, sixty years after it came under British rule. It was a classic example of the 'challenge-response' syndrome. The colony, alongside Shanghai and Canton (now *Guangzhou*), was the cradle of the embryonic Chinese labour movement.

Organised labour in Hong Kong, recalcitrant and closely linked with revolutionary secret societies, engineered a series of early-day successful strikes against Western capital, which climaxed in the abortive Hong Kong-Canton General Strike and Boycott of 1925–1926. It helped inspire the founding of the CCP in 1921. The CCP swiftly penetrated the labour movement, leading to the inception, in 1925, of the All-China Federation of Trade Unions (ACFTU), which played a key role in the General Strike of 1925–1926 (Chesneaux, 1968; Ng, 1985: 428–29).

The General Strike, inspired by the earlier success of the mechanics strike (1920) and the seamen's strike (1922), was a chiliastic response to the vicissitudes of foreign imperialism and capitalism, with the maritime Hong Kong Chinese seamen as the catalyst of Western liberal (socialist) influences. The 'dialectics of capitalism' notion helps explain the 'dualistic faces' of capitalism behind the success and subsequent collapse of the Strike (Ng, 1985; Ng and Ip, 2004: 487–91). The strikers confronted Western capitalism-cum-imperialism and allied with patriotic Chinese merchants, albeit even more exploitative as employers. The Strike paralysed the Victoria Harbour, yet later withered when the Chinese merchants defected. Before long, the Nationalist government in Canton withdrew its support when it broke ties with the CCP to concentrate upon its Northern Expedition against the dissident warlords. The Strike ended when the strikers capitulated, hastening back to Hong Kong for employment.

The Strike, a landmark not only for Chinese-Hong Kong unionism but also in the world's history of industrial conflict, was castigated by the colonial government as a 'civil revolt' of *Bolshevik* anarchists under USSR instigation (Ng and Ip, 2004: 491–4). It swung from former tolerance of Chinese unionism to repression with the enactment of the coercive *Illegal Strikes and Lockout Ordinance* in 1927, which emulated the repressive UK *Trade Disputes Act* of 1927. Unions were banned from political strikes and disallowed links with any external influences. Some vanguard left-wing unions were outlawed. Concomitantly, a Labour Sub-department and a Labour Advisory Board (LAB) were created in 1928 (England and Rear, 1975: 78–82).

Post-war rehabilitation years and industrial 'take-off' (1945–1967)

Post-war unionism was shaped by 'geopolitics'. Reconstruction stimulated militant unions to strike for collective bargaining due to sustained inflation. The labour movement began to split along ideological cleavages. However, union militancy was stemmed when the Liberation of the Mainland by the CCP in 1949 touched off a massive refugee exodus to Hong Kong which glutted the job market. The UN embargo on China in the 1951 Korean War impeded Hong Kong as a trading-port, causing it to industrialise by producing textile and other labour-intensive manufacturing products, made possible by industrial capital and cheap labour fleeing from the Mainland.

Hong Kong excelled as the offshore production workshop for Western developed economies, by enduring 'sweat-shop' conditions in most workplaces. A rudimentary protective labour law regime was in place, but its application, largely to satisfy the International Labour Organisation (ILO), staggered without upsetting the 'free wage equilibrium' (Hughes, 1976: 55–61; Welsh, 1997: 458–62).

The first trade union law, the Trade Unions and Trade Disputes Ordinance, was enacted in 1948, purportedly to foster 'responsible economic unionism of the British tradition'. Unions were legalised upon registration with the government, granted British-styled immunities against common law liabilities for restraint of trade and subject themselves to official governance to safeguard union's democracy and the accountability of union fund, which could not be spent for political purposes (England and Rear, 1975: 210–30). A full-scale Labour Department was established, while the LAB was made 'tripartite' and elected in 1948 (Endacott, 1973: 311–2). The labour movement was formally dissected into two polarised camps, the left-wing Hong Kong Federation of Trade Unions (FTU) and its right-wing competitor, the Hong Kong and Kowloon Trades Union Council (TUC). Uncharacteristically, they were both registered under the Societies Ordinance. It was an official safe-valve flexibility since both were excluded from the purview of the new trade union law which then did not permit registered unions to 'federate across trades or industries'. Unions effaced from organising strikes. Worn by their earlier militancy, they switched to serving the subsistence needs of a destitute working class as welfare fraternities, while functioning as 'hiring halls' for job-seekers (England and Rear, 1975: 83–5; Turner et al., 1980: chapter 3).

Union chiliasm again: the 1967 civil disturbance

Union docility prevailed during the early period of industrialisation, apart from occasional shop-floor protests and the rupturing Kowloon Riots of 1956, which was organised labour's 'civil war' between the TUC and FTU (Welsh, 1997: 456–7; Chau, 2009: 318–30). However, politico-ideological fissures between the colonial regime and the PRC's ginger organisations soon erupted into adversarial confrontation, when the Mainland Cultural Revolution touched off the Civil Disturbance of 1967 (Welsh, 1997: 468–70; Turner et al., 1980: 92–3). British rule was contested by the Communist-controlled 'Anti-Imperial' Struggle Patriotic United Front', with the refractory FTU as the vanguard against the colonial authority. It began with a strike wave, compounded by police intervention. An unpopular and abortive general strike called by the FTU in the public transport sector was ensued by belligerent left-wing reprisals of indiscriminate home-made bombing. Curfew reigned over the city when trapped in a dire state of 'horror' for almost a year. The saga ended as the Cultural Revolution fever subsided. The FTU retreated to an effacing position as its ringleaders faced arrest and penal sanctions (*ibid.,* England and Rear, 1975: 5–8).

Colonial enlightenment: the 'Golden Years' (1970–1985)

The geopolitical context shifted as China ended its diplomatic seclusion in the mid-1970s. In consonance, the recalcitrant FTU switched to accommodation with the colonial authority. It ended its boycott of the LAB and captured an overwhelming majority of union's electoral votes (Turner et al., 1980: 104–6, 160). Membership attrition, sustained after the Civil Disturbance, caused this doctrinal veteran union centre to re-align its union policy. It evolved as a 'secondary association' for the younger cohorts of the labouring mass, less solidaristic as an 'occupational community' but more as an agent of 'collective instrumentalism' (Ng, 1997: 670–2).

The Civil Disturbance alerted the colonial administration to review its 'laissez-faire' policy' of the 1950s. It addressed the pathos of widespread grass-roots grievances exposed by the Disturbance by adopting an extensive agenda of enlightening social-cum-labour reforms. It embraced sizable expansion of social wages, covering public housing and medical service, comprehensive education and rudimentary social security payment. These 'public goods', delivered by the 'public household', usurped unions' providential role. Concomitantly, the government embarked upon an assiduous programme of labour enactments, which dampened further workers' yearning for 'collective bargaining' (Turner et al., 1980: chapter 9).

The Employment Ordinance (1968) provided employees with a 'statutory floor of employment rights'. The Labour Tribunal Ordinance (1972) established the Labour Tribunal which functions as a labour court of informal procedures. The Labour Relations Ordinance (1975) repealed the Illegal Strikes and Lockouts Ordinance to institutionalise 'freedom of strike' and created a state-sponsored escalating machinery of third-party intervention in collective industrial conflict (Ng, 1986: 289–96). This statutory tripod gave labour unions a new role in worker representation for recovering deprived statutory rights but creeping 'legalism' which was compatible with collective voluntarism, still reigned. Unions were less enthusiastic in organising strikes. Most workplace stoppages were spontaneous wildcat actions, to which unions responded (Ng, 1997: 664–70) The Labour Relation Ordinance, enshrined as the 'totem' of 'voluntarism', stayed idle in the statute book.

The FTU-TUC dichotomy gave way to a trichotomy with the inception of a new union centre in 1990. The Hong Kong Confederation of Trade Unions (CTU), backed by a secularised Christian worker education centre, grew to overtake the declining TUC to become the main rival to the FTU (Ng, 1997: 666–8). Concurrently, a 'third sector' of the labour movement emerged as white-collar unionism mushroomed within the civil service, where narrow sectional economic interests caused small grade-specific occupational groups to organise for mutual pay bidding to achieve equalisation (Turner et al., 1980: chapter 11).

Yet such pay haggling fell short of orthodox collective bargaining. The government employer allowed a limited degree of collective pay negotiation at 'staff council joint consultation'. To bargain without the label of collective bargaining was later diffused to the aristocratic 'primary sector' where suspicious management of public enterprises and British corporations practise pseudo collective bargaining while categorically withholding union recognition. Unions were accommodative to wield 'participation' in bilateral pay determination. Employers' apprehension was bypassed when unions acceded to these lesser but more tenable avenues of employee representation (Ng and Warner, 1998: 134–41; Turner et al., 1991: chapter 5). Within the public utility and transport sector where multi-unionism pervaded, a workplace norm of co-existence evolved, for example, to enshrine a novel form of employee representation (Turner et al., 1980: 37–9). Rival enterprise unions communicated separately each year their pay expectations to management, leaving intact with management its ultimate prerogative to announce employers' pay decisions (Turner et al., 1991).

The transition period (1985–1997)

A transition period intervened between the making of the Sino-British accord (1984) and the return of sovereignty of Hong Kong to China. While the care-taking nature of the colonial administration implied a transient polity, the nature of institutions and life-style experienced both continuities and disruptions. The FTU, the mainstream union centre, revitalised itself on three fronts. First, it started penetrating the neighbourhood community with a network of district offices. In resonance with a global trend of 'community unionism', these offices delivered to the local residents an array of union services embracing their needs as wage-earners, consumers, commuters and family members. Second, the FTU clustered its affiliate unions, otherwise dispersed within a trade or industry, to coalesce to form 'federal-like' industry general unions. Third was the FTU's investment in human capital education and training. The FTU, as one of its goods delivered, operated the largest workers' extra-mural centre for vocational training or interest classes. This catered to employees' yearning, for post-entry evening courses for self-enrichment, an ethos of continuous education which was Confucian (Turner et al., 1980; Ng and Ip, 2003: 391–3).

As elsewhere, the British governing elite strived to nurture an elected democratic polity in the process of 'de-colonisation'. Popular elections were introduced, for returning candidates to the law-making Legislative Council and same for the District Councils at the community level. Given the vacuum of an election culture in politics, unions, as elected bodies monitored strictly by the government, excelled as a lay quasi-political parties. The FTU performed second to the People's Democratic Alliance as the second leading party. Its salient elected presence in the Legislative Council altered the relationship between the labour movement and the state. Unions enhanced the weight of their lever of 'legal enactment', in the Webbs' language. Evidently, ascendency in electoral politics enabled them to recoup their dwindling industrial strength by extending into the virgin 'political market' (Ng, 1997: 665–7). Yet the suffrage rule of 'one union, one vote', sustained since the days of the LAB, is conducive to unions proliferation in number (Ng, 1996: 667–8; Chau, 2009: chapter 27).

The 'thirteen-year' transition was indented with politico-economic disruptions. The most traumatic episode was the June Fourth Beijing upheavals of 1989. In its aftermath, China suspended, renewed and escalated its 'market socialism' reforms. In Hong Kong, the 'care-taking' colonial regime hastily erected laws of civil rights and equal opportunities, in an attempt to usher a 'mature' system of 'rule of law' to the colony, as fait accompli. The institutionalisation of 'civil society', heralded as Britain's 'last moral responsibility', was also intended to appease widespread local xenophobia about the predicament of a repressive regime.as the 'overlord' (Welsh, 1997: chapters 16–17).

The FTU positioned itself to be 'ministerial' in the future SAR, while the CTU, more socialist than the FTU, began organising the less acquiescent grass-rooted blue-collars. Both union centres envisaged high uncertainties about post-1997, especially since immigration abroad was too expensive an option for the blue-collars. Their 'strategy' was defensive, aimed at worst to conserve.

An example was the shrewd and vociferous response of organised labour to massive labour importation, a 'stop-gap' de-regulation policy installed by the government which undercut local workers' job security. The alienated labour movement transcended its fragmentation to forge, first time since the 1925–1926 General Strike, a fragile 'united front' in protest. Although labour importation was eventually rescinded, it betrayed the hypocritical contradiction of neo-liberal enlightenment. Liberalisation and coercive co-ordination were 'two in one'. Importation to de-regulate proved to be most regulated by bureaucratic rules, while local unions unmasked their parochial exclusion against foreign migrant workers (Ng, 1997: 666–72; Ng and Rowley, 2000: 183–87). On the eve of the 1997 political changeover, the legislature of the 'last colony' hastily ushered to the statute book a law granting elected workplace unions statutory rights' of collective consultation and bargaining, alongside a basket of statutory labour safeguards, which censured 'unfair dismissal' (Patten, 1999: 104–112; Ng and Ip, 2003: 387).

Hong Kong as China's SAR after 1997

Hong Kong was restored to (socialist) China in 1997 as its SAR, destined to 'preserve stability and prosperity', so that its 'capitalist system' was to continue to reign for another fifty years, up to 2047. This 'borrowed place' was again to live on 'borrowed time'. Since capitalism was non-alienable, any expectations for a 'passing lane' towards the 'estate of the realm' of organised labour proved extravagant. Unions soon found themselves in an uphill struggle of having to engage capital, closely allied with the SAR government (Ng and Ip, 2003: 388–89, 2007: 469–78).

The 1997 pro-labour statutory package was swiftly abrogated by the SAR provisional legislature, while a restrictive clause on public assembly was reinstated to the Public Order Ordinance. The SAR regime sidelined labour affairs so as to appease capital, while 'dogmatically' adopting the 'business model' of the private sector to 'streamline' the civil service (Goodstadt, 2014: 51). Civil service unions were docile in resisting such a transplant of private sector practices superimposed upon their members. Both the Beijing and the SAR authorities castigate the 'welfare state' prescription as detrimental, refuting blind-folded, any blueprint for a territory-wide social pension while defending a low-profit tax regime (Goodstadt, 2014: 11–3). The labour movement is impotent in penetrating such an 'encasement' of the welfare state, even though this institution, a totem of liberal 'capitalist democracies', has been ingrained in the territory. The government unprecedentedly allocates public fund to subsidise private industry, while allowing some key sectors, like housing and food retail, notoriously 'cartelised' by syndicated capital (Cartledge, 2017: 20–1). Unsurprisingly, income and economic inequality has sharpened, as betrayed by the 'Gini coefficient' (Cartledge, 2017: 23–26).

Hong Kong continues as a 'civil society', essential for its 'cosmopolitanism' (Ferguson, 2014: 35–7). Its labour movement is still among the freest in the world. Still intact is a repository of labour laws inherited from the colony, guaranteeing employees such freedoms as to work, associate, strike and bargain, let alone entitlement to a statutory floor of employment rights (Lethbridge et al., 2000: 232–4). Labour may not gain a fair deal but some limited advances. The 'single-industry' rule on union federation and the stringent conditions on unions to affiliate with overseas labour organisations were liberalised (Chan et al., 2000: 90–2). A statutory general wage floor was adopted in 2011. The pro-democratic CTU has been tolerated since 1997, despite the advents of an impending coercive law on 'National Security' (Bland, 2017).

The labour movement has stayed pluralistic and fragmented. The FTU, the second largest political party, is ministerial but sceptical about the docility of the LAB and the SAR regime to accomplish the basics: standard work hours, formalising workplace consultation and legislating to better the protection of non-standard employment, especially in light of quasi-autonomous employment in the shared economy. The CTU is the 'refractory' alternative but its adjunct, the Labour Party, is marginalised in the elected legislature. The FTU, akin to the ACFTU, stays aloof from international unionism, except sustaining a vicarious link with the International Federation of Transport Workers' Unions (ITF) via its seamen's union. As the SAR's 'other conscience', the CTU monitors freedom of association and collective bargaining, not only in Hong Kong but also in the Mainland, tantamount to a non-governmental organisation (NGO).

Partisan polarised politics precludes the FTU from voting consistently for labour's cause in the contested legislature (Kwok, 2018: chapters 4 and 5).

The SAR has been relatively free from large-scale industrial unrest, apart from two landmark trade disputes: the first involving the 'bar-benders' which choked the building and construction trade while the crane drivers in the second paralysed the container port when striking for two months in 2013. In either case, incensed rivalry between the FTU and the CTU stalled effective negotiation. The bar-benders secured a hard won pay rise while the embattled crane drivers were laid-off and had to be re-absorbed by other subcontractors working for the principal operator at the container port (Chau, 2009: 522–39, 2013: 265–9; Ng, 2015: 314–7).

Social protests and street-corner militancy are not simply concerned with political causes but also epitomise alienation with socio-economic inequalities and workplace injustices. In 2005, Hong Kong workers joined hand with farmers from Korea to demonstrate against the ministerial meeting of the World Trade Organisation (WTO) held in Hong Kong (Yuen, 2015: 402–6). The 2013 container port strike was projected as a regional worker's crusade against 'monopoly capital'. In 2014, a 'civil disobedience' movement, targeted against electoral conservatism of the polity, led to a general social 'strike' staged in the banking and metropolitan districts. Media's worldwide coverage labelled it as the 'Occupation Central Movement' or the 'Yellow Umbrella Revolt'. It betrayed grass-roots disenchantment/disaffection with a SAR government perceived as impotent to buttress its legitimacy crisis, to curtail capital greed, urban poverty and workplace labour deprivation. While the FTU doctrinally denounced the 'Occupation' as subversive and betrayal of patriotism, the CTU pledged support, even simply as rhetoric. Like strikes curbed in nineteenth-century Britain by judges' court rulings, the SAR government also exploited court injunctions to quell the Occupation in 2015 (Ng, 2015: 319–21). The episode signalled a syndrome of widening 'legitimation' gap between a plutocratic ruling elite and the grass roots. The divided labour movement was apparently oblivious about the socio-industrial implications of the 'civil disobedience', to which it reacted in an effacing and inhibited way.

Discussion

Labour history in Hong Kong is itself an 'industrial drama' of both continuities and disjoints. Hong Kong unionism, given its specificities, is malleable since as defensive institution, it has responded adaptively to challenges. In order to understand such a union character, the effects of three sets of contextual variables are worth considering.

The industrial and political domains

The first contextual variable is the political economy. Not only the boundary between the 'economic' and 'political' realms is evasive but also the boundary between comparative political economies (CPEs) is often cumbersome and inconclusive (Baccaro and Howell, 2017: 1–11). Economically, most unions in young Asian economies have to face the vicissitudes of capital within the setting of 'international division of labour' fostered by 'globalisation'. Politically, these unions need to confront a 'political market' which, according to Bell (1978: 220–32), pertains to how the state mobilise power and economic resources (the public household) vis-à-vis capital, labour and other key stake-holding groups. Goldthorpe invokes a term 'corporatism' (1984: chapter 3), which himself is sceptical about, to denote the notional equation of stake-holders' participation in the public domain with that in the private domain. Yet the 'first sector' (the state) and the 'second sector' (private enterprises) are never entirely analogous. Earlier, Galbraith examines 'institutionalism' in 'affluent industrial societies' (1970: chapter 2), calling it 'a mix of economic and political ideas assumed as "conventional wisdom"'. His exposition on unionism is Weberian: advancing a technocratic interpretation by labelling unions as 'ministerial' (Galbraith, 1972: chapter 24). Lester epitomises the ethos of 'structural-functionalism' by saying 'as unions mature', being measured by the institutionalisation of 'collective bargaining' (Lester, 1958). To Perlman, unions attain their 'organic consciousness', when emancipated from the political grip of the intellectuals' revolutionary party ideologically driven to rewrite the existing social order (Perlman, 1968: 5). Unions recover their home-made ideology which is economic and non-political.

Orthodox union theories, especially of the British heritage, endorse economic unionism, based upon 'occupational conciousness', while negating unionism as the functionary of partisan politics (Webbs and Webb, 1902, 1920). In the theoretical mainstream which is Weberian, the validity of 'Marxist unionism' has been disputed. The British Trade Union Congress (BTUC) set the pattern of this tradition by hiving off its political arm to constitute an 'independent' Labour Party in 1903 (Pelling, 1971: 123–8; Phelps-Brown, 1986: chapter 4). In Hong Kong, where the political economy dictated otherwise, the FTU, the TUC and later the CTU all evaded such functional demarcation to participate in political elections as 'quasi-political parties'. Role contradictions have emanated as a sequel. The FTU, as both the largest labour centre and the second largest political party, was occasionally castigated for betraying workers' cause when failing to vote for working-people's cause in the Legislative Council (Kwok, 2018: chapters 5–6).

Probably, the bitter experiences of political embattlement of its predecessors in the conflict-ridden 1920s and of the FTU itself in the crises of 1956 and 1967 which alert it the importance of direct participation in electoral politics rather than leaving it to a proxy political party. Given the union centre's historical bonding with the CCP, it is probably Beijng's most trusted functionary in Hong Kong other than its official missions. Besides, the frustration experienced by the British TUC with Blair's 'Third Way' also neutralises the illusion that the partnership between the industrial and political arms of the working-class movement is tenacious.

Even to the recalcitrant CTU, the Labour Party which it sponsored is now more the servant of the middle-class seeking 'mid-way' political solutions than a party of the workers.

As suggested by German sociologists citing Polanyi, 'domestic politics' in post-urban societies address more the theme of 'inclusion', which emphasises 'participation', than concerned with socio-economic 'equalisation'. Indeed, 'equal level playing field' is a trendy human resource management (HRM) jargon beyond comprehension, by idealising the inevitable functional relationship between 'participation' and 'equalisation'. By enrolling actively itself in the participatory polity, it seemingly seeks to help to 'universalize market opportunities and to exclude no one from market citizenship'. Yet, as the minority participant or junior partner vis-à-vis the other 'middle-class' political parties, it is evidently limited to ameliorate 'the classical structure of social inequality' (Dorre et al., 2009: 132). The present decade has passed the 'explicit simplicity' of the 'Dunlop-Ross' debate of the 1960s, so that there is a rationale for the labour centres to transcend both domains of the 'elected polity' and 'industrial/occupational unionism'. As political actors, they can help even 'life-chances' which is leveraged within the 'public household', especially available to employees otherwise trapped in urban poverty. Virtually, such dualism is still 'old wine in new bottles', recasting or modernising the Webbs' union method of 'legal enactment' by shifting from indirect lobbing to direct participation in the polity.

The modern polity always excels with a dosage of the 'welfare state', Hong Kong is no stranger to 'welfare state', which has existed since the colonial government launched the world's earliest mammoth resettlement-cum-public housing programme in the 1950s. Today, both the FTU and the CTU, as the spokesmen of the grass-roots labouring mass, are incessant in pushing a well-endowed 'public household' to erect a basic institution of the modern welfare state, which is an economy-wide state-sponsored social pension. However, the prospects are dim. First, the ruling elite, both at the national (Beijing) and local (SAR) levels, is neurotic about the implant of 'welfare state' for perverting full-swing capitalism in Hong Kong, even what exists now is notably circumscribed, fashioned by 'shareholder capitalism' and not 'stakeholder capitalism' as among the Scandinavian countries (Giddens, 2000: 151–3). Second, the polity is now in disarray, suffering from low legitimacy and lacking political foresight which envisages a credible blueprint for the territory. A disaffected labour movement painstakingly urged a lukewarm SAR administration to curb the perennial syndrome of 'precarious employment', upon which an insensitive SAR authority acted by arresting a random number of 'Uber' drivers.

In Hong Kong, private philanthropies and public subvention coalesce to sustain a feeble 'third sector' of NGOs, the bulk of whom are social enterprises. Few are interested or resourceful to perform as labour pressure groups, leaving unions almost unchallenged for their 'native' tasks of articulating and ameliorating workplace deprivations (Ng and Ip, 2003: 391–2).

As noted earlier when citing Thurley's treatment, Hong Kong employers and employees are relatively independent of state control, but typically, they look to the state for writing a prudent and equitable set of employment norms, as embodied in statute laws and judicial decisions. Where an ethos of 'legalism' reigns in the arena of individual employment relations, there exists a logic for organised labour to participate in the polity where lies the stake-holders' prerogative of determining and writing these legal codes.

Inevitably, organised labour is affected by Mainland-SAR geopolitics. The relationship between the principal and the subsidiary polities has been evidently strained, now two decades after China's resumption, to testify to a widening gulf of mutual distrust between local citizens and the SAR authority. As the 'ministerial union' serving the motherland, the FTU has to participate, by 'activation', in electoral politics to help salvage the withering legitimacy of the SAR government. Likewise, its rival, the CTU also 'activate' its political arm, the Labour Party, in the 'electoral market' to conserve, if not expand, the domain of 'welfare state', supposedly to lever against labour market 'fractionalisation' as precarious employment accentuates. This notwithstanding, neither labour centres, the FTU or the CTU, has excelled in organising the communitarian ethnic enclaves of alien peripheral workers, like foreign migrant workers.

The LAB has been the long and prided 'tripartite' central machinery of consultation which gives organised labour a mandate of 'participation' in the formulation of labour policy. Yet the system, in terms of its purview and representativeness, has become anachronistic. Denied of 'participation' in the LAB, the recalcitrant CTU appeals to the ILO and international trade secretariats on collective bargaining and freedom of association, yet with limited efficacy. Conversely, the FTU was more resourceful in its pursuit, often able to bypass the SAR administration, via its direct link with the Party organ and the ACFTU in the northern backyard. Yet, the FTU has not openly invoked such avenues but prefers to lie low-key (the modest Confucian way) within the new 'third sector', typical of the Hong Kong hybrid.

Economic strikes have been on a secular decline worldwide, alongside the exhaustion of collective bargaining. The threat to both unionism and secondary associations is 'individualism' in an era of 'communication immediacy' (Ferguson, 2014: chapter 4). Collectivism is almost irrelevant to the new 'white-collars', since the nexus of their employment is the individual employment contract and self-representation in negotiation (Atkinson, 2018: chapter 5). However, 'social strikes' have been on the rise as street public demonstrations are now a commonplace in Hong Kong, branded by the Washington Post as 'a city of protest' (Ip and Ng, 2013). Yet the FTU or even the CTU did not identify themselves with the 'Occupation Central' social strike, which posed a nuisance to regular wage-earners as roads were blockaded and their livelihood disrupted. The contradiction was reminiscent of the 'civil war' metaphor. Virtually, Hong Kong workers did not lack a novel history of labour militancy, as epitomised by three landmark agitational episodes: the Hong Kong-Canton General Strike of 1925–1926; second, the 1967 civil-cum-industrial unrest; and third, the container port strike of 2013.

Other than the new aristocracy of knowledge workers and those precarious, there exists a sandwiched stratum of labouring people who find 'collectivism' still bountiful and 'utilitarian'. Post-SAR union density has not receded but slightly ascended to a level of 22%–23% in the 2010s. Organised labour is dichotomous, with the FTU still commanding an edge over the CTU. The ministerial FTU excels as a functionary of 'politicking and a service-providing' agency. These two domains overlap, with its district offices serving delivery of 'community unionism' for the local neighbourhood, which they penetrate to augment electoral support and participation. Conversely, the recalcitrant CTU operates like an NGO within the 'third sector', as the self-appointed bastion of the 'other conscience' on labouring issues in Hong Kong and the Mainland.

Organised labour in Hong Kong represents one 'brand' of Asian unionism, that of diversity and mutual tolerance. The CTU, an offshoot of 'secularisation' of the Church, is expressly hostile towards 'neo-liberal' capitalism: systematically keen at exposing hidden workplace injustices. The FTU, manifesting the 'profaneness' of ideology, embraces the advents of 'knowledge economy' where the individual has a personal stake to invest in his continuous life-long education. The FTU is committed to the standard-bearing role of nurturing painstakingly an esteemed worker education centre, evidently harmonised with the SAR government's ambitious policy to 'galvanise' the manpower hierarchy with the 'qualification framework' (QF) skill accreditation scheme. Simultaneously, it is politically sensitive in conserving such a lower-end share in the education-cum-training industry, especially not to step into the jurisdictional terrain of the tertiary institutions like the (technological) universities.

'Space' and 'temporal' compression: globalisation and late development

The phenomenon of 'globalisation' has provoked almost perennial debates in social science disciplines like economics, sociology, political science and hybrid disciplines like political economy and industrial relations. Whether the issue is 'spatial compression', as when 'globalisation' narrows the horizon of 'distance' or the issue be 'temporal compression', as when 'late development', by diffusion and emulation, enables a nation to catch up from behind, the common interest shared by these disciplines (sub-disciplines) is to gauge the globe's propensity for 'convergence' and 'equalisation'. Such treatment often features a comparative perspective, entailing 'spatial' and 'temporal' comparison across nation-states. The thesis of 'industrialism and industrial man' is now classic as a benchmark notion (Kerr et al., 1973). Its central logic is hastened or 'compressed' economic advance made possible by enhanced performance of the factory type of mass production system. The driving imperative is attributed to technology which, according to Giddens (1991: chapter 1), has transformed and modified fatefully the notion of 'space' and 'distance', as manifest in the 'globalisation' process, which fashions 'late urban cosmopolitanism' (Giddens, 1991: chapter 1). Although the underpinning and unifying overtone is 'convergence', in spite of spurt punctuations by abstract and even extreme ideologies, Bell suggests that societies can vary in the degree of their similarities, discernible at three ascending levels: market and socio-technic capabilities, social institutions and culture (Bell, 2001: xix–xxvii). Unionism worldwide, of the Asian type and the Hong Kong brand, owes their present configuration to this process of 'space' and 'temporal' compression, as epitomised by 'industrialisation' (technology imperative) and 'globalisation' (market and exchange horizon).

Evidently, such a sociological line of exposition is more credible than the 'VoC' thesis, which has dominated the domain of CPE for almost the past decade. The crux of the latter's argument, as pointed out earlier, is problematic for its oversimplification. Economies are typed on a spectrum as VoC. By forcing 'market economies' into either constellation of either 'coordinated' or antithetical, varieties, with the shifting environment taken for granted, it appears 'catch-all' and embracing, with the implication that all forms of variation can hence be accommodated within Western-written universal institutions and their 'adaptive mechanisms' (Baccaro and Howell, 2017: 7–20). However, its embraciveness has been over-exaggerated, as manifest in the 'annex' of an Asian sub-type. Second, the 'coordination' notion can hardly be isolated from that of 'regulation' and 'control', so that the role of the state has to be made explicit, and yet it has not. Woodward's definition of 'technology', denominated in terms of the 'control' variable and Darendorf's patent reference to managerial and ownership control in advanced capitalism, is essential to explain 'coordination' of the capitalist system and yet found missing from the 'VoC' treatment (Woodward, 1965). Besides, any private acts of coordination, if privileged and outside the public domain, is today liable to be deemed as 'collusion' in the marketplace, with unlawful ramifications for infringing upon competition and anti-trust laws.

Benchmark works on 'convergence' by other industrial relations scholars and sociologists like Bell, Kerr, Dunlop and Harbison and Myers, or by political economists like Galbraith, have enumerated both the structural (institutional) and normative systems as the nexus of conceptual models for comparative appraisals on industrialised and industrialising economies. Bell's schema is three-tiered, as above noted. 'The industrialism' thesis of Kerr et al. cites the 'technological imperative' from which emanates the gestation of 'industrialism' and concordant institutions. Galbraith cites the 'technocracy' as the institutional vehicle for the design of the new industrial state, made possible by economic affluence which emphasises specialism-cum-professional competency. Later, Giddens echoes these works by suggesting that all such discourses converge upon, given the social actors, these authors' 'shared interest' to study the 'production and reproduction, continuities, change or dissolution of social systems-cum institutions' (Giddens, 1981: 26–34; 41–48). Such modes of treatment are hence simpler and better focused, less cumbersome and less problematic than the 'VoC' thesis as the theoretical frameworks for dealing 'convergence' under the aegis of 'globalisation'. They are exemplary for studying the union institution and by extension, unionism in the Asian context.

Giddens' critique on 'globalisation' and 'cosmopolitanism', which invokes sociological concepts like control, uncertainty, reflexivity, trust and contract, autonomy and interdependence, the state and the 'welfare state', is instructional for examining Hong Kong unionism (Giddens, 1994: 7–18). Organised labour here, strategically affected by its geopolitical space vis-à-vis China, Britain and the world, has experienced various crises of uncertainty, followed by state coercion or conversely, state and unions' self-reflection to give 'space's for reconciliation, accommodation or even re-definition of their mutual relationship, especially in view of the 1997 'political change'. The industrial relations system is still sustained, notwithstanding the primacy of the individual employment contract, more on unspecified trust, writ collective at enterprises and in the industrial and political realms, than on express collective contracts. Employers articulate their grace typically at year-end with gifts of bonus and extended holidays, some of which are already written into the statute book. However, unions have always maintained their autonomy and 'space', with little direct intervention from either the state or the employers or from the usurping inundation of the NGOs. Since the SAR, despite expectations, such relationship, in terms of mutual power, reciprocal check and balance, has not been sharply altered, apart from wider space of union participation in elected politics, yet confined mainly to the legislature. The practice of the 'welfare state' has remained limited, much in the legacy of the colonial era.

Hong Kong has been exposed to 'globalisation' since it was a British colony, with its distance vis-à-vis the rest of the world compressed first by maritime shipping and later by air transport and now information technology (IT) communication. For this reason, its late development experiences, mirrored in the 'secularisation' of its unions from 'fraternal welfarism' to encompass 'collective instrumentalism' in the 1970s-cum-1980s, have not been that disjointed as to warrant the application of Kuhn's notion of 'Paradigm Shift'. Transformation of the territory's social fabrics and unionism, gradualist, has earlier been noted (Handy, 1999: chapter 12). Still, its 'late development', dated from the Korean War, gave local unions a new momentum when it began to de-industrialise and experiment with participative electoral politics. A distinctive brand of organised labour hence evolved, from which Thurley drew his inspiration on theorising about 'Asian unionism'.

Even ranked as one among the four leading late-developing East Asian economies (others being Singapore, South Korea and Taiwan), Hong Kong is not late but malleable in adapting to the vicissitudes of the global market and capitalism and the whim of shifting geopolitics. Its swift ascendancy to 'post-industrialism' has been made possible by its pre-existent 'cosmopolitanism', which gives it a 'comparative niche' in embracing 'globalisation'. Besides, Hong Kong excels in the global economy on two advantages. First, its city-port and 'the rule of law' heritage entail a congenial normative-physical infrastructure for financial capital and investment destined for China. Second are its stable albeit occasionally volatile political economy and its 'workplace permissiveness', of which non-obstructive unionism (which holds the NGOs at bay) constitutes a part.

Hong Kong's gain from 'globalisation' has to be discounted on the balance sheet for several reasons. It has to be noted that 'globalisation', while bringing firms of different nations together in the compact global production chain, is not always conducive to their 'convergence'. First, its connotation of 'universalisation' is limited by ethnocentrism: namely, the nation-state, nationalism, national unionism and even 'the rule of law', which are institutional prescriptions transplanted to the new or rejuvenated societies under 'globalisation' and yet having their own specificities because of the need for local adaptations. Second, to associate 'equalisation' with 'globalisation' is mythical, since transnational production chains stratify logistically firms of different nationality within an international order of 'division of labour'. It is hierarchical, hence sustaining 'international inequalities' (Atkinson, 2018: chapter 3). In this connection, Hong Kong, second to New York and London as financial centres, never aspires to take over their places. This is partly because the regime of 'rules of the game' in the global financial and commodity markets are still dictated by the institutionalised 'market rule' of Western mega-cities (Fenby, 2017: 130). Constrained by the vicissitudes of an open economy due to, for example, fluidity of its financial capital, demography and human capital, local unions have to be adaptive to be prudent. More exposed to the whims of the global market than other new economies, the territory and its unions always find it luxurious to envisage any far-sighted urban development strategy and union development strategy, which are beyond prediction and attainment. For unions facing such unfathomable perimeters, the strategy of 'adhocracy' tends to prevail. They are cosmopolitan but prefer the flexibility of not forging any formal alliance with unions or labour organisation overseas, even after the law was liberalised by the SAR regime. To a certain extent, the 'adhocracy' analogy applies to the NGOs as well.

Citing Bell, 'globalisation' and its effects are visible at the realms of the market, polity and their regulatory/integrative (coordinating) social institutions. Beyond these realms, socio-economic changes have a normative significance. The aestheticism of work and leisure is hence emasculated as 'distance' is either shortened or extended (especially with the ethos of the contract). This happens when 'Industrialism' sublimes into 'Post-industrialism' and when 'Modernity' evolves into 'Post-Modernity' (Bell, 1978: 46–7; Giddens, 1991: chapters 1 and 2). A local spirit of altruistic welfare collectivism, adaptative instrumentalism and permissiveness for non-exclusive competition (with little room for 'cut-throat' extremes), emergent in Hong Kong since it was a refugee society after the wars, is reflected in unions' cherished tradition of inclusion, entailing freedom to associate, elastic space for diversity, pluralism and competition. Probably, such mutual respect of boundary has not been conducive to the 'zero-sum' type of adversarial collective bargaining of the West.

European critics on social equality like Pickett still dwells upon the income re-distribution effects of union-based collective bargaining (Pickett, 2015: 89–94). Yet, such an allusion, mythical to many (Atkinson, 2018: chapter 4) has long lost its significance for unions here. Relative distribution within the economy, as gauged by the Gini coefficient, improved during the 1970s and 1980s and worsened thereafter, notwithstanding collective bargaining which has never been significant since the early 1950s. Hong Kong had at least two interludes of collective bargaining, first in the 1920s and second in the immediate post-war years of the late 1940s. Paradoxically, unions abdicated such activities exactly when collective bargaining reached a zenith, only to give way to 'arbitration' and its extension, almost economy-wide in 1949–1950. Hong Kong never revives such practices but is vividly cited by the SAR administration as a benchmark case to illustrate the dispensability of collective bargaining for attaining international labour standards as a perquisite of its participation in the global economy.

Labour history in Hong Kong attests to the brewing effects of its century-long exposure to 'globalisation' for local unionism. Yet, its indisputable 'guild and insurgency' legacy, rooted in China's political history, suggests the continuity of 'Oriental collectivism' which transcends, in defiance of the Webbs' classic union theory, the boundary between traditionalism and industrialism (Turner et al., 1980). Hong Kong unionism is in its entirety a cultural hybrid, which combines both traditional Chinese heritage and British institutional legacies diffused to Hong Kong in the colonial days. The labour movement here is pioneered by the maritime unions which were created by seamen on board ocean liners when they, as the most cosmopolitan occupation before the Second World War, were exposed to Western unionism, while inspired at home by the 'May Fourth Intellectual Movement' of 1918 (Leung, 2017). The victorious Seamen Strike of 1922 marked the overture to the General Strike of 1925–1926, which was of a global scale capturing global attention.

From its early days, cosmopolitan Hong Kong was the conduit for Chinese workers to get acquainted with Western unionism and chiliastic strikes. Echoing Marx, such strike experiences helped enrich union consciousness. After the World War, a trade union law borrowed from Britain slowly purged unions of their guild heritages.by requiring them to register with lawful constitutions. Unions showed their malleability by adapting without exception to the law. They still pride it as a source of resilience when they waived the strike weapon, as from the mid-1950s onwards, to free themselves from the bureaucratic rigidities of collective bargaining. They swiftly re-oriented their role to act as the 'stop-gap' providers of providence in the absence of public 'social wages' to relieve industrial pauperism, when 'sweat shops' thrived in the young industrial colony.

Politico-social reforms and economic affluence in the advents of 'globalisation' landed Hong Kong on its 'Golden Years' of the 1980s (Welsh, 1997: chapter 16). With a history of 'cosmopolitan' exposure, 'late urbanism sowed its creeping roots in Hong Kong', which consolidated and refined its body of 'core values' to cherish 'individual autonomy' and 'the rule of law'. By vindicating a global set of 'the rules of the game' or 'the code of practices' governing its participation in the global division of labour and economic order, Hong Kong won international acclaim as a modern civil society (Ng and Poon, 2004: 31–41, Cartledge, 2017: chapters 3 and 4). The 'Hong Kong identity' crystallises from these normative assumptions which exalt, inter alia, permissiveness, aptitude for diversity and ethos of co-existence and mutual aid. These core values, reflective of global cosmopolitanism, also transcend the union sector. Thus, the FTU and CTU, perennial adversaries, never purport to weed out each other. Ironically, 'modern cosmopolitanism' under global (Western) influences breeds a parochial consciousness which resents the Mainland and its people, alongside the northern culture of the motherland. By its power superiority in the domain of geopolitics, Beijing waves its censoring 'stick'; since it cannot tolerate such an 'anomic and unpatriotic' drift of sentiments of local belongingness, essentially harboured by the younger generations, to usurp wider loyalty to the mother nation. The resultant is a Hong Kong with growing disaffection and disillusion about the 'motherland'. Such contradiction has contributed in part to the FTU's apprehension about the onslaught of 'globalisation' and the covert subversion of Western imperialism and hedonistic values.

Given the defensive character of Webbs' or Coleman's economic unionism, which naturally entails a degree of parochialism or localism, the very notion of 'international unionism' is a paradox. Ironically, globalisation serves more to dilute than enhance the relevance of global unionism to the Hong Kong context. The crux is how and where the line between 'inclusion' and 'exclusion' is to be drawn, which depends on 'boundary-demarcation' of the stakeholders on their jurisdiction and jurisprudence. To the FTU, its experiences with externalities abroad have been acidic. First, its forerunning unions in their embattled 1925–1926 Hong Kong-Canton Strike derived their overseas funding support not from the high-profile Comintern (The Second Socialist International) and the British coal miner unions, all pledging moral support in empty rhetorics, but from patriotic Chinese communities abroad. Before that, the Hong Kong seamen succeeded in their general strike of 1922 which witnessed a slight levelling of their relative pay disadvantage vis-à-vis their Western counterparts. Second and in the same vein, when conventional shipping gave way to bulk cargo shipments by container lines in the 1980s, the FTU castigated the overt zeal with which Western maritime unions of the ITF lent 'brotherhood' support to their Asian fraternities by lobbying for the latters' pay surge. The sympathetic campaign of these Western seafarers actually concealed a selfish design to curb competition from their cheaper Asian counterparts. Recently, the ITF pleaded support to the container port dispute of 2013 by dispatching officials from the maritime and wharf unions to join the picket line of the striking crane drivers. Such show of international solidarity won applauds in the media and praises went to the CTU. However, the FTU, when deploring the swift decline of the container handling industry in Hong Kong, lamented that the biggest beneficiary from the strike was the corporate operator of the largest container wharf locked in the strike. The company has skilfully yet unscrupulously re-located the bulk of the handling cargos from Hong Kong to its new container port commissioned in Shenzhen, effectively chocking off this industry in Hong Kong. From topping the world league of container porting, it now drops out the top five. Even if inadvertently, the CTU and its overseas colleagues were seen by the FTU as instrumental to the industry's downturn, alongside its employment capacity.

Interestingly, the above syndrome hints upon an emerging spirit of self-identity of Hong Kong and its people with feeble sentiments of regional affiliation (otherwise based upon ethnic-normative commonalities among some Asian societies, rather than the geopolitics and economics of a shared market for the region, which are hardly pertinent). Hong Kong is now an SAR within China, which provides it with an external buffer diplomatically. Yet, its people and unions cherish its own culture, probably for its unique experience of 'de-colonisation' (in contrast with post-war de-colonisation or the demise of neo-colonialism for most independent nation-states in East Asia), when transiting from a British colony to an SAR of China. The dynamics of contradiction persists after 1997. The union sector, as in many walks of life, needs to face the brewing controversy as how the boundary for the 'one country, two systems' ought to and can be drawn. To the patriotic FTU, it is non-problematic and yet for the purportedly democratic CTU, the boundary is pathetic. Probably, Hong Kong is so pre-occupied with this controversial agenda of addressing such contradiction between the macro and micro identity-cum-image (i.e., Hong Kong in China) that it has little spare enthusiasm to participate diligently in such regional blocs as the 'Asian-Pacific Economic Co-operation' (APEC). Moreover, both the FTU and the CTU, ambivalent about the imprints of 'globalisation' (a process which cannot be negated since by definition, it has been the constant 'life-blood' on which Hong Kong survives and thrives), always elect to keep a 'closed door' for the territory's domestic labour market to other Asian workers, apart from domestic helpers.

For Hong Kong's organised labour, its past experiences attest to its low enthusiasm in joining any Asian-specific labour leagues which have not performed. Again examples help to demonstrate such misgivings. In the 1970s, some new teacher and social worker unions, sponsored by the Catholic

Church, cherished high expectations of participating in a regional forum of the Asian Brotherhood of Trade Unions (BATU), the Asian branch of the Church-sponsored World Congress of Labour (WCL) headquartered in the Philippines. It coincided with an era when the Catholic Church and Christian missionaries penetrated the labour sector in the Third World as a part of their secularisation programme, virtually piloting the beginning of the NGOs. These labour pressure groups appealed to the colonial government for their professed (political) neutrality; even senior labour officials were dispatched to address regional seminars which the BATU hosted. However, the BATU regional movement soon lost steam and such links withered. Later, in the 1980s, civil service unions shifted to 'touch base' with white-collar trade secretariats in the international instead regional domain. Notable examples were the Public Services International (PSI) and the Postal, Telegraph and Telecommunication International (PTTI) (Turner et al., 1980: chapter 11). However, the euphoria again receded when a decade-long sequel of emulative and leap-frogging grade-specific civil service pay disputes largely subsided by the close of the 1980s. Today, the seamen's union in the FTU camp deputises for the ITF in running a Hong Kong office for seafarers, which oversees the 'Great China' sub-region and not wider. It is hence less than a regional office for the Asian sector.

The 'globalisation' syndrome has precipitated a deepening challenge to trade unions due to its stimulus on 'precarious employment', earlier known as 'atypical employment' which stemmed from outsourcing of non-core works by corporate employers. In other words, corporate capitalism rationalises by renewal schemes of 'externalisation' and 'downsizing', which lead to 'flexi hiring' or 'recasualisation' of the labour market.

The responses of the mainstream FTU and the refractory CTU to 'globalisation' have been diametrically opposite. The latter has been vociferous or even agitational, almost emulating labour NGOs in other new Asian economies, while the FTU turns 'ministerial', by seeking to participate in the elected polity and the 'corridor of power' to influence labour enactments. With a growing 'secondary sector' of contract, temporary and part-time workers, income distribution in society has become consistently less even. 'Fractionalisation' of the general labour force breeds an urban 'precariat' sub-class (Kalleberg, 2009; Ip and Ng, 2013). In Hong Kong, the onslaught of the 'precariat' syndrome helped unions to wrestle successfully a general minimum wage law from a reluctant SAR government and its plutocracy in 2011 (Ip and Ng, 2013). Otherwise, organised labour has been frustrated on other fronts in eliciting any legislative betterment for the 'precarious' part-timers, not to mention those emerging in 'platform employment' (Ng and Poon, 2004: chapter 8). Unlike Japan and Europe, Hong Kong still falls short of providing parity benefits of employment safeguards to non-regular employees.

The CTU's agenda is doctrinal, always reiterating its demands for the standard Western recipe, namely, statutory rights of collective bargaining which the government categorically withholds, and statutory regularisation of 'non-standard employment' (to equalise it with 'standard employment'), which employers stubbornly resist. It also appeals to the ILO for support. Conversely, the FTU, even alienated by the state's co-optation with capital, addresses the 'labour fragmentation' agenda with its 'ministerial' methods of legislative lobby, punctuated with token demonstrations on Labour Day. It lobbies, with limited success, the SAR government to better control the outsourcing of peripheral jobs which they hive off. It has also taken employers to task within the LAB, from which the CTU is excluded, for concessions on a corrective to the anomalous MPF 'offset' valve.[1] However, it has met stern resistance from employers and 'lip-service' gestures from a lukewarm SAR government on its proposal on legislating for compulsory standard work hour and enhanced safeguard of part-time non-standard workers. The FTU, expressing agony with unchecked upward drift of the Gini coefficient, can only lament while constrained politically by its institutional role not to mobilise any industrial weapons (such as by calling a 'general strike' to register a collective protest in solidarity) in order to wage pressure upon a non-enthusiastic SAR authority to reform either the low-tax regime or rationalise the social security system for re-distributing income (Pickett, 2015: chapter 1; Cartledge, 2017: 23–26).

Hong Kong dates the inception of its labour law regime, which wins worldwide acclaim for its affinity to 'rule of the law', from the late nineteenth century shortly after its colonisation. To that extent, it is not late developing in this institutional domain, because of its legacy of an international (globalised) horizon. In particular, the official technocracy always prides itself for its proficiency and fair judgement in enforcing labour law. This notwithstanding, the dynamics of enforcement has not been applied evenly over the years. For example, the 1975 Labour Relations Ordinance has hardly been invoked for intervening into trade disputes since its inception. Second, the Trade Boards Ordinance, brought to the statue book since 1940, has been simply window-dressing to satisfy the ritual of reporting to the ILO office. However, this law, if applied conscientiously, would have enabled the authority to answer partly the issue of precarious 'atypical employment'. Specifically, it could enable a tripartite trade board be appointed under official auspices to investigate work hours and pay in a marginal trade, with a view to declaring for the trade a sectoral minimum wage and standard hour norm. However, the government, probably with the silent consent of organised labour, has elected to shelve the law, for fear of upsetting the collective 'industrial relations' equilibrium conserved under 'state absention'. Yet, some labour laws have proved their efficacy at the workplace. This applies especially to the 1968 Employment Ordinance, possibly given its complementarities with the Labour Tribunal Ordinance. Such selectivity of labour law enforcement suggests that the 'rule of law' system is not necessarily homogeneous and excellence cannot be taken for granted in every aspect of labour law application. Often the rigour of enforcing such law is the function of the power relationship among the state, the employers and their employees and their collectivities. The climate of the Mainland-SAR affinity can also be deterministic. For example, the Registrar of Trade Unions in the past de-registered unions from the list as a proscriptive sanction. Although cases have been sparse but the number can surge in future as the purge of societies recently began when a political party registered as a society was outlawed for advocacy of Hong Kong independence, itself a 'taboo' to both the Beijing and the SAR authorities.

Culture, norms and institutions

Daniel Bell, in observing the embedment of society in history, questions the legitimacy of 'unified periodisation', inasmuch as continuities exist between antecedent and succeeding eras. Globalisation of late-modernity is not segregated from industrialism which overlaps with Renaissance-in-feudalism (Bell, 2001: xxi). Civilisations are not discreet occurrences. Cultures are always amorphous and diffusive. The notion of 'culture-relativism' cannot be freed from the 'East versus West' debate (see Patten, 1999; Jacques, 2012; Rachman, 2017). Bell also cites Hess' argument, that 'social institutions are racial creations, racial struggle is primary and class struggle is secondary' (Hess, 1958: 33). Human societies are 'racial', hence saying cultural diversities. Subscription to such a premise suggests that the 'convergence' thesis is not culture-free. Thurley's 'Asian unionism', as an 'Asian make', is naturally culture-bound.

It follows that conceptualisation of society is a hierarchy with three realms. At the core is culture which is most tenacious, the next is the polity where power is deployed for decision-making for the public household by the nation-state and its key players, while at the third level, the techno-economic process governing the market and owed to the management of the firm and economy, which is rational, versatile and changing. From a structural-institutional perspective, most institutions are gestated at the second level to regulate activities at the third level. Institutions as functionaries are resilient and can last, especially after they have been elevated to the realm of culture. Like the schools and banks, they have become axiomatic and blended with the normative perimeters. Concomitantly, institutions often breed vested interests, so that they can be self-perpetuating even after becoming anachronistic. Examples of institutions tending towards self-fulfilling perpetuity when their stakeholders become impervious to admitting and correcting institutional decays, according to Feguson, include, inter alia, the rule of law and civil societies (Ferguson, 2014: chapters 3 and 4). Likewise, unions and collective bargaining can become exhausted and liable to be usurped by 'missionary' NGOs, as earlier noted in this chapter when discussing the FTU's diversion to 'community unionism' since the 1990s.

The longevity of institutions is yet compounded by the propensity for neighbouring nation-states to cluster themselves into regional blocs, either as geopolitical strategy or for shared cultural-normative commonalities

(Ferguson, 2012: 295–325). Examples are the European Union, APEC, Association of Southeast Asian Nations (ASEAN), American trade pacts and the military North Atlantic Treaty Organization (NATO). Such demarcations by regional or sub-regional boundaries exclude outsiders and solidify insiders' togetherness and collaborative participation within the league. Although region-specific 'parochialism', mirrored in shared cultural heritages, can be encased institutionally by legal instruments like treaties of coalition, many regional leagues, political or economic, prove to be tenuous, as illustrated by Britain's divorce from the European Union and Trump's rewrite of the Pan-American trade treaties.

As noted earlier, Hong Kong abstains from active participation in any regional or sub-regional politico-economic forums, Asia or Asia-Pacific. It is not a sovereign nation-state, not to mention its distinctive culture which emanates from its British Sino-heritage. Besides, such regional initiatives of economic cooperation or political dialogue seem to proliferate, only to dampen their appeal to their incumbent or potential members. This notwithstanding, Hong Kong is resonant with many other Asian societies, sharing a colonial heritage and certain cultural traits attributable to Chinese ethnic roots and the Confucian ethos (Ferguson, 2012: chapter 6; Nisbett, 2004: chapters 3 and 4). Against such a wider cultural milieu, Asian unionism, as earlier portrayed by Thurley, also embraces organised labour in Hong Kong. It is the purpose of this book to chart how homogeneous or how heterogeneous Asian unionism is. As a brand of Asian unionism, unions here exhibit a culture of malleability which can spare unions of collective bargaining (the testimonial of Western unionism); yet reminiscent of, nationalist consciousness and anti-colonial recalcitrance, of national development, of growth and poverty alleviation, of lay leadership and of occupational fraternity. Thurley echoed the 'industrial man' thesis of Kerr et al. in pointing to Asian unions' post-decolonisation mission of allying with the state to emancipate the economy from poverty and subjugation to laissez-faire imperialism by hastened late development, a course which Hong Kong has also embraced with seeming success since the closing stage of the colonial days.

There have been two models for Asian economies in the wake of post-war de-colonisation and national economic assertion, the soviet and the capitalist. Hong Kong and Singapore, South Korea and Taiwan belong to the latter category. Whether socialist or capitalist, unions in societies shaped by globalisation and late development are all hybrid, home-made and yet not natively indigenous, due to varying degree of adaptation to universalism on the basis of local exigencies. Like the ACFTU, the FTU early governance system betrays elements of socialist unionism which, however, have been diluted as it evolves in the local milieu as the 'dialectic product of western capitalism'.

This chapter has narrated experiences of Hong Kong unions, as bound by their cultural legacies, constrained by the global economy and conditioned by the political economy. Japanese unionism, perhaps most Confucian, was fashioned by post-war American 'Occupation Administration', which wrote

Japan's modern labour standard and trade union laws (Dore, 1990: 116–9). Both Taiwan and South Korea emulated extensively, after Presidential decree of 'democratisation' which liberalised the polity in 1987, American and Japanese laws in labour reforms. Their democratised polities invited the Church and other democratic Western NGOs to nurture competitive pluralism which altered their pre-reform landscape of monolithic unionism. Singapore's labour movement is annexed closely to the polity while the nation pays homage to its pre-independence British colonial system. The majority of unions in Southeast Asia are within the ambit of state control, except for Japan and Hong Kong. Probably, the latter two are among the few societies in East Asia where the ILO can witness the bona fide vindication of the three basic principles for unionism, freedoms to associate, to bargain and to strike, being genuinely vindicated.

Naturally, intra-regional cultural diversity exists among Asian unions. First, it differs by the extent and nature of borrowing from the West, which cannot be taken at face value. Noting the superficiality of many comparative studies, Kahn-Freund (1974: 27), the labour law authority, cautioned against just charting export/import of legal rules and institutions without considering the environment, with 'the risk of rejection' which perverts or even nullifies the transplant. Within the Asian region, for example, collective bargaining appears little more than nominal in Singapore and the Philippines. In Hong Kong, the statutory immunities from tort and common law restraint bestowed upon the unions by the Trade Unions Ordinance are immaterial since unions have never been taken to court by the state and employers.

Cross-cultural studies yield taxonomies when attempting to cluster and group those which are 'comparable' into categories, or 'types' and 'subtypes'. Yet such classification is also liable to cause 'stereo-typing'. By invoking collective bargaining as the 'natural criterion' for defining unionism, some Western critics dismiss many Asian unions as perfunctory for not having bargained collectively with employers. However, this chapter contends that unions in Hong Kong are unions per excellence, no matter whether they bargain collectively or not. To Thurley, collective bargaining is not definitive for recognising a union.

To reiterate briefly the argument. There can exist a culture of Asian unionism and a sub-culture of Hong Kong unionism as a brand of Asian unionism, given both continuities and disjoints in the evolutionary history of such unionism. For East Asian societies like China, Hong Kong, Singapore and Taiwan, their modern unions are traced back to pre-industrial guilds, ethnic associations and even subterranean revolutionary secret societies, whose activities coincided with the birth of the new nation-state. These Asian unions fall short of the 'ideal-type' unionism by Western definition. The Webb and Webb's authoritative classic definition excluded categorically 'Medieval' guilds. However, it would have impossible to explain how unionism in the China-Hong Kong circuit evolves without tracing back to its guild heritage. The philosophy of Western unionism, centring on 'we-they' working-class consciousness, is 'doctrinally' antagonistic towards capital. However, such 'dialectics' could have been exaggerated. Asian unionism, cherishing the vision and later pride of nationalistic consciousness, can be accommodative towards capital if the latter also subscribe to the shared patriotic goal of defending national interests, especially against colonial/neo-colonial imperialism. Evidently, the horizon of unions' consciousness for 'exclusion' and 'inclusion', for 'continuities' and 'disjoints' varies between Western and East Asian cultures.

The 'union' as an industrial institution is culture-bound. They are the products of the civilisation of 'industrial capitalism'. Yet, as argued above, unionism lacks an existence which is standardised worldwide. Asian unions in different countries never converge wholly with each other, nor will they collectively converge with Western unions in Europe and North America. Moreover, the 'ideology' of 'convergence' conceals Western hegemony, so that Fenby (2017: 130) warns against, as 'extremely short-sighted', the 'axiomatic' assumption that standards written in the Western context are 'the everlasting sanctity of tablets of global law'. By the same token, social scientists, once euphorical in applying Kuhn's notion of 'paradigm' and 'paradigm shift' in physical science to the study of society, has to embrace an extra Chinese 'sub-paradigm' because social premises and theorisation are not as 'transcendental' (Kuhn, 1962: Handy, 1999; chapter 12), Similarly, the 'VoC' thesis, seemingly neat for the taxonomy of market-oriented political economies, has to concede to a non-classifiable 'Asian variety' which does not fall in line with the 'LME'-'CME' locus. Strictly speaking, the 'VoC' typology is just rewrite, as 'old wine in new bottles', of the 'paradigm' schema which can also be employed for typing exercises.

However, the 'paradigm' precept does not risk 'bi-polar' stereo-typing as that of the 'VoC' taxonomy, an excessive dosage of which could regress into nothing more than 'sophisticated empiricism' liable to drift into a 'technician's programming work' (Wright-Mills, 1970: 240–8). Time-honoured labels like Galbraith's 'ministerial unions' and Lester's 'mature unionism' still excel because they are direct as notations of 'kinds' and 'types' and 'brands'. They appeal for being simple and jargon-free.

From a functional-structural perspective, social institutions of the industrial workplace, including webs of rules and unions, are the 'structural prerequisites' of 'industrialism' (Kerr et al., 1973) Today, the rule of law, the welfare state, private property norm, competition and inclusivity as well as NGOs in the 'third sector' are widely considered as litmus tests for the 'civil society' in 'late urbanism' (Patten, 1999: 259–62; Giddens, 2000: chapter 2; Bingham, 2011; Ferguson, 2012:'Introduction'). Yet, such euphoria can be misleading, being romanticised by the 'neo-liberalists' as their accommodative (if not co-optative) strategy with the less powerful and less advantaged by creating an illusion among the latters that they 'participate' and 'share'. Hence, Ferguson laments (2014: chapters 3 and 4) the decay of 'imperialist' (serving the rich and powerful) agencies like 'the rule of law' and the 'third sector', let alone the absurdity of purportedly to enshrine 'free competition' with cumbersome regulations which curb competition. Bell (2001:22–33) also observes that institutions at the economy and polity levels are not 'givens' and 'sacrosanct', but when blended into the culture of 'tradition', they gained resilience and yet also concervatism. Yet, to be so enshrined, institutions need to prove, first, functional and, second, amenable to changes for ease of access to the 'grass-roots community'.

To answer the above, it is noted that institutions have life-cycle. They may evolve and augment, transform, turning either stagnant and withering or adaptive and malleable in greeting changes. For example, 'the rule of law' institution, especially the common law system which helps enshrine Britain as the 'the world's bastion of law', is now anachronistic (still glued to classical economics) but still self-assertive, due to marginal and defensive adjustments of the elitist and powerful legal profession. Trade unions were the custodian institution of the working class, but they are exhausted due to the bureaucratic cage of collective bargaining. Western unionism in the 1980s posited collective bargaining for assisting 'embourgeoisment' of the working class. However, the outcome was that suburban life-style, once the hallmark of the 'middle class', is now emasculated by the 'mega-city ecology' (Bell, 2001: xiv–xvi). Western unions are now subject to peril, with their bases eroded by professionalisation as employment relations of the knowledge workers are individualised, while 'the rule of law' system (especially labour statues) turns hostile towards strikes and unionism (Atkinson, 2018: 128–35). For Asian unions like Hong Kong's, are they more malleable and sustainable? As institutions of industrial relations collectivism, their culture suggests that they have been inactive for collective bargaining, small, pluralistic, lay in leadership which hardly betrays any vestiges of the shop steward system. Yet they have not been exhausted, as the territory's union density surged in the 1990s and now stays at a level of 22%–23% of the employed workforce. This chapter suggests that unions here are more like 'adhocracy', less bureaucratic and less vulnerable to 'bureaucratic paths'.

By its history, Hong Kong unionism is culturally distinct from craft unionism and professional bodies in Western societies, whose 'exclusiveness' is based upon 'calculative rationality'. Instead, many unions in this Confucian society were parochial, cemented by 'normative rationality' attributed to ethnic communitarianism. Today, such traits survive. For example, FTU still excel in cultivating mutual aid, shared amenities and occupational networks for transmitting skill and market knowledge and patriotic fraternity. By tradition, unions are tolerant of adversaries, essentially since they are numerous and behave more as voluntary 'secondary associations' of the 'Third Sector'. Most are non-bargaining but may deputise for members at the Labour Tribunal. Otherwise, they are not necessarily confrontational with enterprises. Affiliates of the FTU are known to project from popular culture, as at singing parties during annual feasts (to which employers are often invited), to buttress loyalty to the nation and the union. Elsewhere in Southeast Asia, including China, NGOs are active in the labour sector, often poising as competitors to local unions as spokesmen representing workers. In Hong Kong, unions eclipse the NGOs.

Yet, Hong Kong does not lack a tradition of philanthropic NGOs organised by the mandarin aristocracy of Chinese merchants. Before the war, they were politically influential but became later increasingly effacing as a 'residual sector', when the state began to institutionalise a net of 'social wages' for poor relief. However, there is now a buoyant market for modern NGOs worldwide, especially among the late-developing/developing economies in Asia, Africa and South America, where they are exalted for performing an 'axe-grinding' role in seeking redress of social injustice, which exceeds their conventional 'welfare-providing capacity' in the past. In many underprivileged quarters, they are viewed almost as the 'panaceas' for ameliorating socio-economic inequalities and articulating effectively social grievances otherwise non-heeded. The image of the 'crusade' is imputed to many NGOs as the standard-bearers of 'civil society'. In Asia and other developing regions, their 'noble' intervention into such vulnerable sectors as the rural peasantry and the urban low-paid groups are readily perceived as the safety-valve to safeguard the 'civil society world-wide' (which overshadows 'foreign aid'). The dearth of ingrained socio-economic deprivations in Hong Kong's affluent society has not generated much deeply hidden worker alienation in Hong Kong otherwise germinate for NGO intervention. Its orthodox unions have so far been proficient in deputising for aggrieved employees at the Labour Tribunal which only grant union officials the right of representation at its proceedings. Unions are comparatively competitive to pre-empt NGOs from usurping their conventional functions.

Moreover, the culture of unionism has been able to penetrate the new pseudo professions more effectively than that of professionalism, the former epitomised by the formation of unions while for the latter, by that of the professional bodies. The 'rule of law' system and the cult of professional 'specialism' constitute partly the cornerstone of modern 'civil society' if both institutional sectors perform with fairness and transparency. However, professional associations tend to 'cartelise' the labour market, such as established professions like the doctors and lawyers (Durkheim, 1997: xxxvi–xxxix). Professional bodies wield social power and status, appealing better than unionism to young knowledge workers. Yet, these 'professions' are often exclusive and self-serving (Ferguson, 2014: 108–9, 134). Just as the glut of union power in the 1970s invited its criticism and containment, the unchecked power of established professions provokes growing scepticism for their growing distance from 'communitarianism' (Earle et al., 2017: chapters 1 and 6). The deficiency of post-modern 'professionalism' hence leaves room for unionism.

From the perspective of normative control, both professional associations and craft (or closed) unionism are soldaristic by fostering 'occupational communities' of 'exclusion' which function as labour cartels, by qualifying their insiders (i.e., professional members or craft union members) for the privileged and exclusive right of practice with a body of entry rules which are backed by statutes (for the aristocratic established professions) or by closed shop agreements negotiated with the employers (for craft occupations). In either case, a professional or occupational culture of a sectarian nature is hence sustained, by which open disclosure of information is often minimum. In Hong Kong, the 'culture embrace' of the 'occupational community', still hegemonic for established professions like medical doctors and lawyers, has largely waned for craft trades, notably wood carving, furniture-building and printing. Federal union centres like the FTU and the CTU are 'open' and diversified in membership. However, the FTU, with a history of 'proletariat' recalcitrance inspired by a 'New China' which climaxed in the 1967 Disturbance, sustains a core community which still cherishes its working-class identity. Such a culture is partly 'industrial' and partly 'altruistic', blended by patriotic sentiments exalting the sanctity of 'the SAR within its motherland'. The challenge of the CTU serves to deepen such a culture anchored upon patriotism.

The FTU is hence rope-dancing between the cult of nationalism and its quest for 'equalisation' in an economy with conspicuous inequalities. The CTU does not face such a dilemma but lacks the same cultural entrenchment as the FTU. Elsewhere, the appeal of nationalism has lessened for many Asian unions as 'globalisation' makes safeguard against exploitative 'international division of labour' a more urgent agenda. These unions are hence likely to find NGOs, many of which, especially among the transnational ones, enchant deprived city workers and rural peasants with their professed mission as the standard bearer of (alternative) human conscience, either competitors or (in most cases) friendly allies. The popular appeal of the NGOs to the grass-roots labour force is understandable, insofar as they can transcend nation-states' parochialism, are not burdened by any constituencies to answer and not fee-charging service providers (Malloch-Brown, 2012: chapter 11). It is beyond the scope of this chapter to investigate the advents of the NGOs, especially since their repercussions on organised labour in Hong Kong have not been significant. However, recent scandals uncovered implicating many famed transnational NGOs cast doubts as whether they should be equated with 'civil societies', writ small. Coincidentally, the ministerial FTU (Hong Kong) and the ACFTU (China) both seek to keep the NGOs 'at arm's length' from the labour movements, if not to co-optate them. For the FTU, it has maintained its competitive niche by evolving an NGO-like wing of 'community unionism', which also helps encase the electoral anchor of the FTU at the district community level. Moreover, a mood of 'reflexivity' society, attributed by Giddens to (post)modernity (1995: 160–72), is conserved since many small unions, by functioning as welfare fraternities and cheap merchandise cooperatives, serve to hedge workers

Internal challenges:

- The ideological/political division between the FTU and CTU appears to constitute a major challenge to building unity within the labour movement any yet there is an implicit consensus of mutual accommodation and aversion from excessive antagonism. Such a phenomenon of 'antagonistic inclusion' is characteristic of the tradition or culture of 'union pluralism in Hong Kong since the close of the Second World War.
- The role of the state: the state abstains from direct intervention. However, the trade unions law and the society law, both governing trade unions and labour organizations, are conducive to their proliferation due to these two laws' permissiveness to union formation.
- The political economy as a determining variable: trade unionism is sensitive to volatility and stability of Hong Kong's geo-politics, its economy and labour market. Episodes like the Hong Kong-Canton General Strike Boycott of 1925-26, the 1949 Liberation of China, the Korea and Vietnam Wars, the Cultural Revolution and the Hong Kong Civil Disturbance of 1967 as well as the Reversion of Hong Kong to Chinese sovereignty are exemplary, all shedding salient effects on labour and unionism in Hong Kong.
- The 'lay leadership lacks the workplace culture of shop-stewardship' but the Trade Union Law prescribes a minimum standard of union governance.
- Survival of the union movement requires the unions to be 'malleable and responsible", as visible in the changing structure and functions of unions in coping with the shifting social and politico-economic context of the territory

External challenges

- The FTU functions as a 'ministerial union' which 'serves the interests' of the PRC However, it is relativistic to say as whether patriotism and national interests, the uppermost and paramount mission of the FTU, constitute an external challenge or an internal prerequisite which legitimates its existence and performance.
- The FTU is 'aloof from international unions except for the ITF'. The FTU is still apprehensive about forging formal links with the rest of the global union movement. However, it prefers informal contacts and exchanges with unions in the Asian-Pacific region. Even its links with the ACTU have always been holistic and yet officially 'informal'.
- Both the FTU and CTU appeared to be uncertain how to react to the 'occupy/yellow umbrella movement' in 2014. The FTU sided with the SAR government while the CTU were supporting the 'occupation' but its pledge of support was more rhetorical than material. The Occupy Central' Movement was in essence a students' movement but compounded by covert political influences which were both anti-establishment and pro-establishment. To generalize, the labour movement still tries to keep itself distinct from the student and social movements. On the other hand, NGOs seems to be more oriented towards social and community services than popular social and political movements.
- The political model of 'One Country, Two Systems', which enshrines Hong Kong as a Special Administrative Region (SAR) of the PRC, has begun to show symptoms of ambivalence and early fatigue. Virtually the notion is itself a political paradox, as contradictions unfold when the SAR matures. For example, trade unions are handicapped in safeguarding Hong Kong employees seconded to the Mainland, as well Chinese workers on transient stay in Hong Kong as imported guest workers.

Figure 5.1 Internal and External Challenges to the Unions in HK.

against 'high consequence risk' where, for example, mandatory providence depends upon performance of a private liquidity market.

Critics of 'late capitalism' warn that the 'self-adaptive' instrumentality of its entire apparatus of institutional leverage, including the unions, may become 'categorically exhausted' (Dorre et al., 2009: 312–3), a theme which this chapter addresses and questions. As Bell predicts, institutions could endure longer if they are elevated to the 'culture' realm. The culture of Hong Kong unions is not pivoted around adversarial collective bargaining, but excels because of its tolerance for diversity and its guild legacy. Like the wider culture, the culture of Hong Kong's organised labour is hybrid, structured

- **Reform of union structures**:
- A review of the post-war history of the Hong Kong labour movement reveals the following metamorphosis in the structure and functions of trade unions. First, there was a conspicuous shift of Hong Kong unionism towards 'instrumental collectivism' in the 1970's from fraternal friendly societies of the 1950's. The FTU's reforms in the 1990's and early 2000's, after the reversion back to China, were reminiscent of these reform measures: i) ministerial unionism by converting parts of its functionaries into electoral and quasi-political agencies; ii) coalescing small and dispersed member unions in the major industries into industry-specific and federal-like general unions; and iii) evolving a type of 'community unionism' in face of the exhaustion of workplace conventional unionism. A host of district offices to cater to the neighbourhood communities has hence been established by the FTU under its organizational auspices. Yet, the CTU still has to betray any conspicuous reforms in their union structure due to its relative youthful history. However, it has a less bureaucratic structure and is hence more versatile and malleable than the FTU. Besides, the trade union law prescribes certain basic perimeters of union governance and of union internal structure. These rules are less amenable to changes.
- **Organising strategies**: Both the FTU and the CTU have been capitalizing on trade disputes and strikes for recruitment. However, the FTU has been attracting new members also by the popular appeal of its workers' after-work education and amenity centre. The CTU, behaving more like a labour NGO, penetrates the neighbourhood labouring mass more effectively since it has been able to project a more dedicated and missionary image than the FTU. The common challenge which both trade union centres will face are two-fold: i) the growth of 'atypical employment' in light of the creeping expansion of the shared 'gig' economy and ii) the aging of the population and providential safeguard of the 'old-aged' sector of the population and the labour force.
- **International solidarity**: The CTU has successfully forged links with the International Federation of Trade Unions (the former ICFTU) and the international trade secretariats. It has habitually appealed to the various functional committees of the ILO on alleged breach of labour standards in Hong Kong. By contrast, the FTU has been effacing in establishing solidarity abroad. However, it always been a close fraternity to the ACFTU in China, while it has also maintained friendly ties with the NTUC in Singapore. At law, international links have also been made easier when the trade union law was liberalized in the late 1990's by the SAR government, thereby allowing unions to be associated with overseas unions and labour organizations without prior official consent. However, there was little ramification for the FTU and the CTU, since both operate under the Societies Ordinance, rather than the Trade Unions.

Figure 5.2 Strategies Adopted by the Union Movement to Secure Their Future.

- **Labour-management partnerships:**
- By comparison, collective bargaining practices are better developed in the public sector than in the private sector where the norm is 'individual haggling of the market'. It epitomizes a kind of Hong Kong union flexibility when it is possible for both sides to conceal collective bargaining as 'joint consultation'.
- The Labour Advisory Board (LAB) has been a consultative organ of tripartite participation (government officials, employee and employer representation) on the formulation of labour policy and labour law at the top level of official policy-making. It used to excel, almost like the top labour policy forums in Japan and Singapore. However, it has recently been plagued by pursuit of sectional interests leading to confrontational haggling between capital and labour, especially in the SAR era. Besides, its prerogative is limited to simply consultation and not policy-decision. It is now consistently over-shadowed by the fully elected law-making assembly, the Legislative Council in the labour domain.

- **Political action:** As 'ministerial unionism', the FTU cannot hive-off its political arm but needs to enhance such a functionary to operate as a quasi-political party. This was due to the vacuum of 'partisan' politics and culture in Hong Kong when electoral democracy was introduced in the 1980's and now the FTU has become the second largest political party. This notwithstanding, the FTU has to rope-dance its industrial functions and political mission, the latter now often overriding because patriotism is at its core. The FTU is working within the 'corridor of power', which is also reminiscent of the ACFTU. The dilemma of the FTU is that it has to operate directly as a 'quasi political party' since it is perhaps the CCP's most trusted agent in Hong Kong. The CTU has always experienced difficulties in making inroad into the official consultation system. For example, it strives to but still cannot participate in the Labour Advisory Board and the Senior Civil Staff Council in the public sector. It blamed such failures to the pre-emptive strategies allegedly deployed by its rivals.

- **Coalition building:** Organized labour has never been perceived by the civil societies as a fertile 'greenfield' for the NGOs. The only known case is a quasi-union like NGO which serves, almost exclusively, an old industrial-cum-suburban district in Hong Kong, called the 'Street Workers'. Most NGOs are more interested in cultivating the field of generic social services and social welfare, due to the relative ease of obtaining resources from government subvention. The CTU does operate like an NGO, especially since it has also an interest on labour and union freedom in the Mainland. Besides, it is rather well connected with other NGOs in Hong Kong. On the other hand, the FTU 's countervailing strategy has been its development of a spatial network of community district offices, which can, however, be competing with the NGOs in terms of social services, especially in assisting the socially and industrially disadvantaged and for the pursuit of justice in cases of deprivation and extortion. It appears that organized labour is sufficient viable and malleable on its own, hence with little incentive to build coalition with the NGOs which seem to have a sparse interest in labour and employment matters.

Figure 5.2 (Continued).

by British-inherited union law, yet blending an altruistic dosage of patriotism (FTU) or a quest for democracy (CTU).

The internal and external challenges to the trade union movement in Hong Kong and the strategies which have been adopted by the unions to revitalise the movement are shown in Figures 5.1 and 5.2.

Conclusions

To a large extent, unionism in Hong Kong coalesces with Thurley's notion of 'Asian unionism'. It is perhaps a distinctive brand of Asian unionism, for three historical reasons. First, Hong Kong from its early days of British rule was the bastion and spring-board of the embryonic Chinese labour movement which cradled the gestation of the CCP in the 1920s. Second, it was the hybrid product of home-grown Chinese unions, rooted in traditional guilds and revolutionary insurgencies, fashioned by the British heritage of trade union law and ethos of 'collective laissez-faire'. Third, union pluralism in Hong Kong epitomises a permissive culture of 'inclusion', which has been conserved in spite of its transition in 1997 from a British colony to China's SAR.

The Hong Kong 'union type' also helps to vindicate the Thurley model on, for example, a twofold dimension. The first is the market or occupational orientation of Hong Kong workers who are not focused around the 'enterprise' identity. Their mobility lends themselves more to occupational and industrial unionism than enterprise-specific unionism. The second is the relationship between the unions and the state which prescribes for organised labour the 'rule of the game' but abstains from direct control and coercive repression, apart from the turbulence of 1925–1926 and 1967. However, since the inception of the SAR, the FTU has become 'ministerial' and professedly nationalistic, purporting to support unreservedly the motherland's national enterprise of accelerated development.

Bell suggests that a history of an institution is essential for understanding its character. Unions are 'bona fide' defensive workers' combinations, as proven by the history of union struggles. In Hong Kong, unions excel as the territory's oldest secondary voluntary associations, sometimes emasculated and yet later recouping and occasionally innovative, as the environment changes. As workers' collectivities bound by law of democratic governance, unions have diversified into the realm of electoral politics launched by the colonial government in the mid-1980s. From the 1990s, the FTU enhanced its direct participation in the elected polity, in anticipation of its 'ministerial' transformation in the SAR era. However, unions continue to elect the path of reflective quasi-adhocracies rather than 'bureaucratisation', with lay leadership and dispensing with any workplace culture of shop-stewardship and collective bargaining.

Unionism has stayed resilient beyond the 1997 threshold, when the colony transited into the SAR. Union density has ascended and stabilised at a formidable level of 23%. The SAR regime, constrained by its mission to harbour 'free' capitalism, embraces organised labour with ambivalence. Following its predecessor, the state abstains and intervenes with 'discretion'. It is permissive towards organised labour, allowing unions free to operate either as trade unions proper or societies under the law, in spite of some fears that it may become coercive.

Thurley's notion of 'Asian unionism' hence largely applies when charting Hong Kong's union history. This chapter addresses unionism of this heritage in the context of political economy and space compression owed to 'globalisation' and 'late-development'. The later processes and the advents of the NGOs were not yet explicit in Thurley's treatise. However, his scheme envisaged that Asian unionism was not encased in 'we-they' adversarial collective bargaining, which is the Hong Kong case. Apart from the nexus of nationalism which splits the SAR's labour movement, its local parochialism is attested by its consistent negation of labour importation. Given urban spatial compactness, unions can avert the expenses of maintaining an elaborate tree of locals, pointing to their propensity for adhocracies. Instead, unions are resourceful in supporting members' self-learning and education-cum-skilling with after-work courses in amenity centres. Globalisation, by compressing 'space', has made Hong Kong unions 'amphibious' and adaptive, capable of instigating and waiving strikes, let alone to bargain collectively under the effacing disguise of 'joint consultation'. The Thurley prognosis largely applies to Hong Kong.

Note

1 The 'Mandatory Provident Fund (MPF) scheme was a hastily and ill designed 'welfare state' project ushered to the working citizenry of Hong Kong by legislation on the eve of 1997 and duly adopted and implemented after 1997 by the SAR government. If falls short of a state pension for old-age retirement. Its main weakness lies in the abstention of any public sponsorship but is fed only upon the parity contribution of the employee and his employer. However, the most objection is the compromise of the employee's rights by allowing the accrual of such MPF to the retired employee balanced against his legal entitlement to his long-service payment or severance pay.

References

Atkinson A (2018) *Inequality: What Can be Done?* Paper back edition, Cambridge, MA: Harvard University Press.

Baccaro L and Howell C (2017) *Trajectories of Neoliberal Transformation: European Industrial Relations since the 1970s*, Cambridge: Cambridge University Press.

Bell D (1978) *The Cultural Contradictions of Capitalism*, Paper Edition with a Foreword, New York: Basic Books.

Bell D (2001) *The End of Ideology: On the Exhaustion of Political Ideas in the Fifties*, Cambridge, MA: Harvard University Press.

Bingham T (2011) *The Rule of Law*, London: Penguin Books.

Bland B (2017) *Generation HK: Seeking Identity in China's Shadow*, Australia: Penguin Books, Random House.

Brown K (2017) *CEO, China: The Rise of Xi Jinping*, London: I. B. Tauris.

Cartledge S (2017) *A System Apart: Hong Kong Political Economy from 1997 until Now*, Australia: Penguin Books.

Chan M, Ng SH and Ho E (2000) Labour and Employment. In Ng SH and Lethbridge D (eds.), *The Business Environment in Hong Kong*, 4th ed., Hong Kong: Oxford University Press, 74–96.

Chau Y (2009) *A Labour History of Hong Kong, in Chinese*, Hong Kong: Nice Publishing Company.

Chau Y (2013) *Labour History of Hong Kong: an Abbreviated Version*, Hong Kong: Nice Publishing Company.

Chesneaux J (1968) *The Chinese Labour Movement 1919–1927*, Stanford, CA: Stanford University Press.

Clegg HA (1983) Otto Kahn-Freund and British Industrial Relations, In L. Wedderburn, Lewis R and Clark J (eds.), *Labour Law and Industrial Relations: Building on Kahn-Freund*, Oxford: Clarendon Press, 14–28.

Child J (ed,) (1973) *Man and Organization,* London: George Allen & Unwin

Dahrendorf R (1959) *Class and Class Conflict in an Industrial Society,* London: Routledge and Kegan Paul.

Dore R (1990) *British Factory-Japanese Factory*, with a new foreword, Berkley: University of California Press.

Dorre K, Lessenich S and Rosa H (2009) *Sociology, Capitalism, Critique*, London: Verso.

Durkheim E (1997) *The Division of Labour in Society*, with an introduction by Lewis Coser, New York: The Free Press.

Earle J, Morgan C and Ward-Perkins Z (2017) *The Econocracy: On the Perils of Leaving Economics to the Experts*, United Kingdom: Penguin Books, Random House'.

Endacott G (1973) *A History of Hong Kong*, 2nd ed., Hong Kong: Oxford University Press.

England J and Rear (1975) *Chinese Labour under British Rule*, Hong Kong: Oxford University Press.

Fenby J (2017) *Will China Dominate the 21st Century?* Cambridge: Polity Press.

Ferguson N (2012) *Civilization*, London: Penguin Books.

Ferguson N (2014) *The Great Degeneration: How Institutions Decay and Economies Die*, London: Penguin Books.

Flanders A (1974) The Tradition of Voluntarism, *British Journal of Industrial Relations*, XII (3), pp. 352–70.

Galbraith JK (1972) *The New Industrial State*, 2nd ed., Harmondsworth: Penguin.

Giddens A (1973) *The Class Structure of the Advanced Societies*, London: Hutchison University Library.

Giddens A (1981) *A Contemporary Critique of Historical Materialism*, volume 1, Power, Property and the State, Berkeley: University of California Press.

Giddens A (1991) *The Consequences of Modernity*, Cambridge: Polity Press.

Giddens A (1994) *Beyond Left and Right: The Future of Radical Politics*, Cambridge: Polity Press.

Giddens A (2000) *The Third Way and its Critics*, Cambridge: Polity Press.

Goldthorpe JH ed. (1984) *Order and Conflict in Contemporary Capitalism: Studies in the Political Economy of Western European Nations*. Oxford: Clarendon Press.

Goodstadt LF (2014) *Poverty in the Midst of Affluence: How Hong Kong Mismanaged its Prosperity*, 2nd ed., Hong Kong: The University of Hong Kong University Press

Hall and Soskice DW (eds.) (2001) *Varieties of Capitalism: The Institutional Foundations of Comparative Advantage*, New York: Oxford University Press.

Hamann K and Kelly J (2008), Varieties of Capitalism and Industrial Relations. In Blyton P, Herry E, Bacon N and Fiorito J (eds.), *Sage Handbook of Industrial Relations*, New York: Sage, 129–148.

Handy C (1999) *Understanding Organisations*, 4th ed., with a new foreword and a new introduction, London: Penguin Books.

Hess M (1958) *Rome and Jerusalem*, New York: Philosophical Library.

Hughes R (1976) *Borrowed Place, Borrowed Time: Hong Kong and its Many Faces*, 2nd ed. London: Andre Deutsch.

Ip O and Ng SH (2013) Labour and Employment in the Tsang Administration. In Cheng YS *The Second Chief Executive of Hong Kong SAR: Evaluating the Tsang Years 2005–2012*, Hong Kong: City University of Hong Kong Press, pp. 409–433.

Jacques M (2012), *When China Rules the World: The End of the Western World and the Birth of a New Global Order*, 2nd ed., London: Penguin.

Kahn-Freund O (1974) On Uses and Misuses of Comparative Law. *Modern Law Review*, 37, 1–27.

Kalleberg AL (February 2009) Precarious Work, Insecure Workers: Employment Relations in Transition. *American Sociological Review*, 74, 1–22.

Kerr C, Dunlop JT, Harbison HF and Myers CA (1973) *Industrialism and Industrial Man*, 2nd edition with Foreword and Postscript, Harmondsworth, Penguin Books.

Kwok J (2018) Labour Selling out Labour, an unpublished Master of Philosophy thesis, Government and Public Administration, The Chinese University of Hong Kong, Hong Kong.

Kuhn TS (1962) *The Structure of Scientific Revolutions*, Chicago: University of Chicago Press.

Lester RA (1958) *As Unions Mature*, Princeton, NJ: Princeton University Press.

Lethbridge DG, Ng SH and Chan M (2000) Is Hong Kong Entering a New Paradigm? In Ng SH and Lethbridge DG (eds.), *The Business Environment in Hong Kong*, 4th ed., Hong Kong: Oxford University Press.

Leung PL (2017) *Sweat Shop in Victoria City: The Early Days of Hong Kong's Workers and Labour Movement, in Chinese*, Hong Kong: Chung Wah Bookshop Publishing Company.

Lewis R (1976) The Historical Development of Industrial Relations. *British Journal of Industrial Relations* XIV(1), 1–17.

Malloch-Brown M (2012) *The Unfinished Global Revolution: The Limits of Nations and the Pursuit of a New Politics*, London: Penguin Books.

Mintzberg H (1983) *Structure in Fives*, New York: Prentice-Hall.

Ng SH (June 1982) Labour Administration and 'Voluntarism': The Hong Kong Case. *The Journal of Industrial Relations*, 24(2) 266–281.

Ng SH (1985) *A Report on the Thurley-Turner Visit to the All-China Federation of Trade Unions, 1985*, Hong Kong: Centre of Asian Studies, University of Hong Kong.

Ng SH (1985) A Revisit to the Chinese (Canton-Hong Kong) Labour Movement and Perlman's Model. *The Australian Journal of Politics and History*, 31(3), 418–434.

Ng SH (1986) Labour. In Cheng Y S (ed.), *Hong Kong in Transition*, Hong Kong: Oxford University Press, 268–299.

Ng SH and Ip O (2004) Dialectics of Capitalism: A Re-visit to the Hong Kong Chinese Labour Movement and Perlman's Model. *Labour History*, 45(4), 496.

Ng SH and Warner M (1998) *China's Trade Unions and Management*, London: Macmillan Press.

Ng SH (1997) Reversion to China: Implications for Labour in Hong Kong. *International Journal of Human Resource Management*, 8(3), 660–676.

Ng SH (2015) *Labour Law in Hong Kong*, 2nd ed., Alphen, The Netherlands: Wolters Kluwer.

Ng SH and Ip O (2003) Phenomenon of Union Exhaustion: Is there A 'Third Way' for Trade Unionism in Hong Kong. *The Journal of Industrial Relations*, 45(3), 378–394.

Ng SH and Poon C (2004) *Business Restructuring in Hong Kong: Strengths and Limits of Post-Industrial Capitalism*, Hong Kong; Oxford University Press.

Ng SH and Rowley C (2000) Globalization and Hong Kong's Labour Market: The Deregulation Paradox. *Asian Pacific Business Review*, 6(3 and 4), 174–192.

Nisbett, RE (2004) *The Geography of Thought*, New York: Free Press.

Patten C (1999) *East and West*, 2nd ed., London: Pan Books.

Patten C (2018) *First Confession: A Sort of Memoir*, London: Penguin.

Pelling H (1971). *A History of British Trade Unionism*, 2nd ed., Harmondsworth: Penguin.

Perlman S (1968) *A Theory of the Labour Movement*, New York: Kelly.

Phelps Brown H (1986), *The Origins of Trade Union Power, with Additional Materials*, Oxford: Oxford University Press.

Pickett T (2015) *The Economics of Inequality*, translated by Goldhammer A, Cambridge, MA: Belknap Press of Harvard University Press.

Rachman G (2017) *Easternization*, London: Vintage.

Rogin M (July 1962) Voluntarism: The Political Foundation of an Anti-Political Doctrine. *Industrial and Labour Relations Review*, 15(4), 521–535.

Streeck W (2014, *Buying Time: The Delayed Crisis of Democratic Capitalism,* London: Oxford University Press

Thurley K (1983), The Role of Labour Administration in Industrial Society. In Ng SH and Levin DA (eds.), *Contemporary Issues in Hong Kong Labour Relations*, Hong Kong: Centre of Asian Studies, University of Hong Kong, 106–120.

Thurley K (1988), Trade Unionism in Asian Countries. In Jao YC, Levin DA, Ng SH and Sinn E (eds.), *Labour Movement in a Changing Society: The Experiences of Hong Kong*, Hong Kong: Centre of Asian Studies, University of Hong Kong, 24–31.

Thurley K and Wirdenius H (1989), *Towards European Management*, London: Pitman.

Turner HA, Fosh P, Gardner M, Hart K, Morris R, Ng SH, Quinlan M and Yerbury D (1980). *The Last Colony: But Whose? A Study of the Labour Movement, Labour Market and Labour Relations in Hong Kong*, Cambridge: Cambridge University Press.

Turner HA, Fosh P and Ng SH (1991) *Between Two Societies: Hong Kong Labour in Transition*, Hong: Centre of Asian Studies, University Press.

Webb S and Webb B (1902) *Industrial Democracy*, London: Longmans.

Webb S and Webb B (1920) *The History of Trade Unionism*, 2nd ed., London: Longmans.

Welsh F (1997) *A History of Hong Kong*, 2nd ed., London: HarperCollins.
Woodward J (1965) *Industrial Organization: Theory and Practice*, London: Oxford University Press.
Wright-Mills C (1970) *The Sociological Imagination*, Harmondsworth: Penguin Book.
Yuen KS (2015) *Almanac on Hong Kong Since Reversion Back to China 2002–2007*, Hong Kong: Joint Publishing Company.

6 Trade unions and globalising India

Towards a more inclusive workers' movement?

K.R. Shyam Sundar and Rahul Suresh Sapkal

Introduction

Workers collectivise to not only enhance their bargaining power vis-à-vis their employers but also create their own social identities. Workers' representation takes several forms such as trade union, non-governmental organisation (NGO), workers' committee and other forms. Trade unions are a classic and dominant form of workers' representation. They are collective bodies operating on the principles of democracy and thus constitute a vital part of democratic and pluralistic political systems. Unions seek to protect and promote economic and non-economic interests of workers both at the workplace and in the larger society. They have, over the decades, earned recognition through struggles with both the state and the employers, although this is now at risk. Unions pursue several methods (industrial, legal enactment, political and so on.) not only to protect their real wages but also to fight for their rights and entitlements. They act as 'swords of justice' and provide 'voice' to the voiceless. However, trade unions are not always viewed benevolently. Trade unions are seen to introduce rigidities in the working of free labour market. They are held to hurt economic efficiency in several ways, such as obstructing technological changes, interrupting and slowing down production. Unions are accused of creating unemployment by raising wages above the market clearing level.

The nature, structure, objectives and other aspects of institutions in a country are contingent on various factors such as history and the nature of economic and political systems. Hall and Soskice (2001) have developed a theory of 'Varieties of Capitalism' (VoC) in which they distinguish between two ideal but polarised types of capitalism: liberal market economies (LMEs) and coordinated market economies (CMEs), in order to understand the working of institutional structures in capitalistic systems. However, the 'institutional distance' or varieties, *between* the two polar types is so huge as to provoke identification of 'in-between types' such as 'hierarchical market economies' (HMEs), and the Mediterranean type. Even as we discuss these types, it is evident that they relate more to the developed Western economies rather than the developing ones like the 'Asian Variants' (see Verma and Shyam Sundar, 2017: 336).

While the VoC framework addresses broader issues, including capital markets, some researchers extend their analyses to incorporate the role of state or the variations in union behaviour operating in similar systems (Traxler, 1999; Frege and Kelly, 2003) which are necessary to understand the varieties framework much better. In fact, the 'Varieties of Unionism' (VoU) literature has its origin due to a sordid context, namely: the decline of trade unions, but it has provided an analytical framework (in terms of context, processes and strategic choices) which can be used to examine the differential strategic responses to revive unionism in some of the advanced economies. Again we witness academic deficits with near-absence of literature concerning the Asian variety or varieties – though some works do exist that helps us understand the working of trade unions and employers' organisations in Asia (e.g., Benson and Zhu, 2008; Benson et al., 2017). This volume seeks as a whole to comprehend the VoU in Asia, and this chapter relates to India. The basic argument of our chapter, following Verma and Shyam Sundar (2016), is as follows. The reforms initiated since the mid-1980s have transformed the product market from a command economy to a market economy (or LME). We submit that *complex* institutional varieties exist in workers' representation owing to the huge presence of the informal labour economy and rising informalisation of labour in the labour market, as well as the continued relevance and intervention of the state in the industrial relations system (IRS). Hence it is difficult to fit the IRS as a whole approximating to LME.

The structure of this chapter is as follows: In Section 1, we briefly describe the institutional framework of the IRS in India and the institutional features of trade unions during the planned economy period. In Section 2, we note the changes in the product and labour markets sparked by forces of globalisation. Section 3 maps out the challenges faced by trade unions in the post-reform period. In Section 4, we describe the strategies of trade unions and other organisations and bring out the dynamics in them. In Section 5, we propose an agenda for trade unions and workers' organisations. Finally, we end with some concluding remarks.

Trade union movement during the planned economy period, 1947–1991

Due to various reasons, such as the adoption of economic planning, and the unequal distribution of power within the IRS, the central government in the post-Independent period preferred state intervention in the IRS to 'voluntarism' in order to regulate it (Ramaswamy, 1984). The main aspects of the state interventionist system comprised comprehensive labour laws, compulsory adjudication and conciliation of industrial disputes, labour administration and inspection system, judge-made laws and so on. The aforementioned state institutions determined the substantive and the procedural rules of the IRS. Collective bargaining was held to be incompatible with economic planning and hence was accorded a secondary role, and this intended to continue until the IRS matured (Ramaswamy, 1984). Since 'Labour' is on the Concurrent List of the Constitution of India, the legal framework of the IRS comprised labour laws made by both the central and the state governments (see Shyam Sundar 2009a, 2009b, 2018, for a detailed discussion of the institutional framework of IRS in India).

Typically, trade unions at the unit or industry or occupation levels affiliate themselves to political parties (so-called political unionism)[1] or remain independent. Political unionism became the dominant union model for several reasons, namely: continuation of a rich colonial history of interface between political parties fighting for freedom from colonial rule, trade unions in the post-Independence period, the ruling parties' desire to gain better control over industrial relations, ease of access to power centres in the government, members' desire to capitalise on political connections for stronger bargaining power (Ramaswamy, 1984, 1988, see Table 6.1 for details of political unions).

Even though political unionism was the dominant 'type' of unionism, trade unions also developed along other forms. For example, tired of 'cleavage politics' of these unions, workers in many regions in India (especially in Bombay, Pune, Madras, Calcutta) formed enterprise-based unions (also known as enterprise unions or independent unions, see Davala, 1996; Ramaswamy, 1988). Trade unions have also developed along caste, gender, regional, occupation lines, even though some of them may be affiliated to a political party or remain independent (see Table 6.2 for details on the types of unionism). The overall result is a highly fragmented and diverse pattern of organisation of workers.

Unionism during the command economy period suffered from three shortcomings. First, these unions (for convenience we call them as traditional unions) were battling over limited organisational space, that is: the organised sector[2] which constituted less than 10% of total workforce. Hence the organising efforts of the traditional unions were largely spent on 'competitive union politics' of capturing the 'already organised spaces'. This created intense battles both within and between trade unions. Second, a strong interface between unions and political parties produced 'mixed' outcomes for workers as political interests often dominate industrial interests. Third, they largely ignored non-standard workers (e.g., contract, casual, temporary workers and women workers). As a result, union density, based on household surveys by government, comprised less than 12% in 2009–2010[3] (see IHD 2014: Figure 5.2, p. 122).

However, there was a major exception to the above narrative. As the concept of informal sector entered into the lexicon of labour market, the self-employed women in Gujarat formed Self-Employed Women's Association (SEWA) in 1972, following a unique combination of three movements, namely: the labour movement, the cooperative movement and the women's movement (see the contributions in George and Sinha, 2017).

Table 6.1 Details regarding Major Trade Unions India

Major Trade Unions	*Alliance or Proximity with Political Party (Currently)*
All India Trade Union Congress (AITUC) (1920)	Communist Party of India (CPI)
Indian National Trade Union Congress (INTUC) (1947)	Indian National Congress
Hind Mazdoor Sabha (HMS) (1948)	Non-political[(1)]
United Trade Union Congress (UTUC) (1949)	Revolutionary Socialist Party (RSP)
All India United Trade Union Centre (AIUTUC)[(2)] (1951)	Socialist Unity Centre of India (Communist)
Bharatiya Mazdoor Sangh (1955)	Non-political[(3)]
National Front of Indian Trade Unions – Dhanbad (NFITU-DHN)	Non-political[(4)]
National Front Indian Trade Unions – Kolkata (1967)[(5)]	Non-political[(5)]
Centre of Indian Trade Union (CITU) (1970)	Communist Party of India (Marxist) (CPI-M)
Self-Employed Women's Association (SEWA) (1972)	Non-political
Trade Union Coordination Centre (TUCC) (1970)	All India Forward Bloc
Labour Progressive Federation (LPF) (1969)	Dravida Munnetra Kazhagam (DMK) (Regional political party)
All India Central Council of the Trade Unions (AICCTU) (1989)[(6)]	Communist Party of India (Marxist-Leninist) Liberation
National Trade Union Initiative (NTUI) (2006)	Non-political
Indian Federation of Trade Unions (IFTU)[(7)]	Communist Party of India (Marxist-Leninist) New Democracy

Notes:

1 See www.hindmazdoorsabha.com/new-ideology.php, accessed 17 February, 2018, but generally known to be aligned with Socialist Party.
2 Till 2008 known as United Trade Union Congress (L-S).
3 Claims to be non-political (see http://bms.org.in/pages/DistinctFeatures.aspx, accessed 17 February 2018) but known to be close to Bharatiya Janata Party (BJP) and Rashtriya Swayamsevak Sangh (RSS).
4 https://www.facebook.com/pg/nfitu/about/, accessed 17 February 2018.
5 Ahn (2010: 22).
6 http://archive.cpiml.org/liberation/year_2008/february/aicctu.html, accessed 18 February 2018.
7 http://cpimlnd.org/category/iftu/, accessed 18 February 2018.

Though fragmented, the trade union movement was powerful in the organised sector: especially in manufacturing, plantations, mining, public sector enterprises, banking, insurance and education, as reflected by the number of collective agreements reached and the high incidence of strikes in them during much of the planned economy period 1950–1985 (Venkata Ratnam, 2006; Shyam Sundar, 2010a).

Table 6.2 Different Types of Unions in India

Nature of Union Organisation	*Comments*	*Level*
CTUOs	Mostly political, affiliated to central political parties	National
Regional TUOs	Political or non-political affiliated to regional political parties	Regional
Industry/sector organisations/ federations	Mostly in public sector like banks, insurance, railways, aviation, electricity, affiliated to political parties, or independent, e.g., All India Stock Exchange Employees Federation)	National/ regional
Caste-, ethnic- or gender-based organisations	Organisations by scheduled caste and tribes, tribals and women employees	Enterprise/ regional/ industry
Craft organisations	Railways, textiles, coal, aviation	Industry/ national/ regional
White-collar organisations	Clerical/managerial/professional	Enterprise/ sectoral/ national
Enterprise unions	Mostly non-affiliated	Enterprise
Firm-level federations of enterprise unions	Non-affiliated	National
Unity organisations	Political or non-political	National/ regional/ enterprise
Informal-sector organisations	Trade unions (political/non-political), NGOs	National/ regional/ industry

Source: IHD (2014: Table 2, p. 119).

The economic reforms and allied aspects

In response to the criticisms of the planned and regulated economic model such as low growth, poor performance of public sector, unsustainable fiscal deficits and triggered by the balance of payments crisis in 1990, the central government has, since June 1991, introduced a slew of economic reforms which can be classified under liberalisation, disinvestment (selling shares of public sector enterprises while retaining state control and character) and globalisation (the LDG model). These economic reforms have transformed India from a tightly controlled command economy to a market economy (LME type). Employers and the critics of labour market regulation have demanded reforms concerning labour laws and governance so as to enable firms to achieve and sustain competitiveness so necessary in a highly competitive context in the globalised world. At the same time, firms have adopted certain managerial strategies to achieve labour flexibility.

Labour market – towards informality

Public (government) employment declined during much of the post-reform period, although recently there has been slight revival. Organised private sector employment also declined during 1997–2003 period, though it rose later as the result of faster growth rates (see Figure 6.1 in the Appendix). An International Labour Organisation (ILO) Labour Market Update, based on household survey conducted by the government, noted that in 2011–2012: '79 per cent of non-agricultural wage workers had no written contract and only 23.8 per cent were eligible for social security benefits' (ILO 2016, see also Sapkal and Shyam Sundar, 2017: 346). The employment elasticity for total workers declined from 0.30 during 1993–1994–2004–2005 to 0.07 during 2004–2005–2011–2012 (Papola and Kannan, 2017: Table 4.1, p. 31). The share of informal workers in total employment remained almost stable during the 2000s at 92% (ILO, 2016). The share of informal employment (which is the sum of those in both the organised and the unorganised sectors) has risen in manufacturing, construction, services sectors during the period 1999–2000–2011–2012 (see Ghose, 2017: Table 4). The share of contract workers in the total workers in the organised factory sector rose from 13.34 in 1993–1994 to 35.35% in 2014–2015 (see Figure 6.2 in the Appendix). Employment has been growing in the emerging new service sectors like information technology (IT), gig economy, e-retail and e-commerce, but reliable estimates of employment are not available.

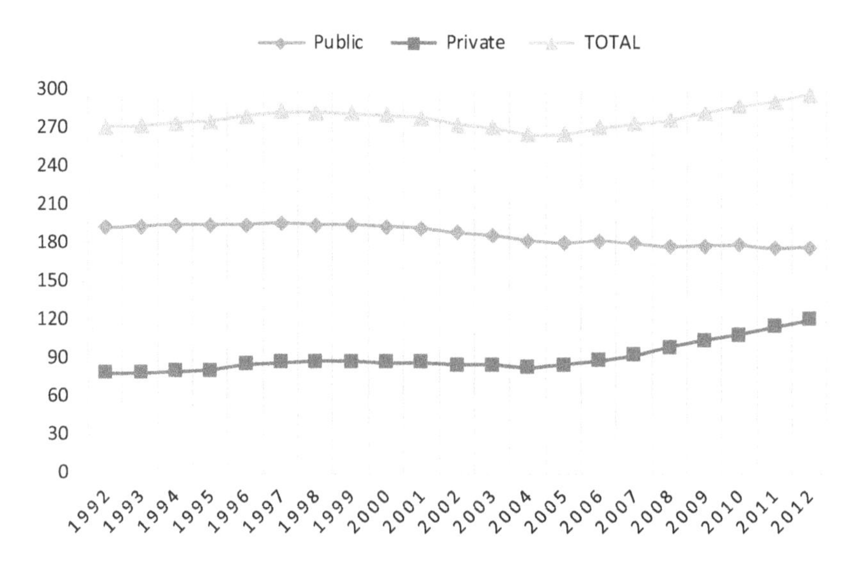

Figure 6.1 Trends in Employment in the Public, Private Sectors and Total Organised Sector, 1992–2012.

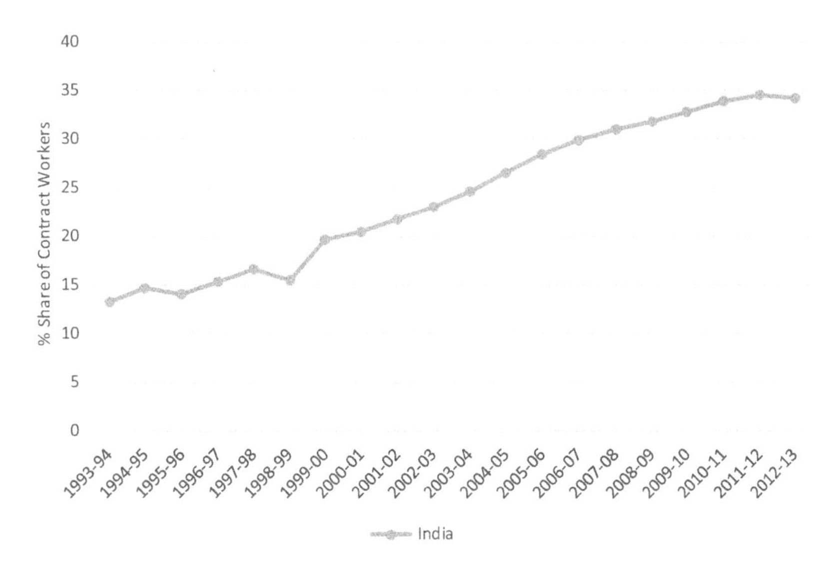

Figure 6.2 Per cent Share of Contract Workers in the Total Employment in the Organised Manufacturing Sector in India, 1993–1994 to 2014–2015.

Labour law and governance reforms by the government

Employers' major demands broadly include two sets of reforms: first: reforming of labour laws to provide for numerical flexibility (free firing of workers, easier closure of firms, free employment of contract labour in core and non-core activities, etc.) and second: liberalising the labour inspection system and the rationalisation and modernisation of records and data reporting systems. These strategies are expected to attract and retain foreign capital and help domestic capital to increase investment levels in the economy.

Both the central government and many state governments in India have, in their respective labour administrative spheres, liberalised labour inspection system considerably to reduce the frequency and scope of labour inspection, remove surprise inspections, introduce self-certification and accredited third-party certification, exempt several sectors (like the Special Economic Zones) from inspection. Several state governments like Rajasthan, Gujarat, Assam, have reformed labour laws to reduce the coverage of important labour laws and hence not only create informality but also increase various forms of insecurity like voice insecurity, employment insecurity.

The current National Democratic Alliance (NDA) government at the centre has sought to rationalise numerous central labour laws into four codes (on Industrial Relations, Wages, Social Security and Occupational Safety), and the proposed codes offer a mixture of measures that serve the interest of labour (like universal social security) but also disadvantage them (reduced employment security, legalising informal work such as fixed-term contracts) (see for a comprehensive discussion of labour law and governance reforms, Shyam Sundar, 2015b, 2018).

Managerial strategies

Employers have been using strategies that generally seek to increase labour flexibility and weaken collective institutions and practices. Scholars have observed that many of these practices have been deliberately allowed by the government as it has not been able to effect such reforms formally by changes in the relevant labour laws. These amount to reforms on the sly or by stealth (see Shyam Sundar, 2009b, for an elaborate discussion of these arguments). Such strategies include employment of contract labour, trainees and apprentices on regular work, refusal to negotiate with legitimate trade unions, banning of outside union leaders, shutting shops in the unionised metro areas and relocate them in union-free regions, reduce regular workers' strength by coercion and incentives, outsourcing, aggressive lockouts, adopting cheap labour strategy and creating wage flexibility (see Shrouti and Nandkumar, 1995; Bardhan, 2002; Shyam Sundar 2016, 2017, for detailed discussion of these strategies). Rising informality, rising non-unionism and poor compensation are some of the major outcomes.

Challenges faced by trade unions in India

The foregoing mapping of the past and the recent developments throw up several challenges to trade unions, and we highlight a few major ones here. One, fundamentally, trade unions have to not only defend the historically determined rights and the earned ones but also fight to create new rights for the informal workers. Two, high politicisation and fragmentation has weakened trade union power. Hence forging some form of unity and aggregation and political dissociation will be a big challenge. Three, they should organise not only informal workers but also employees in the modern and emerging sectors. Four, the institution of workers' representation should not only comprise the conventional trade unions but also newer forms of organisations and NGOs. There must be alliances between trade unions, NGOs and other organisations. Five, it has been observed that the battle for reforms is carried out more in the realm of ideas than on the streets; then, trade unions need to build intellectual support for their cause. Six, trade unions need to enhance their negotiation and lobbying capacities so as to enhance their bargaining power to match with that of big and global capital (Ramaswamy, 1999; Roye, 2007; Shyam Sundar, 2009a, 2011, 2017).

Strategies and responses by trade unions and others organising the unorganised

The central trade union organisations (CTUOs) have adopted three strategies to organise and address the concerns of unorganised workers. First, they have organised particular occupational groups among informal economy workers such as *hamals* (porters), hawkers, beedi workers, domestic workers, *kisan* (agricultural workers) under their banners. Second, they have included issues concerning informal workers in struggles, negotiation and legal action at both the national and local levels (e.g., social security for the unorganised sector workers, right to trade for street vendors, employment security and equal wages for equal work for contract workers). Third, by involving the organisations representing workers in the informal economy, unions have facilitated wider participation of workers in the labour movement (Ahn, 2010; Shyam Sundar, 2011; IHD, 2014). As a result, the CTUOs' total verified (by government agencies) membership rose from 12.27 million in 1989 to 24.60 million in 2002. This increase in union membership was primarily due to the rise in membership within the unorganised sector like agriculture and construction (John, 2007). The total *claimed* membership of the CTUOs for 2011 is between 90 and 100 million. Unions attribute the spectacular increase in their membership to the growth in informal workers joining the movement (Menon, 2013). New non-political national trade union organisations, like the National Trade Union Initiative (NTUI), organise workers in both the organised sector and the unorganised sector (Mohanty, 2009).

Given the vast size and heterogeneity of the informal sector, it will be well-nigh impossible to cover the numerous associations of informal workers that have mostly emerged in the post-reform period. We seek to provide a summary of their features, organisational methods, their struggles and so on. Alternative forms of organisations have risen to suit the peculiarities of organisation and delivery of work in the informal sector. The unorganised workers' organisations (UWOs) use several organisational models like self-help groups (SHGs), networks, micro savings families/groups, union-cum-cooperatives, social security and mutual insurance models, community-based organisations, NGOs, business associations, campaign committees, advocacy groups. The rise in the number of workers' cooperatives has also been significant, but it is not covered in this chapter due to space constraints (see Sapovadia and Patel, 2013, for a discussion on this issue). The location of UWOs ranges from public spaces like streets, construction sites, *nakas* (public hiring spaces), waterways, local clubs, to private homes. These organisations register not only under the Trade Unions Act, 1926, but also other laws like the Cooperative Societies Act, 1912, the Public Trust Act, 1950, Society Registration Act, 1860, the Companies Act, 1956.

The UWOs encompass wider canvas in which they view workers' rights not merely in terms of wage and employment issues but also through a larger lens such as women's rights, labour freedom and holistic human rights. They strive to achieve identity, security and dignity by elevating the status of those working in the unorganised sector like *anganwadis* (health centre volunteers) or street vendors to that of 'workers' in order to achieve legal identity. Legal identity is important to access labour judiciary (Ahn and Ahn, 2012; Kabeer et al., 2013; George and Sinha, 2017; Shyam Sundar, 2011; Krishnaprasad and Peer, 2019).

Modern sectors

IT is a modern sector in which the supply and demand for trade unions have been problematic. On the demand side, employees either fear victimisation from employers if they join unions. They also consider themselves as 'professional', and it is below their dignity (which is socially associated with blue-collar workers) to become a union member. On n the supply side, conventional trade unions do not have enough resources (including ideas for organising a-typical sector like IT) to organise these employees. Furthermore, employers do not welcome unions for fear of losing competitive advantage enjoyed by India (see Noronha and D'Cruz, 2017) as in the absence of unions they can hire employees at competitive wage rates and have uninterrupted work, which will enable them to meet the market needs.

Though the Union for Information Technology Enabled Services Professionals (UNITES), West Bengal Information Technology Services Association (WBITSA, affiliated to Centre for Indian Trade Unions (CITU)) and Centre for BPO Professionals (CBPOP) were formed during the first half of the 2000s, they did not sustain their membership over time for various reasons. For example, there was ferment concerning the functioning of the UNITES due to a lack of transparency and centralisation of power. Furthermore, its affiliation to Indian National Congress and its labour wing Indian National Trade Union Congress (INTUC) was problematic (Noronha and D'Cruz, 2017).

The Forum for IT Employees (FITE) and Karnataka State IT/ITES Employees Union (KITU) are new organisations, and they operate in a few states which have a prominent IT presence like Tamil Nadu, Telangana and Maharashtra. Three factors have contributed to their growth. First, the massive lay-offs effected in the IT industry in the last two years due to technological developments (like artificial intelligence) and cost optimisation; second, intervention by the state labour departments in some states like Telangana, Tamil Nadu; and third, judicial awards setting aside dismissals by the IT companies. The unions are fighting legal battles to secure the status of 'worker' under the ID Act for the employees in these sectors so that they can enjoy protections assured by the Act. So long as the IT employees are able to use the 'exit' (quit) option, the demand for unions in this industry is likely to remain poor. However, as the labour market for IT workers has slackened, the workers have increased search for 'voice' options. Hence, the demand for unions in the IT sector has risen, reflecting the classic exit-voice trade-off.

Political dissociation

The globalisation logic has compelled the ruling governments at the centre and the states to frame liberal industrial, labour and tax policies to attract capital. As a result, political parties, when in power, follow 'capital appeasement' policies to attract capital and attack such policies when in opposition. This has been an 'opportunistic policy'. Hence, significant cracks have appeared in the relationship between the political parties and their labour wings during the post-reform period. This has occurred, for example, between the Communist Party of India (Marxist) and its labour wing CITU in West Bengal, as well as between the Indian National Congress and its labour wing INTUC at the national level and also between the Bharatiya Janata Party (BJP) and its labour wing Bharatiya Mazdoor Sangh (BMS) (Shyam Sundar, 2009a, 2009b; Nanda, 2017; Outlook, 2018). Political dissociation assumes importance for the trade union movement as labour issues take prominence over politics and hence this lends intensity to their struggles. To be sure, labour wings have not completely split off from their political allies or sympathisers, and they continue to strategically use their alliance to further their organisational and labour interests.

Unity and coordination efforts

In the wake of globalisation and reforms, in the post-reform period trade union organisations, which are generally at or around the left of the centre position, have formed an alliance to counter the economic and labour policies of the governments. The non-left larger CTUOs like INTUC and BMS stayed away from this coalition for quite some time. The pressure of adverse reforms and rising political dissociation of CTUOs has eventually brought INTUC to the Joint Platforms of unions and later with the BMS. Currently, the major unions are a part of Joint Platform for Actions. However, trade union organisations insist that unity is issue based and rule out organisational mergers (see Shyam Sundar 2009a, 2017, for a discussion of these developments).

Trade unions and civil society organisations

The interface between the mainstream trade unions and the NGOs in India is marked by tension, due to mutual distrust. But there are positive sources for synergy between the two, given their common concerns of contesting globalisation as trade unions are realising the potential for synergy between the two. During the 1990s, trade unions were instrumental in creating a wide social movement forum called the National Platform for Mass Organisations (NPMO), although it is now not so active. Trade unions have widened their agenda to include not only employment relations but also social and environmental issues. Recently, trade unions as well as diverse organisations of farmers, youth, women, NGOs and rights groups have jointly launched a national platform called 'people's parliament for unity and development' to sensitise people across rural India (Kurian, 2017). Trade unions have participated in struggles concerning industrialisation of rural areas and tribal-allocated areas and for closure of industries causing pollution (see Sangvai, 2007; CITU, 2015).

However, a possible source of division is that labour and other rights such as those concerning the environment often conflict. For example, demands by Green groups to relocate industries from metro centres to rural areas to avoid pollution as well as protests against ship breaking are not endorsed by trade unions as they may reduce employment for union members (Chattopadhyay, 2005; Sucheth, 2014). During 2018, trade unions and workers participated in the people's movement seeking closure of Sterlite Industry on account of damage which it inflicted on the environment. Yet in 2013, workers had demanded re-opening of the same factory in order to create jobs (*The Hindu*, 2013). Hence there is a major need to weave labour rights into the larger human rights discourses (Shyam Sundar, 2009a).

Globalisation of struggles

With the advent of economic reforms, foreign direct investment (FDI) has been allowed in many sectors to reach 100%. This contrasts with a few sensitive sectors like defence and insurance; the proportion of FDI has been limited to between 24% and 49%. However, the trade unions have objected that the multinational corporations (MNCs) pursue 'dual' industrial relations policies, namely: observing labour standards in their home countries but violating them in the host countries. At the basic level, some MNCs deny trade union and collective bargaining rights. The Global Union Federations (GUFs) such as Industrial (operating in mining, energy and manufacturing sectors, worldwide), the International Union of Food, Agricultural, Hotel, Restaurant, Catering, Tobacco and Allied Workers' Associations (IUF) have designed a counter strategy to MNCs' global production strategy. The IUF builds interfaces with local enterprise unions at the MNC's plants and offer forms of support for the local union's industrial campaigns. The GUFs invoke the Organisation for Economic Co-operation and Development (OECD)'s MNE Guidelines, 2011, where possible. The GUFs have successfully intervened in MNCs such as Nestle India, GlaxoSmithKline Horlicks, Coca Cola, Holcim-*La Farge* cement factories, etc. by establishing and defending trade union and collective bargaining rights. They have successfully pressured the MNCs to recognise a trade union of the workers' choice and to enter into collective agreements with it. In several cases, the actions by GUFs have secured employment security for contract and casual workers (Shyam Sundar, 2011, 2016).

Strikes and larger struggles

The aggressive pursuit of economic and labour law and governance reforms by the governments, as well as employers' initiatives to achieve labour flexibility at the firm level, have ironically united even the fragmented trade union movement in a country as large as India. Further, developments in technology and transportation have aided transmission of information in real time and helped in struggles through 'whatsapp', email and so on. Over fifteen *national* strikes and struggles have taken place in India in the post-reform period. Recent strikes are reported to have achieved the participation of around 180 million workers, and this includes a vast majority from the unorganised sector (Sharma, 2016, CITU, 2016).

Protest sites include social dialogue forums, legislative bodies and streets. Actions by unions and associated worker organisations include strikes, demonstrations, marches to law-making bodies, fasts, petitioning, demonstrations at significant places, *jail bharao* (getting arrested), leafletting, *bandhs* (total stoppage of economic activity), industrial violence (violence by both workers and management), sit-in strikes, plant occupations, litigations. The unorganised sector workers like domestic workers, *beedi* workers, *anganwadis* (health centre volunteers) and street vendors have also conducted several nationwide strikes against the government demanding economic benefits, identity and social security. More significantly, along with platform and app-driven workers like Ola, Uber drivers are litigating and striking for worker identity, better terms of contract and so on. As a result, contrary to popular perception, industrial conflict in the post-reform period has been high and not declined (see *The Hindu*, 2011; Shyam Sundar, 2010a; Shyam Sundar 2015a; Sharma, 2016; Shyam Sundar and Sapkal 2017; Sundaram, 2018). It is important to note that the macro struggles (at the systemic level or industry or occupation or industry) by workers' organisations in both the formal and informal sectors target the state – union in the organised sector protest against the reform efforts and asking for universalisation and effective implementation of laws; either jointly or independently workers' organisations demand that the state (in the absence of employer-employee relationship) should provide the welfare measures including work and social security. Hence, the state is not only a contested terrain but also hugely relevant. Further, the state's role is required even to deregulate and, in the case of the latter, to appoint regulatory bodies (such as the Pension Fund Regulator if pension funds need to be invested in equities and other market assets). Hence, the state in the developing countries assumes a continuing strong role.

Major achievements of the trade union movement

During the period of the planned economy, 1950–1991, trade unions adopted a variety of strategies such as industrial action, political lobbying, legal action, collective bargaining, participation in the consultative forums like Indian Labour Conference (ILC) and secured a body of labour rights. The sustained rise in the union density and the significant increase in industrial conflict during the planned economy period are reflective of the labour struggles. It is significant that unions secured several labour rights despite several repressive measures taken by the government such as enacting often the Essential Services Maintenance Ordinance/Act) to deny the right to strike, employing the state's powers (like conciliation machinery, police) to side with capital in industrial conflicts. The state also passed laws to prohibit strikes and demonstrations (see Shyam Sundar 2009a, 2009b; Sen, 2013).

The major labour rights secured by unions during the planned economy period included protection for union activities, a formula for determination of minimum wages (backed by judicial awards), institutionalised cost of living allowances, statutory bonuses not linked to profits (called deferred wages), protection against unfair dismissals even for so-called acts of indiscipline, employment security, the legal power to demand prohibition of employment of contract labour system in perennial jobs, non-discrimination against women employees in terms of employment and pay, medical insurance, provident fund, gratuity, pensionable government sector employment with post-retirement benefits (including medical). They were/are embodied in laws, collective agreements (which set precedence), judgements and so on. The labour market outcomes during the planned economy period comprised a steady growth of employment at 2% per annum during 1960–1990, real wage growth rates during the mid-1970s and the 1980s, gradual rise in bi-partism (implying acceptance of collective bargaining), significant rise in the organised sector employment (especially the public sector employment) and substantive outcomes such as passage of a series of labour protective laws which covered almost all aspects of employment relations and the establishment of labour welfare boards for the unorganised sector workers (see Papola and Sharma, 2004; Sharma, 1982; Sen, 2013; Papola and Kannan, 2014, for a comprehensive history of union struggles and achievements).

During the post-reform period (i.e., 1992 onwards), trade unions have achieved a fair amount of success in not only resisting the dilution of labour rights via labour law and governance reforms but also creating new labour rights, especially for unorganised labour. At the central level, the labour rights such as employment security, contract labour rights, minimum wages, social security, maternity benefits, accident compensation were enshrined in the major labour laws (up to twenty-four of them). These rights remain virtually intact and, in some cases, such as maternity benefits or accident compensation, have been enhanced. Furthermore, the applicability of some of these laws, although not yet universal, has been applied to a greater number of workers by enhancing the thresholds of applicability (see Shyam Sundar, 2018). In the case of the unorganised workers, important legislation has been enacted which provides some form of social security albeit limited (The Unorganised Sector Workers Social Security Act 2008), the statutory right to work (The Mahatma Gandhi National Rural Employment Guarantee Act 2005) and statutory rights for street vendors (Street Vendors (Protection of Livelihood and Regulation of Street Vending) Act, 2014). Due to relentless pressure by the inclusive trade union movement, the current NDA government at the centre has proposed to introduce universal social security as well as gradually extending health insurance to 500 million people, in financially vulnerable households, which is in the Budget for 2018–2019.

An agenda for trade unions

We have mapped the challenges and the strategic choices made by workers' organisations to widen the 'voice' coverage. Globalisation forces have, in fact, forced workers' organisations to innovate, reinvent their strategies and make significant ideological compromises (such as the coming together of trade unions following polarising ideologies and coalitions between workers' organisations and social organisations). But there is still an unfinished agenda for the workers' movement. A brief summary is outlined below.

Wider and long-term alliancing

Trade unions have already taken several measures not only to forge unity within the trade union movement but also with other like-minded organisations. But there are some outstanding issues. Even though political dissociation has taken place, there are still serious differences between trade unions and political parties. During 2017–2018, BMS distanced itself from the larger unity front of CTUOs in protest against the NDA government's policies. Politics has become quite competitive at all levels, and if political affiliations continue to dominate the trade union movement, sustaining unity will be difficult. Some organisational reforms such as mergers need to take place to reduce the number of peak organisations.

The traditional unions need to strengthen their ties with NGOs and other like-minded organisations. A productive interface is needed between trade unions and other civil society organisations. Globalisation is challenging not only the interests of people as workers but also as consumers of goods and natural resources. Trade unions and other labour social-political organisations are opposed to globalisation and also rising inequality within the capitalistic system. Pure industrial relations issues are now entangled with larger economic, environmental and political issues – such as mergers between a global player like Walmart with a domestic player like Flipkart thus creating a duopoly market context in retail industry. In this case, traders' association, trade unions and others have come together to oppose the merger (Choudhury and Chakraborty, 2018). Trade unions have been the vanguard of the working-class movement, but they should lead a coalition of like-minded organisations to increase working peoples' voice, especially in the informal sector.

Capacity building exercises

Trade unions have often relied upon organisational resources and workers' emotions, besides taking recourse to legal action to secure and protect their rights. However, trade unions need to enhance their capacities of negotiation and lobbying through training, to be familiar with, if not command over, ideas and to make their demands based on research in order to shape outcomes at all levels. There are three aspects to this:

a Interface: The interface between trade unions and academics must be established (in cases where it is non-existent) and strengthened (where it is present). Trade unions possess vast amounts of information and experience which could be used to create credible and policy-oriented research purposes by academics, and trade unions can, in turn, benefit from academics. Further, as noted earlier, the battle for reform is being waged in the realm of ideas, and policies and laws are sought to be formed on the basis of lobbying power, research evidence and the so-called economic logic. For example, employers legitimise their demands for reforms of labour laws and inspection system by citing research works and the poor ranking of India in terms of the ease of doing business or competitiveness of Indian economy (see Shyam Sundar 2017, 2018, for a discussion of this aspect). Trade unions need to adopt two strategies to confront employers' arguments. First, they should rely on counter intellectual research and point out faults in the pro-flexibility research evidence. Second, they should create a counter argument to the 'ease of doing business' case by drawing attention to institutional deficits or labour rights deficits. Trade unions in India do not have credible research capacity, and hence they need to create interfaces with academics.

b Labour market and IRS intelligence and research: Human resource management (HRM) experts undertake benchmarking surveys before wage bargaining, and they often cite macroeconomic and market fundamentals as a result of their training and education and focus. Trade unions primarily rely on emotions and their bargaining skills backed by the threat of strikes. But in modern times, these tactics often do not work. Trade unions could use labour market intelligence and research as tools to conduct their collective bargaining and improve the efficiency of social dialogue activities. They could build alternate database on flexi-categories of workers to challenge official data that under-report them. The battle against flexibility needs a strong database and official sources provide limited and often unreliable data. Unions need to build database innovative collective agreements and provide access to unions so as to emulate them in their bargaining exercises.

c Training: Management officials usually have a sound academic background and frequently undergo training to update their knowledge and skills, but trade union leaders often have to depend on poor training resources. There needs to be a level playing field in both social dialogue and negotiations between management and trade unions. Training is indispensable for better and informed negotiation outcomes. Trade unions should be capable of funding themselves or find resources from the external agencies to be trained. In other words, training expenditure should be considered as a form of investment by the trade unions.

Conclusion

Political union was a dominant type of unionism during much of the planned economy though alternative types of organisations were cropping up here and there. Multiple forms of organisations representing workers have cropped up. It is not so much union revival as correcting the historical blunder of narrow union coverage thanks to a huge informal economy. There is a huge "scope" for organisation thanks to low macro union density. However, there are encouraging developments to show that union movement is transforming into a labour movement and perhaps carries a potential for a people's movement. With a sure sense of incomparable history of organising workers, trade unions shall remain in the vanguard of transforming the union movement into a working-class movement and eventually a people's movement. There are two ironies in this story of globalisation and workers' organisations. One, the very forces of globalisation that seek to challenge collectivisation have shaken the unions in several ways and pushed them to form unity fronts, build wider alliances, use internet and mobile devices during the struggles, etc. Another irony is that as much as the state desires strongly to withdraw from the labour market under the influence of neo-liberal pressure groups, workers' organisations in both formal and informal sectors target the state to not only protect and even enhance labour rights in the formal sector but also to provide right to work and social security cover to those in the informal sector.

These pages and the literature cited in this chapter should provide some idea of the complexities inherent in the IRS in general and also with respect to the actors like the workers' organisations. Varieties of workers' organisations ranging from conventional trade unions to union-cum-cooperative to labour NGO to a network model have emerged due to the dynamics of labour market and organisation of production in the globalising India. The role of state is complex and assumes greater significance in the context of workers' struggles to protect existing rights and demand for more labour rights rightly covering the huge informal economy. While the product market has surely been moving from a command economy to a neo-liberal economy (LME), the foregoing discussion of developments in the IRS negates association of the IRS to LME type. It is quite important to recognise that even in the post-reform period in India, the state is a 'contested terrain'. In the same vein, we submit here that given the complex inter-sectionalities in the labour market and varieties of workers' categories (wage to self-employed workers), in a large economy such as India, VoU serve as intra-texts to the varieties of unions across countries.

Notes

1 Trade unions given their mandate and methods are inevitably 'political' in nature in several senses, viz. as organisations they deal with power distribution within and across organisations, have political aspirations and adopt political methods, define and driven by ideology. The ideological foundation has gained greater currency in the post-liberalisation period as unions struggle and contest a certain political dispensation for mass mobilisation.

2 In India, the organised sector comprises non-agricultural establishments which employ ten or more workers and are governed by labour laws and regulations. Most labour laws in India apply to establishments employing at least ten workers though the coverage could vary across laws.

3 For more information, visit www.iuf.org/nestle/2010/01/nestle_india_unions_win_recogn.html, http://www.industriall-union.org/lafargeholcim-contract-workers-achieve-fair-settlement-in-india, accessed 3 March 2018, for some examples.

References

Ahn PS (2010) *The Growth and Decline of Political Unionism in India: The Need for a Paradigm Shift*. Bangkok: ILO DWT for East and South-East Asia & the Pacific.

Ahn PS and Ahn Y (2012) Organising Experiences and Experiments among Indian Trade Unions: Concepts, Processes and Showcases. *The Indian Journal of Labour Economics* 55(4): 573–593.

Bardhan P (2002) The Political Economy of Reforms in India. In: Mohan R (ed.) *Facets of the Indian Economy*. New Delhi: Oxford University Press, pp. 221–223.

Benson J and Zhu Y. (2007) *Trade Unions in Asia*. London and New York: Routledge.

Benson J, Zhu Y and Gospel H. (2017) *Employers' Associations in Asia: Employer Collective Action*. London and New York: Routledge.

Centre of Indian Trade Unions (CITU) (2015) All India General Strike, September 2015, Available at: http://citucentre.org/77-collective-resistance-against-the-government-s-anti-people-policies, accessed 10 August 2018.

Chattopadhyay K (2005) Class Struggle and Environmental Activism. Available at: www.europe-solidaire.org/spip.php?page=article_impr&id_article=1188, accessed 2 March 2018.

Choudhury K and Chakraborty S (2018) Fearing Job Losses, Traders Plan to Fight Walmart-Flipkart Merger. *Business Standard*, 5 May 2018.

CITU (2016), 2nd September 2016 General Strike – Reflection of Workers' Anger, Available at: www.citucentre.org/component/k2/103-2nd-september-2016-general-strike-reflection-of-workers-anger, accessed 10 August 2018.

Davala S (1996) *Enterprise Unionism in India*. New Delhi: Fredrich Ebert Stiftung.

Frege Carola M and Kelly J (2003), Union Revitalization Strategies in Comparative Perspective. *European Journal of Industrial Relations* 9(1): 7–24.

George S and Sinha S (Eds.) (2017) *Redefined Labour Spaces: Organising Workers in Post-Liberalised India*. London: Routledge.

Ghose Ajit K (2017), Informality and Development. *Indian Journal of Labour Economics* 60(1):1–16.

Hall PA and Soskice D (2001) *Varieties of Capitalism: The Institutional Foundations of Comparative Advantage*. Oxford: Oxford University Press.

Institute for Human Development (IHD) (2014) *India: Labour and Employment Report 2014*. New Delhi: Academic Foundation and The Institute for Human Development.

International Labour Organisation (ILO) India Labour Market Update, ILO Country Office for India, July 2016, Available at: www.ilo.org/wcmsp5/groups/public/—asia/—ro-bangkok/—sro-new_delhi/documents/publication/wcms_496510.pdf, accessed on 10 august 2018.

John J (2007) Overall Increase and Sectoral Setbacks: Lessons from Trade Union Verification 2002 Data (Provisional). *Labour File*, Jan–April: 13–25.

Kabeer N, Milward K and Sudharshan R (2013) Organising Women Workers in the Informal Economy. *Gender and Development* 21(2): 249–263.

Krishnaprasad S and Peer K. (2019) An Ongoing Battle for Rights: The Case of Anganwadi Workers with Special Reference to Maharashtra. In: Shyam Sundar KR (ed.), *Globalization, Labour Market Institutions, Processes and Policies in India – Essays in Honour of Lalit K. Deshpande*. Singapore: Palgrave Macmillan, pp. 341–367.

Kurian V (2017), Trade Unions, NGOs, Civic Groups Form 'People's Parliament for Unity and Development *Business Line*, July 25, 2017.

Menon S (2013) Indian Trade Unions Are Getting Bigger, Coinciding with Slowdown *Business Standard*, 7 April, 2013.

Mohanty M (2009) *A Note on New Trends in Unionisation in India*, Working Paper Series WPS No. 641, IIM Calcutta, June 2009.

Nanda PN (2017) RSS Affiliate Bharatiya Mazdoor Sangh Stages Massive Rally against NDA Govt. *Live Mint*, 18 November, 2017.

Noronha E and D'Cruz P (2017) New Identities Require New Strategies: Union Formation in the Indian IT/ITES Sector. In: George S and Sinha S (eds.), *Redefined Labour Spaces: Organising Workers in Post-Liberalised India*. London: Routledge, pp. 181–207.

Outlook (2018) Indian Labour Conference Postponed After RSS-Affiliated BMS Threatens to Boycott Prime Minister Narendra Modi. *Outlook* 20 February, 2018.

Papola TS and Kannan KP (2017) *Towards an India Wage Report*. ILO Asia-Pacific Working Paper Series. Geneva: ILO.

Papola TS and Sharma AN (2004) Labour: Down and Out. *Seminar*. Available at: www.india-seminar.com/2004/537/537%20t.s.%20papola%20and%20alakh%20n.%20sharma.htm, accessed 10 June 2018.

Ramaswamy EA (1984) *Power and Justice: The State in Industrial Relations*. New Delhi: Oxford University Press.

Ramaswamy EA (1988) *Worker Consciousness and Trade Union Response*. New Delhi: Oxford University Press.

Ramaswamy EA (1999) Changing Economic Structure and Future of Trade Unions. *Indian Journal of Labour Economics* 42(4): 33–34.

Roye D (2007) *All India Convention of Contract Workers in Oil & Petroleum Enterprises*. New Delhi: CITU Manifesto.

Sapovadia VK and Patel A. (2013) *What Works for Workers' Cooperatives? An Empirical Research on Success & Failure of Indian Workers' Cooperatives*, Available at: SSRN: https://ssrn.com/abstract=2214563 or http://dx.doi.org/10.2139/ssrn.2214563, accessed August 9, 2018.

Sangvai S. (2007) The New People's Movements in India. *Economic and Political Weekly* 42 (50): 111–117.

Sapkal RS and Shyam Sundar KR (2017) Determinants of Precarious Employment in India: An Empirical Analysis. *Research in the Sociology of Work* 31: 307–33.

Sen S (2013) *Working Class of India: History of Emergence and Movement, 1830–2010*. Hyderabad: Prajasakti Book House.

Sharma GK (1982) *Labour Movement in India (Its Past and Present From 1885 to 1980)*. New Delhi: Sterling Publishers.

Sharma YS (2016) Strike by 18 Crore Workers All Over India to Push Government to Raise Minimum Wages. *The Economic Times*, 2 September 2016.

Shrouti A and Nandkumar (1995) *New Economic Policy Changing Management Strategies - Impact on Workers and Unions*. New Delhi: Friedrich Ebert Stiftung/ Maniben Kara Institute.

Shyam Sundar KR (2009a) *Labour Institutions and Labour Reforms in India: Trade Unions and Industrial Conflict (Vol. I)* Hyderabad: ICFAI Press.

Shyam Sundar KR (2009b) *Labour Institutions and Labour Reforms in Contemporary India: The State and Labour Reforms Debate (Vol. II)* Hyderabad: ICFAI Press.

Shyam Sundar KR (2010) *Industrial Conflict in India: Is the Sleeping Giant Waking Up?* New Delhi: Bookwell.

Shyam Sundar KR (2011) *Non-regular Workers in India: Social Dialogue and Organisational and Bargaining Strategies and Practices*, Social Dialogue. Geneva: ILO.

Shyam Sundar KR (2015a) Industrial Conflict in India in the Post-reform Period: Who Said All is Quiet on the Industrial Front? *Economic and Political Weekly* 50(3):3–53.

Shyam Sundar KR (2015b) *Labour Law and Governance Reforms in India: Some Critical Perspectives*. New Delhi: Synergy Books India.

Shyam Sundar KR (2016) *Aspects and Dynamics of Collective Bargaining and Social Dialogue in the Post-reform Period in India*. New Delhi: Synergy Publications.

Shyam Sundar KR (2017) *Industrial Relations in India: Working Towards a Possible Framework for the Future*. New Delhi: ILO, ACTRAV, Bureau for Workers' Activities.

Shyam Sundar KR (ed.) (2018) *Contemporary Reforms of Labour Market and Industrial Relations System in India: Ease of Doing Business Versus Labour Rights*. New Delhi: Academic Foundation.

Shyam Sundar KR and Sapkal RS (2017) Labour laws, Governance Reforms, and Protests: Are They Legitimate? *Economic and Political Weekly* LII(38): 59–66.

Sucheth PR (2014) Locals Up in Arms against SILK Ship-breaking Unit. *New Indian Express*, 26 May 2014 Available at: http://recyclingships.blogspot.in/2014/05/locals-up-in-arms-against-silk-ship.html accessed 3 March 2018.

Sundaram R (2018) Ola, Uber Drivers Strike Affects Commuters in Chennai, Rides Get Expensive. *The Hindu* 3 January, 2018.

The Hindu (2011) Domestic Workers Strike Work. *The Hindu*, 9 January, 2011.

The Hindu (2013), Sterlite Employees, Contract Workers Seek Reopening of Plant, March 31.

Traxler F. (1999) The State in Industrial Relations: A Cross-national Analysis of Developments and Socioeconomic Effects. *European Journal of Political Research* 36(1): 55–85.

Venkata Ratnam C.S. (2006) *Industrial Relations*. New Delhi: Oxford University Press.

Verma A and Shyam Sundar KR (2016) India. In: Bamber G, Lansbury R, Wailes N and Wright C (eds.), *International & Comparative Employment Relations: National Regulations, Global Changes* Australia: Allen & Unwin, pp. 303–340.

7 Bucking the trend

Union renewal in democratic Indonesia

Michele Ford

Introduction

In their seminal discussion of varieties of capitalism, Hall and Soskice (2001) identified two ideal types of capitalism, each of which is characterised by different 'institutional complementarities' that push firms in different directions, in turn reinforcing the institutional structures of the economies in which they operate. Much has been written about the limitations of this approach as revealed by its application to different economies in Asia (see, for example, Amable, 2003; Nottage, 2002; Ritchie, 2009; Tipton, 2009). Critics are right to point to the lack of fit between Hall and Soskice's two ideal types – liberal market economies (LMEs) and coordinated market economies (CMEs) – and Asian economies. However, a third ideal type proposed by Schneider and Soskice (2009) to describe the hierarchical market economies (HMEs) of Latin America is more salient to Asia's developing economies (Ford, 2014a), including Indonesia.[1] Like the HMEs, Indonesia has a large informal economy and its formal economy is dominated by domestic conglomerates, through which it is integrated into global supply chains in labour-intensive industries, as well as a weak employer association and low union density (Ford and Sirait, 2016).

But while the varieties of capitalism framework is useful for explaining broad differences between union movements, it cannot explain variations between union responses in countries that fall within the same ideal type or, indeed, variations over time (Kelly and Frege, 2004). In order to address this limitation, Kelly and Frege (2004) compare union renewal strategies in LME, CME and Mediterranean economies, bringing into focus other determinants of union behaviour, most notably union strategy and their interactions with other actors including the state. This approach provides an important correction to the firm-centred approach of varieties of capitalism. But varieties of unionism, too, assumes that 'institutional change is gradual and incremental rather than fundamental and abrupt' (Ford and Gillan, 2016: 171). Yet, as the Indonesian experience demonstrates, serious ruptures – in this case, regime change – can fundamentally transform the opportunity structures available to the labour movement and, consequently, the path taken by unions.

This chapter documents a process of union renewal that has transformed Indonesia's labour movement from one of the weakest in Southeast Asia to its strongest. Since the advent of democracy in 1998, Indonesian unions have employed all of the six strategies for union revitalisation identified by Frege and Kelly (2003) in their discussion of varieties of unionism. In contrast to the European experience, however, coalition-building and international solidarity have been just as important as the 'more traditional strategies' of restructuring, partnership with employers, organising and political action (Kelly and Frege, 2004: 187). As the discussion also reveals, the Indonesian government responded harshly to unions' growing influence, undermining many of their most important gains.[2]

Challenges facing Indonesia's labour movement

During Suharto's New Order (1967–98), Indonesia's developmentalist state formed a strong alliance with local and foreign capital in its efforts to achieve rapid economic growth, guaranteeing political and industrial stability in return for unquestioning loyalty and financial support. Its authoritarian corporatist political system, coupled with a low-wage, high-control industrial climate, was well-suited to the needs of foreign firms seeking to expand their production base in labour-intensive industry (Hadiz, 1997). A key feature of this system was its use of unions to manage rather than represent workers. This model was directly challenged when the growth of export-oriented production from the mid-1980s led to the emergence of an unofficial labour movement, driven by middle-class labour non-governmental organisations (NGOs) and student groups, which engaged in advocacy and community-based organising (Ford, 2009). It was not, though, until the regime fell that independent unions were legally permitted.

Following the resignation of President Suharto in May 1998, the country underwent a dramatic political transformation as it embraced liberal democracy. Coupled with decentralisation and democratisation, the restructuring of the industrial relations system allowed workers, through their unions, to engage in a meaningful way in policy national debates, for example, on social security (Cole and Ford, 2014). In addition, unionists leveraged their position on local wage councils and the local electoral cycle to achieve significant increases in minimum wage levels in union-dense districts (Caraway et al., 2019). In some cases, unions have also developed a stronger workplace presence, which they have used to demand access to minimum wages, engage in collective bargaining and push back against measures that undermine job security, such as the increased use of short-term contract work and labour outsourcing. In short, unions have developed a series of tactics that allowed them to take on both workplace-level and broader concerns. And, in doing so, they have established themselves as important actors in Indonesian society.

This rapid transformation notwithstanding, the Indonesian labour movement continues to face a series of internal and external challenges (Table 7.1).

The internal challenges experienced by Indonesia's unions are experienced by unions in other developing country contexts. External challenges, meanwhile, are a consequence of the structure of the country's economy and the nature of institutional relationships within it. In particular, they reflect Indonesia's dependence on labour-intensive manufacturing for export as a source of foreign revenue and employment. From the perspective of workers, the impact of Indonesia's integration into global supply chains had many positive effects. In the 1980s and 1990s, it drove growth in formal-sector employment and the development of industrial communities, which gave rise to a nascent independent labour movement in the 1990s. It also focused the international spotlight on poor labour practices (see Ford, 1999). Although these pressures alone were not sufficient to effect real change in the country's authoritarian corporatist structures of industrial relations, they fostered a range of independent forms of organising outside the structures of the state-sanctioned union that helped build the momentum for regime change (Ford, 2009).

Despite its increasing momentum, then, the union movement continues to face many obstacles. For example, the industrial workforce may have grown, but the structure of the labour market still acts as a barrier to greater union

Table 7.1 Internal and External Challenges facing Indonesia's Unions

Internal Challenges	*External Challenges*
• Fragmentation of the labour movement • Weakness of the confederations • Unevenness in union capacity in the workplace but also regionally and nationally • Poor processes for leadership renewal in many unions • Low levels of member engagement in many unions • Weak funding base through dues, and in some cases an over-reliance on financial support from the international labour movement	• Low-wage, export economy • Size of the informal sector • Increasing levels of precarious employment within the formal sector • Legacies of authoritarian period approaches to industrial relations • Employer anti-unionism • Lack of institutionalisation of union involvement at the workplace level • Weakness of employer organisations • Low capacity of labour officials, in part because of the decentralisation of the industrial relations system • Lack of enforcement of pro-worker elements of the regulatory framework • Introduction of new anti-worker legislation • Threats to freedom of association in industrial parks and special economic zones • Resurgence in military involvement in labour disputes and increasing criminalisation of striking workers

influence. There was a marked shift from agricultural employment to manufacturing and service sector employment over latter part of the twentieth century. The informal sector nevertheless remains large. Employment patterns also reflect the continued prevalence of micro and small enterprises in an economy where large and medium enterprises comprise just 0.07% of private sector enterprises and employ only 37.5% of the private sector workforce (BPS, 2016a, 2016b, 2016c, 2016d). An additional issue is the level of precarious employment, even within the formal sector. Under the 2003 Manpower Law, employers can employ workers on fixed-term contracts for a period of two years, with the option of a single extension. Under the same law, 'outsourcing', which involves employing workers through an agency, is allowed in 'non-core' business activities. A subsequent regulation limited the scope of outsourcing to five areas (cleaning, catering services for employees, security, support services in mining and oil sectors and transportation services for employees). However, unions argue that the regulations limiting contract work and outsourcing are poorly enforced (interviews with union leaders, various years).

Unions also struggle with the legacies of an industrial relations system that privileged management's role in the workplace. Regardless of whether they are located in the formal or informal sector, Indonesia's small and medium enterprises continue to run almost exclusively on the 'family' model of employment relations, with little or no regard to the requirements imposed upon them by the formal industrial relations system. Even where there are unions, it is most likely that management essentially sees itself as a unitarist actor. Business owners and managers maintain either that unions are not necessary or that their purpose is to safeguard the prosperity of the company and, through that, ensure that workers continue to have a job (employer focus group discussions (FGDs), July 2017). They may tolerate a union's presence but frequently take steps to undermine them if they begin to disrupt workplace harmony. For their part, most enterprise unions have very little clout, as evidenced by very low levels of collective bargaining or even use of the bipartite committee mechanisms legally required in workplaces with more than fifty employees. As a consequence, many unionised workplaces have at best a collective bargaining agreement that simply restates the provisions of the national law, but more commonly no collective bargaining agreement at all.

The situation is exacerbated by a lack of capacity – but also political will – on the part of government in relation to the enforcement of worker rights enshrined in the country's legal system. Local manpower officials cannot be relied upon to force companies to comply with their legal obligations on issues such as payment of the minimum wage, the use of outsourced labour or even freedom of association. Another legacy of the Suharto period is the fact that employer associations and government officials are poorly equipped to participate in the industrial relations processes mandated by law. Many nominally formal-sector firms operate with little or no reference to industrial relations system, while anti-union behaviour on the part of employers, including the illegal outsourcing of core production work and active union-busting measures, goes largely unpunished even in unionised firms (Ford, 2013). As a consequence of these low levels of institutionalisation and poor regulatory enforcement, much of what could be considered formal-sector employment lies beyond the reach of the formal industrial relations system (Ford and Sirait, 2016).

Faced with these obstacles, unions struggle to maintain membership density even in the country's relatively small formal sector. Union membership was officially verified in 2005 at approximately 3.5 million (Ministry of Manpower, 2013). A second verification exercise was attempted in 2015, when membership was measured at just 1,678,364 – a finding questioned by the Ministry of Manpower itself, which subsequently released revised union membership figures for that year of 2,171,961 (data provided to the author by the Ministry of Manpower).[3] Based on this figure, just over 2% of Indonesia's workforce are union members. Unionisation rates are low even in secondary industry. While union members account for approximately 15% of industrial workers, many factories and other kinds of formal-sector workplaces have no union presence at all.

Strategic responses and their outcomes

In responding to these dramatic changes in context, the Indonesian labour movement has employed all six strategies for union revitalisation identified by Frege and Kelly (2003). As Lee and Lansbury (2014) point out, however, the utility and implications of each of these strategies are quite different in a developing country context like Indonesia's than in the advanced Western economies upon which Frege and Kelly based their analysis (Table 7.2).

Table 7.2 Union Renewal Strategies and their Outcomes in Indonesia

Strategy	*Applicability*	*Benefits*	*Risks*
Reform of union structures	Overarching characteristic of Indonesia's most successful unions within a context of national institutional reform	Stronger financial base, leadership renewal, delivery of more benefits to members, increased member engagement	Splits in the union and poorly planned and/or executed reforms exacerbate already-weak position
International solidarity	Has underpinned the growth of some of Indonesia's strongest unions	Has helped generate financial and non-financial resources for the movement and has increased collaboration between unions, especially among affiliates of IndustriALL	Has acted as a barrier to dues collection and a lack of accountability to members in some cases; also a risk of accusations from governments and employers of external control

(*Continued*)

Strategy	*Applicability*	*Benefits*	*Risks*
Labour–management partnerships	Primary strategy of most unions	Increase firm-level institutionalisation; avoidance of poorly managed government processes	Co-optation by management
Organising	Feature of Indonesia's most successful unions, has generated significant mobilisational power	Stronger financial base, stronger bargaining power, increased member engagement, large-scale increases in minimum wages	Expensive and difficult work, may increase the risk of union-busting through targeting of union officials or members at the workplace level or adverse regulatory measures at the national level
Political action	Important and highly successful strategy in policy terms through policy advocacy at the national level and engagement with candidates in local executive elections but less successful where unions have fielded candidates for the legislature	Introduction of more pro-worker policy at the national or local level, increased likelihood of programmatic politics, formation of a worker voter bloc	Increased negative attention from government, divisions within and between unions over political strategy, reputational risk, diversion of resources from unions' industrial functions
Coalition-building	Has underpinned successful policy campaigns (national level) and increases in the minimum wage (national and local levels)	Has provided greater voice on the national and regional stage and underpins capacity to achieve substantive policy changes	Increased negative attention from government, risk of intra-coalition competition, vulnerable to differences in members' strategic approaches and capacity

As discussed below, each of these strategies has played an important role in union renewal. At the same time, each brings with it not only potential benefits but also potential risks.

Reform of union structures

Since the advent of democracy, the labour movement has transformed itself from one where workers were formally represented by a national-level peak body but had little opportunity to act independently to one that is complex and ideologically diverse, and where unions are free to engage in workplace organising and to advocate for pro-worker policy at the national level. Within months of Suharto's resignation, reformists within the single, state-sanctioned union federation permitted in the Suharto period had responded by establishing a series of break-away sectoral unions, many of which went on to become affiliated to a new national centre called the Confederation of Indonesian Trade Unions (Konfederasi Serikat Pekerja Indonesia, KSPI). A second confederation, known as the Confederation of Indonesian Prosperous Labour Unions (Konfederasi Serikat Buruh Sejahtera Indonesia, KSBSI), grew out of the most influential of three alternative unions that had emerged in the 1990s but had not been permitted to register. However, the legacy union, which reconfigured itself as a confederation called the Confederation of All-Indonesian Workers Unions (Konfederasi Serikat Pekerja Seluruh Indonesia, KSPSI), remained the largest confederation. Several of the small independent worker associations that had emerged with the support of labour NGOs or leftist student groups in that same period also reconfigured themselves as regionally based unions. In addition, unions were formed in key state-owned enterprises, whose employees had not been permitted to unionise under the New Order regime.

Internally, some of the large unions went to great lengths to engage in leadership renewal, shore up their financial base and develop a stronger focus on members. The strongest example of all three of these elements of restructuring is the powerful Federation of Indonesian Metalworkers Unions (Federasi Serikat Pekerja Metal Indonesia, FSPMI), which not only went through a process of leadership regeneration but also increased dues and restructured the relationship between enterprise unions, the provincial branches and the central structure in order to give the upper levels of the union the resources to engage strategically with employers and government (Ford, 2014b). Other key unions within KSPI have followed suit, over time opening their top leadership ranks to new talent and attempting to loosen enterprise unions' stranglehold on dues. In other cases, there are instances of grassroots dynamism within larger union structures. In general, however, national-level unions limp along on a legacy membership, having made few changes in terms of personnel or strategy, or live with the consequence of failed attempts to implement reforms, in many cases leading to damaging splits, and thus the further fragmentation of an already-fragmented movement.

International solidarity

International solidarity has been a key driver in the process of union renewal since 1998. The American Federation of Labor and Congress of Industrial Organisations (AFL-CIO), some European unions and a number of national governments provided support for the labour NGOs and unofficial unions that worked to harness and systemise spontaneous labour protests within the alternative labour movement during the New Order period. During this period, the international union movement engaged almost exclusively with the state-sanctioned union. Upon the advent of democracy, however, the international labour movement began engaging intensively in Indonesia.

Determined to demonstrate that unionism had a future in the developing world, the International Trade Union Congress (ITUC) supported the establishment of KSPI, while the Global Union Federations (GUFs) supported the establishment of the new sectoral unions. Since that time, GUFs including Education International, IndustriALL, the International Union of Food, Agricultural, Hotel, Restaurant, Catering, Tobacco and Allied Workers' Association (IUF), Public Services International and Union Network International (UNI) Global Union have worked closely with unions in their sectors to strengthen their internal processes and provide leverage for their campaigns internationally. Solidarity Support Organisations from Europe, North America and Australasia – but in particular the Fredrich-Ebert-Stiftung and the Solidarity Centre, both of which have country offices in Indonesia – have also played an important role, supporting particular unions, facilitating opportunities for collaboration across union lines and developing an evidence base to support the broader work of the international labour movement.

Links to international NGOs like Oxfam or the Clean Clothes Campaign have also continued to be important for some of the smaller national unions and union federations in the textile, clothing and footwear sector, many of which grew out of NGO-sponsored worker groups in the late New Order period (Ford, 2009). In addition to providing direct support to some of these unions, these international NGOs sponsored attempts to leverage brands' corporate responsibility programmes to promote unionism. From 2009, for example, the Fair Play Alliance, represented by the Clean Clothes Campaign and Oxfam Australia, along with the International Textile, Garment and Leather Workers' Federation, supported direct discussions between brands, supplier factories and unions. These discussions resulted in the signing of a guidelines for brands and their suppliers to adhere to regarding the implementation of freedom of association, known as the FOA Protocol, in 2011 (Gardener, 2012).

The level of international support channelled to Indonesian unions in the first two decades of democracy brought some risks to the labour movement. Large amounts of external money – sometimes provided with little demand for any form of accountability – meant that some unions had few incentives to engage with their membership, let alone to collect dues (Ford, 2006). There is also the risk of accusations of foreign control and jealousy between unions that receive international support and those that do not. On balance, however, the benefits have far outweighed these challenges. Without the financial resources provided by the international labour movement and international NGOs, Indonesia's nascent independent unions would have had little chance of developing in the early post-Suharto period. In the absence of advice and examples on questions of how unions should operate, moreover, it would have been much more difficult for Indonesian unionists to imagine an alternative model of unionism to the one in place for over thirty years.

Labour–management partnerships

Partnership with management is the primary strategy adopted by the majority of Indonesian unions. In addition to enshrining the right to organise, the new regulatory environment supported independent unions by identifying and outlawing various kinds of anti-union activity such as campaigning against the formation of a union, termination or temporary suspension of employment of union officials, demotion or transfer and withholding or reducing payment (Ford and Sirait, 2016). In a context where firm-level institutionalisation is low and government processes unreliable, however, only the most organised and militant plant-level unions can survive in the face of serious employer opposition.

Even where management is open to working with plant-level unions, both sides face serious challenges in doing so effectively. Although workplace collective bargaining was permitted under the New Order, management and plant-level unionists had little experience of social dialogue or collective bargaining before the advent of democracy. For their part, human resource managers are often poorly trained and unaccustomed to negotiating – a fact acknowledged by representatives of the Indonesian Employers Association (Asosiasi Pengusaha Indonesia, Apindo) and officials from the Ministry of Manpower (interviews, July 2017). Plant-level unionists, meanwhile, may have a poor understanding of their workplace rights and/or little experience of collective bargaining.[4]

National union officials seeking to promote labour–management partnerships at the firm level are aware of the risks to this strategy of having poorly skilled shop stewards. As one high-ranking official noted, 'We need better plant-level officials who understand the issues and communicate well, so that companies understand we're a serious partner' (interview, July 2017). In an attempt to address this problem, a number of national unions have implemented programmes – most often with international support – that focus on capacity building for plant-level officials. Plant-level unionists who have participated in these programmes report that they have been useful. Being part of a national federation also means that they have opportunities to meet with other plant-level union officials and compare conditions within their respective factories, as well as being able to ask the advice of branch officials (plant-level union FGDs, July 2017). Yet even the best-resourced national-level unions struggle to meet demand for these kinds of opportunities.

Where unions' partnership strategies succeed, they result in the establishment of effective processes for resolving issues within the workplace. Such processes have the added benefit of avoiding the involvement of local government officials, who seldom have the skills or resources to resolve industrial disputes and who too often expect some kind of pay-off for their services (employer FGDs and plant-level union FGDs, July 2017). In cases where unions have low capacity, however, they run the risk of co-optation by management. This risk is particularly strong with unaffiliated enterprise unions but also affects workplace units of national unions.

Organising

While most of Indonesia's unions remain weak at the plant level, some have adopted an explicit focus on organising. Organising is expensive and difficult work, which can increase the risk of union-busting within plants or adverse changes in policy at the national level. However, in a context where access to a check-off system is declining even in large workplaces, it has become increasingly important not only to unions' ability to secure benefits for their members but also to their financial viability. In best-case examples, concerted plant-level organising campaigns have resulted in increased member engagement and stronger bargaining power with management. In most, though, there has been little change at the workplace level.

Organising also underpins, and benefits from, unions' capacity to mobilise beyond a particular plant. One of the best examples of such a mobilising strategy are the factory raids (*grebek pabrik*) that took place in the industry-dense district of Bekasi in 2012 (Mufakhir, 2014). In response to the widespread use of outsourcing and contract employment, striking workers, often joined by workers from surrounding factories, occupied their workplaces until an agreement was reached with management to provide permanent employment. Between May and October, over one hundred factories were the target of such raids. As Mufakhir (2014) has argued, the raids shored up unions, whose position in unionised workplaces was threatened by outsourcing. They were also an important organising tool, as they provided an opportunity for workers in non-unionised factories to make contact with a union. The unions would then assist them in negotiations with management, and use the factory raid tactic to force management back to the table when negotiations broke down. Ultimately, however, employers developed counter-measures including prolonging negotiations, use of police, military and thugs in responding to rallies and accusing union activists of criminal activities to clamp down on the unions' activity.

The government also took steps to reduce union activity of this kind. Two key initiatives that have affected unions in industrial zones are a Ministerial Decision No. 620/M-IND/Kep/12/2012 on National Vital Objects in Industry and Government Regulation No.96/2015 on Facilities and Concessions in Special Economic Zones. Ministerial Decision No. 620/M-IND/Kep/12/2012 applied Presidential Decision No. 63/2004 on Securing

National Vital Objects – a regulation initially put in place to manage threats of terrorism – to industrial parks. Ten industrial parks and thirty-eight corporations/factories were initially identified as industrial vital objects worthy of direct protection by the state. By February 2018, that number had grown to nineteen industrial parks and seventy-two manufacturing companies (Siregar, 2018). As unions feared, the 'vital object' designation has been used to limit their capacity to mount demonstrations within industrial parks. Although strikes are still permitted, police are allowed to take action to protect national vital objects against 'threats and/or disturbances' and can invite the military to assist them in their dispersal.[5] Government Regulation No.96/2015, meanwhile, allows for the establishment of specialised tripartite cooperative committees within industrial parks formed with the stated aim of creating a harmonious and conducive manpower climate. These special committees include not only representatives of unions, employers and government but also of the management of the industrial park.

An area where unions had more sustained mobilisational success was in the annual process of minimum wage-setting, which is the responsibility of local tripartite wage councils. There, having established a baseline that took into account the cost of a basket of goods designated as reflecting a decent standard of living, unions could negotiate for a higher base wage. In a context where workplace-level collective bargaining is weak, the local minimum wage is important, as it effectively represents a wage ceiling, rather than a safety net in the majority of workplaces (Caraway et al., 2019). Their ability to back up their demands with large-scale protests, particularly at sensitive times in the electoral cycle, also gave them unprecedented political clout at the local level (Caraway and Ford, 2014, 2020). This practice proved to be very effective in union-dense areas, achieving increases worth many times the value of inflation.

Unions' use of this tactic infuriated employers, who pressured the national government to intervene. In 2013, the Yudhoyono government attempted to reign in wage increases by issuing a presidential instruction calling on local government officials to consider productivity and national economic growth when setting minimum wages. This instruction had little effect. In 2015, the Widodo government made a further attempt to control wages, passing Government Regulation No.78/2015 on Wage Determination, which effectively replaced the bargaining process within the local wage councils with a formula that required minimum wages to be set based on inflation and economic growth. This measure proved to be very effective in undercutting unions' capacity to leverage their mobilisational power to drive up the minimum wage, seriously undermining union strength.

Political action

Unions' mobilisational power has also underwritten political action in both the policy and electoral domains. A key strategy for the labour movement as a whole has been a series of campaigns aimed at pressuring policymakers to consider the needs of workers in a wide range of policy domains, some of which have focused on labourist concerns such job security, and others on broader social issues, such as fuel subsidies and social security. Unions have, for example, been quite successful in their campaigns against changes to the legal framework that governs labour relations. Successive protests against the 1997 Manpower Law, passed just before the fall of Suharto, saw its implementation delayed a number of time, and the law ultimately dropped. The law that replaced it – the 2003 Manpower Law – ensured the right to strike and payment of wages during strikes over 'normative' issues, placed restrictions on outsourcing and contract labour, prohibited the replacement of workers during legal strikes, provided higher pay for workers suspended during the labour-dispute resolution process and higher severance pay (Caraway, 2004). Successive attempts by government to water down these pro-worker provisions have been met by large-scale worker demonstrations, which were surprisingly effective in blocking anti-worker change (Caraway and Ford, 2020).

Unlike street-based mobilisation against anti-worker policies or employer behaviour, which was common in the late New Order period, unions' engagement in the electoral domain represents a fundamental departure from the economic model unionism that dominated that period (Ford, 2005; Caraway and Ford, 2020). Several unions have supported the campaigns of execute candidates in exchange for promises that, if elected, they will support workers. Sometimes this support took the form of resources, for example, the provision of a building to serve as a union secretariat (Ford, 2014b; Caraway and Ford, 2020). More commonly, support was sought from government within the context of minimum wage negotiations. In the industrial district of Bekasi, for example, an incumbent who had not been a particularly close ally of labour-supported unions in wage negotiations in the late 2011 in the hope that the unions would support him in the district head election a few months later (Caraway and Ford, 2014). A more ambitious strategy was adopted in the 2014 presidential election, when KSPI secured a political contract with Prabowo Subianto, one of just two presidential contenders, which committed him to act on ten demands relating to wages, pensions, healthcare, outsourcing, honorary teachers, better protection for domestic workers, universal social security, public transport, affordable housing and education. The other two main union confederations supported his opponent, the successful candidate, Joko Widodo, who also promised to implement pro-worker policy (Ford and Caraway, 2014). The presidential candidates' engagement with the unions was unprecedented and attested to the level of influence they had gained on the political stage (Caraway and Ford, 2020).

A smaller number of unions also ran institutional candidates in local, provincial and national legislative races in 2009 and 2014. This was not the first time that a union had adopted an institutional approach to the legislative elections and certainly not the first time that unionists had run for office.

KSPSI and KSBSI had both formed a series of labour parties in the early years of the democratic period, none of which were particularly successful (Ford, 2000, 2005). Union leaders had run for these parties on an institutional ticket but also as individuals for a range of other parties. However, in 2009, two key sectoral unions associated with KSPI developed a new strategy centred around institutional collaboration with a number of parties, most notably a cadre-based Islamist party that had long courted labour called the Prosperous Justice Party (Partai Keadilan Sejahtera, PKS) (Ford, 2014b). As part of this strategy, parties would run candidates identified by the union in industrial districts in the hope of securing the worker vote. The strategy was divisive, and ultimately only marginally successful, but it did represent an important step in the development of workers' identity as voters.

The union movement's engagement in the policy sphere has been quite successful, but its forays into electoral politics have met with more mixed results. Union candidates invested a great deal of time, money and effort into campaigns for legislative office, but few were elected. Once in office, moreover, they realised that they had little chance of influencing the behaviour of the legislature. In the context of executive races, unions gained considerable traction with candidates for at the local and even provincial levels in some cases. In others, union leaders staked their reputations on a particular candidate, only to be ignored when that candidate gained office or shunned by the victor if their candidate lost. At the national level, KSPI's president, Said Iqbal, risked his reputation, but also the cohesiveness of the confederation and his own union, by choosing to back Prabowo, a businessman and former general with a record of human rights abuse (Ford and Caraway, 2014; Caraway and Ford, 2020). When Prabowo lost, KSPI also forfeited any chance of patronage from the successful candidate. Finally, political engagement necessarily diverts union attention from its industrial functions and is resource-intensive, which has serious implications in a context where their industrial presence is fragile.

Coalition-building

An important element of regional organising initiatives around the minimum wage, but also unions' policy campaigns, has been coalition-building. Indonesia's labour movement is highly fragmented, but the opportunity structures available to it at the local level through the minimum wage-setting process encouraged unions to form local alliances across confederation lines. It is these local alliances that underpinned unions' capacity to achieve massive wage increases from 2012 to 2014 (Caraway et al., 2019, Caraway and Ford, 2020). They have also translated into the electoral domain, where union alliances have at times worked together to secure a deal with a candidate in an executive race or even in support of a labour candidate.

Unions have found it more difficult to collaborate at the national level, but coalition-building has nevertheless been important, particularly in the policy arena. The most successful example of coalition-building for policy change has been the social security campaign, in which several key unions were actively involved. This campaign, which succeeded in forcing the government to implement a system of universal social security, was particularly notable because it combined street-based protest with other tactics, including collaboration with NGO activists and sympathetic legislators to secure support from a reluctant parliament (Cole and Ford, 2014).

The success of the social security campaign spurred an attempt by the three major confederations to form a more permanent coalition at the national level, called the Indonesian Labour Council (Majelis Pekerja Buruh Indonesia, MPBI). Formed in 2012, MPBI proved to be a formidable force, mounting several successful policy campaigns. The coalition was short-lived, however, as a consequence of intra-coalition rivalry, differences in capacity and disagreements about strategy and tactics. Unions' alliances with the few labour NGOs that survived after the first decade or so after the fall of Suharto have also proven to be short-lived and incidental, despite those NGOs' fundamental role in laying the foundations of the independent labour movement in the late New Order period.

Conclusion

A process of union renewal – driven by a dramatic change in opportunity structures and underwritten by international solidarity – has transformed Indonesia's labour movement from one of the weakest in Southeast Asia to undoubtedly the strongest in the region. While unions continue to struggle with a range of internal and external challenges, they have nevertheless succeeded in establishing themselves as a serious player in both the industrial and policy domains. In addition to drawing on the resources of their international allies, these successes have been achieved through internal reform in key unions and the adoption of approaches to organising, political action and coalition-building previously confined to the alternative labour movement.

Yet at the same time that improved access to freedom of association and other changes in the framework of industrial relations have generated new opportunities for unions to be more active in the workplace, weaknesses in the industrial relations system, along with ongoing hostility towards unions and low internal capacity, mean that most unions have struggled to establish a strong workplace membership base or engage in productive partnerships with management that produce positive outcomes for workers. Instead, unions have continued to rely heavily on extra-workplace activity, and in particular large-scale mobilisations around minimum wage-setting and other policy issues of concern to their membership, to pursue a labourist agenda. It is this policy advocacy, rather than sustained workplace-level engagement, that has underwritten organising efforts and promoted coalition-building among unions and with other forces within civil society.

As a consequence of these internal and external challenges, the gains secured in the first decade and a half of the democratic era ultimately proved to be quite fragile in the face of backlash from employers and the state. As the labour movement became more powerful, unions faced increasingly punitive treatment not only by employers but also by government, which has introduced new anti-union policies and legitimised the heightened involvement of the military in the handling of industrial actions. Restrictions on the right to stage protests in industrial parks and on union influence in minimum wage-setting have been particularly detrimental to the mobilisational power of the labour movement, which had underpinned its electoral experiments and driven many of its successes in the policy domain. While it remains to be seen whether unions can initiate another cycle of renewal, it is clear that the institutional volatility of post-authoritarian contexts such as Indonesia's requires further theorisation if we are to understand its impact on unions' position and practice.

Notes

1 The introduction of the HME ideal type was one of a number of innovations made by the framework's architects in their attempts to address criticisms of the limitations of the model, and, in particular, its inability to explain economic and political change. See also Iversen and Soskice (2009) and Hall and Thelen (2009). While Hall and Soskice (2001) had focused firmly on Western Europe and the advanced democracies of the Anglophone settler world, they asserted that the model has relevance in the South. They also made passing reference to varieties of capitalism to a 'Mediterranean economy' but did not develop this model.

2 The research on which this chapter is based was funded by an Australian Research Council Future Fellowship and an Australian Research Council Discovery Project grant (FT120100778, DP130101650). Focus group discussions were funded by the International Labour Organisation as part of a consultancy project on garment workers in Asia.

3 These figures are extremely rubbery, as verification exercises are poorly run. They also exclude the public-sector membership of the massive teachers' union.

4 Sirait's study (2014) found that firm-level unions in the retail sector with connections to national and/or international unions are more likely to have an effective strategy of partnership with management than those without external connections.

5 The role of the military in the handling of industrial disputes was formally expanded in 2018 with the signing of an MOU between the police and the army on security and public order, which explicitly mentioned a role for the military in handling demonstrations and strikes (*Kumparan News,* 2 February 2018).

References

Amable B (2003) *The Diversity of Modern Capitalism.* Oxford: Oxford University Press.

BPS (2016a) *Jumlah Perusahaan Industri Besar Sedang Menurut SubSektor (2 digit KBLI), 2000–2015.* Available at: www.bps.go.id/dynamictable/2015/09/14/896/jumlah-perusahaan-industri-besar-sedang-menurut-subsektor-2-digit-kbli-2000-2015.html.

BPS (2016b) *Jumlah Perusahaan Industri Mikro dan Kecil Menurut 2-digit KBLI, 2010–2015.* Available at: www.bps.go.id/dynamictable/2015/11/24/1011/jumlah-perusahaan-industri-mikro-dan-kecil-menurut-2-digit-kbli-2010-2015.html.

BPS (2016c) *Jumlah Tenaga Kerja Industri Besar dan Sedang Menurut Subsektor, 2000–2015.* Available at: www.bps.go.id/statictable/2011/02/14/1063/jumlah-tenaga-kerja-industri-besar-dan-sedang-menurut-subsektor-2000-2015.html.

BPS (2016d) *Jumlah Tenaga Kerja Industri Mikro dan Kecil Menurut 2-digit KBLI, 2010–2015.* Available at: www.bps.go.id/dynamictable/2015/11/24/1012/jumlah-tenaga-kerja-industri-mikro-dan-kecil-menurut-2-digit-kbli-2010-2015.html.

Caraway T (2004) Protective Repression, International Pressure, and Institutional Design: Explaining Labor Reform in Indonesia. *Studies in Comparative International Development* 39: 28–49.

Caraway T and Ford M (2014) Labor and Politics under Oligarchy. In: Ford M and Pepinsky T (eds.) *Beyond Oligarchy: Wealth, Power and Contemporary Indonesian Politics.* Ithaca, NY: Cornell Southeast Asia Program, 139–156.

Caraway T and Ford M (2020) *Labor and Politics in Indonesia.* New York: Cambridge University Press.

Caraway T, Ford M and Nguyen O (2019) Politicizing the Minimum Wage: Wage Councils, Worker Mobilization, and Local Elections in Indonesia. *Politics & Society* 47(2): 1–25.

Cole R and Ford M (2014) *The KAJS Campaign for Social Security Reform in Indonesia: Lessons for Coalitions for Social Change.* Singapore: Friedrich-Ebert-Stiftung.

Ford M (1999) Testing the Limits of Corporatism: Reflections on Industrial Relations Institutions and Practice in Suharto's Indonesia. *Journal of Industrial Relations* 41: 371–392.

Ford M (2000) Continuity and Change in Indonesian Labour Relations in the Habibie Interregnum. *Southeast Asian Journal of Social Science* 28: 59–88.

Ford M (2005) Economic Unionism and Labour's Poor Performance in Indonesia's 1999 and 2004 Elections. In: Baird M, Cooper R and Westcott M (eds.) *Reworking Work: Proceedings of the 19th Conference of the Association of Industrial Relations Academics of Australia and New Zealand, February 9–11, Sydney, 2005 Volume 1 Refereed Papers.* Sydney: AIRAANZ, 197–204.

Ford M (2006) Emerging Labour Movements and the Accountability Dilemma: The Case of Indonesia. In: Dowdle M (ed.) *Public Accountability: Design and Experience.* Melbourne: Cambridge University Press, 153–173.

Ford M (2009) *Workers and Intellectuals: NGOs, Trade Unions and the Indonesian Labour Movement.* Singapore: NUS Press.

Ford M (2013) Employer Anti-Unionism in Democratic Indonesia. In: Gall G and Dundon T (eds.) *Global Anti-Unionism: Nature, Dynamics, Trajectories and Outcomes.* Bassingstoke: Palgrave Macmillan, 224–243.

Ford M (2014a) Developing Societies – Asia. In: Wilkinson A, Wood G and Deeg R (eds.) *The Oxford Handbook of Employment Relations: Comparative Employment Systems.* Oxford: Oxford University Press, 431–447.

Ford M (2014b) Learning by Doing: Trade Unions and Electoral Politics in Batam, Indonesia, 2004–2009. *South East Asia Research* 22: 341–357.

Ford M and Caraway T (2014) Rallying to Prabowo's Cause. *New Mandala. Available at: https://www.newmandala.org/rallying-to-prabowos-cause/*

Ford M and Gillan M (2016) Employment Relations and the State in Southeast Asia. *Journal of Industrial Relations* 58: 167–182.

Ford M and Sirait G (2016) The State, Democratic Transition and Employment Relations in Indonesia. *Journal of Industrial Relations* 58(2): 229–242.

Frege C and Kelly J (2003) Union Revitalization Strategy in Comparative Perspective. *European Journal of Industrial Relations* 9: 7–24.

Gardener D (2012) Workers' Rights and Corporate Accountability – the Move towards Practical, Worker-Driven Change for Sportswear Workers in Indonesia. *Gender & Development* 20: 49–65.

Hadiz V (1997) *Workers and the State in New Order Indonesia.* London, New York: Routledge.

Hall P and Soskice D (2001) An Introduction to Varieties of Capitalism. In: Hall P and Soskice D (eds.) *Varieties of Capitalism: The Institutional Foundations of Comparative Advantage.* Oxford, New York: Oxford University Press, 1–68.

Hall P and Thelen K (2009) Institutional Change in Varieties of Capitalism. In: Hancké B (ed.) *Debating Varieties of Capitalism: A Reader.* Oxford: Oxford University Press, 251–272.

Iversen T and Soskice D (2009) Distribution and Redistribution: The Shadow of the Nineteenth Century. *World Politics* 61: 438–486.

Kelly J and Frege C (2004) Conclusions: Varieties of Unionism. In: Frege C and Kelly J (eds) *Varieties of Unionism: Strategies for Union Revitalization in a Globalizing Economy.* New York: Oxford University Press.

Lee B-H and Lansbury R (2014) Refining Varieties of Labour Movements: Perspectives from the Asia-Pacific Region. *Journal of Industrial Relations* 54: 433–442.

Ministry of Manpower (2013) *Organisasi Pekerja/Buruh di Indonesia.* Available at: pusdatinaker.balitfo.depnakertrans.go.id/viewpdf.php?id=318.

Mufakhir A (2014) "Grebek Pabrik" in Bekasi: Research Note on Unions' Mobilisation Strategy. In: Suryomenggolo J (ed.) *Worker Activism after Reformasi 1998: A New Phase for Indonesian Unions?* Hong Kong: Asia Monitor Resource Centre, 93–114.

Nottage L (2002) Japanese Corporate Governance at a Crossroads: Variation in 'Varieties of Capitalism'? *North Carolina Journal of International Law and Commercial Regulation* 27: 255–299.

Ritchie B (2009) Economic Upgrading in a State-coordinated, Liberal Market Economy. *Asia Pacific Journal of Management* 26: 435–457.

Schneider B and Soskice D (2009) Inequality in Developed Countries and Latin America: Coordinated, Liberal and Hierarchical Systems. *Economic and Society* 38: 17–52.

Sirait M (2014) Employment Relations in Indonesia's Retail Sector: Institutions, Power Relations and Outcomes. PhD Thesis. The University of Sydney.

Siregar B (2018) 72 Perusahaan Jadi Objek Vital Industri. *Warta Ekonomi.*

Tipton F (2009) Southeast Asian Capitalism: History, Institutions, States, and Firms. *Asia Pacific Journal of Management* 26: 401–433.

8 Changes in the labour market and employment relationships in Japan

Katsuyuki Kubo

Introduction

This chapter examines changes in the labour market and employment relations in Japan. First, the traditional characteristics of employment practices in Japan, such as long-term employment, seniority wages and enterprise-based unions, are examined. We describe how these characteristics are related to employees' incentives and firm behaviour. Previous studies show a correlation between these practices and firm productivity (Aoki, 1988; Itoh, 1994; Koike, 1988). Because employees and employers expect long-term relationships, employees have an incentive to accumulate firm-specific skills. Firms are less likely to reduce the number of employees and thus are less likely to close low-productivity divisions. Because trade unions operate at the enterprise level, and as their leaders have information on various managerial issues through the joint labour–management committee (JLMC) of the firm, union leaders have an incentive to cooperate with senior managers to maximise firm productivity. Employees also have an incentive to pursue productivity improvements as they will yield better employment conditions.

Some newspapers and business magazines argue that these characteristics of labour markets have become outdated because the mechanisms no longer work effectively. We examine whether there have been any changes in any of these characteristics. Long-term employment relationships exist for regular workers in large firms, and at the same time the proportion of non-regular workers is increasing. Therefore, the number of workers in long-term employment relationships is decreasing. Furthermore, the relationship between employees' ages and wages is becoming weaker.

Because of globalisation and institutional changes, many adjustments have occurred in financial markets. For example, it has become easier for firms to reorganise themselves through mergers or acquisitions, and the proportion of shares held by foreign shareholders and investment funds has increased. These changes in financial markets have impacted labour markets, because firms are now more likely to emphasise shareholder value. Empirical studies show that firms with foreign shareholders are more likely to reduce the number of employees. We describe the possible impacts of financial markets on employment practices.

The remainder of this chapter is as follows: Section 2 describes the traditional features of labour markets in Japan, such as long-term relationships and seniority wages. Section 3 reviews employment representation with particular emphasis on enterprise unions and the JLMCs. Section 4 focuses on the institutional changes in financial markets and their impact on labour markets. An analysis of the union response is provided in Section 5, and Section 6 concludes this chapter.

Labour markets in Japan

There are several important characteristics of the labour market in Japan, including long-term employment and seniority-based wages, both of which have been examined in many studies. Some investigate the extent to which these characteristics are observable and find that they are observed mainly among male workers in large firms who are regular employees. Recently, several attempts have been made to detect changes in these characteristics.

One of the most important questions is whether these characteristics have positive or negative impacts on firm performance. Some studies suggest that they are effective in motivating employees to acquire various sets of skills, in particular firm-specific skills that increase productivity. In contrast, others argue that these employment characteristics are among the major causes of the stagnation of the Japanese economy. Firms may not be able to close loss-making divisions to protect employees. In this section, I examine these views and recent studies on these characteristics.

Long-term employment

Long-term employment practices were developed in the high-growth era following Second World War, when it was difficult for firms to attract and retain skilled workers. Typically, workers enter a firm after they graduate from school and continue working for that firm for many years. It is often the case that workers remain with the firm they joined after school for their entire working life. They develop their career within the firm and are promoted to increasingly senior positions. Firms tend to fill managerial positions by promoting employees from lower levels rather than hiring from outside the firm. It is often the case that workers' salaries decrease when they move from one large company to another. Therefore, the easiest way to earn more money is to keep working for the same company over the long term and gain promotion.

Employees typically accumulate firm-specific skills for promotion to higher positions. They also acquire a wide range of skills through job rotation. A firm will not dismiss its employees unless the firm is in severe financial distress. This practice is supported by case law that limits the firms' right to dismiss employees. According to a rule called the 'Doctrine of Abusive

Dismissal' (Hanami and Komiya, 2011; Kambayashi, 2011), firms can dismiss regular employees only when they are in severe financial distress. As a result, large firms rarely lay off employees if they are making a profit.

Previous studies show that firms tend to reduce the number of their employees when they experience negative profits for two consecutive years (Koike, 1983; Suruga, 1998). As it is difficult for firms to dismiss employees, firms reduce the number of employees by other means, such as by soliciting voluntary retirement with an additional retirement bonus and by limiting the hiring of new employees. In addition, large firms dispatch their employees to group firms to prevent job losses (Kato, 2001; Kester, 1991).

Several recent studies using large micro datasets examine whether there have been changes in the nature of long-term employment practices (Hamaaki et al., 2012; Kambayashi and Kato, 2012; Ono, 2010; Shimizutani and Yokoyama, 2009). These studies show that large firms have maintained their long-term employment practices. For example, the separation rate – which is the proportion of workers who leave the firm – for employees aged 25–59 years was stable between 1991 and 2003 (Ono, 2010). Ono (2010) also shows that the proportion of 'lifetime workers' who work at only one company was 23% for male employees in 2000.

To examine whether there has been a change in long-term employment practices, we examine the average length of service of employees and the separation rate. Figure 8.1, based on data from the Basic Survey of Wages, shows no change in the length of service for regular employees from 1976 to 2017. In fact, this has increased slightly for both male and female workers. For example, the average length of service for male workers was 9.5 years in 1976 and 13.5 years in 2017.

Figure 8.1 Employees' Length of Service.

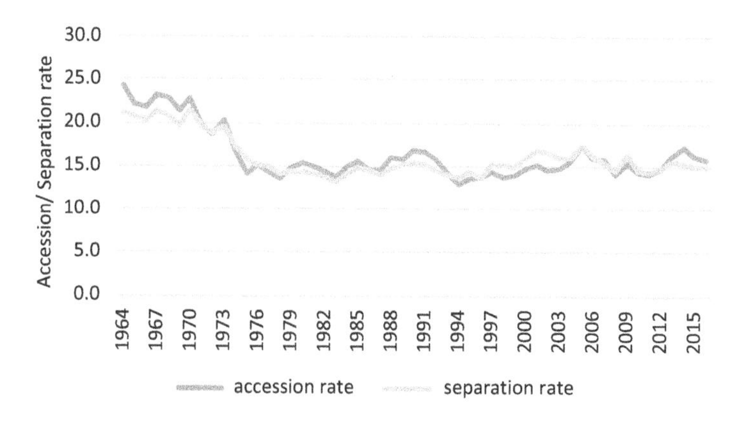

Figure 8.2 Change in Employees' Turnover Rate.

Figure 8.2 shows the separation rate and accession rate for the period 1964–2016. These data are from the Survey of Employment Trends. The separation rate is the ratio of workers who leave a firm to the total number of the firm's employees, while the accession rate is the ratio of employees hired in one year to the total number of employees. The separation rate is stable. There is little change in employees' tendency to leave the firm, with a separation rate of 15.1% in 1976 and 15.8% in 2016. These results indicate that there has been little change in long-term employment among regular employees.

Not all types of workers follow the practice of long-term employment. This applies mainly to male workers with a university degree, and those who are regular workers in a large firm. According to Ono (2010), of male workers aged 50–54 years in firms with more than 1,000 employees, 55.2% have worked for the same firm since graduation.

Figure 8.3 shows the proportion of non-regular workers among male and female workers from 1984 to 2015. The data are taken from the Labour Force Survey. This figure clearly shows that the proportion of non-regular workers has increased for both male and female workers. The proportion of non-regular workers who are male was 22% in 2015. The proportion of non-regular workers who are female is large, at 57%. The increase in the proportions of non-regular workers can be partly explained by the legal change that makes it easier for firms to utilise non-regular workers. For example, the Worker Dispatch Law was introduced in 1986 and subsequently amended several times.

Seniority-based wage

Another important characteristic of employment practices in Japan is seniority-based wages. Previous studies have shown that the correlation between wage and length of service is larger in Japan than in other countries

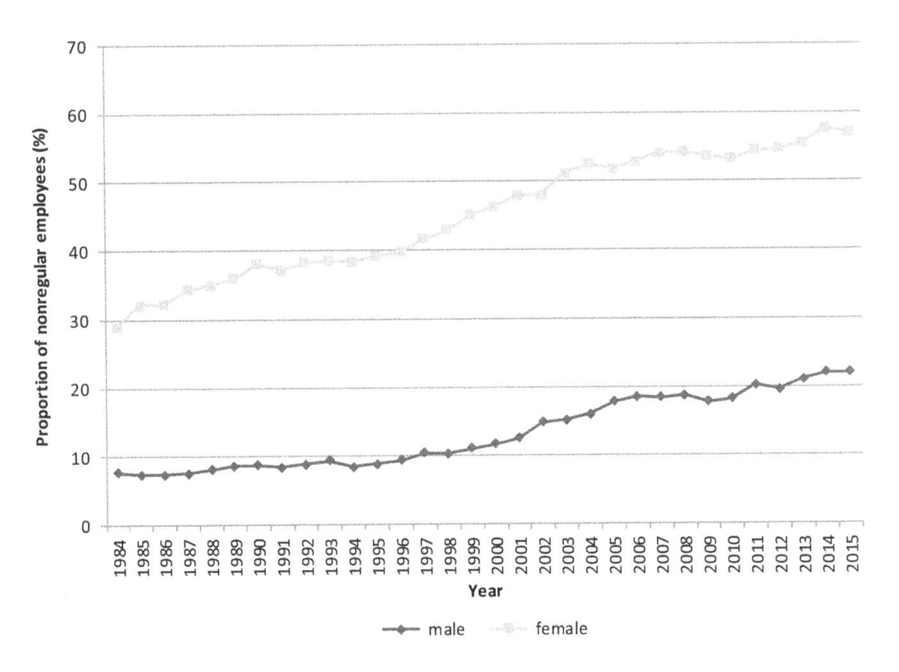

Figure 8.3 Proportion of Non-Regular Workers.

(Mincer and Higuchi, 1988; Shimada, 1981). Clearly, there is a strong correlation between long-term employment and seniority-based wages.

When firms determine the salary of each worker, they do not consider the employee's age or length of service. In fact, some employees earn a relatively low wage even though they are elderly. There are significant variations in salaries among older employees. The observed correlation between age and wages is a result of the pay structure.

Typically, there is an internal-rank system within firms, which is often called the competence-rank system (Uehara, 2009). All the employees in the firm are subject to ranking, which determines base pay. New employees who enter the firm after they graduate from school belong to the lowest rank. As they acquire skills, they move to higher ranks and receive higher wages. It takes a certain number of years to move to a more senior position. As there is no 'fast track', employees need to spend a significant number of years within the firm to be in a managerial position. Thus, there is a correlation between length of service and wages. It should be noted that not all employees move to a higher rank despite spending a significant number of years in their firm. Employees have an incentive to acquire firm-specific skills for promotion.

However, firms are finding it difficult to retain this system, partly because of the ageing of the workforce. Therefore, the relationship between age and wages is expected to weaken. In addition, many firms have changed their wage structure so that wages are more dependent on performance, in particular for employees in managerial positions.

Figure 8.4 shows the change in the relationship between age and wages, using data from the Basic Survey of Wages. It shows the age–wage profile of workers with a university degree working in large companies in 1981, 2000 and 2014. In this figure, the wages of workers below the age of

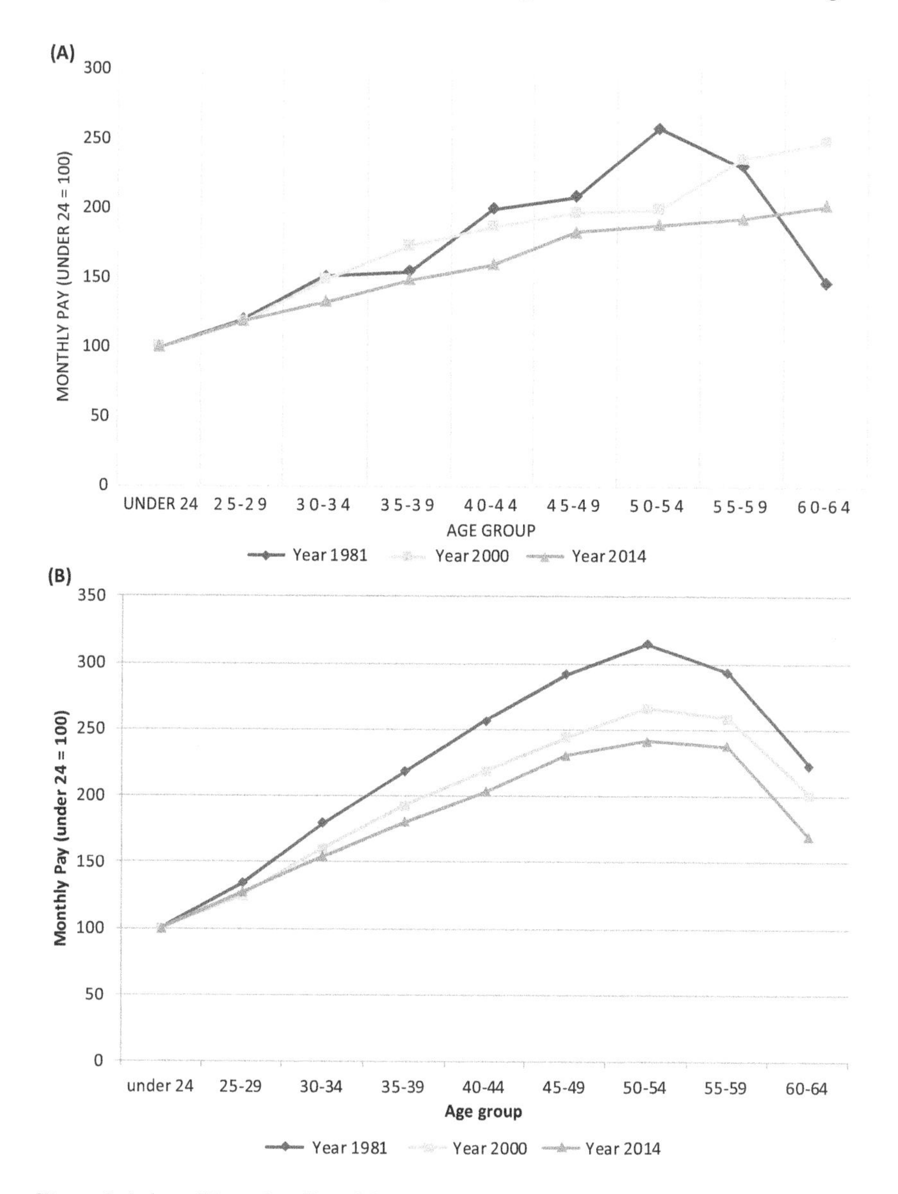

Figure 8.4 Age–Wage Profile of Employees: (A) Male Employee and (B) Female Employees.

twenty-four years are standardised to one hundred to enable a comparison of the slopes across the years. Panel A of Figure 8.4 shows the relationship between age and wages for male workers. In 1981, employees aged 50–54 years received a wage more than three times that of employees aged below twenty-four years. However, the gap is smaller in later years. Panel B shows that the relationship between age and wages has become smaller for female workers as well.

Employee representation

In this section, we examine trade unions and worker representation in Japan. In particular, we focus on enterprise unions and the JLMC. These organisations are believed to influence long-term employment and the seniority-based wage system. In addition, it is believed that these worker representation organisations affect firm productivity. Below, we describe the operations of these organisations and their recent changes.

Enterprise-based unions

One of the most important elements of employment relationships in Japan is that unions are organised as enterprise unions rather than industrial or occupational unions. Enterprise unions are organised by employees of the same company. They consist of both non-manual and manual workers, while non-regular workers are typically not part of the union.

Enterprise unions often belong to the union federation of the associated industry, such as *Denki Rengo* (Japanese Electrical Electronic and Information Union), and the industrial-level federations belong to national organisations such as *Rengo* (JTUC, Japan Trade Union Confederation). *Rengo* is the largest national centre, with around 6.82 million members in 2015.[1]

Wage bargaining occurs at the enterprise level; however, most firms conduct wage negotiations at the same time, usually in spring (Sako, 1997). This annual negotiation is called *Shunto*, which literally means 'spring offensive'. Wage bargaining in one company is influenced by the results of bargaining in other companies. In particular, smaller companies use the results of wage negotiations in large companies as a reference.

There is often a cooperative relationship between employers and enterprise unions. The main reason for this is that they share the same objective: the growth of the firm. Under conditions of long-term employment and a seniority-based pay system, employees expect to be promoted to higher positions within the same company and to receive higher salaries. In addition, the salaries of employees depend on the profitability of the firm, as a significant proportion of their salaries comes from bonuses (Hart and Kawasaki, 1999). From the perspective of the employees, it is important for firms to grow to ensure sufficient managerial positions for future promotions.

One of the most important problems for trade unions is their declining participation rate. Figure 8.5 shows the change in the unionisation rate from 1947 to 2016. It also shows the unionisation rate for part-time workers after 1990, with the exception of 2011.[2] The data are from the Basic Survey of Labour Unions.

Figure 8.5 shows that the unionisation rate was around 35% until the 1970s and decreased steadily subsequently. It dropped from 33.7% in 1976 to 17.3% in 2016. The number of union members declined from 12.37 million in 1976 to 9.88 million in 2016. The unionisation rate for part-time workers is below that of regular workers, although it is increasing.

There are several possible reasons for the decreasing unionisation rate. One reason is that the proportion of female and non-regular workers has increased. The unionisation rate is lower among female and non-regular workers, as shown in Table 8.1, which shows the proportion of union members across different employee groups. The data are from the Basic Survey of Labour Unions. The unionisation rate of female employees is 12.5%. The rate for part-time workers is only 7.5%, with only 1.13 million of the 15.17 million part-time workers being union members. At the same time, the proportion of non-regular workers is increasing, as shown in Figure 8.3.

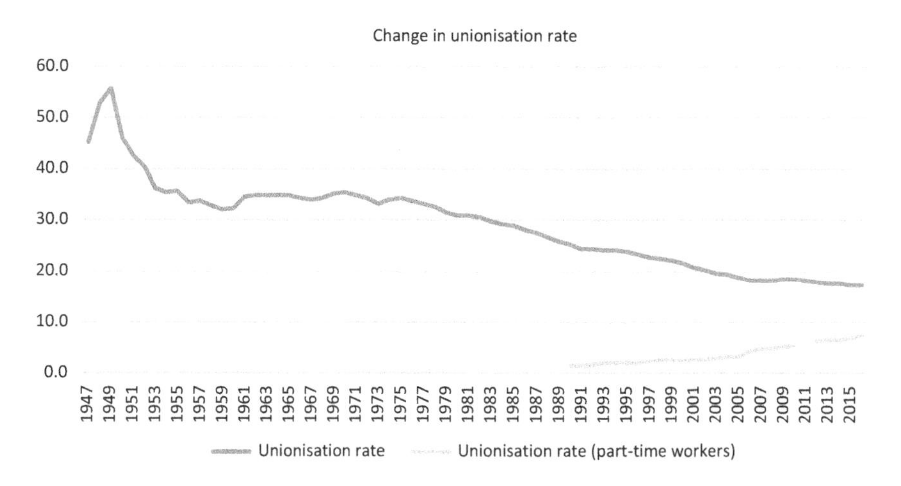

Figure 8.5 Unionisation Rate.

Table 8.1 Union Participation by Various Types of Workers

	Total	*Female*	*Part-time*
Number of workers (1,000 persons)	57,400	25,440	15,170
Number of union members (1,000 persons)	9,940	3,192	1,131
Unionisation rate (%)	17.3	12.5	7.5

Source: Basic Survey of Labour Unions.

One reason for the very low union membership rate among non-regular workers is that enterprise unions are usually comprised of regular workers, although some unions encourage membership of non-regular workers. There is a possible conflict of interest between regular and non-regular workers. Suppose a firm experiences severe financial distress and needs to reduce labour costs. The firm will attempt to reduce the number of non-regular workers it employs to protect regular workers. It is easy for union leaders who are regular employees to agree to firm proposals to reduce the number of non-regular workers employed.

According to the 'Doctrine of Abusive Dismissal' (Hanami and Komiya, 2011; Kambayashi, 2011), firms are required to make every effort to avoid the dismissal of regular employees, which indicates that firms should dismiss non-regular employees before they dismiss regular employees.

Another possible reason for the declining unionisation rate is the increase in the number of workers in the service sectors. Using data from the Basic Survey of Labour Unions, Figure 8.6 shows substantial differences in the unionisation rate across sectors. The rates are highest in sectors such as electricity, gas and water, and finance and insurance. One reason might be that these sectors are comprised of relatively large firms. The unionisation rate in the services sector is 4.3%, which is much lower than in other sectors.

JLMCs

A JLMC is an important mechanism for employment relationships. In many large companies, the JLMC is used as a channel through which representatives of employees communicate with the employer on various topics (Kato and Morishima, 2002; Morishima, 1991a, 1991b; Shirai, 1983). It is usually

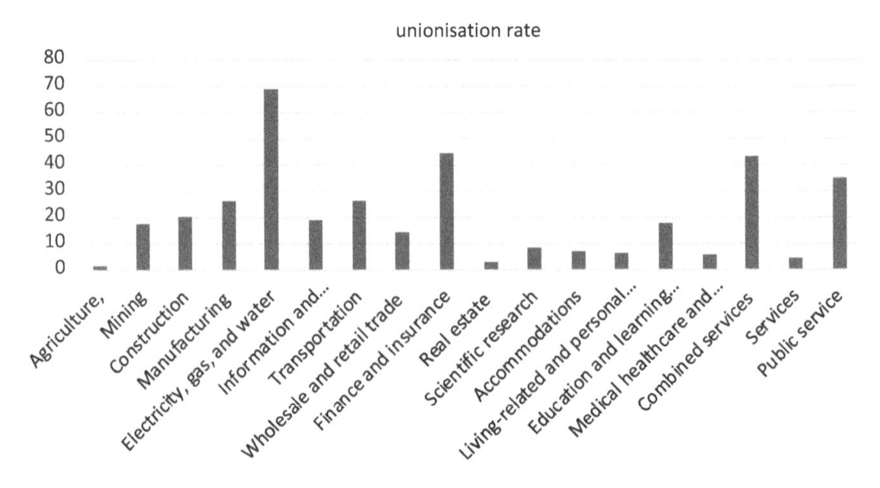

Figure 8.6 Unionisation Rate by Sector.

the case that union representatives become workers' representatives in the JLMC when the union is established.

It is not compulsory to have a JLMC, although most large firms have one. According to the Survey on Labour–Management Communication in 2014, 74.7% of firms with more than 5,000 employees have a JLMC. For firms of all sizes, 40.3% have a JLMC. One important characteristic of JLMCs is that they include non-regular workers. According to the survey, 93.3% of firms with JLMCs had both regular and non-regular workers involved in them. Non-regular workers are sometimes chosen as worker representatives on JLMCs.

The issues dealt with by JLMCs are not limited to labour conditions. Management informs workers about general business conditions and about possible future important business plans such as large investments and plant relocations. JLMCs discuss issues such as working hours, holidays, workplace safety, wages, mandatory retirement and other employment issues. In 54% of the firms with a JLMC, the committees formally discuss management policy. Moreover, they often discuss the labour conditions of non-regular workers.

Employees may learn about business conditions through the JLMC. This information sharing affects wage bargaining. As both employers and employees share information, the wage negotiations are likely to be more efficient. According to Morishima (1991a), the duration of wage negotiations is shorter in firms with information sharing. Union leaders may agree with management plans, for example, to reduce the number of employees because they understand that it is important for firms to do so.

There are several studies that show positive and significant relationships between JLMCs and firm productivity (Kato and Morishima, 2002; Morishima, 1991b). For example, Kato and Morishima (2002), who examine the performance of firms from 1973 to 1992, show that there is a difference in the productivity of firms with participatory employment practices such as those with a JLMC and those without. Firms with participatory employment practices achieve 8%–9% higher productivity than those without.

Changes in financial markets and their effect on employment relationships

In this section, we describe the changes in financial markets in Japan and their effects on labour market relationships. It is often assumed that there was a change in firm behaviour in Japan after the 1990s because of the significant changes in financial markets in that period. These changes include the introduction of the Amendment of Anti-Monopoly Law in 1997, the introduction of the Company Act in 2005 and the introduction of the Financial Instruments and Exchange Law in 2006. The Company Act of 2005 was introduced to consolidate the earlier Commercial Code and the Limited Liability Company Law and other related laws. The Financial Instruments and Exchange Law of 2006 was introduced with the intention of enhancing the development of financial markets. This law is an amendment of the Securities and Exchange Act of 1948. One of the important objectives of these changes was to revitalise financial markets.

There was a significant change in the ownership structure of listed companies. One important change was the advent of investment funds. Investment fund activity, such as that by private equity (PE) funds and activist hedge funds, is observable from the late 1990s (Buchanan et al., 2012; Inoue and Kato, 2007; Nose and Ito, 2009, 2011; Sugiura, 2010). According to Sugiura (2011), the first buyout transaction by a PE fund occurred in 1998 and became increasingly common thereafter. The total value of transactions was 1.24 trillion yen in 2008. Nose and Ito (2009, 2011), who examine the impact of PE funds on firm performance, show a positive and significant effect on profitability and shareholder value. According to Inoue and Kato (2007), the reaction of the stock market to acquisitions by activist hedge funds is positive and significant.

Traditionally, large Japanese firms have owned shares in closely related firms. By creating a network of cross shareholdings, senior managers of the firms are less likely to face pressure from shareholders to maximise shareholder value. However, according to Miyajima and Kuroki (2007) and Miyajima and Nitta (2011), firms are more likely to dissolve these relationships. At the same time, the proportion of foreign shareholders is increasing. According to the Japan Exchange Group, the proportion of shares owned by foreigners increased from 11.9% in 1996 to 30.1% in 2016.

These changes in financial markets increase the pressure on senior managers to improve shareholder value to avoid hostile takeovers. If this is the case, firms are more likely to emphasise the interests of shareholders than those of employees. Hirota (2015) conducted a questionnaire survey of listed companies in Japan, asking the same questions as Yoshimori (1995): whether firms should reduce the number of employees or cut dividends when they experience poor business conditions. He shows that there was a slight change in the behaviour of large firms. According to his analysis, 21.73% of managers believed that firms should leave dividend payouts unchanged, while 31.3% believed that firms should maintain employment levels by cutting dividends. In other words, the proportion of managers who emphasise the interests of shareholders is increasing.

There are several reasons why these changes in financial markets have affected employment relationships. First, new owners of a firm who have acquired a significant proportion of the firm's shares may have little incentive to prioritise the interests of employees. One example is Top Tour, a travel agency acquired in 2004 by Activ Investment Partners Ltd., a PE fund. Top Tour used to be a subsidiary company of a railway firm, but the parent firm decided to sell the agency to the fund. It is reported that the new owner has weakened the traditional employment relationship to maximise profit. To weaken the power of the enterprise trade union, the firm established an 'employee association'. The firm pays bonuses only to those employees who belong to the employee association and refuses to pay bonuses to employees who are members of the trade union.

There are several empirical studies that examine the effect of ownership on employment.[3] Nose and Ito (2011) examine cases in which a significant proportion of shares was acquired by a PE fund and find a significant reduction in the number of employees. According to Ahmadjian and Robbins (2005), who analyse large Japanese firms from 1991 to 2000, firms with foreign shareholders are more likely to reduce the number of employees. These studies are consistent with the view that employees are more likely to lose their jobs in firms with strong shareholder influence.

Union response to the challenges

Previous sections show that employers and employees achieve both high productivity and employment protection through these practices. At the same time, there are several challenges for these practices from the viewpoint of unions. The conditions that support enterprise-based unions are changing. Tables 8.2 and 8.3 summarise the challenges for the unions and their responses.

One important change is in financial markets. Senior managers face greater pressure from the stock market to maximise short-term profits. The number of firm reorganisations through mergers and acquisitions is increasing. Because of these changes, senior managers are less likely to protect long-term employment. Trade unions need to be reorganised when firms conduct reorganisations, such as mergers (Watanabe and Kobayashi, 2017). When a company splits into multiple firms, the enterprise union will often be divided into multiple unions as well. When a company sells part of its business, the workers sometimes form new trade unions or join the enterprise union of the company that bought the business. The number of union members decreases significantly when the firm experiences such a reorganisation.

Table 8.2 Union Challenges in Japan

Internal Challenges	*External Challenges*
The number of non-regular workers is increasing. The number of workers covered by long-term employment relationships is reduced.	Senior managers face greater pressure from the stock market to maximise short-term profits. The number of firm reorganisations through mergers and acquisitions is increasing. Trade unions need reorganisation when firms conduct reorganisations, such as mergers.

Table 8.3 Union Strategies in Japan

	Applicability	*Benefit*	*Risk*
Organising	Some unions attempt to organise non-regular workers.	Regular and non-regular workers have better communication.	It is not easy to persuade regular workers to include non-regular workers.
Organisational restructuring	Trade unions of the companies that belong to the same company group form a unified union.	Workers in subsidiary firms have a chance to bargain with senior managers of the parent company.	Union members of parent companies, who receive higher wages may not be willing to merge.
Coalition-building	Trade unions seek cooperation with NGOs.	Both unions and NGOs benefit from the cooperation.	
Partnerships with employer	Most large firms have joint labour–management committees through which they communicate their views on business situations and future plans.	Communication between senior managers and employees is improved.	When the organisation of the company becomes larger and more complex, it is not easy for a union to represent workers of the whole group.
Political actions	*Rengo* exerts significant efforts to promote various policies on employment, such as raising the minimum wage, promoting decent work and realising a gender-equal society.	It has close relationships with opposition parties.	Each union may have different opinions on political issues.
International links	*Rengo* works together with international organisations. It also encourages multinational corporations to be aware of international business rules.	Some companies, such as Takashimaya, Mizuno and the Aeon Group, have signed a global framework agreement to enhance constructive employment relationships.	Both companies and enterprise unions tend to focus on domestic issues.

One response to such firm reorganisations by enterprise unions is to form an association of enterprise unions that represents the same company groups. In some cases, the trade unions of the companies that belong to the same company group form a unified union. In 2004, seven trade unions in companies of the Kenwood Group, which is a manufacturer of audio equipment, merged into one union. According to Oh (2011), this enables union members of subsidiary companies to communicate with senior managers of the parent company. By forming one large union, the number of union members increases. At the same time, union members from the parent companies, who receive higher wages, may not be willing to merge as wage differentials between parent and subsidiary firms may decrease.

Many companies extend their businesses to foreign countries. As a result, unions are aware of the importance of international business rules. *Rengo*, the largest trade union federation, works together with organisations such as Global Union Federations and the International Trade Union Confederation to promote decent work. *Rengo* also encourages multinational corporations to become conscious of international business guidelines such as the Organisation for Economic Co-operation and Development (OECD) Guidelines for Multinational Enterprises and the International Labour Organisation (ILO) Tripartite Declaration of Principles concerning Multinational Enterprises and Social Policy. These actions have helped to promote decent work in multinational companies. Some multinational companies, such as Takashimaya, Mizuno and the Aeon Group, have signed a global framework agreement to enhance constructive employment relationships.

Another important change in the Japanese labour market is the increased number of non-regular workers. When there is a dispute between non-regular workers and the employer, enterprise-based unions may not be involved, as enterprise-based unions are comprised of regular employees.

In response to these changes, some trade unions and federations of trade unions, such as *Rengo*, are attempting to organise non-regular workers. In spite of these efforts, many enterprise unions consist only of regular workers. One reason for this may be that there is a conflict of interest between regular workers and non-regular workers. Firms can protect the employment of regular workers by cutting non-regular workers. At the same time, several labour unions have begun to organise non-regular workers (RENGO-RIALS, 2009). One example is unions that belong to UA ZENSEN, which is an association of trade unions in industries such as textiles and garments. Of its 1.72 million members, 57.6% are non-regular workers. The Aeon Retail Workers' Union belongs to UA ZENSEN. Aeon Retail is the core company of the Aeon Group, which is composed of retail and financial service companies. As of 2008, the number of workers in the company was 107,000. Among them, 83% were non-regular workers. Until 2004, the labour union was composed only of regular workers. The union decided to organise non-regular workers in 2001. One reason for this was to facilitate communication between regular workers and non-regular workers. It started organising non-regular workers after 2004, and in 2008, the union was composed of 15,800 regular workers and 64,800 non-regular workers.

There are other unions that incorporate are not enterprise based. One example is the Capital Area University Part-Time Teachers' Union, which is comprised of part-time university teachers (Ishii, 2018). Ishii (2018) describes how this union helps part-time teachers to obtain better working conditions. In 2013, one university set a new rule for its part-time teachers that the maximum length of contracts would be five years. This university proposed this rule as a response to a labour contract law amendment enacted in 2012. According to the law, workers with a fixed-term contract can request their employer to change their contracts to one without a fixed term once they satisfy certain conditions. One of these conditions is that the employment period exceeds five years. This is believed to be the reason that the university introduced the rule. After several negotiations between the branch of the union and the university, the university changed the rule. One important change was that the rule to limit the contract to five years was lifted.

Several unions have attempted to strengthen their relationships with other non-governmental organisations (NGOs). In 2004, the Forum for NGO–Trade Unions in International Cooperation was established by NGOs and trade unions to enhance international cooperation to deal with problems mentioned in UN Sustainable Development Goals (SDGs). NGOs that have experience in international cooperation can work with trade unions, which have a wide network in Japan. For example, trade unions promote various products of NGOs.

Conclusion

This chapter has examined the labour market and employment relations in Japan as well as the responses of unions. It has been shown that there are complementarities among various employment practices, such as long-term employment, enterprise-based unions and JLMCs. These practices help employees to acquire firm-specific skills for promotion. Firms seek to avoid dismissing employees to promote long-term employment, which improves productivity. Finally, it should be noted that one important driver of these changes in employment relations is the change in financial markets which has emphasised the interests of shareholders. Previous studies have shown that firms become more likely to reduce the number of employees following changes in financial markets.[4] Hence, an important theoretical implication of these results is that we need to further examine changes in financial markets, because they have significant effects on labour conditions.

Acknowledgements

The author acknowledges the financial support of a Grant-in-Aid for Scientific Research from the Japanese Ministry of Education, Science, Sports, and Culture (15K03560, 15H01958), funding from JSPS Core-to-Core Program A, Advanced Research Networks and a Waseda University Grant for Special Research Projects.

Notes

1 *Rengo* exerts significant political efforts to promote various employment policies, such as raising the minimum wage, ensuring decent work and realising a gender-equal society. It has close relationships with opposition parties. However, it should be noted that unions may have different opinions on political issues.
2 Statistics are incomplete for part-time workers in 2011 because of the Great East Japan Earthquake.
3 Kubo (2014) analyses the effect of investment funds on employees.
4 Some studies report that employees of firms with larger proportions of foreign ownership have better working environments. Olcott (2009) shows that the proportion of female managers increases significantly in large Japanese firms acquired by foreign firms. Kubo (2018) examines the determinants of firm policy regarding the work environment using data from 1,258 listed firms and finds that firms with a large proportion of foreign shareholders are more likely to have better work environments.

References

Ahmadjian C and Robbins G (2005) A clash of capitalisms: Foreign shareholders and corporate restructuring in 1990s Japan. *American Sociological Review* 70(3): 451–471.

Aoki M (1988) *Information, Incentives and Bargaining in the Japanese Economy*. Cambridge: Cambridge University Press.

Buchanan J, Chai DH and Deakin S (2012) *Hedge Fund Activism in Japan: The Limits of Shareholder Primacy*. Cambridge: Cambridge University Press.

Hamaaki J, Hori M, Maeda S and Murata K (2012) Changes in the Japanese employment system in the two lost decades. *Industrial and Labor Relations Review* 65(4): 810–846.

Hanami T and Komiya F (2011) *Labour Law in Japan*. Alphen aan den Rijn: Kluwer Law International.

Hart R and Kawasaki S (1999) *Work and Pay in Japan*. Cambridge: Cambridge University Press.

Hirota S (2015) *Corporate Finance and Governance in Stakeholder Society: Beyond Shareholder Capitalism*. London: Routledge.

Inoue K and Kato H (2007) Advantages and disadvantages of activist funds. *Kezai Kenkyu* 58: 203–216.

Ishii T (2018) Employment conditions and emerging labour movements of non-regular workers in Japan. *Asia Pacific Journal of Human Resources*. Epub ahead of print 6 March 2018. DOI: 10.1111/1744-7941.12177.

Itoh H (1994) Japanese human resource management from the viewpoint of incentive theory. In: Aoki M and Dore R (eds.) *The Japanese Firm Sources of Competitive Strength*. Oxford: Oxford University Press, pp. 233–264.

Kambayashi R (2011) Dismissal regulation in Japan. In: Hamada K, Otsuka K, Ranis G and Togo K (eds.) *Miraculous Growth and Stagnation in Post-War Japan*. London: Routledge, pp. 74–90.

Kambayashi R and Kato T (2012) Trends in long-term employment and job security in Japan and the United States: The last twenty-five years. CJEB Working Paper #302.

Kato T (2001) The end of lifetime employment in Japan? Evidence from national surveys and field research. *Journal of the Japanese and International Economies* 15(4): 489–514.

Kato T and Morishima M (2002) The productivity effects of participatory employment practices: Evidence from new Japanese panel data. *Industrial Relations* 41(4): 487–520.

Kester C (1991) *Japanese Takeovers: The Global Contest for Corporate Control*. Boston, MA: Harvard Business School Press.

Koike K (1983) Modern Japanese industrial relations from the viewpoint of dismissals. In: Moriguchi C, Aoki M and Sawa T (eds.) *Analysis of Japanese Economic Structure*. Tokyo: Sobunsha, pp. 109–126.

Koike K (1988) *Understanding Industrial Relations in Modern Japan*. New York: St. Martin's Press.

Kubo K (2014) Japan: Limits to investment fund activity. In: Gospel H, Pendleton A and Vistols S (eds.) *Financialization, New Investment Funds, and Labour: An International Comparison*. Oxford: Oxford University Press, pp. 290–312.

Kubo K (2018) The effect of corporate governance on firms' decent work policies in Japan. *Asia Pacific Journal of Human Resources*. Epub ahead of print 23 February 2018. DOI: 10.1111/1744-7941.12176.

Mincer J and Higuchi Y (1988) Wage structure and labor turnover in the United States and Japan. *Journal of the Japanese and International Economies* 2(2): 97–133.

Miyajima H and Kuroki F (2007) The unwinding of cross-shareholding in Japan: Causes, effects, and implications. In: Aoki M, Jackson G and Miyajima H (eds.) *Corporate Governance in Japan: Institutional Change and Organisational Diversity*. Oxford: Oxford University Press, pp. 79–124.

Miyajima H and Nitta K (2011) Kabusiki syoyukozono tayokato sono kiketsu (Diversification of ownership structure and its effect on performance). In: Miyajima H (ed.), *Nihon no Kigyo Tochi (Corporate Governance in Japan)*. Tokyo: Toyokeizai Shimposha.

Morishima M (1991a) Information sharing and collective bargaining in Japan: Effects on wage negotiation. *Industrial and Labor Relations Review* 44(3): 469–485.

Morishima M (1991b) Information sharing and firm performance in Japan. *Industrial Relations* 30(1): 37–62.

Nose Y and Ito A (2009) Baiauto fandoniyoru baisyuno inpakutoni kansuru bunseki (The impact of the buyout fund). *Gendai Finance* 26: 49–66. [In Japanese]

Nose Y and Ito A (2011) Kokai izigata biauto zisshi kigyo no choki pafomansu (The long-term performance of PIPEs in Japan. Hitotsubashi IS-FS Working Paper Series FS-2011-J-002, Hitotsubashi University.

Oh HS (2011) Kigyo guru-pu roshi kankei no nozomashii sugata (Good example of group employment relationship). *Business Labour Trend* 11: 5–11.

Olcott G (2009) *Conflict and Change: Foreign Ownership and the Japanese Firm*. Cambridge: Cambridge University Press.

Ono H (2010) Lifetime employment in Japan: Concepts and measurements. *Journal of the Japanese and International Economies* 24(1): 1–27.

RENGO-RIALS (2009) Research Report on the Organising of Non-Regular Workers. Tokyo: Research Institute for Advancement of Living Standards.

Sako M (1997) Shunto: Employer and union coordination for pay determination at the industry and inter-sectoral levels. In: Sako M and Sato H (eds.) *Japanese*

Labour and Management in Transition: Diversity, Flexibility and Participation. London: Routledge, pp. 236–264.

Shimada H (1981) *Earnings Structure and Human Investment: A Comparison between the United States and Japan*. Tokyo: Keio Economic Observatory.

Shimizutani S and Yokoyama I (2009) Has Japan's long-term employment practice survived? Developments since the 1990s. *Industrial and Labor Relations Review* 62(3): 313–326.

Shirai T (ed) (1983) *Contemporary Industrial Relations in Japan*. Madison: University of Wisconsin.

Sugiura K (2010) History of buy-out market in Japan. In: Sugiura K and Koshi J (eds.) *Praibeto Ekuitei (Private Equity)*. Tokyo: Nihon Keizai Shinbumsha, pp. 1–26. [In Japanese]

Suruga T (1998) Employment adjustment in Japanese firms: Negative profits and dismissals. In: Ohashi I and Tachibanaki T (eds.) *Internal Labour Markets, Incentives and Employment*. London: Macmillan Press, pp. 196–221.

Uehara K (2009) Early or late promotion/ screening? Empirical analysis of career ladders for Japanese white-collar workers using employees' list. *Japan Labor Review* 6(3): 25–58.

Watanabe H and Kobayashi T (2017) Soshiki hendo ni tomonau rodo kankeijo no shomondai ni kansuru chosa (Research on the problems concerning firm reorganisation and employment relations). Tokyo: Japan Institute of Labour Policy and Training. [In Japanese]

Yoshimori M (1995) Whose company is it? The concept of the corporation in Japan and the west. *Long Range Planning* 28(4): 2–3, 33–44.

9 Malaysian trade unions in the twenty-first century

Failed revitalisation in a market economy

Peter Wad

Introduction

The national strategy symposium of Malaysian Trades Union Congress (MTUC) on the Island of Langkawi in April 1997 had, according to G. Rajasekaran, Secretary General of the MTUC (1993–2010), the purpose to 'identify the challenges and evolve trade union strategies to counter them' (MTUC, 1997: 10). The challenges identified by the 150 trade union participants were

> to increase union membership; to build the Malaysian trade union movement as an effective voice of labour; to seek changes in labour legislation to permit greater freedom to organise and to obtain union recognition; to compel employers to respect and implement Ministers' lawful order and Industrial Court Awards.
>
> (MTUC, 1997: 10)

In the MTUC Langkawi Charter, under the subtitle 'The Role of the Labour Movement in the 21st Century', strategies were outlined regarding labour organising, labour laws, minimum wages, consumerism, home ownership, privatisation, environmental protection and formation of a Labour Institute (MTUC, 1997: 12–13). The core strategy for membership expansion held that 'MTUC shall organise 1 million workers within its fold by the year 2000' by means of door-to-door campaigns, accessing private service employees and would '[c]ontinue to demand an industrial union for electronic workers but in the meantime [MTUC] will assist thee workers to organise themselves into enterprise unions for their immediate protection and interests' (MTUC, 1997: 13). The strategy for political-institutional change stated that

> [t]he MTUC shall continue to demand amendments to labour laws to enable workers to organise, secure union recognition, achieve fair gains through collective bargaining, enjoy check-off rights, enjoy protection against unfair dismissals and be free to administer the unions without undue interference from authorities

and 'that the discretionary and arbitrary powers of the Director General of Trade Unions and the Human Resources Minister be repealed' (MTUC, op. cit.).

The subjects of 'Multi-Racial Unity' and 'Culture and Religion' were not included in the Langkawi Charter as they were in the former MTUC 1989 strategy paper, 'Labour's Struggle Towards The Year 2000'. Workers' social identity as a united community in solidarity was assumed to override and overrule ethno-political identities and potential conflicts, and no strategy for a workers' collective identity formation was outlined in a context where the ethnic composition (Malays vs. non-Malays) of employees, union members and national union leadership positions correlated by and large (Jomo and Todd, 1994; Ariffin, 1997). Gender inequality persisted.

The symposium was supported by the International Labour Organisation (ILO) and the International Confederation of Free Trade Unions (ICFTU) Asia-Pacific Regional Organisation (APRO), and MTUC Langkawi strategy was approved by the MTUC General Council (Ramasamy, 2008). An assessment of the strength of the Malaysian trade union movement in the late 1990s also called for much more union integration, collaboration and capacity building (Rasiah and Chua, 1998).

The MTUC strategy of 1997 has not been achieved when viewed by the trade unions in 2018. When the Council of Eminent Persons, established as an advisory body by the new oppositional political alliance ('Alliance of Hope') (PH) government after the defeat of the Barisan Nasional (BN) government in May 2018, invited the Secretary General of MTUC, J. Solomon, to specify labour issues left behind by the former government, J. Solomon mentioned cost of living, job insecurity, inadequately skilling of workers for digital economy, dysfunctional tripartism, inflow and precarious situation of foreign migrant workers and lack of trade union rights in legal and administrative terms (the edge 14 May 2018, uploaded at the MTUC webpage).

MTUC's list of challenges 2018 includes many of the grievances discussed at the Langkawi symposium two decades before and added new issues of migrant workers, job security and 'industry 4.0' (digitalised production). The old problems have generally persisted and new problems have emerged with increased trade liberalisation, rising labour immigration and rapid technological change. So why have Malaysian trade unions not been able to revitalise and carve out a larger space for labour empowerment?

Within the broader picture of organised labour in Malaysia, this chapter is focused on trade unions in the manufacturing sector of Peninsular Malaysia (PM), on the one hand, and the MTUC, the peak association ('society') of unions that relates politically to the Malaysian government and labour-related state institutions, on the other. The reasons for this delimitation are as follows. First, manufacturing has been the main source of economic development and the sector reached the highest proportion of Malaysian employment during the 2000s, although the service sector (private and public) held the largest share of the labour force (Rasiah, Crinis and Lee, 2015).

Second, industrialisation has also been a core economic development strategy of Malaysian governments since independence 1957 enabling Malaysia to become a Newly-Industrialised Country in the 1990s (Jomo, 2007). Third, the MTUC is the only national and cross-sector labour body that is allowed to voice workers and unions' concerns in labour-related state institutions.[1]

This chapter is structured in the following way. After the introduction, there is a methodological section on theoretical and empirical choices. Thereafter, the generic issues of union revitalisation are addressed: the core challenges to organised labour in Malaysia in the last 20 years; the strategic changes undertaken; the results achieved and why; alternative forms of labour representation; and finally, this chapter concludes with theoretical implications of the revitalisation strategies employed by Malaysian unions during the twenty-first century.

Methodological clarifications

This chapter addresses the generic issues of the union revitalisation with a focus on the core challenges confronting Malaysian unions after the East Asian financial crisis in 1997–1998. The strategies of the unions and MTUC to deal with these challenges appear to include the typical strategies of 'union revival' identified in the 'varieties of unionism' (VoU) approach (Frege and Kelly, 2004). While 'strategy' in the VoU terminology means the successive deliberate configuration of ends and means pursuing medium and long-term goals, we use the term to describe the ongoing strategising process of formulating, implementing, evaluating and adjusting the combination, switching and sequencing of various specific strategies. The generic revitalisation strategies are organising, reform of union structures, international solidarity, labour–management partnership, political action and coalition-building (Turner, 2004: 4).

Although the union revitalising agenda is pertinent in Malaysia in 1997 as well as in 2018 and all types of revitalisation strategies seem to have been used, No generic union strategy from the VoU approach deals with the particular challenge of ethnic and national diversity that pervades the Malaysian workforce and society and embeds the trade unions in an ethno-political environment with an 'ethnocratic' political regime (ruling coalition) based on mono-ethnic political parties from Independence 1957 until 2018.

The VoU thinking is derived from studies of union revival in three types of large advanced industrial countries: liberal market economies (LMEs; USA, UK), coordinated market economies (CMEs; Germany) and Mediterranean market economies (MMEs; Spain and Italy), and VoU is framed by the structural-institutional analytics of 'varieties of capitalism' (VoC) (Hall and Soskice, 2001). Hence, the original VoC approach does not properly comprehend state-governed developing economies or smaller internationalised market economies like Malaysia. Ben Schneider's (2012) expanded 'typology' is more relevant but still insufficient.

How can the Malaysian trade union trajectory of the last twenty years be adequately conceptualised and understood in a revised VoC/VoU perspective. This theoretical question is addressed after the empirical analysis in the concluding section of this chapter, but it should be noted that this chapter is also informed by a larger 'worker empowerment' perspective that takes 'worker power' to be configured by and vary with workers' collective structural-economic, political-institutional, civic-societal and organisational powers (Wad, 2017; Dinah, 2018).

The empirical insights on which this chapter relies are drawn from field studies with visits, interviews and surveys on-and-off from 1983. During the two weeks visit in January–February 2018, the author updated his knowledge through consultations and interviews with a few mostly 'active' (but also retired) non-partisan 'non-establishment' (general secretary and industrial relations (IR) officers of industry unions, female non-governmental organisation (NGO) leader) and 'anti-establishment' partisan trade unionists (general secretaries, MTUC branch secretary and IR officers), labour-oriented NGOs (male activists) and politicians (one leading and one internal opposition figure of a core oppositional party) accessed through my personal network. To balance the critical perspective on the 'establishment' of the hegemonic United Malays National Organisation (UMNO) and the governing 'National Front' (BN) of mono-ethnic political parties, secondary sources from authorities and ruling organisations are used, too.

Core challenges confronting Malaysian trade unions in the early twenty-first century

From a worker empowerment perspective, associational or organisational power is the first pillar of power constituted by independent and democratic trade union formation and operation. It also includes total union membership, relative membership of the eligible workforce (union density) and collective agreement (CA) coverage with employers. Anything that impedes or prevents organisational empowerment is a challenge for the unions and their officials and staff and more generally worker empowerment, and such challenges amount in Malaysia in the twenty-first century (see Table 9.1).

The challenges vary in their importance and depth. The *first order* of core challenges is the low union density, small and fragmented unions and low levels of collective bargaining agreements which foster weak resources, finance and organisational capacity. Although total union membership increased from around 735,000 in 2000 to more than 900,000 from 2013 and women's membership exploded from above 300,000 in the early 2000s to more than 500,000 in the mid-2010s, MTUC's share of union membership declined from 66% in 2000 to 43% in 2014 (Kumar et al., 2013; MTUC, 2007; International Trade Union Congress (ITUC), 2015; Khairi and Faisal, 2017). Moreover, trade union density is below 10% for Malaysia[2] and has

Table 9.1 Internal and External Challenges for Trade Unions in Malaysia 1997–2018

Internal Challenges	*External Challenges*
• Fragmentation of the trade union movement organisationally, industrial, ethnically, politically and gender wise. • One peak national labour centre with status as 'society', not 'trade union', and with low organisational capacity for union support, labour advocacy and social mobilisation. • Small unions due to narrow legal and administrative space and scope of organising, collective bargaining, agreement and action. • Unevenness in unionisation (union density) of various industries and sectors but also regionally and nationally. • Democratic governance of membership by constitution but senior male dominance in practice due to organisational skills, learning or capturing union leadership by small group of leaders. • Intra- and especially inter-union cleavages preventing or weakening inter-union collaboration and consolidation (e.g., mergers). • Low levels of member engagement in many unions. • Weak financial base through member dues, yet check-off system and company paid time off for union officials obtainable by collective agreements. Unions' financial problems spill over to MTUC due to delayed or none payment and/or exit. Low levels of corruption due to intense control regime by state authorities. • Little reliance on external financial support for union daily operations from the international labour movement and ILO due to Malaysia's upper-middle-income status.	• Trade unions considered irrelevant in socialisation, schooling and public media mostly controlled by UMNO-led governments 1957–2018 and based on coalitions of mono-ethnic parties. • Low-wage (immigrant) labour reliant but diversified, foreign controlled and globalising export economy. • Huge government-linked business sector and export sector controlled by foreign MNCs. • Increasing levels of precarious employment within the formal sector especially among foreign migrant labour and domestic servants. • Institutionalised anti-union policies and practices by state authorities (extensive managerial rights, narrow legal space for union formation, bargaining and action and even worse in export-processing zones). • Legalistic IR system where some employment, trade union and collective bargaining rights are rudimentary legalised and secured by the Industrial Court but can be challenged in civil courts. • Weak employer organisations and pressure for company level and individualised wage bargaining. • Foreign and local employers' preferences for union-free companies with anti-union policy targeting industry unions while in-house unions might be temporarily accepted if industry union is threatening. • Employers apply civilian legalistic means of union-busting if defeated in the Industrial Relations system incurring high costs on unions in legal battles. • Macro-tripartism instituted but hollowed out during the twenty-first century. No mandatory institutionalisation of micro-bilateralism, but in-house unionism and voluntary labour–management consultations are allowed and accepted by the authorities. • Partisan politics by trade unions prohibited.

been declining most of the last twenty years. The average union membership is a little above 1,000 members and only one union has more than 50,000 members (National Union of Teaching Profession PM with 113,019 members in 2005). In the manufacturing sector, union density declined from around 13% in 1994 to 11% in 2005 (own estimations). More dramatically, the Electrical Industry Workers' Union (EIWU) that evolved into one of the largest trade unions and peaked with around 28,000 members in 2002 went down to around 11,000 members in 2017 (EIWU, 2017; Ministry of Human Resources Registrar of Trade Unions (MHR RTU), annual reports).

Centralised collective bargaining and agreement making (CBA) were conducted in the private and export-related sectors (plantations, mining, banking) in the 1960s, but it was only achieved briefly in automobile assembly manufacturing during the 1970s (Dass, 1991; Wad, 2004). Since the 1980s, CBA has been conducted at the company level in manufacturing, while centralised CBAs still prevail in the commercial plantation and the banking sectors for rank-and-file employees. While the National Union of Plantation Workers (NUPW) declined from near 110,000 members in 1980 to 40,000 in 2000, the National Union of Bank Employees (NUBE) rose from around 11,000 members in 1980 to more than 30,000 members in 2000 (RTU, annual reports). CBA is allowed in the private sector but forbidden in the public service sector since the 1970s. CBA coverage is at least as low as the overall union density in the private sector and that is below 5% on average (with industry variety). Collective bargaining coverage has been estimated to be at the very low level of 2.4% in 2008 and further down to 1.1% in 2012 and up to 1.3% in 2016 (ILO, 2018b).[3]

The *second order* of core challenges of Malaysian unions in the twenty-first century is the narrow legal-administrative space for union formation and operations and the low level of union recognition and poor legitimacy among employers, public authorities and the general public system (Peetz and Todd, 2000; Todd, Lansbury and Davis, 2006; Ramasamy and Rowley, 2008). In 2010, the International Trade Union Confederation (formerly the ICFTU until 2006) classified Malaysia as a country with systematic violations of international labour rights, and this classification has not been changed since then (ITUC 2018). For example, the ILO Covenant 87 on employees' freedom to form trade unions is not adopted by Malaysia, and trade unions must register with the authorities (RTU) and stay within narrow domains of industry, trade, occupation or establishment and are confined to bargain on a limited scope of labour-related issues. Trade unions at the federal level is not permitted, at best regionally (PM or below) or state-wise.

Collective actions, such as strikes, are nearly impossible to undertake and disputes are predominantly refereed to mediation and arbitration by the Industrial Court, while sympathy strikes are forbidden. The limited space for CBA and action is driven by an anti-union political establishment (UMNO and its governing alliances 1957–2018) and anti-union foreign and domestic employers of multinational corporations (MNCs), business groups and small- and medium-sized firms (Kumar et al. 2013). These two ruling forces have conducted institutionalised union-busting that has weakened organised labour from the early days of Malaysia's Independence.

The *third order* of challenges relates to the increasing flexibilisation of labour in the wake of globalisation and the ethnic composition and political regime of 'ethnocracy'. Union-busting has been deepened with the adoption of export-oriented labour-intensive and low wage industrialisation as a core economic development strategy since the 1970s, based on foreign direct investment by MNCs and especially by market-leading American corporations in the global electronics industry (Rasiah, Crinis and Lee 2015; Rasiah, 2017). National and industry-based unionisation has been prohibited in leading export industries (textile and garments, electronics) and fragmented in the government-linked sector of industrial or services companies (GLCs). Textile and garment workers were only allowed to form state-based unions. Even though the five state-based textile and garment unions formed a union federation in 1989 at the peak of their membership strength and a declining union density (from around 22% in 1981/1982 to 14% in 1993/1994, own calculations) the state-based unions ended up approximating enterprise unions. The unions were later allowed to form a national union in the 2000s, but the leaders were not keen on the idea and nothing happened (Crinis, 2017:26).

With economic globalisation speeding up since the 1990s (World Trade Organisation, WTO) and 2000s (ASEAN Free Trade Area (AFTA), China) new business strategies of outsourcing and offshoring became prevalent in the Global North and over time also among East Asian NICs, newly industrialising and industrialised countries. In Malaysia, temporary, fixed employment contracts and hiring of foreign labour under precarious conditions in manufacturing became prevalent during the 2000s and reached a point of providing labour contractors with employer status derailing labour organising. However, in the mid-2010s, the Malaysian and the US governments signed the 'Labour Consistency Plan' as a prerequisite for the labour-related chapter of the Trans-Pacific Partnership (TPP) Agreement (Dinah 2018, 14). Thus, Malaysia had to adapt to US demands for less restrictions on trade unions. After the election of Donald Trump as US President, the USA withdrew from the TPP in 2017, but the remaining countries signed in 2018 a modified agreement, the Comprehensive and Progressive Agreement for TPP. This agreement has not yet been ratified and enforced, and it is less 'progressive' for trade unionism.

Strategic changes undertaken by Malaysian unions

The Malaysian trade unions and their single cross-sector umbrella organisation, the MTUC, have been quite consistent adhering to a union strategy for an independent, democratic trade union movement consisting of larger (industry-based) unions with branch or worksite committees, ongoing organising campaigns to widen membership, counter-partnership with employers (not getting too close with non-trusted management) based on CBAs to improve members' (and by law all workers within the orbit of the CA) wage and working conditions, political-corporate tripartism at macro level and ideological-political support for politicians and parties that protected and promoted workers' and unions' interests (MTUC, 1997, 2013; Jomo, 2014; Jomo and Todd, 1994). This 'mission' was framed and supported internationally by the affiliation of Malaysian unions to the International Conference on Fourier Transform and Uniform Continuity (ICFTUC) and its trade secretariats (since 2006 ITUC and Global Union Federations (GUFs)) and Malaysia's membership of the ILO and UN.

At the Langkawi symposium in the late 1990s, the MTUC formulated a strategy that only slightly deviated from the traditional approach of accepting enterprise unionism for electronics workers as a stepping stone to industry-based unionisation and the downplaying of affirmative policy-making in union matters. But in-house unionism never gained momentum among electronic workers, leadership of new unions were often co-opted into 'company' unions and made defunct. Unions pushed for an industry union, and a compromise was struck in 2010 when the Ministry of Human Resources allowed the formation of four regionally based, multi-state Electronic Industry Employees Unions (EIEUs) in PM (Wad, 2012).

During the 2000s, issues of domestic (women) workers and immigrant workers rose on the MTUC agenda and MTUC took a more proactive approach with externally funded project activities and concomitant influence (ILO, ITUC, GUFs, national donors) (Ford, 2013; Crinis, 2017; Dinah 2018). Increasing economic globalisation during the 1990s continued after the East Asian financial crisis 1997–1998 with intensifying regionalisation through AFTA and China's access to the WTO followed by deeper regional economic integration. The attack on decent work conditions (such as regular employment and living wages protected by CAs and legislation against unfair dismissal) in favour of precarious employment caused unions to question the conditions for immigrant and domestic workers and call for minimum wage legislation for a living wage, unemployment insurance scheme, regulation of labour contracting and admission of immigrant labour. Also the cost of living like consumer prices and taxation, housing rents, road tariffs, etc. were targeted through public campaigning by labour organisations.

The trade unions had diverging opinions and favoured different tactics and strategies to promote these issues, choosing to align with government and BN-coalition forces ('the establishment'), to oppose it by engaging individually in oppositional parties or in NGOs and civil society organisations (CSOs) ('anti-establishment') or to stay free of partisan controversies and pursuing a political but non-partisan agenda ('non-establishment'). During the East Asian financial crisis 1997–1998, tripartism was reactivated by the government and pro-government actors within MTUC gained momentum. But with the political showdown followed by the anti-establishment 'reformasi' movement tripartism was again brought into disarray. Since the mid-2000s, the MTUC has engaged more actively with civil, political and social rights movements. However, during the early 2010s, the MTUC became increasingly marginalised in tripartite institutions. More recently, during the TPP free trade negotiations, the MTUC again called for labour laws to be reformed.

The 2010s were a turbulent time for the leadership of MTUC. Events reached a climax in 2016 with the creation of an anti 'anti-establishment' alliance which elected the current leadership for 2017–2019 (interviews with general secretary, MTUC branch secretary, union IR officers, January–February 2018). The new leadership immediately was in crisis as the result of the MTUC general secretary, J. Solomon public supporting the PH while the union's president, Abdul Halim, supported the governing alliance (BN) during the run-up to the General Election 2018. These divergent positions taken by the general secretary and president of the MTUC contravened the unions' traditional approach and put the whole organisation in jeopardy as a non-partisan socio-political organisation.

Table 9.2 summarises the strategies applied and combined during the last 20 years. The next section will discuss the results of union strategising and the conditions that have influenced the lack of achievements.

Table 9.2 Union Renewal Strategies and Their Implications in Malaysia 1997–2018

Strategy	*Applicability*	*Potential Benefits*	*Potential Risks*
Reform of union structures	MTUC and industry unions prefer a limited number of larger national industry unions. Union federations are formed. In-house and then regional unions allowed in the key export-oriented electronic industry.	Besides generic benefits of 'licence to organise' in-house unionism failed and regional unionism was invented for the electronic industry (2010) but has only made limited advances so far.	Mergers are prohibited across related industries and seldom used within industries. Federations do not work as the power lies within the union. Management has often captured in-house unions and used them against industry unions.
Organising	Generic feature of multi-company unionising but not among in-house unions and depending on organisers (union staff and activists) and financial resources.	Organising new members among its existing base or new segments (migrant workers) generates additional resources of activists, finance, ideas, etc. Use of multiple strategies necessary.	Anti-union employers and authorities react with harassment and union-busting, blacklisting of activists, company restructuring, outsourcing, legal and prolonged disputes that drain unions for financial means.

Strategy	*Applicability*	*Potential Benefits*	*Potential Risks*
International solidarity	Malaysian unions are by and large excluded from international development aid due to middle-income status of country. Projects for migrant workers supported. GUF intervention important and on the rise.	GUFs are consolidating their presence, e.g., IndustriALL Malaysian Council and UNI National Labour Centre. International support can be decisive for union recognition by MNC subsidiaries or affiliates.	Accountability of union leaders and beneficiaries redirected to foreign donor organisations. GUFs have been criticised for supporting Northern vested interests, e.g., Northern MNCs.
Labour–management partnerships	Union recognition and collective bargaining at the workplace level are constitutive for union work, but management's widespread and deep-seated anti-unionism prevent trustful and fair partnerships.	Limited legal-administrative scope of organising, collective bargaining and action reduce potential benefits. Adversarial labour–management relations reduce employee productivity and engagement, invite to resistance and militancy.	Union leaders in the private sector fear co-optation by management. Union leaders might shift side becoming HR-managers or getting career minded and less concerned about union and membership issues.
Political action	Unions are legally defined as socio-economic organisations and prohibited from partisan politics. Macro-tripartism has been preferred for union involvement in labour-related policies via MTUC, the only national labour centre in the twenty-first century. Ambivalent relationships with the political parties.	Transforming anti-labour policies, laws and administrative practices requires political power. Concessions have been achieved by internal mobilisation and external pressure via international trade negotiations (between Malaysia and USA). Appeals to ILO have backfired with government sanctions.	Constituted as a 'structural opposition' to the dominant political-ethnocratic regime (1957–2018) trade unions have been subordinated national development strategies and risk severe retaliation if intervening in partisan politics and general elections. Unions have temporarily been involved during macro-economic or political crises (1997–1998).
Coalition-building	Ambivalent relation with NGOs and CSOs where these voluntary organisations criticise unions and position themselves as labour organisations. Unions consider themselves as hegemonic in labour affairs.	Trade unions mobilised and engaged selectively with civil rights and social movements in the 2000s in relation to unfair development of workers' livelihood. Multi-ethnic or trans-ethnic learning took place through grass-root engagement and mobilisation for just causes.	Being squeezed politically into a weak tripartite position (MTUC) and kept financially fragile trade unions were also ambivalent taking on social movement unionism and they lost momentum relative to the 'reformasi' sociopolitical movement during the twenty-first century.

Achievements of union strategising

No significant increases in union empowerment have occurred during the last twenty years. However, small concessions have been obtained by way of applying and combining different revitalisation strategies that addressed key organisational and political challenges see Table 9.2.

Within the electronics industry, regional (multi-state)-based unions have been permitted by the government, but not a national (PM) industry union for electronics workers. The government has still not ratified the ILO Covenant 87, and electronics MNCs are still fighting unionisation with all means (MTUC Selangor, 2014): harassment and busting of activists and unionists, restructuring or relocation of companies, formation of 'company' (in-house) unions if union-free shops are impossible to sustain but busting in-house unionists if they do not comply with management (e.g., German Infineon Technologies Melaka in 2016). In the Northern Region, around Penang, the new union finally succeeded overcoming management resistance and administrative obstructions organising around 3,500 members in three companies and extracting recognition and a CA from one company, but it took years (interview with IR officer of the EIEUNRPM, 04 February 2018). Less progress was made in the other three regions.

GUFs have some impact, especially on European MNCs, not least if they have Global Framework Agreements (GFAs) with the MNCs. Management–labour partnerships, based on mutual recognition and fairness, have been promoted with external support (e.g., Infineon Technologies Kulim, Kedah) and might have a demonstration effect among anti-union managers, but their sentiments are deep-seated and difficult to change (interview with union IR officer, 4 February 2018).

Massive hiring of foreign migrant labour has created another barrier to organising workers due to their extremely precarious employment situation. Domestic workers do not even count as workers but as 'domestic servants'; they are not covered by labour laws and they do not have the right to unionise (Dinah, 2018). Both these segments have been addressed by the unions and MTUC with the support from international unions, ILO and international aid donors. These efforts may partly explain the significant rise of female union membership during the twenty-first century from above 300,000 in the early 2000s to more than 500,000 in the mid-2010s (comments by Kumar et al., 2013; Khairi and Faisal, 2017; Ariffin, 2018).

Union domains have not been widened in law or administrative practice to form national industry unions, with the possible exception of the textile and garment industry where state-based industry unions have a union federation and were allowed to a former national industry union but were declined by union leaders (Crinis, 2017). The integration of in-house unions and the industry union into a union federation in the automotive industry also failed. However, in-house unions among the nationally protected automobile companies formed an enterprise union federation (interview with general secretary of industry union, 30 January 2018).

The concession by MTUC to temporary accept enterprise unionism, even in industries with industry unions, did not result in increased union density in the electronics industry (Wad, 2012). Failure also occurred in other industries where management exploited the 'in-house' union card if industry unions knocked on the factory gate (Wad, 2004). In terms of union organising and union fragmentation, this strategy backfired and may have created a bad reputation for in-house unions as 'company' unions. It is an open question if the rise of enterprise unionism in Malaysia's manufacturing sector will result in more harmonious IR at the company level, as sought by the government's micro-corporatist policy of in-house unionism (Jomo, 2014). Alternatively, in the longer term, it might generate more militant workers and unions. The South Korean trajectory has demonstrated an alternative option and outcome of this kind of workplace unionism that was instituted top-down by law in 1980 only to see the 'Great Worker Struggle' being triggered in 1987–1989 as part of the larger democratisation movement (Lee and Yi, 2012).

The efforts to improve the legal-administrative space for unions through tripartite institutions and advocacy largely failed. Administrative practices were not made more legal, effective or efficient: such as processing recognition claims by unions for workplaces which they organised. Employers could exploit the legalistic IR system of Malaysia and at least postpone the enforcement of union recognition, if not prevent it. Legislative changes did not assist unions in any important cases. One exception, however, was the enforcement of minimum wage legislation in 2013 and the unemployment insurance scheme in 2018. Both of these successes, however, only indirectly empower organised labour, and they illustrate the importance of partisan politics and the powerlessness of organised labour when it is excluded from party politics, and it becomes marginalised in tripartite negotiations by the ruling elite. Only when there was external pressure for labour reforms, following the TPP negotiations with the USA, the Malaysian government opened up for consultations with the MTUC. However, this window closed with the election of Donald Trump as President of the USA and the withdrawal of the USA from TPP in 2017 (Kishnam, 2016).

Table 9.2 provides an overview of union strategies and counter-strategies and actions by authorities and employers and the outcomes of union strategising for the period 1997–2018.

Alternative forms of worker representation

Workers at the (micro) enterprise level have few alternative forms of representation than being member of a trade union and the union's worksite committee. Company-level joint consultation committees (JCCs) or labour–management committees (LMCs) are not mandatory, but these mechanisms were recommended in the Code of Conduct for Industrial Harmony of 1975. JCCs or LMCs can be established by management or by CA.

Occupational safety and health committees (OSHCs) with management and non-management representation (including union representatives) were required by the occupational safety and health (OSH) law of 1994 in companies with forty employees or more. MTUC established an OSH department and programme after the Langkawi symposium with the support of Danish LO-FTF Council for Development based on development aid. MTUC announced an OSH policy in 2002 targeting OSH in electronic and construction industries (MTUC, 2009: 26). Based on a survey in 2003, MTUC stated that a majority of big electronic companies had established OSHCs, but most employee representatives had been selected by the management and not elected by the employees as stipulated by law (MTUC, 2009: 26–27). In 2008, 4,337 manufacturing firms had OSHCs estimated to a coverage of around 50% and without performing quite well (Farouk, Richardson and Santhapparaj, 2011).

Although labour parties with explicit socialist or labour-oriented objectives have been allowed, they have enjoyed little electoral support and attracted few members, but some have been part of a chain that generated strong oppositional parties. Recently, the Malaysian Workers' Party (MWP), established around 1980, combined with the moderate Islamic party, Amanah which had been denied registration. The MWP was reshaped into a party that joined the PH-oppositional alliance and is now part of the PH-governing coalition. The largest opposition party, People's Justice Party (PKR), was formed through a merger of the National Justice Party (PKN) that initiated the 'reformasi' movement, and the Malaysian People's Party (PRM), a former socialist party. PKR is basically a social-liberal party committed to social justice, equality, equal rights, rule of law and a liberal democracy in an open and regulated market economy.

Low and declining numbers of union membership, in both absolute or relative terms, weakened the voice, resources and public impact of MTUC and the trade unions in the eyes of political parties. As a consequence, the labour movement lost the mediating role that unions played between the workers as voters and the political parties, in the past. In the run-up to the general election 2018 one leading opposition politician frankly described the situation as follows:

> We announce a policy, and if the workers like it, they work for us. The unions lost that mediator role. In that sense I say that the unions now are much weaker. It's big time outside the labour movement.
>
> (Interview with leading opposition politician, 31-01-2018)

The main avenue for alternative worker representation has been the Malaysian civil society that has included several NGOs or CSOs with a labour orientation or agenda. One is the Labour Resource Centre (LRC) that was set up by grass-root-oriented unions as a labour information and training centre with a strong international network (e.g., Asian Workers Solidarity Links) that could mobilise international support for union recognition at MNC transplants (Dass, 1991; Wad, 2013). The NGO, Tenaganita, took an initial interest in the cause of plantation and factory (women) workers in the early 1990s. It subsequently developed into an internationally known NGO when it concentrated on issues of migrants and refugees in Malaysia, within a broader human rights framework. Environmental NGOs, such as Friends of the Earth Malaysia (SAM), have also investigated and exposed OSH problems in plantations. With NGO support from abroad, the Malaysian Association of Working Women (MAOWW) was established in 2002 by a former female trade unionist to promote the cause of single working mothers and pursued an agenda of establishing women centres with child care institution and consultation, education and legal assistance services for women irrespective of their employment status.

Probably, the politically most influential NGO has been the Coalition for Free and Fair Elections (Bersih) that was established by five oppositional political parties in 2005 with support by MTUC and many NGOs. It was restructured into a pure NGO in 2010. Bersih mobilised tremendous support for election reform and genuine democratisation. It paved the way for the political transition in 2018. However, the electoral system continues to be rigged through gerrymandering, disproportional allocation of mandates, unequal access to public media, money politics, etc. Bersil mobilised across ethnic and social lines against a corrupt and authoritarian regime led by Prime Minister, Najib Razak that became increasing linked to the 1 Malaysia Development Berhad (1MDB) corruption scandal where billions of Malaysian Ringgits (RMs) disappeared (Rewcastle, 2018).

Theoretical implications of the Malaysian union trajectory in the early twenty-first century

The structure and institutions of Malaysia's political economy made revitalisation of organised labour a Sisyphean endeavour blocking or impeding strategising that occurred, in advanced market economies. According to the VoU perspective, participating in labour market struggles of organising, collective bargaining and actions was the primary option in LMEs, while engaging in industry-wide CBA and multi-level tripartism was more appropriate in CMEs. Joining a partisan political battle seemed most relevant in the Southern European or MMEs. None of these three ways of strategising worked in Malaysia. Why?

The Malaysia pattern does not fit directly into the classic or even the revised and enhanced typology of the VoC theory (Schneider, 2012). The strong state and the ethno-political regime obscure the match between Malaysia and the hierarchical market economy type of Latin America and Southeast Asia (Gomez and De Micheaux, 2017; Gomez et al., 2018). However, the dual hierarchical dimension of Latin American market economies, with foreign MNCs and domestic business groups dominating the economy against weakly organised and skilled workers, could be differentiated further by adding a third and fourth dimension of state-linked firms and ethno-political cleavages, respectively. In this VoC type, the labour market is segmented into three main territories: first, a state-linked sector (government-linked investment companies (GLICs) and GLCs) with Malay labour in in-house unions; second, a foreign-controlled export sector increasingly hiring non-unionised foreign migrant labour, and third, Malaysian big businesses which dominate the domestic market and employ a mix of plural ethnic Malaysians unorganised, company- or industry-unionised workers. This complex economy is again embedded in a regional and global economy that is deepened by the AFTA and the inroads made by China and India into Southeast Asia via WTO and bilateral trade agreements.

Considering the three-pronged structure of the Malaysian market economy Malaysia can be classified as a particular sub-type of a hierarchical market economy with a strong state-governed sector and a state that is authoritarian and ethno-politically construed (at least until 2018) and severely restricts social classes from organising and acting politically, economically and ideologically or discursively. Accordingly, the Malaysian trade unions and the labour movement have not been able to drive labour empowerment, socio-economic upgrading and political democratisation with the available strategies of union revitalisation, except where there is ambivalent coalition-building with civil society groups and indirect partisan political engagement. A political regime change was necessary to transform anti-labour institutions and allow organised labour more space for action.

Although the 'reformasi' (political reform) movement of 1998, in its first round, failed to achieve a political regime change, as happened in Indonesia, the mobilisation of civil rights and social justice activists and NGOs paved the way for a second round during the twenty-first century. Organised labour aligned with middle-class CSOs and movements that created more pluralistic and multi-ethnic discourses and attitudes (Croucher and Miles, 2018). This civil society movement gained increasing electoral support in the general elections of 2008 and 2013 and finally the PH unseated the UMNO-led government after sixty years of rule. The PH won with a broad agenda for social justice, democratic reforms, anti-corruption, recognition of core labour rights and promotion of a decent working life including abolition of a goods and service tax. But can and will the new government transform the ethno-political hierarchical market economy of Malaysia?

The old and the new political establishment both subscribe to the 'Vision 2020' whereby Malaysia seeks to achieve the status of an advanced or developed market economy by year 2020. But in the revised VoC perspective, there are three options available to high-income economies: LME, CME and MME. These offer different roles for organised labour to play. Moreover, the static VoC theory does not explain how a higher-middle country can make the transition and catch-up. The VoC must be translated into a more dynamic theory of structural and institutional transformation. The obvious question is whether the VoU approach might add such a dynamic dimension considering its emphasis on strategy and agency of unions in relation to labour, capital and state?

One strategy for the achieving LME status is transforming the economy to a radical or incremental manufacturing (and business service) economy through massive investment in R&D, vocational and higher education, innovative clusters of state institutions and corporations. Rising external and internal corporate competition could generate such a transformation if domestic companies were supported to overcome competitive disadvantages, without relying too much on cheap and unskilled labour through, e.g., labour immigration. For such a transformation to occur, the state-linked financial and corporate entities would have to be privatised thoroughly and developmental state features dismantled. However, the transition would empower labour structurally through industrial-technological upgrading of workplaces and value chains and though labour market upskilling and human resource development for employability in a high-income economy.

A development strategy aimed at achieving a more labour-friendly advanced market economy is to strategise for CME or MME status. This sociopolitical construction of an innovative industrial economy would entail freeing up labour market, organising and allow free union restructuring and partisan or civil society participation. Moreover, trade unions should be able to push for higher wages and better work conditions and social benefits through CBA and collective action. Acknowledging the dialectical relations of capital and labour, having converging and diverging interests inclusive and comprehensive tripartist institutions, must be in place to accommodate industrial strife. Such trilateral or multilateral collaboration or partnership could also enable employee innovation and participation and facilitate collective forms of organisational innovation (institutional advantages). This could stimulate massive and targeted investment for higher productivity and 'green' growth. It could require the development of a sustainable society with highly skilled workers and strong worker-oriented or controlled financial (pension) funds undertaking social responsible investments. This endeavour could be supported by the new global organisations of organised labour, the ITUC and the GUFs and their regional affiliates together with the ILO and the UN within the comprehensive sustainable development goals (SDG) agenda.

A dynamic interpretation of Malaysia's development, in a VoU/VoC perspective, would not necessarily forecast a pro-labour outcome. In Malaysia, processes of social transformation may also be exploited by forces of the old establishment for the re-creation of a more political-hierarchical market economy with an authoritarian and neo-ethnocratic political regime. Such an outcome would marginalise and disempower organised labour and progressive CSOs and networks. The future is not predetermined.

Acknowledgement

Thanks to all Malaysians who took time off for interviewing or discussions; to the editors of the anthology and Patricia Todd, Vicki Crinis, Rohana Ariffin and Syed Shahir for reviews and constructive comments; and to Arokia Dass for housing the author during his fieldwork in 2018. The usual disclaimers prevail.

Notes

1 MTUC has affiliates among both private and public unions. The public sector employees' union federation, Congress of Union of Employees in the Public and Civil Services Malaysia (CUEPACS), is also participating in tripartite institutions. The Union Network International (UNI)'s local affiliate, Malaysian Labour Centre (UNI-MLC) is a service sector-based umbrella organisation that was formed in early 2000s and claims to be an alternative national labour organisation with seventy-five union members with around 300,000 members (Dinah 2018, 9 note 8).
2 Malaysia is a federation and constitutional monarchy and composed of thirteen states and three federal territories that geographically cover Peninsular Malaysia, Sabah, Sarawak and Labuan.
3 These figures are probably too low because non-union members of a company with collective agreement (CA) are by law covered by the CA, too (Campbell 2001, 431). Public sector unions are not allowed to strike CAs with their state employers.

References

Ariffin R (1997) Changing employment structures and their effects on industrial relations in Malaysia. *Economic and Labour Relations Review* 8 (1): 44–56.

Campbell D (2001) Social dialogue and labour market adjustment in East Asia after the crisis. In: Betcherman G and Islam R (eds.) *East Asian Labor Markets and the Economic Crisis. Impacts Responses & Lessons*. Washington: Word Bank and ILO, 423–465.

Crinis V (2017) The fragmentation of the clothing and textile trade union movement in Malaysia. In: Crinis V and Vickers A (eds.) *Labour in the Clothing Industry in the Asia Pacific*. London: Routled, 43–59.

Croucher, R. and Miles L (2018) Ethnicity, popular democratic movements and labour in Malaysia. *Economic and Industrial Democracy* 39 (2): 294–311.

Dass A (1991) *Not Beyond Repair. Reflections of a Malaysian Trade Unionist*. Hong Kong: AMRC.

Dinah V (2018) *Trade Unions in Transformation. Organising Migrant Workers in Malaysia: Ways out of Precarity*. Berlin: Friedrich-Ebert-Stiftung.

Electrical Industry Workers' Union (EIWU) (2017) *Laboran Majlis Tertinggi 2014–2017*. Subang Jaya: EIWU.

Farouk U Richardson S and Santhapparaj A (2011) Occupational safety and health committees: how fares the pulse of the self-regulatory system in Malaysian manufacturing firms? *International Journal of Trade, Economics and Finance* 2 (5): 412–418.

Ford M (2013) The global union federations and temporary labour migration in Malaysia. *Journal of Industrial Relations* 55 (2): 260–276.

Frege C and Kelly J (eds.) (2004) *Varieties of Unionism. Strategies for Union Revitalization in a Globalizing Economy.* Oxford: Oxford University Press.

Gomez, ET and De Micheaux EL (2017) Diversity of Southeast Asian capitalisms: evolving state-business relations in Malaysia. *Journal of Contemporary Asia* 47 (5): 792–814.

Gomez T et al. (2018) *Minister of Finance Incorporated. Ownership and Control of Corporate Malaysia.* Petaling Jaya: SIRDC/palgrave macmillan.

Hall PA and Soskice D (2001) *Varieties of Capitalism. The Institutional Foundations of Comparative Advantage.* Oxford: Oxford University Press.

ILO (2018) ILO Stat. Collective bargaining coverage rate (%). Accessed on 21–06–2018.

International Trade Union Confederation (ITUC) (2018) *The ITUC Survey of violations of trade union rights.* Geneva: ITUC, https://survey.ituc-csi.org/Malaysia.html?lang=en. Accessed 21–06–2018.

International Trade Union Confederation (ITUC) (2015) List of Affiliated Organisations 2014.

Jomo KS (2007) Industrialization and Industrial Policy in Malaysia. In: Jomo KS (ed.) *Malaysian Industrial Policy.* Singapore: NUS Press, 1–34.

Jomo KS (2014) 'Malaysia Incorporated': Corporatism a la Mahathir. *Institutions and Economies* 6 (1): 73–94.

Jomo KS and Todd P (1994) *Trade Unions and the State in Peninsular Malaysia.* Oxford: Oxford University Press.

Khairi M and Faisal A (2017) Where are we. *Slides* to ILO Regional on Strengthening Governance in EPZS/GSC Through Promoting GFA and Other Instruments, Jakarta 29th – 31th May 2017.

Kishnam G (2016) MTUC Urges Malaysia To Implement Labour Laws Reforms Regardless of TPPA's Uncertainty, www.mtuc.org.my/mtuc-urges-malaysia.... Accessed 14–08–2018.

Kumar N, Lucio MM and Rose RC (2013) Workplace industrial relations in a developing environment: barriers to renewal within unions in Malaysia. *Asia Pacific Journal of Human Resources* 51: 22–44.

Lee B-H and Yi S (2012) Organisational transformation towards industry unionism in South Korea. *Journal of Industrial Relations* 54 (4): 476–493.

Malaysian Trades Union Congress (MTUC) (1997) *MTUC Langkawi Charter – the Role of the Labour Movement in the 21st Century.* National Symposium, 14–16 April 1997. Pulau Langkawi, Kedah: MTUC.

Malaysian Trades Union Congress (MTUC) (2007) www.mtuc.org.my/membership.htm, Accessed 20–08–2007.

Malaysian Trades Union Congress (MTUC) (2009) *MTUC 60th Anniversary Commemorative Publication.* Subang Jaya: MTUC.

Malaysian Trades Union Congress (MTUC) (2013) About MTUC, www.mtuc.org.my/about-us/. Accessed 14–08–2018.

MTUC Selangor (2014) Memorandum calling for an end of all forms of union busting and violation of worker rights, www.mtuc.org.my/memorandum calling for an end of all forms of union busting and violation of worker rights. Accessed 14–08–2018.

Ministry of Human Resources (MHR) *Annual Report of the Trade Union Registry (RTU)* MHR: Kuala Lumpur, various years.

Peetz D and Todd P (2000) Malaysian Industrial Relations at Century's Turn: Vision 2020 or a spectre of the past, www.mngt.waikato.ac.nz/airaanz/.

Ramasamy N (2008) The Future of the Trade Union Movement in Malaysia. *Paper* presented at the MTUC/ACILS National Workshop, 21.22 January 2008.

Ramasamy N and Rowley C (2008) Trade unions in Malaysia: Complexity of a state-employer system. In: Benson J and Zhu Y (eds.) *Trade Unions in Asia. An Economic and Sociological Analysis.* London: Routledge, 121–139.

Rasiah R (2017) The industrial policy experience of the electronics industry in Malaysia. In: Page J and Tarp F (eds.) *The Practice of Industrial Policy. Government-Business Coordination in Africa and East Asia.* Oxford: OUP, 123–144.

Rasiah R and Chua T (1998) Strength of trade unions in Southeast Asia. In: Rasiah R and Hofman N (eds.) *Workers on the Brink. Unions, Exclusion and Crisis in Southeast Asia.* Singapore: Friedrich-Ebert-Stiftung, 15–46.

Rasiah R Crinis V and Lee H-A (2015) Industrialization and labour in Malaysia. *Journal of the Asia Pacific Economy* 20(1): 77–99.

Rewcastle C (2018) Notes on a scandal. *Mekong Review* 3 (4): 3.

Schneider B (2012) Contrasting capitalisms: Latin America in comparative perspective. In: Santiso J and Dayton-Johnson J (eds.) *The Oxford Handbook of Latin American Political Economy.* Oxford: Oxford University Press, 381–402.

Todd P, Lansbury R D and Davis E (2006) Industrial relations in Malaysia: Some proposals for reform. *Philippine Journal of Labor and Industrial Relations* 61 (1): 70–84.

Turner L (2004) Why revitalize? Labour's urgent mission in a contested global economy. In: Frege C M and Kelly J (eds.) *Varieties of Unionism. Strategies for Union Revitalization in a Globalizing Economy.* Oxford: Oxford University Press, 1–10.

Wad P (2004) Transforming industrial relations: the case of the Malaysian auto industry. In: Elmhirst R and Saptari R (eds.) *Labour in Southeast Asia. Local processes in a Globalised World.* London: RoutledgeCurzon, 235–264.

Wad P (2012) Revitalising the Malaysian trade union movement – the case of the electronic industry. *The Journal of Industrial Relations* 54 (4): 494–509.

Wad P (2013) Getting labour rights right at a foreign controlled company in Malaysia. A global labour network perspective. *Geoforum* 44: 52–61.

Wad P (2017) The Asian automotive industry and labour organising. In: Hansen A and Nielsen K B (eds.) *Cars, Automobility and Development in Asia. Wheels of Change.* London: Routledge, 36–61.

10 Worker representation in a segmented and globalised Philippine economy

Rene E. Ofreneo

Introduction

The right of workers to form unions and to be consulted on labour policies is recognised in the Philippine legal system. Kate Bailey (1996), former director of the Manila office of the International Labor Organisation (ILO), observed that the Philippines 'has one of the most advanced labour enactments in Asia-Pacific Region' (p. 34).

The labour enactments that Bailey was referring to are the provisions in the *Labour Code of the Philippines* (1974), which draws inspiration from the 1935 Constitution and the 1987 Constitution (Anvil, 2005). The 1935 Constitution mandates the State, under Section 5, Article II, to promote 'social justice to insure the well-being and economic security of all the people'. It also guarantees the right of the people 'to form associations or societies not contrary to law' (Section 1, Article III).

On the other hand, the 1987 Constitution is even more explicit and emphatic on the various rights of the workers. Section 3, Article XIII, provides for the following:

> *The State shall afford full protection to labour, local and overseas, organised and unorganised*, and promote full employment and equality of employment opportunities for all.
>
> *It shall guarantee the rights of all workers to self-organisation, collective bargaining and negotiations*, and peaceful concerted activities, including the right to strike in accordance with law. *They shall be entitled to security of tenure, humane conditions of work, and a living wage. They shall also participate in policy and decision-making processes affecting their rights and benefits as may be provided by law.*
>
> *The State shall promote the principle of shared responsibility between workers and employers* and the preferential use of voluntary modes in settling dispute...
>
> (underscoring supplied)

The above rights are reflected in the *Labour Code*. Although enacted in 1974 by a martial-law government, the *Labour Code* expressly recognises the right of workers to form unions, bargain collectively and participate in policy and decision-making processes affecting their rights, duties and welfare. The *Labour Code* also enshrines the principle of tripartism in the formulation of government policies related to employment, wages, social security, dispute settlement and workers' rights.

And yet, the number of workers organised into unions in the Philippines for collective bargaining purposes is appallingly small. As gathered by the ILO Manila Office, in its *Decent Work Country Diagnostics* (2017), there were 17,245 registered unions in the private sector in 2016, and yet, only 1,126 of these unions have collective bargaining agreements (CBAs).These CBAs covered a total of 200,476 workers, a figure equivalent to half of 1% of the total employed of 40 million. Moreover, the CBA rates have been going down since 2003.

So, what accounts for the low rate of unionism and declining CBA coverage despite what is supposedly to be a favourable and pro-union legal system in the Philippines?

The thesis of this chapter is simple: Despite the relatively long history of unionism and pro-CBA labour law system, the trade union movement has remained weak and divided due to the fragmented character of the industrialisation process and the anti-union attitude among corporations and the political leadership. These developments are further accentuated in the era of globalisation. And yet, the trade union movement, despite its limited base, has managed to push for a number of protective labour laws and keep a seat in the tripartite industrial relations system, precisely because of the impact of decades of union struggle for workers' rights under various administrations.

This chapter begins with a historical overview of industrial development, labour law development and unionism. This is followed by a summation of the structure of the labour market under economic globalisation and the challenges facing trade unions in asserting workers' voice in industry and society.

Historical overview

The struggle for workers' rights during the American colonial period

Trade unionism in the Philippines has a fairly long history. It dates back to the turn of the twentieth century when the American imperialist forces took over from Spain control over the archipelago.

However, the field for trade union organising in the first decade of American rule was naturally limited. The American colonisers inherited a backward agrarian archipelago producing a few export crops – sugar, abaca, tobacco and coconut – for the world market. The Americans strengthened further this export crop orientation by imposing a one-sided free trade policy on the colony through the Payne-Aldrich Tariff Act passed by the US

Congress in 1909 (Abelarde, 1947). Free trade allowed all the American goods to enter the Philippines free of duty and in unlimited quantities. These were mostly in the form of finished products, given the advanced industrial development of the United States. The same duty-free treatment was accorded Philippine exports, mainly primary products, given the underdeveloped character of the colony.

In terms of trade union development and government policy towards unionism, the American colonial period can be divided into the following phases:

1900s: Decades of union suppression. The first workers' federation in the Philippines – *Union Obrera Democratica (UOD)* – was formed in 1902 on the initiative of the printing workers belonging to the *Union Impresores y Litograficos de Filipinas* (Carrol, 1961). Operating under a highly repressive atmosphere and with a limited industrial base, UOD was remarkably radical. The UOD members actively organised unions in various enterprises and even waged a number of strikes in Manila. In a petition submitted to the American colonial government, UOD asked that 'the laws of protection of the working man be studied, adopted, and brought to the notice of the honorable civil commission, especially in regard to dwellings for workmen, accidents while at work, and a protective law for women and children'.

UOD also advocated political independence. The anti-imperialist orientation of UOD was due to a great extent to its founding president, Isabelo de los Reyes, who was imprisoned by the Spaniards in the 1890s for his anti-clerical and anti-Spanish writings. However, de los Reyes' career as a union man was short-lived. In August 1902, de los Reyes was arrested on a framed-up charge that he was attempting to assassinate striking workers wishing to return back to work, a ridiculous charge that was later changed to labour conspiracy (Scott, 1982).

1910s: Decade of union toleration. In 1908, the American colonial government adopted a more tolerant attitude towards trade union formation. Trade unionists from the moderate American Federation of Labor (AFL) visited the Philippines to promote welfare unionism. This led to the formation of the *Union del Trabajo de Filipinas* (UTF), which co-operated with the colonial government and tried to minimise labour's involvement in political affairs. Its officers even sent their constitution and by-laws to Governor Taft for approval (ILMS, 1983).

1920s: Return of radical unionism. Radical and political unionism crept back in the third decade of American rule (Ofreneo, 2010a). A charismatic labour leader, Crisanto Evangelista, organised the *Congreso Obrera de Filipinas* (COF) in 1919 and revived the demand for Philippine independence, proclaiming COF's overall goal of '*lalong ganap na kalayaan*' (greater freedom). Subsequently, Evangelista and his followers founded the *Partido Obrero* in 1924, the *Katipunan ng mga Anak-pawis ng Pilipinas* (KAP) in 1929, and the *Partido Komunista ng Pilipinas* (PKP) in 1930. Evangelista and followers dominated the labour scene in the 1920s.

1930s: Labour reforms in the 'red decade'. The decade of the 1930s was a 'red decade' because of the unprecedented incidence of labour strikes and peasant mass actions launched by Evangelista's followers and other radical political groupings that sprouted in the different parts of the country such as the peasant-based Socialist Party of the Philippines and '*pulajanes*[1]' messianic groups (Ofreneo, 2010a). The labour and social unrest of the 1930s was rooted in the crisis of the export crop economy under the free trade regime, which was greatly aggravated by the Great Depression that plagued America in 1929–1933.

To contain the social and labour unrest, the 'Philippine Commonwealth' government, which was established by the Americans preparatory to the proposed 'granting' of independence to the colony, launched a 'Social Justice' programme in 1936. Manuel Quezon, the first elected Commonwealth President, in emulating the 'New Deal' programme of US President Franklin Delano Roosevelt, pushed for the enactment of an eight-hour labour law, workmen's compensation, minimum wage in government, establishment of the Government Service Insurance System, legal protection to members of legitimate labour unions and the establishment of a Court of Industrial Relations (Ofreneo, 2010a).

Japanese interregnum. Japan invaded the Philippines in 1940. During the war, the export-crop-based economy built around the US market went haywire, causing massive job displacements. Pre-war political and civic organisations, including trade unions, were dissolved. Crisanto Evangelista was arrested and executed (UIF, 1982).

The economic and labour landscape in the post-war period

In 1946, the Philippines gained its political independence. And yet, the country remained an economic appendage to the United States. The rigid pre-war free trade rules were re-imposed by the Americans via the threat that no American war damage assistance would be extended under the Philippine Rehabilitation Act and the Philippine Trade Agreement enacted by the US Congress in 1946. The Trade Act also tied the Philippine peso to the American dollar and granted American businessman 'parity rights' in the exploitation of natural resources and operation of public utilities (Constantino and Constantino, 1978).

The free trade re-imposition derailed recovery in the war-ravaged economy. The Philippine market was swamped with duty-free non-essential American commodities. By 1949, the country was facing a balance of payment (BOP) crisis. In 1948, the number of unemployed was estimated to be 1.23 million out of 7.49 million labour force or an unemployment rate of 16.4% (Ofreneo, 1993).

The post-war economic crisis provided the general backdrop to the inevitable confrontation between the Philippine government and the Communist-led labour and peasant movement. The labour dimension of the crisis was reflected in the numerous strikes and street demonstrations launched by the radical Congress of Labour Organisations (CLO) and the *Federacion Obrera de Filipinas* (FOF). The CLO united under its fold some seventy-eight unions with more than 100,000 members in Luzon, while the FOF had 70,000 plus members in the Visayas and Mindanao (Ofreneo, 1993).

The government's response to the CLO-FOF challenge was twofold: repression and reform.An all-out campaign to supress the militant CLO and FOF was undertaken and culminated in their formal outlawing in 1951. On the reform side, the government enacted labour laws aimed at improving labour–management relations and upgrading of the wages of workers (Ofreneo, 1993), namely: the National Minimum Wage (1951), Industrial Peace Act (1953) and the Social Security Law (1954).

The Industrial Peace Act was patterned after the US 'New Deal' National Labour Relations (Wagner) Act of 1935, as amended by the Labour–Management Relations (Taft-Hartley) Act of 1947. The twin US measures made collective bargaining between labour and management mandatory. One reason for the adoption of American-style collective bargaining was the calculation that such bargaining fosters economic unionism because issues are localised and solved at the plant level, not through a concerted national action of workers such as what the CLO and pre-war Philippine labour organisations tried to accomplish. After the conclusion of a CBA, workers go back to their work, for better or for worse, and have to wait for three years before the contract is renewed. Blas Ople (1958, p. 7), a journalist-labour activist who would later become Secretary of Labor himself, explained that under the American model, '*Political activity has leaped into a purely secondary – even indifferent – place in the scale of priorities of organised labor*'.

The shift to import-substituting industrialisation (ISI)

Because of the economic crisis, the Philippine government was forced to modify the pre-war free trade arrangement with the United States, which acquiesced somehow to the policy changes. Import and foreign exchange control measures were imposed to balance the trade situation and stop the outflow of critical foreign exchange. These control measures became the instruments for the promotion of new industries under the ISI strategy that the Central Bank (CB), created in 1949, pushed hard under the leadership of a fiercely nationalistic CB Governor Miguel Cuaderno (Ofreneo, 1993).

A decade after, Philippine Senate President Gil Puyat (1959, p. 33), an industrialist himself, proudly described the changes in the industrial landscape as follows:

> …the Philippines now has factories for the production of a wide variety of manufactured goods including hollow blocks, galvanized iron sheets, corrugated cartons, plastics, steel windows, fluorescent lamps, steel manufactures, automobile tires, glass, pianos, knitted goods, plywood, fishing nets, caustic soda, cement, textiles (cotton, rayon, ramie, silk), foundries, paper, pulp, sodium carbonate powder, hydrochloric acid, chlorine and other chemicals, virginia-blend cigarettes, kitchen utensils, zippers, batteries, barbed wires, crayons, chalk, jute bags, phonograph records, amplifiers, cosmetics, perfumes, pharmaceuticals, lead pencils, steel cabinets, steel fixtures, bathroom materials, aluminum products, ammonium sulfate fertilizers, sulfuric acid, industrial gases, and other essential commodities and consumer goods. Most of these items were previously imported from abroad, particularly from the United States….

A 1962 World Bank report, appended to the State of the Nation message of President Diosdado Macapagal, summed up the economic changes in the 1950s as follows:

> The major structural change since the war has been the growth of domestic manufacturing. Organised manufacturing (15 workers and over), which was limited to processing of agricultural products before the war, expanded more than 10% per year during the 1950's… A vigorous entrepreneurial class has emerged and the nucleus of skilled labour force has been formed….
>
> (p. 6)

Ironically, the Macapagal Administration reversed the economic programme that gave birth to the above structural change. A programme of 'decontrol' was instituted, per advice of the International Monetary Fund (IMF), which gave the Philippines in 1962 its first IMF standby loan. The IMF also recommended the devaluation of the peso to correct the BOP situation (Ofreneo, 1993). Miguel Cuaderno, the proponent of controls as instruments for industrialisation, was replaced as CB Governor.

The rise of 'free' trade unions

The changing industrial structure naturally had a profound impact on the composition of the industrial workforce. The establishment of the ISI factories required the employment of an increasing number of blue-collar workers and the services of professional and technological manpower such as corporate lawyers, bankers, managers, engineers, accountants, supervisors, secretaries, advertising personnel and so on.

In turn, the rise of these ISI industries and the enactment of the law promoting collective bargaining paved the way for the emergence of a new generation of labour leaders. Unions tried to avoid the anti-Communist witch hunt in the Cold War decades of the 1950s–1960s. Thus, some federations added the word 'free' in their names, for examples: Federation of Free Workers, National Association of Free Labour Unions and Federation of Free Farmers, to emphasise their alignment with the anti-Communist campaign of the United States for a 'Free World' (Ofreneo, 1993).

Nonetheless, radical political unionism kept creeping back. The vehicle for its re-emergence was the anti-imperialist movement launched by Senator Claro Recto in the 1950s. Recto's crusade got the support of the more radical federations such as the National Association of Trade Unions (NATU) and the Philippine Association of Free Labor Unions (PAFLU) (Ofreneo, 1993).

The economy and labour under martial law

In September 1972, martial law was declared throughout the archipelago. This altered once more the economic and labour landscape of the country.

President Ferdinand Marcos issued General Order No. 5, which prohibited 'all rallies, demonstrations and other forms of group actions by persons within the geographical limits of the Philippines, including strikes and picketing in vital industries' (Ofreneo, 2010a). A number of militant labour leaders were arrested during the early months of martial law.

The martial-law government also changed the focus of industrial development. The ISI programme was abandoned in favour of a 'labour-intensive export-oriented' (LIEO) industrial strategy. The shift to LIEO was pushed by a group of American-educated technocrats who openly espoused freetrade economics, criticised the ISI industrialists of the 1950s–1960s as 'rent-seeking', welcomed the entry of foreign investors, and enjoyed the backing of the IMF and the World Bank (Ofreneo, 1993).

One outcome in the shift to the LIEO programme was the emergence in the Philippine import-export statistics of 'non-traditional manufactured exports' and 'non-traditional agricultural exports'. The former consists mainly of garments, electronics, toys, footwear and handicrafts; the latter, pineapple and banana. The growth of the non-traditional export manufacturing was facilitated with the establishment of export-processing zones (EPZs) and the licensing of bonded warehousing manufacturing (BWM) facilities for investors engaged in re-export manufacturing under international subcontracting arrangements (Macaraya, 1987).

Marcos tried to balance the repressive effects of martial law by maintaining the protective labour laws (Macaraya, 1987). He required employers to get prior clearance from the Department of Labor before an employee could be separated from the service. He issued a number of wage decrees mandating 'emergency cost of living allowances' and minimum wage adjustments.

As to dispute settlement, Marcos abolished the old CIR, and created in its place an ad hoc National Labor Relations Commission (NLRC), which was later institutionalised as a regular agency. Collective bargaining was promoted within the framework of compulsory arbitration. The idea was to make compulsory arbitration provided by the NLRC mandatory in the resolution of various disputes that were not settled through negotiation and conciliation proceedings.

In 1974, Marcos issued Presidential Decree No. 442, promulgating the *Labour Code of the Philippines*. All the pre-martial law labour laws were put under one codified book. The Code also came up with a number of 'reforms' that hewed closely to the government's corporatist vision of labour order such as the elevation of tripartism into a state policy (Macaraya, 1987). To streamline representation in tripartite meetings and bodies, the government called on the various labour federations to unite under the government-supported Trade Union Congress of the Philippines (TUCP). For the management side, the Philippine Chamber of Commerce and Industry (PCCI) organised the Employer Confederation of the Philippines (ECOP).

Martial law weakened the trade union movement. The *Labour Code* withdrew the right to self-organisation of the following employees: supervisory employees, security guards and personnel of government-owned or controlled corporations. In the pre-martial law period, some of the strongest unions were formed by the supervisory and public sector employees (Ofreneo, 1993).

More importantly, wages were repressed with the weakened system of unionism and collective bargaining. Perfecto Fernandez (1983) of the U.P. College of Law contended that the overall objective of the government labour policies was to depress wages for the LIEO enterprises, which he said required a 'cheap labour policy'.

However, the strike-free period did not last long. Towards the end of 1975, a strike at the La Tondena distillery, supported by some priests and nuns, shook the regime.

As to the proposed unification of the labour movement under the TUCP umbrella, there was little progress given the intense intra- and inter-union rivalries among them. The Bureau of Labour Relations reported that as of December 1979, there were 7 trade union centres, 106 federations and 1,463 local affiliates/independent unions, with a total claimed membership of 1.9 million. This membership claim was an exaggeration since only 287,450 workers were covered by CBAs registered in 1979 (Ofreneo, 1993).

Economic crisis, structural adjustment programme and 'temporary' migration programme

In the mid-1970s, the economy registered 6%–7% annual growth rate. But by 1979–1980, the economy was sputtering. The high growth achieved in the mid-1970s was due to the massive infrastructure spending undertaken by the Marcos government with the help of loans from the IMF/World Bank-led creditors. But by the late 1970s, the government had difficulty in servicing the debt. Eventually, the government's inability to service the debt, amounting to over US$24 billion, became a full-blown debt crisis in the 1980s (Lim, 1992).

The debt crisis was partly rooted in the LIEO programme to deliver its promises for the country of greater industrial dynamism, less import dependence and better balance in trade and payment accounts. The growth of the non-traditional manufactures was miniscule and constituted some kind of an enclave, accounting in 1977 for only 4.3% of the total manufacturing output (Ofreneo, 1993).

The limited growth of LIEO industries is one reason why the government adopted in 1975–1976 a 'manpower export' programme aimed at deploying 'overseas contract workers' (OCWs) to the petrodollar-rich Saudi Arabia and other Middle East countries. Labour Secretary Blas Ople argued that this was 'temporary' and was needed because the LIEO programme had not yet fully taken off. But the economy never took off and the government's manpower export programme, instead of declining, kept increasing each year. Around 50,000 OCWs were initially deployed (Ofreneo, 2010b).

As to the economic technocrats of the Marcos regime, their response to the failure of the LIEO programme to take off was to push harder for its implementation. They re-baptised the LIEO as the 'export-oriented industrial' (EOI) programme and negotiate with the IMF-World Bank group for 'structural adjustment loans' or SALs. These SALs were in support of a 'structural adjustment programme' (SAP) that called for the wholesale liberalisation of the trade and investment regimes, the deregulation of key sectors of the economy and the privatisation of a number of government corporations and assets (Fair Trade Alliance, 2006).

The irony is that the SAP, introduced in 1980–1982, only deepened the crisis of an economy that was on the recessionary path in 1980–1983. SAP had a crippling effect on the home industry because trade protection was removed. Second, SAP, to succeed, needed the stimulus of a vibrant export market, which, following the 1979 oil shock, was relatively sluggish in the early 1980s. Fred Elizalde, President of the Philippine Chamber of Commerce and Industry, openly attacked the government's SAP policies of import liberalisation, interest rate deregulation and tight monetary policy. Elizalde (1982) wrote:

> We must be as innovative as our competitors who live and succeed in similar environments... Operating with interest rates twice as those of those countries, and at the same time being subjected to liberalised importation, is more than Philippine industries can take under arduous global economic conditions.

In 1983–1985, the dire warning of Elizalde happened, with the economy sinking into a depression as the gross domestic product (GDP) growth turned negative. This forced many firms to engage in all kinds of downsizing exercises. The Labour Ministry recorded an average of 65,000 workers being laid-off annually in 1980–1982 and 82,000 workers yearly in 1983–1985 (Ofreneo, 1993).

Not surprisingly, industrial relations in 1980–1985 were tumultuous. Both militant and moderate trade unions conducted all kinds of mass protest actions and work stoppages. The most affected was domestic manufacturing, which had the highest concentration of unions and which was severely injured by the SAP and the shrinking domestic market. But labour unrest was also intense in the EOI sector. The EPZ in Bataan (BEPZ), a strike-free area in the 1970s, witnessed the unthinkable: the whole zone paralysed by workers from fifty or so companies who walked out voluntarily from their jobs (Ofreneo, 1993).

The labour control system established under martial law quickly crumbled. To placate the workers, two laws – BP 130 and BP 227 – were enacted in 1981 by the Marcos regime to 'restore' the right to strike. However, these laws were denounced by both the moderate and militant unions as meaningless because they gave management the right to 'free ingress or egress' or bring in and out products in companies affected by strikes.

After the assassination of opposition leader Benigno Aquino in 1983, the labour unrest further deepened and became part of the general political agitation against the Marcos regime. Actual strikes increased by 82% from 155 in 1983 to 282 in 1984, and by 32% to 371 in 1985 (Ofreneo, 1993).

Continuity of the SAP and seesawing labour policy under the Aquino Administration

The LIEO/EOI crisis became a debt crisis in the early 1980s. In turn, this debt crisis rapidly evolved into a multi-sided politico-economic crisis that led to the downfall of the Marcos regime in 1986. A 'People-Power Revolt' led by a faction of the military installed Mrs. Corazon Aquino as the leader of the country.

But upon assumption to power, the Aquino Administration opted to maintain and deepen the SAP. A January 1989 World Bank report lauded the Aquino government for its vigorous implementation of the SAP-related measures such as the introduction of the value-added taxation system, lifting of import controls on 'a wide variety of industrial raw materials and capital goods', elimination of price controls, interest rate deregulation, foreign exchange deregulation and privatisation of over 100 public corporations (Macaraya and Ofreneo, 1992). In brief, there was no change in the orientation of the people managing the nation's economic planning department.

As to the regulations governing unionism, the Aquino Administration swung from a policy of liberalisation to tight regulation. In 1986, the Administration issued Executive Order No. 111, which (a) eased the rules on the conduct of a strike and the requirements for certification election for purposes of determining collective bargaining agent; (b) ordered the police force to'keep out of the picket lines until actual violence or other criminal acts occur therein'; and(c) opened the door to public sector unionism (Ofreneo, 1993). Because of the liberal atmosphere, the first year of the Aquino Administration saw an unprecedented rise in the number of strikes, with 581 recorded strikes in 1986, the highest in the country's history (Ofreneo, 1993).

However, employers were not happy with the liberalisation process. ECOP and the business chambers also expressed alarm over the 'radical' pronouncements of Labour Secretary Augusto Sanchez, a human rights lawyer. Sanchez was quoted attacking the exploitative practices of transnational corporations and recommending corporate profit-sharing with workers. He was denounced as a 'one-man wrecking crew' to investors (Ofreneo, 1993).

In response to the pressures of the business community, the Aquino Administration replaced Sanchez by appointing Franklin Drilon, a corporate lawyer and an officer of ECOP, as the new Labour Secretary. Drilon, however, did not introduce any major policy changes on the regulation of strikes. He tried to cool down the strike fever by seeking police assistance in the dismantling of 'illegal' strikes and by reviving the enforcement of the rules on strikes based on the provisions of BP 130 and BP 227 (Ofreneo, 1993).

On the promotion of industrial peace, Drilon reiterated the martial-law era policy of promoting collective bargaining within the broad framework of compulsory arbitration. He complemented this by strengthening the machinery for dispute settlement through the establishment of the National Conciliation and Mediation Board (NCMB), the hiring of more NLRC arbiters, the convening of tripartite fora to discuss various industrial relations issues and the promotion of voluntary arbitration and bipartite labour–management councils (LMCs). In 1990, the government issued Executive Order 403, which formally established the Tripartite Industrial Peace Council (TIPC). Finally, in 1999, wage fixing was 'regionalised' through the creation of Regional Tripartite Wages and Productivity Boards.

With the foregoing measures, the total number of strikes declined. However, the number of cases compulsorily assumed by the government through the NLRC and its arbiters rose. In 1986, over 20,000 cases were handled by the NLRC; in 1991, the number was over 34,000 cases (Ofreneo, 1993).

Labour in an open but fragmented economy

The 1980s to the present are decades of trade and economic liberalisation for the Philippines. The Aquino Administration and the succeeding Presidents – Fidel Ramos (1992–98), Joseph Estrada (1998–2002), Gloria Macapagal-Arroyo (2002–2010), Benigno Aquino (2010–2016) and Rodrigo Duterte (2016-present) – have continued the EOI programme/SAP. Today, the Philippines is one of the most open economies in Asia.

At the same time, the industrial relations policy framework that the government formulated in the tumultuous decade of the 1980s has remained. So what then is the situation for the labour force and the trade unions in a liberalised, deregulated and globalised economy? To answer this, several points need to be clarified: first, the economy is growing despite the failure of the EOI/SAP to promote industrial transformation; second, both the national economy and the labour market have become increasingly segmented; and third, there is a general trend towards labour flexibilisation in the formal labour market.

On the whole, industrialisation under the EOI/SAP growth framework has been stagnant, as amply captured in Table 10.1. The contribution of the agricultural sector to the GDP shrank by 150% from 1980 to 2015, although the sector still accounts for almost 30% of the employed. In brief, what Table 10.1 indicates is that the Philippines has become a services-led economy without having experienced an industrial revolution and without the benefits of agricultural modernisation. Services sector now accounts for more than half of the GDP and employment.

And yet, the economy has been growing. One explanation for this is the rise of a remittance-driven economy. The 'temporary manpower export' programme of the 1970s has become a huge pillar of the economy. In 1975–1976, the government processed around 50,000 OCWs. Today, it is around 2 million a year, with 6,000 plus overseas Filipino workers (OFWs) leaving daily. The total number of migrant workers, now called as the OFWs, reached a total of over 10.2 million in 2013, or roughly 10% of the total resident population. OFW remittances totalled US$25.7 billion or some 10% of GDP in 2015 (ILO Country Office for the Philippines, 2017). The OFWs and their families have disposable incomes that have contributed to the tremendous expansion of the service sector industries such as the remittance

Table 10.1 Sectoral Composition of Economy, Output and Employment (Percentage, 1980 and 2015)

Sector	*1980*	*2015*
Output Share		
Agriculture	25.1	10.3
Industry	38.8	30.7
Services	34.3	58.9
Employment Share		
Agriculture	51.8	29.2
Industry	15.4	16.2
Services	32.8	54.6

Source: Philippine Statistics Authority.

business, mall/retailing, fast-food, nostalgia (unique Filipino goods), housing, transport, education and other industries catering to the consumption needs of OFWs and their families.

Another explanation for the positive growth of the economy is the phenomenal growth of the call center – business process outsourcing (CC-BPO) sector in the last two decades. And yet, this sector was not in the original EOI/SAP equation. The CC-BPO sector has developed on Philippine soil because providers of customer service for America's top 500 companies have found it cheaper to offshore such service in a country with a good supply of English-speaking, ICT-literate and American-acculturated workforce who are paid a fraction of what American CC agents would normally get (Ofreneo, Ng and Pasumbal, 2007). Of course, advances in modern communications, e.g., internet and VOIP, have served as facilitating factors. In 2013, the sector generated US$15.3 billion and employed 851,782 Filipinos (Errighi, Khatiwada and Bodwell, 2016).

However, the overall picture of the economy and labour market is one of segmentation. The three sectors – services, industry and agriculture – have segments with varying sizes, technology and complexity. The industrial sector is composed of two major segments: the EOI firms, which are usually based in EPZs and ecozones, and the domestic-oriented companies, a number of which were nurtured in the ISI era. But both segments have big, medium, small and micro participants. In the case of the EOI sub-sector, a system of subcontracting between big exporters and small and home-based subcontractors was common in the 1970s and 1980s in the garments industry.

As to the agricultural sector, it accounts for 10% of the GDP and 30% of the employed. This shows the low level of productivity in agriculture and explains why poverty is widespread in the countryside. The poorest of the poor are coastal fisherfolks, indigenous tribal people and the numerous landless farm workers.

Services sector has two major sub-sectors: formal and informal. On the formal side, the biggest employers are government and industries providing education, logistics, finance, transport, entertainment and wholesale-retailing services. Outside of the CC-BPO sector and banking segments, many of the service industry workers are low-paid non-unionised casual workers.

The informal side of the service sector is the catch basin for the millions of workers who cannot get jobs in the formal labour market. It is composed of numerous micro and informal income-generating activities undertaken by the poor, such as hawking, vending, unregistered repair and personal services, and similar activities. ECOP (Ortiz-Luis, 2008) estimated the informal economy in 2007 to be over 70% of the employed; this figure was arrived at by adding the statistics on unpaid family workers (around 12% of the total), underemployed (22%) and the self-employed (32%).

Because of the weak industrialisation process and the fragmentation of the labour force, the base of traditional unionism has been limited.

The trade unions lament that many jobs in the formal labour market are not being 'regularised' by employers. They denounce the phenomenon of 'contractualisation', or what labour economists simply call as 'flexibilisation', through the short-term hiring of workers. A popular Filipino slang for a short-term worker is '*Endo*', literally an abbreviation of the phrase 'end of contract'.

In the contractualisation process, employers and recruiters classify short-term workers as 'non-regulars' because they are hired as temporaries, probationaries, 'project employees' and 'trainees'. The utilisation of the services of third-party job/service contractors who bring in their short-term hires is also widespread. In addition, there are workers compensated on a commission basis, on a 'boundary' arrangement (transport drivers turn over a fixed daily earning to transport owners), and on a piece-rate basis (Kapunan and Kapunan, 2006).

The rights of workers limited by missing laws

Under the Philippine Constitution, all workers enjoy the same rights when it comes to membership in a union and coverage of collective bargaining. In reality, such rights are enjoyed only by a minority among workers in the formal labour market. The non-regulars, who constitute the majority, are excluded. Countless cases handled by the court system recognise only the right of regular or permanent employees to join a union for collective bargaining purposes. Managerial and so-called confidential rank-and-file employees are also explicitly excluded (see discussion in Azucena, 2016).

As to the right to strike, this is respected under the legal system, but its exercise is subject to established rules (see Azucena, 2016) such as the filing of a strike notice, conduct of a strike vote, observance of a cooling-off period, respect of the 'free ingress/free egress' provisions of the strike laws, submission to NCMB preventive mediation and compliance with the return to work orders issued by the Department of Labour or the NLRC. A defiance of any of the strike rules can lead to the declaration of a strike action as 'illegal', which means the employers may terminate the services of striking workers legally without any compensation.In the 1990s, a number of big companies such as the Philippine Air Lines and the MERALCO power company terminated striking workers or union officers without giving them any separation pay simply because their strikes had become illegal when the strikers defied the return-to-work orders issued by the DOLE Secretary. Thus, since the turn of the millennium, the number of strikes has been declining.

In the public sector, unionisation has been in a limbo because there is still no enabling law on public sector unionism and industrial relations. However, some organisers have succeeded in forming a number of public sector unions despite the absence of such law and the limited bargaining power of the unions.

As to workers in the vast informal economy, unionism and collective bargaining are unheard of. However, there are all kinds of organising in the sector undertaken by civil society and community organisations to advance a variety of socio-economic causes such as microfinance, housing right, land reform, vendors' rights and so on.

Conclusion: the future of worker representation under globalisation

In its 'diagnostics' on 'decent work' in the Philippines, the ILO (2017) lamented that union formation and collective bargaining have been declining. The explanations are not difficult to find. The environment for organising in an open but segmented and uneven economy is generally hostile to unionism. The ISI industries, which bred strong unions in the past, have either crumbled or weakened under economic globalisation.

In the case of the EOI industries, the most successful union organising happened in the export-led garments industry, in the 1970s–1980s. However, most of the garment unions have disappeared because garment investors and exporters based in the Philippines have been relocating to other Asian countries since the 1990s in search of cheaper and malleable labour. In the case of the electronics industry, the rate of unionism is very low. This is because many companies have 'proactive' human resource management practices, which tend to keep the unions at bay. Thus, out of 400 plus electronic companies, there are only a dozen or so successful cases of organising.

As to the CC-BPO sector, none of the union organisers have succeeded in registering a union and concluding a CBA. Employment in the industry is 'project-based' and the nature of work usually leads to a very high rate of turnovers, which naturally affects any sustained organising campaigns.

The flexibilisation processes and narrow legal framework on the enforcement of workers' union rights in the formal sector further limit the area for unionism and the scope of collective bargaining. In the huge informal economy, there are no enabling labour laws.

Unions retain a voice in society

Despite the foregoing, the unions' position on various issues is amply covered by the Philippine mass media. The policy of tripartism, put in place by the martial-law government in the 1970s and formally enacted into law in the 1980s by the Aquino Administration, gives worker representatives belonging to different labour centres and federations an opportunity to be heard in official consultation meetings on labour matters, at the national and regional levels. Worker representatives are also appointed in different tripartite bodies such those dealing with social security, health and safety, dispute settlement, wage boards and so on. There are also worker-based political parties given special seats in Congress.

Meanwhile, a number of progressive unions have been collaborating with enlightened academics and civil society organisations (CSOs) to advance broader worker organising through an adjustment in the traditional way workers are organised and their interests are advanced. The concept of 'social movement unionism' (SMU) has been accepted and articulated by some labour leaders, who realise the importance of covering under the union umbrella all workers, regular and non-regular, formal and informal (Aganon, Serrano and Certeza, 2009). Also, union organisers in the non-unionised CC-BPO sector are now discussing the need to shift organising and representation framework by helping call centre agents and BPO programmers to form 'professional IT associations' based on skills which, in a way, is a revival of skills-based guild organising.

There is a proposal currently before Congress for a 'Magna Carta for Workers in the Informal Economy' (MCWIE), which seeks to establish a system of registering organisations of informal workers at the local and national levels. But despite the absence of enabling laws, a number of CSOs and people's organisations (POs) have been active in organising different segments of the labour force, such as migrants, domestic workers, tribal people, home-based workers, non-wage transport workers, ambulant vendors, coastal fisherfolks, landless rural poor and so on.

The point is that labour empowerment in a liberalised and globalised economy need not be confined to organising qualified workers to forge a CBA contract with a formal-sector employer. This is clearly too narrow, while the *Labour Code* provisions on union organising and collective bargaining have become meaningless to the majority of workers even in the small formal sector of the labour market.

New theorising on unionism in Asia: the case of the Philippines

The Philippines needs a new and more inclusive *Labour Code*, which is able to provide protective mantle for all workers. There is a need to revisit the industrial relations framework such as the one conceptualised by John Dunlop (1958). The Dunlop framework guided a number of developing countries in the 1960s in the formulation of labour policies for the emerging 'modern sector' of their economy. This is what the Philippines did with the promulgation of a new *Labour Code* in 1974. However, the Dunlop model based on tripartite rule-making among the three actors – industry, unions and government – is narrow and outdated.

In a segmented, uneven and globalised Philippine labour market, there is clearly a need for new industrial relations theorising, that can give voice to all segments of the workforce and, at the same time, enable the government to pursue an inclusive programme of social and economic development. There is also a need for the trade unions to continue reflecting on the multi-dimensional challenge of how to develop new forms of worker organising, new forms of worker representation and various forms of worker empowerment. Table 10.2 provides a summary of major challenges facing the Philippine trade union movement. Table 10.3 lists organising and advocacy

Table 10.2 Challenges Facing the Philippine Trade Union Movement

Internal Challenges	*External Challenges*
Shrinking membership	Weak government support to unionism
Rivalry and lack of unity	Strict *Labour Code* rules on union formation and collective action
Weak organisational capacity (limited legal and financial resources)	Missing laws on public sector unionism
	Uneven, segmented economy and labour market, compounded by overseas migration
	Labour precarity widespread, aggravated by Race to the Bottom culture among capitalists (e.g., squeezing wages and labour rights)
	Informal sector widening
	Emerging industries (e.g., those using digital platforms) difficult to unionise
	SAP or economic development blueprint not inducive to unionism

Table 10.3 Union Revitalisation in the Philippines: Issues and Organising and Policy Advocacy Options

Issues	*Organising and Policy Advocacy Options*
1 Restrictions on union registration, coverage and representation	1 Review and overhaul of the Labour Code and Implementing Rules, purging them of restrictive provisions
2 Limited application of tripartism (mainly on conflictual minimum wage fixing)	2 Tripartite social dialogue should focus too on labour law reforms and industry/firm consultation on personnel policies and adjustment to technology modernisation, etc. Bipartism and tripartism supplemented by multi-partism involving other actors, e.g., Church, civil society organisations
3 Exclusion of large segments of the labour force from scope of unionism	3 Enactment of enabling laws on the rights to form unions and bargain collectively/pursue collective action for all workers, e.g., non-regulars (e.g., casuals, project workers, etc.), informal-sector workers (e.g., transport, home-based, farmers, fisherfolks, etc.) Promotion of all-sector organising
4 Missing laws on public sector unionism	4 Enactment of enabling laws on public sector industrial relations
5 Divisions in trade union movement	5 Code of Conduct on union raiding and settlement of inter/intra-union disputes; unity efforts on issue-to-issue basis (for example, unified stand on social protection for all)
6 Negative public image of unions to some sectors	
7 Leadership in society and national governance	
8 Weak and uneven industrial and agricultural development	
9 Race to the Bottom at the national, regional and global levels weakening labour rights	

(*Continued*)

Issues	*Organising and Policy Advocacy Options*
	6 Union modernisation programmes to make unions attractive to middle class, millennials and freelancers 7 Demonstrating capacity of union leaders in 'alternative' politics (e.g., advocacy of non-elitist development agenda) 8 Campaign for comprehensive, inclusive and balanced industrial and agricultural development 9 Solidarity among unions at all levels on how arrest Race to the Bottom and promote a Race to the Top based on enlightened industrial relations ideas.

options that the trade unions could pursue to build a truly broad and representative social movement. These challenges and organising/advocacy options could provide a starting point for new theorising about the future of unionism in the Philippines.

Note

1 *Pulajanes*' means 'reds'. They were generally millenarian messianic groups promising members redemption from poverty and misery.

References

Abelarde P (1947) *American Tariff Policy towards the Philippines.* New York: King's Crown Press.

Aganon M, Serrano M and Certeza R (2009) *Union Revitalization and Social Movement Unionism in the Philippines: A Handbook.* Quezon City: Friedrich Ebert Stiftung.

Anvil (2005) *The Constitutions of the Philippines.* Mandaluyong: Anvil Publishing.

Azucena C (2016) *The Labor Code: With Comments and Cases.* Quezon City: Rex Publishing.

Bailey K (1996) The Labor Code: One of the Most Advance Labour Law Enactments in the Asia-Pacific Region. In Foz V (ed.) *Amending the Labor Code for Philippines 2000.* Quezon City: Philippine Law Gazette 13 (1): 34–35.

Carrol J (1961) *Philippine Labor Unions. In Philippine Studies.* Quezon City: Ateneo de Manila University, IX (2): 223–224.

Constantino R and Constantino L (1978) *The Philippines: The Continuing Past.* Quezon City: Foundation for Nationalist Studies.

Dunlop J (1958) *Industrial Relations System.*Boston: Harvard University Press.

Elizalde F (1982) The Commerce and Industry Sector. In Dialogue on the Financial Situation. Manila: Central Bank.

Errighi L, Khatiwada S and Bodwell C (2016) *Business Process Outsourcing in the Philippines: Challenges for Decent Work*. Bangkok: ILO Asia-Pacific.

Fair Trade Alliance (2006) *Nationalist Development Agenda: A Road Map for Economic Revival, Growth and Sustainability*. Quezon City: Fair Trade Alliance.

ILO Country Office for the Philippines (2017) *Decent Work Country Diagnostics: Philippines 2017*. Makati: ILO Manila Office.

Institute of Labor and Manpower Studies (1983) *Towards an Achieving Society*. Manila: Ministry of Labor and Employment.

Kapunan R and Kapunan R (2006) *Labor-Only Contracting in a "Cabo" Economy*. Quezon City: C & E Publishing.

Lim P (1992) Structural Adjustments in the Philippines. In *Philippine Labor Review*. Manila: ILS-DOLE 16 (1): 1–23.

Macaraya B (1987) *Workers' Participation in the Philippine People Power Revolution*. Manila: Friedrich Ebert Stiftung.

Macaraya B and Ofreneo R (1992) Structural Adjustments and Industrial Relations: The Philippine Experience. In *Philippine Labor Review*. Manila: DOLE 16 (1): 24–86.

Ofreneo R (1993) Labor and the Philippine Economy. Unpublished Doctoral Thesis, University of the Philippines College of Social Sciences and Philosophy.

Ofreneo R (2010a) *Ed Balik-Tanaw, BagongPananaw*. Quezon City: Department of Labor and Employment.

Ofreneo R (2010b) Migration and Development: When Will the Turning Point Come? In Sta Ana F (Ed) *Philippine Institutions: Growth and Prosperity for All*. Quezon City: Action for Economic Reforms, 263–284.

Ople B (1958) The History and Direction of Philippine Labor. In *The Saturday Mirror Magazine*. Manila, 7.

Ortiz-Luis S (2008, May) The Practical Approach to Benefit the Majority. In Philippine Employer. Makati: ECOP: 13–17.

Philippine Statistics Authority (2016). Labor Force Statistics for 2016. Available at https://psa.gov.ph/statistics/survey/labor-force.

Puyat G (1959) The Need for a Dynamic Spirit of Economic Nationalism. In *NEPA Silver Anniversary Handbook*. Manila: NEPA.

Republic of the Philippines (1935) The Constitution of the Republic of the Philippines.

Republic of the Philippines (1987) The Constitution of the Republic of the Philippines.

Republic of the Philippines (1974) The Labor Code of the Philippines.

Scott W (1982) The Union ObreraDemocratica, First Filipino Labor Union. In *Philippine Social Sciences and Humanities Review*. Quezon City: New Day Publishers.

World Bank (1962) Economic Growth in the Philippines: Preliminary Report. Appendix to the State of the Nation Message of President Diosdado Macapagal. Manila: Malacanang.

Union de Impresores de Filipinas (1982) *Crisanto Evangelista: Kasaysayan ng Isang-DakilangLider ng UringAnakpawis*. Manila: UIF-Katipunan.

11 From worker representation to worker empowerment

The case of Singapore[1]

Chew Soon Beng and Ryan Tan Hin Tuan

Introduction

Bereft of natural resources and impoverished, Singapore was thrust into the deep waters of nationhood when it gained independence in 1965. Two years later in 1967, the British military forces which accounted for 20% of Singapore's economy, started their withdrawal from the island. This fuelled massive unemployment and resulted in severe industrial unrests amid the heated political rivalry between the communist elements and the government. Singapore's GDP per capita of US$512 then was beneath that of Jamaica, South Africa, Chile and Uruguay (Sng and Chia 2011).

During the next five decades, Singapore's economy was transformed. By 2016, Singapore's GDP (PPP) per capita of US$88,003 was ranked third as a country, just behind Qatar and Luxembourg by the World Bank. Singapore was also placed third behind Switzerland and the United States in the 2017–2018 World Economic Forum Global Competitiveness Index. Furthermore, Singapore consistently enjoyed low inflation rates, healthy fiscal budget balances and growing foreign exchange reserves while achieving excellence in key social areas such as education, health and housing. Singapore also deftly dealt with five major economic crises by adopting pragmatic policies. Singapore's economy not only emerged unscathed from these major tests but also became successively more robust.

Many observers have attributed Singapore's economic miracle to good governance and hard-headed policies. This chapter examines the key factors that calmed the turbulent labour relations in the earlier years and ushered in an era of industrial peace. In turn, this afforded a conducive environment where pragmatic policies could be earnestly planned and promoted by Singapore's leaders, rationally understood by the workforce and supported by the overall population. It is, therefore, crucial to understand the role of the labour movement in Singapore's economic development. To do so, we visit the formation of Singapore's labour movement and its progressive role in developing Singapore's workforce. We then examine its constant evolution to stay relevant to a diverse and rapidly changing workforce. We also explain how the labour movement, together with the tripartite partners, collaborate to restructure Singapore's economy given the global challenges ahead. Finally, we discuss the uniqueness of Singapore's labour movement using two contemporary theoretical frameworks in the context of industrial relations.

The early years of Singapore's labour movement

Singapore's first labour union was the Singapore Trades Union Congress (STUC) established on 13 June 1951. Endorsed by the colonial government, it served as an umbrella organisation to wean unions away from Communist influence (Sim 2015). Lee Kuan Yew, who later became Prime Minister, had returned from his overseas studies and began to represent unions and workers in court cases. Eventually, he formed the People's Action Party (PAP) and won the national elections in 1959. His substantial involvement in the legal representation of the working class had been a favourable factor in his party's victory (Sutherland 2015). Many party members of the ruling PAP were leaders of the STUC. In July 1961, the ruling party encountered an internal split which also disrupted the labour union. The unionists who supported the break-away faction of the PAP formed the Singapore Association of Trade Unions (SATU), with more than eighty unions under its fold. Pro-PAP unionists, on the other hand, established the National Trades Union Congress (NTUC) with only twelve unions on their side on 6 September 1961.

SATU and NTUC contrasted starkly in their approaches to labour relations. While SATU engaged in acrimony such as mass strikes, the NTUC focused on pragmatic labour relations to maximise employment in Singapore. By November 1963, the majority of SATU's affiliates had defected to NTUC rendering SATU quite irrelevant. Eventually, SATU's application for registration was rejected on the grounds of unlawful activities. NTUC then assumed the official role of the national confederation of trade unions in Singapore. Within a decade, the number of man-days lost in strikes fell to zero (Figure 11.1).

The early symbiosis between the NTUC and PAP afforded Lee with political support to focus on harmonious industrial relations which made Singapore attractive to foreign investments. In November 1969, the NTUC launched a four-day 'Modernisation of the Labour Movement' seminar. The NTUC declared that collective bargaining would be collaborative and non-confrontational in the interest of industrial harmony. It reiterated the fundamental belief that better worker welfare would be achieved through their economic relevance to the economy. It was also at this milestone event that NTUC announced its decision to participate in Singapore's economic and social development through social enterprises. The Modernisation Seminar was deemed by Lee Kuan Yew to be 'the most significant transformation of the trade union movement' (Lee 2011).[2]

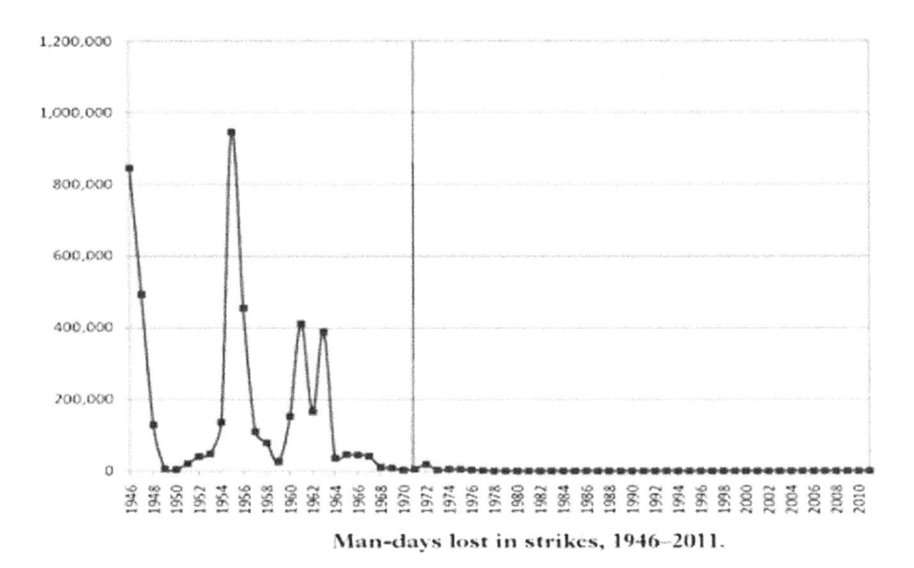

Figure 11.1 Days Lost in Strikes, 1946–2011.

The labour movement during non-crisis periods

In the earlier years, NTUC engaged substantially with workers on their welfare during the non-crisis and crisis periods. During non-crisis periods, NTUC played a significant role in nation building by steadily improving the socio-economic welfare of the workers. In crises periods, NTUC rallied workers to respond decisively to the challenges at hand. Because of her deep involvement with Singapore society at all times, the NTUC is instrumental to Singapore's economic and social development.

One approach which the NTUC took to improve workers' lives was to set up social enterprises for the working class. After the Modernisation Seminar in 1969, NTUC initiated three major social enterprises to stabilise the Singapore society (National Library Board 2014). The first social enterprise launched in September 1970 was **NTUC Income**, which provided low-cost insurance coverage to low-income workers for protection against unplanned financial difficulties in the event of mishaps. Today, the NTUC Income is one of the largest insurers in Singapore. The second social enterprise launched just two months later was the **NTUC Comfort** which harmonised the large, fractious private taxi transportation market by subjecting all taxi drivers to proper licensing and regulations. Many became owners of their taxis and shareholders of the social enterprise. This development enabled them to become responsible members in the economy. Subsequently rebranded as **ComfortDelGro** and listed on the Stock Exchange of Singapore in 2003, it has remained as an active key component stock of the Straits Times Index. The third social enterprise, **NTUC Welcome**, was launched in July 1973 to provide essential consumer items at reasonable prices to combat rampant profiteering. Renamed as **NTUC FairPrice**, it has remained as the largest supermarket chain in Singapore today. These three inaugural social enterprises of the NTUC were fundamental to stabilising Singapore's volatile society in the earlier years. They have been well managed and this outcome attests to NTUC's organizational capability.

In July 1982, NTUC initiated a nation-wide programme called Basic Education for Skills Training (BEST) to equip lowly educated workers with basic English and Mathematics literacy skills. This initiative enabled them to enrol in essential skills courses to become useful to the job market. In December 1996, NTUC launched the Skills Redevelopment Programme (SRP) to enhance the training culture among workers by promoting the national certification of courses to equip workers with quality portable skills.

As ordinary workers strove to improve their lives, the NTUC sought to ensure that the finer lifestyle aspirations were accessible to the working class. NTUC launched the Pasir Ris Resort in October 1988 followed by the Orchid Country Club in December 1994. Both were excellent world-class recreational facilities for workers at affordable prices. This was to ensure that the working class did not feel excluded from enjoying the fruit of Singapore's economic success.

The National Wages Council (NWC) was formed in February 1972[3] to deliberate on annual wage increase recommendations (Tan 2013). It was structured as a tripartite committee with equal representation from the government, the employers' federation and the NTUC (Lim 2011). The NTUC represents the interests of the workers and negotiates with her tripartite partners to find common ground where wages can be adjusted to maximise the national employment. In challenging economic times, the NTUC has supported wage reduction to sustain industries in Singapore by explaining the economic challenges and the rationale for lower wages to workers. Conversely, the NTUC has championed for higher wages to the NWC when the economy excelled.

The labour movement during crisis periods

We shall highlight two economic crises that demonstrate NTUC's role as a responsible tripartite partner and as a representative for workers.

Singapore encountered an economic crisis in 1985 when the domestic economy contracted in stark contrast to a thriving global economy. Singapore's GDP suffered its first negative growth of 1.8%. Unemployment reached 6.1% with about 95,000 jobs lost. Menon (2015) noted that the recession exposed structural deficiencies in the economy which were masked by strong economic growth in the preceding years. Lim (2017), on the other hand, attributed Singapore's recession to the collapse of commodity prices in the neighbouring countries of Indonesia and Malaysia, as well as to the high direct taxation and contribution rates of the social savings scheme known as the Central Provident Fund (CPF). The government convened the Economic Committee (EC) in April 1985 to review Singapore's economic situation and to identify new directions for its future growth. A raft of measures was proposed by the EC to turn around Singapore's economic situation. The NTUC supported a proposal by the EC to drastically reduce the employers' part of the monthly mandatory contributions to the CPF from 25% to 15%. Separately, the NWC also recommended severe wage restraint which saw that the average earnings increase of 7.9% in 1985 plunged to 0.5% in 1986. These combined cost-cutting measures in 1986/1987 reduced the unit labour costs in manufacturing by more than 15%. Hence, the number of deregistered companies declined and there was an increase in new registrant firms (Figure 11.2). Consequently, many jobs were saved and the resulting cyclical unemployment rate was kept relatively low. It was clear that both the CPF reduction and the wage restraint measures, supported by the NTUC, helped the economy buffer against extraneous job losses. Singapore's GDP growth rate rebounded from −1.8% in 1985 to 1.2% in 1986, then soared to 6% in 1987.

Remarkably, the temporary but drastic effects on the individuals' savings scheme and wages did not spark social unrest in Singapore which might have occurred elsewhere. This further lent credence to the NTUC as a trustworthy body that protects workers' interest without detriment to the economy. As part of further wage reform efforts, the NWC recommended that wages be made more responsive to economic conditions. Thus, the NWC introduced the Flexible Wage System (FWS) which was composed of the variable bonus, performance-driven assessment, profit-sharing scheme and Key Performance Indicator bonuses. Firms which adopted the FWS reward workers with year-end bonuses instead of according them fixed annual wage

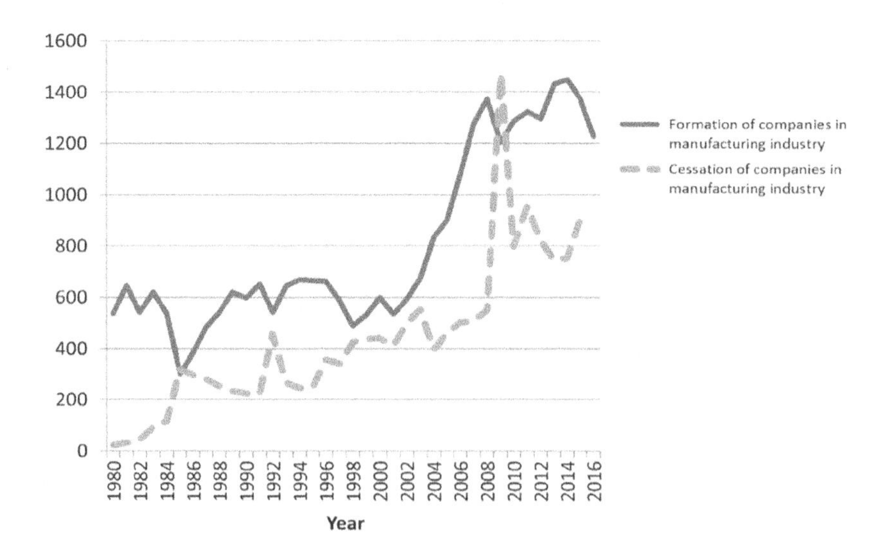

Figure 11.2 Number of New Firms and Deregistered Firms in the Manufacturing Sector of Singapore.

increases. This approach enabled firms to adjust wages according to their annual business performance. The FWS was therefore a departure from the seniority-based compensation system which was unaligned with the firm's performance. NTUC's support of the FWS and the constant engagements with workers to explain its rationale were instrumental to its acceptance by workers.

Another economic crisis that struck Singapore was the infamous Asian Financial Crisis. Starting with the collapse of the Thai baht in July 1997, the crisis quickly engulfed Indonesia, Malaysia, the Philippines and South Korea over the subsequent months (Chew 2016). While Singapore's currency was relatively unscathed, she eventually felt the effects of the crisis around September 1998 when seasonally adjusted unemployment rate edged up to 4.5% compared to 2.2% in March of that year (Lim 2013). By then, productivity further declined by 2.5% and most sectors experienced negative productivity growth. More than 20,000 people were retrenched in Singapore for the first nine months of 1998 which was double the 9,784 workers laid-off for the whole of 1997. In response, the government convened the Committee on Singapore's Competitiveness (CSC) in May 1997 to review and strategise Singapore's competitiveness for the next decade. Together with the NWC, various harsh economic austerity measures were recommended while the NTUC engaged with workers on the rationale of the necessary measures and ensured that affected members were properly compensated. By the first quarter of 1999, the Singapore economy reverted to positive growth with reduction in retrenchments. The overall GDP for 1999 grew by 7.2% which far exceeded the government's initial forecast of between −1% and 1%.

Worker representation in Singapore

The genesis of the PAP together with the ensuing formation of the NTUC by pro-PAP unionists saw that successive NTUC Secretary Generals were party stalwarts. The founding Secretary General, Devan Nair, was a PAP veteran who later served as the President of Singapore. Successive NTUC Secretary Generals were Cabinet Ministers. Similarly, Ng Chee Meng, the current NTUC Secretary General appointed in May 2018, is a Minister in the Prime Minister's Office. Critics of this long-standing symbiosis question the independence of the labour movement, but proponents argue that the voices of the workers can be heard by the Cabinet and, ultimately, the Parliament.

Over the years, the NTUC has progressively widened its representation, strengthened its organisation and rejuvenated its offerings to workers. By October 2015, the NTUC had a total of sixty affiliated trade unions and affiliated associations with 888,000 union members. The NTUC has twenty-one Central Committee members comprising of senior members from the industrial sector, services sector and the public service sectors.

As a labour movement, the credibility of the NTUC is tied to the size of its member base. This is important for the NTUC to be able to rally and influence as much of the workforce as possible. Chew (2017) noted that the macro-focused union has been cooperating rationally with employers and the government for sensible rather than maximum wage increases to maximise the national employment pie for workers' benefit. Inherently, all workers in the economy and not only the union members would have been benefitting from this approach. This paradox of free-ridership meant that there is little incentive for workers to be union members. Chew (2017) noted that the objective of maximising national employment by a macro-focused union undermines its other objective of maximising its membership base. These twin objectives are in conflict because with free-ridership, all workers stand to benefit regardless of their membership status with the NTUC. Chew and Chew (2012) proposed that the macro-focused union could circumvent this dilemma by offering non-collective bargaining benefits to entice new memberships. These are the benefits which are not associated with union representation rights and are enjoyed by all union members. Thus, union membership can be attractive and eligible to all regardless of their union representation entitlement.

Although all members enjoy non-collective bargaining benefits, it is important that members are identified according to their union representation status. This is done by using two types of NTUC memberships: Ordinary Membership and General Branch Membership. Ordinary members are union members who work in unionised firms and are represented by the unions in wage negotiations and workplace issues. General branch members are union members who work in non-unionised firms and do not have union representation rights. Both types of memberships enjoy the same level of non-collective bargaining benefits. In contrast, non-union members have no access to any of the non-collective bargaining benefits. Thus, to be effective enticements, non-collective bargaining benefits are generally practical and appealing to the typical worker. Examples are discounts for consumer items purchased from NTUC FairPrice supermarkets and participating vendors, and member subsidies for approved educational and skills courses. Chew (2017) established that on average, an NTUC member enjoys S$65 worth of non-collective bargaining benefits compared to the S$9 membership fee on a monthly basis. Thus, the economic rationale for a typical worker in Singapore to join the NTUC is indeed compelling.

The potency of the General Branch Membership was proven in 1985. Between 1980 and 1984, there was a decline in total union membership. It was reversed in 1985 when NTUC started to offer the General Branch membership. Since then, the membership base has progressed on a positive trajectory (Figure 11.3) to 888,000 by October 2016. The union density of the Singapore resident workforce increased from 23% to 27% during the period 2009–2013 in contrast with only 1% growth for the period 2005–2009 (Xue 2014). The NTUC enjoyed a consistent growth in the professionals, managers and executives (PMEs) category with one in five members being

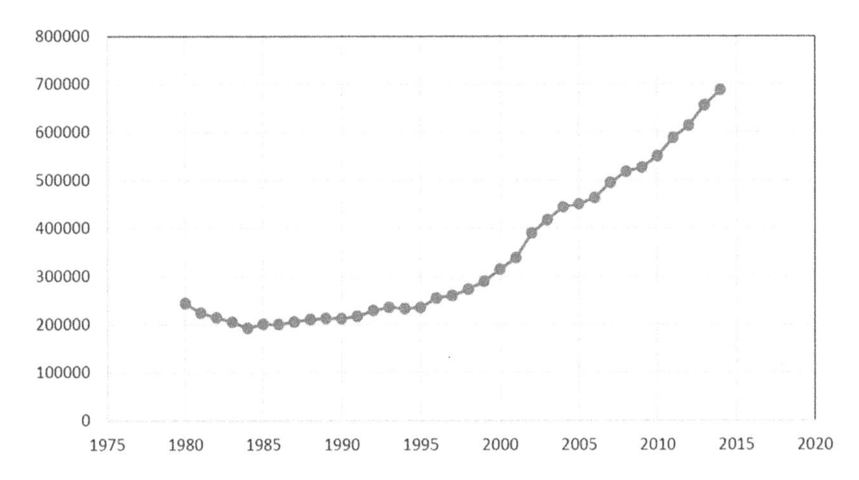

Figure 11.3 Union Membership in Singapore (1980–2014).

a PME in end 2017 compared to one in six a decade ago. These trends of NTUC memberships contrasted sharply with the decline in union memberships around the world.

Corporatising tripartism for better worker representation

An important milestone was achieved by the tripartite partners when they incorporated a legal entity for the first time in March 2017. Known as the Tripartite Alliance Limited (TAL), it is equally owned by the tripartite partners and subsumes two prior tripartite entities, namely: Tripartite Alliance for Fair and Progressive Employment Practices (TAFEP) and Tripartite Alliance for Dispute Management (TADM). This setup enables resources to be better pooled and shared to represent workers (Chuang 2017).

To appreciate the TAL, it is important to understand the complementary functions of the TAFEP and TADM with respect to representing workers' interest. TAFEP was formed in 2006 to champion fair employment practices against labour discrimination. It publicly lauds organisations which demonstrate desirable employment values and it also equips participating companies with resources such as tools, processes and training to encourage the adoption of fair and progressive employment practices (Lim 2016). TAFEP discourages unfair employment practices by citing companies with persistent breaches to the Ministry of Manpower for punitive measures. In addition, TAFEP promotes labour productivity. Singapore's workforce growth has declined from 4% in the period 2011–2014 to 1% in 2016. However, the labour productivity improved marginally from 0% in 2011–2015 to 1% in 2016. Since then, the government has been encouraging businesses to shift from 'manpower-led' to 'manpower-lean' strategies (Lim 2017). TAFEP supports this initiative by championing a wider adoption of innovative practices to attain higher productivity. For example, it encourages all companies to be supportive of flexible work arrangements and foreign companies to facilitate knowledge transfer to the local workforce.

The TADM, which has become the other sub-entity of the TAL, was originally established in April 2017 to strengthen Singapore's ability to resolve employment disputes. Currently, the Employment Act in Singapore covers only employees who earn up to S$4,500 implying that employees who earn above this amount are not protected by the Act.[4] The TADM addresses this interim gap by covering all employees who earn more than $4,500. It resolves disputes holistically by engaging with support organisations for other forms of assistance such as legal and financial help for affected workers. Finally, the TADM seeks to resolve non-salary disputes such as disagreements on performance appraisals and justifications for termination.

Challenges facing the labour movement in Singapore

Earlier, we discussed the effectiveness of the NTUC during the non-crisis and crisis periods of Singapore's development. As Singapore's economy developed and overcame successive economic challenges, workers may have become complacent with the NTUC. In a study, Chew and Neo (2013) established that 75% of union members joined NTUC primarily for the monetary savings at the social enterprise, NTUC FairPrice. Similarly, in a NTUC corporate video, the former Secretary General Chan commented that '*Very often when we talk about NTUC, many people only think of FairPrice and the welfare benefits we give. Actually, the most important thing the labour movement provides for our workers must be over and beyond all these welfare benefits and that is training, upgrading and career opportunities*' (National Trades Union Congress 2017).[5] He noted that the call to workers to pursue life-long learning to stay relevant to the job market has become crucial given Singapore's exposure to technological disruptions and globalisation. In a typical employment lifecycle today, workers are likely to transition across different jobs involving different skills. They will have to adapt to working in large corporations, small medium enterprises and freelancing while acquiring different skill sets to meet job demands. The challenge for the NTUC is to empower workers across the continuum of employment options over their entire working lifecycle.

In other words, if NTUC is to be successful in promoting the importance of life-long learning in career opportunities to workers, it must be able to rally workers to exert their personal efforts in these areas. In turn, workers are more likely to heed NTUC's rallying call if NTUC remains highly relevant to their career aspirations (Chan 2017). While the NTUC has proven itself to be an effective organisation over the years, its relevance to individual workers is determined by their perception of its usefulness to achieve their aspirations. Thus, the distinction between 'effectiveness' and 'relevance' is nuanced but important. To raise its relevance with the workforce, NTUC has been addressing two important dimensions.

The first dimension is the scope of representation. Aside from the traditional rank-and-file workers, NTUC has been extending her representation scope by reaching out to four other workforce segments (Toh 2017c). These are:

- the professionals, managers and executives
- the workers in small and medium enterprises
- freelancers and the self-employed
- domestic and migrant workers

The second dimension of boosting NTUC's relevance relates to the usefulness of its products and services to the workforce. Technological disruptions and globalisation have been rapidly creating new job roles and obsoleting many existing ones, thus generating volatility in the labour market. The tripartite partners are encouraging workers to take ownership of their employability through life-long learning. In 2015, the Singapore Government launched SkillsFuture as part of a national movement to provide Singaporeans with the opportunities to develop their fullest potential through life-long learning regardless of their socio-economic status and age. With the support of NTUC, the government has created a training account for all citizens above the age of twenty-five. In the first instance, the government has credited each citizen with S$500 to choose the right training programme to enhance their skills and avoid unemployment. To bolster support for SkillsFuture, the NTUC has expanded on the courses it offers to public members, covering many domains including IT, HR, languages, leadership and even workplace safety and health. NTUC has also partnered with institutes of higher learning in Singapore to offer 'bite-sized' learning modules delivered through a mobile application called U Leap (Learning Enabled through Active Participation) (Toh 2017a). Aside from campaigning for life-long learning, the NTUC has started the **U Career Network** in April 2017 to offer professional career coaching to individual workers, with the involvement of industry professionals as mentors to workers and provisioning of guidance on the myriad of job resources available. Thus, there is now a maturing of NTUC's role from that of a national marshal that drives workforce improvements *en masse* to one that seeks to be an active partner for each individual worker throughout his employment journey.

In January 2016, the Singapore Government convened the Committee of Future Economy (CFE), a tripartite committee, to review and chart Singapore's economic strategies. This need arose from the observation that major global changes are expected to have substantial impacts on Singapore. Following consultations with 9,000 stakeholders[6], the CFE assessed that the economy together with twenty-three industries covering 71% of the workforce required restructuring (Ministry of Communications and Information, Singapore 2017). As a tripartite partner, the NTUC was called upon to support the economic restructuring in four main ways. First, the NTUC will continue to help displaced workers regain employment through placement services. Second, the NTUC will continue to prepare workers for the future by supporting life-long learning and reskilling programmes. Third, the NTUC is to continue collaborating closely with the tripartite partners to transform 23 key industries. Lastly, the NTUC will help to improve working conditions for low-wage workers in selected industries by supporting the implementation of the Progressive Wage Model (PWM). The PWM introduces entry-level wages for low-wage workers in landscaping, security and cleaning services and matches wage increases with productivity improvements. Many of these workers have encountered suppressed wages and are not expected to have sufficient retirement savings (Sapari 2018). Since 2016, NTUC's support for the PWM has included extensive lobbying of the government to consider more holistic measures given its limited effectiveness (Sapari 2016).[7]

Throughout this chapter, several core challenges and responses of the NTUC have been discussed. Some of these challenges are internal and are within the NTUC's sphere of influence and control. Other challenges tend to be externally driven which entail collaboration with external stakeholders. A summary of the core challenges as well as responses is given in Table 11.1.

Table 11.1 Challenges Confronting the Singapore Labour Movement

Internal Challenges to NTUC	*External Challenges to NTUC*
• Ensure strong relevance and sustainability of the many social enterprises that it operates in the Singapore economy. • Need to accurately perceive and effectively convey worker sentiments and expectations to tripartite partners on important issues. This is achieved through grass-root engagements with workers, surveys, labour trend analysis and leadership engagements. This multi-mode approach is important at a time when the Singapore workforce is becoming increasingly diverse in their career and lifestyle aspirations. • Enhance relevance to workers by empowering them for career resilience by helping affected workers in job placements and rallying them to embrace life-long learning. The NTUC subsidizes members for training and works closely with the tripartite partners on initiatives such as SkillsFuture to reskill the working population. NTUC also collaborates with institutes of higher learning to deploy new innovative modes of learning for workers such as modular courses through mobile applications that are stackable towards tertiary degrees.	• Maximise national employment levels by working closely with tripartite partners. This requires NTUC to be an effective voice for workers to the tripartite partners. Conversely, NTUC also serves as a voice of reason to workers they can understand economic constraints and challenges. • Globalisation and technological disruptions are blurring the distinction between 'white-collar' and 'blue-collar workers'. NTUC continues to lobby the tripartite partners for more workers to be protected by the Employment Act and the Industrial Relations Act. • More 'blue-collar' workers are becoming PMEs or freelancers as the economy evolves. Many of these workers are still independently focused on their own career development efforts. NTUC is constantly finding ways to embrace these workers. For example, NTUC has started engaging with professional associations (e.g., IT, banking) to provide better domain support to workers. It has also formed a new National Instructors and Coaches Association to look after the interests of freelancers who teach sports, enrichment and wellness.

Internal Challenges to NTUC	*External Challenges to NTUC*
	• NTUC has been constantly concerned with the plight of low-wage workers. Market practices such as 'cheap sourcing' which award tenders solely based on lowest cost, tend to suppress the wages of low-skilled workers in the outsourcing industry. e.g., cleaners and security guards. NTUC has engaged with the government to promote 'best sourcing' where other criteria besides cost are considered in awarding tenders especially in low-skilled manpower-intensive areas. At the same time, NTUC actively supports the Progressive Wage Model to help low-wage workers attain better wages and working conditions.

Comparative perspectives of the labour movement in Singapore

One prominent theoretical approach, 'varieties of capitalism' (VoC) by Hall and Soskice (2001), provides a comparative framework for political economies based on studies of several Organisation for Economic Co-operation and Development (OECD) economies. The VoC framework examines the strategic interactions of the firm with other institutions in a political economy, which is archetypically characterised as either liberal market economies (LMEs) or coordinated market economies (CMEs). Both types of political economies differ markedly and, therefore, bestow different institutional complementarities on the firm.

The VoC analysis posits that globalisation, with its highly disruptive effects, tends to be more damaging on LME unions compared to those in the CMEs. An initial application of the VoC framework suggests that the Singapore economy could be associated more with CMEs given its relatively more stable, regulated market. However, Ritchie (2008) asserts that Singapore has been able to adopt portions of both the LME and CME models to generate long-term, sustainable economic development and, therefore, does not easily fit into the LME or CME mould.

Lim Aik (2010) argues that the success of Singapore's state-led economy is substantially due to the heavy involvement of state-sponsored institutions such as the government-linked companies, CPF and the Economic Development Board in the economy. The aligned interests and functions of these organisations lend institutional complementarities which propel Singapore's economy. Thus, Lim Aik (2010) proposes that the relative success of Singapore's state-led economy has made a powerful case for the VoC framework to accommodate the role of political power in institutional mechanisms. This can be done by including a third model that reflects state leadership in the market economy. Even so, the VoC framework may still be limited in explaining Singapore's political economy as its analysis is firm-centric and unsuited to account for Singapore's tightly woven tripartite model. This multifaceted nature of the NTUC as a responsible state-led tripartite partner in nation building does not fit well with the conventional industrial relations described in the VoC framework.

Another theoretical approach, the 'varieties of unionism' (VoU) by Frege and Kelly (2004), argues that unions remain crucial for the proper functioning of capitalist economies and political democracy despite underlying changes due to globalisation. It outlines six strategies that the labour movements in the US, UK, Germany, Italy and Spain have undertaken to respond to their challenges of union decline.

Since the formation of the NTUC in 1961, it has exercised all six strategies to a rather high degree of effectiveness due to the coordination linkages that can be attributed to the cohesiveness of the partners in Singapore's tripartite model. It is instructive once again to recall the powerful symbiotic relationship between the NTUC and the PAP which enables the NTUC to be well aligned with the State to achieve social and economic objectives. Table 11.2 summarises the VoU strategies that have been corroborated by NTUC's experiences since its formation.

Many of the major achievements of the NTUC are possible only with state direction and support from the tripartite partners. The labour movement, therefore, cannot be viewed in isolation. The VoU perspective can be made more relevant to Singapore's labour movement if the structures and dynamics of the Singapore's state-led tripartism can be included in its analysis.

Table 11.2 Varieties of Unionism Strategies

Strategy	*Applicability*	*Benefits*	*Risks*
Reform of union structures	Highly applicable. Since the formation of the NTUC in the 1960s, the labour movement has continually reformed itself to progress from worker representation in terms of wage and benefits bargaining to worker empowerment through reskilling for the new economy. Similarly, the labour movement adapts itself to cater to the social needs of Singapore through its social enterprises over the years.	The continuous reformation momentum has enabled a much wider coverage of workers from diverse backgrounds and salary levels. The revitalisation of the labour movement has enabled a paradigm shift that empowers workers to take responsibility for their own career aspirations through the myriad of career enhancement schemes made available to them.	As the labour movement continues to be successful in revitalising itself to accommodate the working population, workers may become overly dependent on the labour movement for career progression. Ironically, if this dependence manifests excessively, it may inhibit the resilience of workers in becoming more adaptable to changes in the global economy.

Strategy	*Applicability*	*Benefits*	*Risks*
International solidarity	Applicable. The labour movement works closely with international bodies to promote good labour practices. For example, the labour movement actively supports an agreement between ILO and Singapore's Ministry of Manpower to share its belief in tripartism with ASEAN member states to promote good employment and workplace practices in the region.	Positive outcomes, such as the Decent Work Agenda in ASEAN, to bring about good employment and workplace practices are being promoted (Seow 2018a). Such initiatives support the desired integration of ASEAN economies to enable better exchange of labour among member states and consequently a more robust and growing ASEAN regional economy.	Very limited risk of any unexpected misrepresentation in the international arena as engagements are usually done as a tripartite structure comprising the Singapore government, employers' federation and the labour movement.
Labour–management partnerships	Highly applicable. In Singapore, the labour movement, employers' federation and Singapore government cooperate, collaborate and negotiate within a tripartite framework with the aim of maximising the national employment level and worker welfare. The focus and dynamics of these negotiations are usually state-led.	The tripartite arrangement allows labour issues, employer challenges and government priorities to be discussed in earnest without public discord. This allows agreements to be jointly agreed by the tripartite partners. In turn, such institutional partnerships enable economic policies to be coherently formulated and systematically executed by stakeholders.	The tripartite partnership was established by the ruling party, PAP. As the main union body is helmed by political appointees, uncertainty with the leadership of the labour union will arise in the event of a change of the ruling party.
Organising	Highly applicable. The strategy of organising is used very well to increase membership and union density, in stark contrast to the general trend of declining union memberships in other developed economies. The labour movement organises itself to provide very favourable member benefits through its social enterprises to entice new memberships.	Increases the credibility of the labour movement as a tripartite partner, in representing the workforce to the government and employer federation. Increases the moral position of the labour movement to rally the working population during peaceful and crisis periods.	Continual revitalisation efforts must be sustained so that the offerings of the labour movement continue to be relevant to the workforce to sustain their interest and participation in union activities. Expectations of the labour movement by worker members may unexpectedly exceed what the labour movement can reasonably achieve if unmanaged.

(*Continued*)

Strategy	*Applicability*	*Benefits*	*Risks*
Political action	Highly applicable. The labour movement, as a tripartite partner, regularly consults the government and employer federation on crucial matters relating to the working population. During times of crises, the labour movement mobilises grass-root leaders to communicate critical issues and rally the working population.	The labour movement is aligned with the tripartite partners to achieve national priorities. It helps to channel resources and rally the workforce to achieve national economic objectives and to overcome national crises.	The labour movement may be perceived by detractors as being excessively present in all areas of civilian life. Detractors may also view the labour movement as being too closely aligned to the ruling party and, hence, may opt to avoid the labour movement altogether.
Coalition-building	Applicable. The labour movement partners with some civil groups to promote social causes, e.g., the Singapore Council of Women's Organisations to promote gender equality. Furthermore, the labour movement has also partnered institutes of higher learning to promote reskilling and life-long learning to all members of the public and not just union members alone (Davie 2016).	Increases institutional power of the labour movement by leveraging on the resources and capabilities of non-labour civil organisations. Expands desired social norms that contribute to higher social and economic well-being of Singapore.	Civil groups may occasionally deviate from specific social norms and cause social divisions. This may put the labour union at odds with the civil groups in question, e.g., the labour movement publicly withdrew its support for a call by a coalition partner to repeal a long-standing but socially divisive penal code on homosexuality (popularly known as 'Section 377A') (Toh 2017b).

Conclusion

The NTUC has been instrumental in shaping the Singapore workforce and looking after the wider interests of the population as well. Singapore faces unprecedented challenges from disruptive forces such as technological advancement and globalisation which have resulted in the creative destruction of jobs where old jobs are being replaced by new ones requiring different skill sets. Workers are now required to adapt to different forms of employment to thrive in the new economy.

The NTUC continues to transform herself to offer better support and to be more relevant to the workers. It has expanded beyond representing the traditional rank-and-file workers to accommodate new segments of the workforce. It maintains an active, responsible role in Singapore's drive for more judicious use of human capital by encouraging progressive employment practices among employers and supporting continuous reskilling among workers. Thus, the NTUC is expanding its paradigm of worker representation to include worker empowerment through a culture of life-long learning. Individual workers will be empowered to advance their own career and lifestyle aspirations. Collectively, this empowerment forms a national resilience against future employment uncertainties.

Singapore's unique model of tripartism is crucial for its social stability and competitiveness. Arguably, Singapore's approach cannot be duplicated by unions in other countries since it has been uniquely forged out of Singapore's political history. The NTUC continues to be a steadfast, responsible and adaptive economic actor in Singapore's economy and society.

Notes

1 The authors would like to thank Prof. Lim Chong Yah for his invaluable, insightful suggestions on the earlier draft. We are also grateful to Prof. David Wan for his very useful comments. Usual disclaimer applies.
2 Speech by Mr. Lee Kuan Yew during the NTUC's 50th Anniversary in 2011.
3 NWC was first chaired by Prof. Lim Chong Yah (1972–2001).
4 The salary cap is in effect at the time of writing (October 2018). Parliament has decided that from April 2019 onwards, the salary cap will be removed entirely from the Employment Act so that the Act is applicable to all PMEs.
5 Released via social media platform YouTube on 25 April 2017.
6 Comprising of unions, trade associations and chambers, public agencies, companies, workers, academics and students.
7 Asst. Secretary General of NTUC and Member of Parliament, Mr. Zainal Sapari, has frequently voiced out about the plight of low-wage workers in the outsourcing sectors through the Parliament, official media and corporate blogs.

References

Chan CS (2017) *A Representative and Relevant Labour Movement.* In: NTUC. Available at: https://ntuc.org.sg/wps/portal/up2/home/news/article/articledetails?WCM_GLOBAL_CONTEXT=/Content_Library/ntuc/home/about%20ntuc/newsroom/media%20releases/defbf725-cf7c-4b59-888b-5914ecee33bc (accessed 21 January 2018).

Chew SB (2017) *Labour Economics and Public Policy: Managing the Labour Markets for Competitiveness.* Singapore: World Scientific.

Chew SB and Chew R (2012) A New Form of Union Representation to Meet the Challenges of a Globalized World. In: *16th ILERA World Congress*, Philadelphia, 02–05 July 2012.

Chew SB and Neo A (2013) *Unions and Union Benefits as Part of the Inclusive Growth Strategy: The Case of Singapore.* Report for the Economic Growth Centre Nanyang Technological University. Report No. 2013/02, 31 January.

Chew V (2016) *Asian Financial Crisis (1997–1998)*. In: Singapore Infopedia Online Encyclopaedia, National Library Board. Available at: http://eresources.nlb.gov.sg/infopedia/articles/SIP_1530_2009-06-09.html (accessed 21 August 2018).

Chuang PM (2017) *Tripartism Movement Gets Formal Body to Push for Fair, Progressive Workplaces*. Available at: www.businesstimes.com.sg/government-economy/tripartism-movement-gets-formal-body-to-push-for-fair-progressive-workplaces (accessed 03 April 2018), *The Business Times*, 01 April, 2018.

Davie S (2016) NTU Sets Up New School Offering Courses to Working Adults Under Tie-up With NTUC. *The Straits Times*, 01 May 2016.

Frege C and Kelly J (2004) *Varieties of Unionism – Strategies for Union Revitalization in Globalizing Economy*. Oxford: Oxford University Press.

Hall PA and Soskice D (2001) *Varieties of Capitalism – The Institutional Foundations of Comparative Advantage*. Oxford: Oxford University Press.

Lee KY (2011) *Speech at NTUC's 50th Anniversary Dinner (May 2011)*. Available at: www.ntuc.org.sg/wps/portal/siseu/home/workingforu/workingforudetails?WCM_GLOBAL_CONTEXT=/content_library/ntuc/home/working+for+u/e411bf8046d6b92e9657b6cd32e0f7cd (accessed 11 February 2018).

Lim A (2010) Varieties of Capitalism: Locating Singapore's State-Led Model. *Singapore: USP Undergraduate Journal*, Vol 3, No. 1, pp. 36–44.

Lim CY (2011) The National Wages Council (NWC) and Macroeconomic Management in Singapore. In: Sng HY and Chia WM (eds), *Crisis Management and Public Policy: Singapore's Approach To Economic Resilience*. Singapore: World Scientific, pp. 3–17.

Lim CY (2013) *Singapore's National Wages Council – An Insider's View*. Singapore: World Scientific.

Lim SS (2016) *Speech by the Manpower Minister at the TAFEP Exemplary Employer Award Presentation Ceremony at the Grand Copthorne Waterfront Hotel Singapore*. Available at: www.tafep.sg/sites/default/files/speeches/Minister (accessed 12 February 2018).

Lim SS (2017) *Speech by the Manpower Minister at the Human Capital Partnership Conversations Event at Fairmont Hotel*. Available at: www.tafep.sg/sites/default/files/speeches (accessed 07 January 2018).

Menon R (2015) *An Economic History of Singapore: 1965–2065- Keynote Address Singapore Economic Review Conference 2015*. Available at: www.mas.gov.sg/News-and-Publications/Speeches-and-Monetary-Policy-Statements/Speeches/2015/An-Economic-History-of-Singapore.aspx (accessed 08 February 2018).

Ministry of Communications and Information, Singapore (2017) *Report of the Committee on the Future Economy for the Prime Minister's Office*, 8 February.

National Library Board (2014) *National Trades Union Congress is Formed – 6th Sep 1961*. Available at: http://eresources.nlb.gov.sg/history/events/def653e3-0756-460c-a8e7-05fcebde6634 (accessed 19 January 2018).

National Trades Union Congress (2017) *A Representative and Relevant Labour Movement*. Available at: https://www.youtube.com/watch?v=jFiENk6YXf4 (accessed 20 January 2018).

Ritchie Bryan K. (2008) Economic Upgrading in a State-coordinated, Liberal Market Economy. *Asia Pacific Journal of Management*. September 2009, Vol. 26, Issue 3, pp. 435–457.

Sapari Z (2016) Time for Government to Do More for Low-wage Workers. *Today*, 14 February 2016.
Sapari Z (2018) *Slavery of the Poor*. In: LabourBeat. Available at: www.labourbeat.org/2018/02/14/slavery-of-the-poor/ (accessed 03 February 2018).
Seow BY (2018a) *Renewed Partnership to Push for 'Decent Work' in ASEAN*. Available at: www.straitstimes.com/singapore/manpower/renewed-partnership-to-push-for-decent-work-in-asean (accessed 19 August 2018).
Seow J (2018b) Freelancers May Get Help with Payment Disputes, Insurance. *The Straits Times*, 22 February 2018.
Sim C (2015) *National Trades Union Congress*. In: Singapore Infopedia Online Encyclopaedia, National Library Board. Available at: http://eresources.nlb.gov.sg/infopedia/articles/SIP_2015-03-11_160912.html (accessed 21 January 2018).
Sng HY and Chia WM (2011) *Crisis Management & Public Policy*. Singapore: World Scientific.
Sutherland, D (2015) *Lee Kuan Yew*. In: Singapore Infopedia Online Encyclopaedia, National Library Board. Available at: http://eresources.nlb.gov.sg/infopedia/articles/SIP_2013-03-18_164023.html (accessed 05 January 2018).
Tan CL (2013) *The Story of NWC – 40 Years of Tripartite Commitment and Partnership*. Singapore: Straits Times Press.
Toh EM (2017a) Bite-size Modules and Crowdsourced Learning Features in New ULeap App. *Today*, 17 November. Available at: www.todayonline.com/singapore/bite-size-modules-and-crowdsourced-learning-features-new-uleap-app (accessed 02 February 2018).
Toh WL (2017b) Women's Groups Withdraw Support for Joint Report on Gender Inequality. *The Straits Times*, 29 September 2017. Available at: www.straitstimes.com/singapore/womens-groups-withdraw-support-for-joint-report-on-gender-inequality (accessed 05 May 2018).
Toh YC (2017c) NTUC to Bring More Workers into Its Fold. *The Straits Times*, 26 April 17.
Xue J (2014) Union Membership Growing at Faster Rate: NTUC. *Today*, 21 August 2014. Available at: https://www.todayonline.com/singapore/union-membership-growing-faster-rate-ntuc (accessed 30 February 2015).

12 Labour unions and worker representation in South Korea

Byoung-Hoon Lee

Introduction

South Korea (Republic of Korea, hereafter Korea) is an exemplary case of successful late industrialisation. Its late development can be explained by Japanese colonial occupation (1910–1945), division of the nation (1945–1948) and the Korean War (1950–1953). Despite its late industrialisation, Korea achieved a 'compressed' economic growth under the developmental state from 1960s until 1987, thereby being typically characterised as a state-led market economy during this period. The democratisation of 1987 and the economic crisis of 1997 combined to produce a fundamental transformation in the country's political economy regime and labour market system. Since the 1997 economic crisis, in particular, democratic governments in Korea have adopted neo-liberal reforms and institutionalised social dialogue among interest groups (Lee & Lee, 2003). During the past twenty years, the Korean political economy regime has seemingly evolved into a hybrid model of liberal market economies (LMEs) and coordinated market economies (CMEs; Lee & Kang, 2012), going beyond the ideal typology of LMEs and CMEs as outlined by Hall and Soskice (2001). In other words, the country's political economy has been reshaped by neo-liberal deregulation policy of the LME model, while simultaneously embracing the persistent legacy of 'strong state' and the involvement of interest groups in CME-style social dialogues, within the context of globalisation.

Along with the extensive transformation of Korea's political economy, the labour movement in the country experienced the ups and downs of fortune over the past three decades. The democratisation of Korea, beginning in 1987, led to the dismantling of the labour regime of the developmental dictatorship, which had enforced a militaristic labour control policy, and established the industrial citizenship of organised labour at workplace by guaranteeing their labour rights of unionisation and collective bargaining. As a result, the labour union movement achieved explosive growth immediately after political democratisation and, until the mid-1990s, was viewed as a new front-runner of the global labour movement due to its militancy. At the same time, there occurred sustained decline in union density to the level of around 10% during 1990s and the notable shrinkage of organised labour's social influence, particularly after the economic crisis of 1997, even though union representatives continued being invited to engage in social dialogue. During the post-1997 period, however, unions have been confronted with a new crucial challenge of increased labour market fragmentation, demonstrated by a sharp increase in the non-regular workforce and triggered by the government's neo-liberal labour reforms and business-driven employment relations flexibilisation.

Given the worsening labour market segmentation since 1997, the union movement in Korea has been widely criticised for being entrapped by the exclusionary tradition of enterprise unionism which focuses exclusively on the interest protection of insiders, who are union members within the boundary of enterprises. During the post-1997 period, however, there have been meaningful attempts to represent and organise the unorganised workforce, who are under the precarious working conditions, by reshaping the organisational structure of the existing unions into industry unionism and organising those unrepresented workers in various new ways of unionisation and worker representation. This chapter delineates the historical evolution and the current state of unions and worker representation, major challenges to unions and noticeable strategic actions of labour movement and their achievements. It concludes with theoretical implications for the varieties of union revitalisation.

Historical evolution and current state of unions and worker representation

Prior to democratisation in 1987, the union movement in Korea was chiefly influenced by political contingencies. The first unions were formed in the period of Japanese colonial industrialisation (1910–1945). Many unions had strong political orientation towards national liberation and socialist activism and mounted resistance against Japanese imperialistic occupation. Immediately after national liberation of 1945 from Japanese colonialism, the General Council of Korean Trade Unions (GCKTU) was the first national centre formed by the direction of a leftist political party, the South Chosun Labour Party. Following the communist party line on union movement, this national centre integrated the existing and newly organised enterprise unions into several industry unions. However, the GCKTU was short-lived, since its political general strikes, led by the Communist party, were met with extensive suppression by the US Military Administration in 1947 and replaced by the General Federation of Korean Trade Unions (GFKTU), which aimed to defy the leftist-led national centre. The GFKTU was formed in 1946 under the political tutelage of Rhee, Syngman, who was the leader of the rightist party and later became the first president of South Korea. The affiliates of the GFKTU were organised by the framework of enterprise unionism, which was rooted during the period of Japanese colonialism. The GFKTU-led union movement supported President Rhee as a submissive adherent group during his twelve-year dictatorship (1948–1960).

There were some attempts to reform the union movement after the Civil Revolution in April 1960, which ousted the President Rhee. However, attempts at union reform were frustrated by the military coup, led by General Park, Chunghee, who took power in the 1962 presidential election. President Park forced unions to transform their organisational structure into a centralised industry union model, so that his authoritarian government could effectively control them. In the early 1980s, however, President Chun, Doowhan, who gained power through military coup in December 1979, became aware that these industry unions had challenged the state' control in the late 1970s and forced the organisational reshaping of unions into an enterprise unionism model by revising the labour union law in early 1980s. Consequently, from 1962 to 1987, industrial relations and the union movement in Korea were primarily controlled by the authoritarian government's interventionist labour policy. This policy sought to guarantee the sustained supply of cheap and strike-free labour which was deemed necessary for economic development. To a large extent, the so-called developmental state prevented workers from organising unions and taking industrial action. Hence, unions were too weak to voice their members' discontent, and employment conditions were unilaterally determined by the state and employers during this period. The Federation of Korean Trade Unions (FKTU), the official national centre, and its affiliates were controlled by the authoritarian state and colluded with management at workplace. However, from the mid-1970s, the so-called democratic unions emerged to actively represent the rank and file's interests. As illustrated in Figure 12.1, despite restrictions by the state, unions continued growing from the 1960s to the 1980s, mainly owing to the country's remarkable industrialisation.

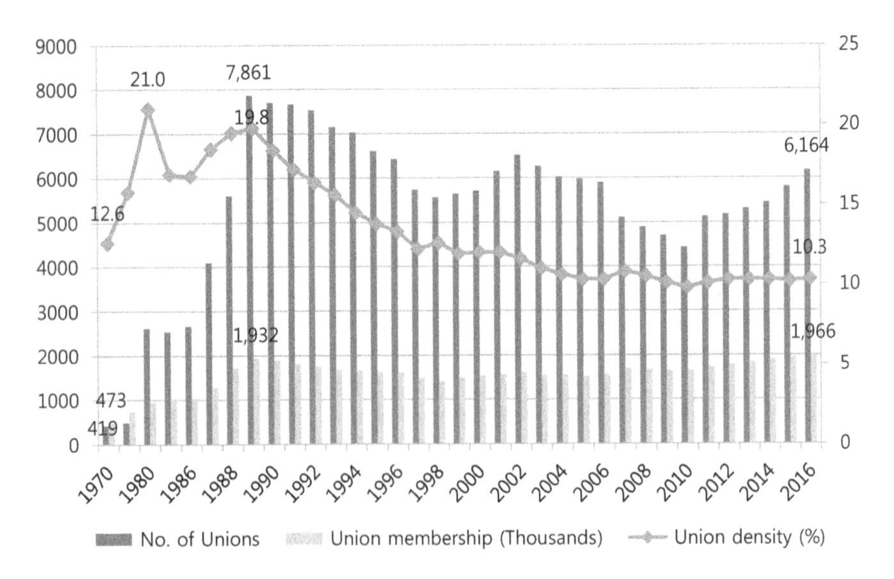

Figure 12.1 Trends of Union Statistics (1970–2016).

The number of unions sharply increased from 362 in 1965 to 2,534 in 1985, and the size of union membership more than tripled from 301,000 to 1,000,000 during the same period. As a consequence, union density grew from 12.6% in 1965 to 16.9% in 1985, with a short upsurge to 20.8% in 1980.

In the late 1987, the 'Great Labour Struggle', which followed political democratisation, led to the dismantling of the state-controlled labour regime, which triggered an explosive growth in unionisation and an upsurge in industrial action. Within the context of political democratisation, the number of unions nearly tripled from 2,742 to 7,883 between 1986 and 1989. During this period, union membership nearly doubled from about 1,036,000 to 1,932,000, while union density grew from 16.8% to 19.8%. It should be noted that many of the newly organised unions were critical of the FKTU's submissive support for the government's labour control policies before 1987 and rejected affiliation with the FKTU. The independent unions espoused 'democratic unionism' and organised their own federations, which resulted in the formation of a second national centre, the Korea Confederation of Trade Unions (KCTU), in 1995.

In 1990s, union membership decreased from 1,887,000 in 1990 to 1,402,000 in 1998. The decline of union membership during 1990s can be explained by various factors, including an economic recession, workers' growing indifference to union activities, derived from substantial improvements in their pay and working conditions and waning public sympathy towards militant unionism after the collapse of the Soviet bloc in the early 1990s (Lee & Lee, 2003). The downward trend in union membership halted from the early 2000, when teachers and civil servants were given the legal right to organise their unions in accordance with the 1998 Social Pact.[1] The unionisation of teachers and civil servants (organising around over 300,000 union members) helped the then-stagnant union movement gain new membership in 2000s. In addition, the increasing unionisation of non-regular workers has subsequently contributed to the continued expansion of union membership up to 1,966,000 in 2016. Despite the increase of union membership during 2010s, however, union density has remained at around 10%, largely due to the sustained growth in the total wage workforce.

By 2016, the unions were divided with four groups by their affiliation, as follows:

- The Federation of Korean Trade Unions (FKTU): 2,395 unions (842,000 members: 42.8% of the total union membership) in twenty-seven industrial organisations
- The Korea Confederation of Trade Unions (KCTU): 368 unions (649,000 members: 33%) in thirteen industrial organisations
- The Korean Labour Union Confederation (KLUC) & Public Service Union Confederation (PSUC): sixty-seven unions (34,000 members: 1.7%) in three industrial organisations
- Independent unions: 3,333 unions (442,000 members: 22.5%), which are not affiliated with the above national centres.

It is noteworthy that the membership of independent unions withdrawing their affiliation from the FKTU and the KCTU increased sharply from 176,700 in 2006 to 442,318 in 2016. The growing membership of independent unions might reflect their concern with the prohibition of employers paying wages to union officials, likely to have a damaging impact on union finances, which was legislated in 2010.

The Labour–Management Council (LMC) is another institutionalised vehicle for representing workers' interest, as well as promoting communication between employees and management. President Chun's government enacted the *Labour–Management Council Act* in 1980, making it mandatory for all establishments with more than fifty workers to establish a council. Despite this statutory obligation, only a limited number of enterprises formed LMCs until 1987. However, confronted with increasing labour disputes after political democratisation in 1987, management tried to promote cooperation with workers by implementing the LMC. As a result, enterprises with LMCs rapidly increased, up to over 14,000 in the early 1990s.

In 1997, the *Labour–Management Council Act* was replaced with the *Act Concerning the Promotion of Worker Participation and Cooperation.* The new Act stipulates that all enterprises with more than thirty workers should form a council and hold meetings every quarter. In accordance with the new law, the number of enterprises that formed LMCs almost doubled between 1996 (15,234) and 2001 (29,348). The number of LMCs continued to grow, reaching 51,034 in 2015. The LMC is composed of equal numbers of representatives from employees and management at workplace. When an enterprise has a union that represents a majority of workers, the union's leaders are entitled to participate in the LMC as employees' representatives. According to *the* Act Concerning the Promotion of Worker Participation and Cooperation, workplace issues to be dealt with by the LMC fall into three categories: first, issues requiring prior consent by employee representatives (i.e., training and development plans, fringe benefit programmes, in-house welfare funds, grievance handling and joint labour–management committees); second, issues of consultation with employee representatives (i.e., human resource planning, workplace renovation and new technologies, prevention of industrial accidents, redundancy adjustment, working time rescheduling, pay system changes and revision in work rules); and third, issues to be reported (i.e., corporate strategies and performance, quarterly production plan, personnel issues and the enterprise's financial situation). Note that many unions use LMC meetings as an extension of their collective bargaining, while top management at many enterprises is indifferent to the feasibility of cooperation and communication promoted by the LMC.

Challenges confronting unions and worker representation

The major challenges which unions and worker representation have been faced with during 2000s are labour market polarisation and proliferation of non-regular workers. As illustrated in Figure 12.2, wage gaps of full-time workers between large and medium-small firms continued expanding since the late 1980s, when the political democratisation occurred and the authoritarian state's labour cost (or wages) control came to an end. The relative ratio of total wages at small firms with 10–29 employees in comparison to large firms with 500 employees and more sharply declined from 90% in 1986 to 59.2% in 2007[2], while that of medium-sized firms with 100–299 employees decreasing from 91.6% to 72% during the same period. Labour market polarisation is also evident in workers' fringe benefits and human resources development. The discrepancy in enterprise-level expenditures on fringe benefits and training between large and small firms has increased. For example, the relative ratio of fringe benefits expended by large enterprises with 300 employees and more, in comparison with small- and medium-sized firms with 10–299 employees, grew from 179% in 2008 to 251% in 2016, while that of training expenditure by the large firms increased from 646% to 867% in the same period.

The 1997 economic crisis came as a great shock to labour markets. Many large firms dismantled the conventional human resource policy of 'lifetime employment', which had existed before 1997, and undertook extensive restructuring of their businesses and employment practices in the context of the economic crisis. According to an enterprise-level survey conducted by the Korea Labour Institute in 2000, 66% of respondents downsized after the economic crisis, while 74% carried out spin-offs and 58% outsourced part of their business (Park & Roh, 2001). Those enterprises recruited non-regular workers to fill what previously had been regular jobs, after the economy recovered in 1999.

As a consequence, the number of non-regular workers increased sharply along with the proliferation of various non-regular employment types after

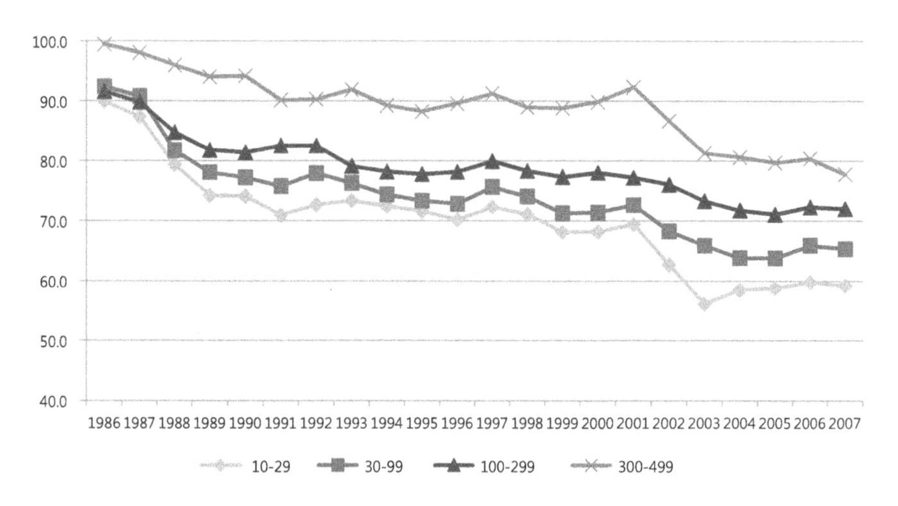

Figure 12.2 Trends in Wage Gaps by Firm Size (1986–2007).

the economic crisis. As demonstrated in Figure 12.3, the share of the contingent workers (i.e., temporary and daily workers), whose statistics has been monthly estimated by the economically active population (EAP) survey, among the total wage workforce, rose sharply from 41.8% in 1995 to 52.1% in 2000. The government began conducting the EAP supplementary survey to capture the total size of non-regular workforce, comprised of various employment types (i.e., temporary or fixed-term, part-time, dispatched, contracted, dependent self-employed and on-call) and their working conditions annually since 2001. According to the EAP supplementary survey, the share of non-regular workers grew from 26.8% in 2001 to 37% in 2004 and has since then declined to 32.8% in 2016.[3]

Non-regular workers, who had a growing presence in the post-crisis working population, suffered from discriminatory compensation and inferior working conditions, so that their precarious employment status became an additional fracture line to contribute to the deepening of labour market polarisation. The wage gap between regular and non-regular workers widened between 2003 and 2016. The ratio of non-regular workers' average hourly wage in comparison with that of regular workers declined from 71.6% in 2003 to 65.4% in 2016. In 2017, the average tenure of non-regular workers was thirty months, less than one third that of regular workers (ninety-one months) (KLI, 2017b). It is also noteworthy that a large number of non-regular workers are excluded from the institutional protection of statutory welfare and labour standards, as shown in Table 12.1. Although the protective coverage of social welfare and labour standards for workers, over the past fourteen years (2003–2017), has expanded to some extent, the majority (54.7%–75.8%) of non-regular workers (and some portion of regular workers who are mainly employed in small firms) are still excluded from legal protection, except the case of written contracts (40.4%). In addition, the widespread nature of informal employment practices in the Korean labour

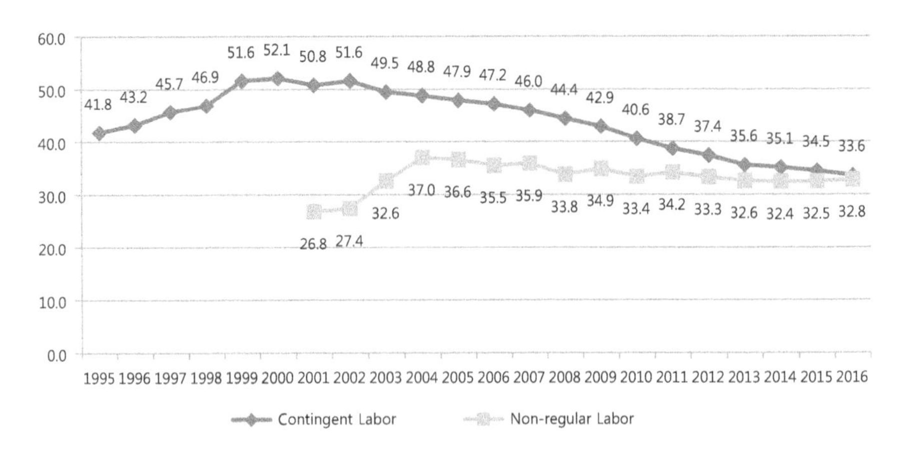

Figure 12.3 Trends in Non-regular and Contingent Labour Force (1995–2016).

Table 12.1 Comparison of Worker Protection: Regular vs. Non-Regular Workers

	2003		*2017*	
	Regular	*Non-Regular*	*Regular*	*Non-Regular*
National pension	70.8	30.5	85.0	36.6
Medical insurance	72.5	32.6	88.4	45.3
Employment insurance	59.7	29.2	85.9	44.1
Severance pay	66.4	24.8	87.8	41.5
Extra work allowance	52.1	15.4	59.3	24.2
Paid vacation	58.0	22.7	75.7	31.7
Written contract	10.8	25.7	62.1	59.6
Union density	15.3	3.4	17.1	2.9

Source: KLI (2017b).

Note: Economically Active Population – Supplementary Survey in August, each year.

markets is identified by the fact that by March 2015, 12.4% (2,330,000) of total workforce is paid below national minimum wage (Kim, 2015).

Along with the widening disparity between the primary (regular workers at large firms) and the secondary (workers at small firms and in the non-regular employment) sectors, the sustained decrease of good jobs in the primary sector has posed another crucial problem. The loss of good jobs at large enterprises was due mainly to corporate policy to carry out downsizing and outsourcing as well as expanding the use of non-regular labour. The share of employment at enterprises with more than 500 employees decreased from 17.2% (2.11 million) in 1993 to 10.2% (2.03 million) in 2014 (KLI, 2017a). Moreover, the process of de-industrialisation has accelerated since the mid-1990s, resulting in a reduction of manufacturing employment, having relatively a good job quality, compared with service jobs. Between 1995 and 2016, the percentage of employment in the manufacturing sector declined from 21.3% to 11.7%, while that of service sector increasing from 62.9% to 82.0% (KLI, 2017a).

The proliferation of non-regular employment and labour market polarisation both posed a critical challenge to the union movement and worker representation. Given the widening gaps between primary and secondary labour market segments, the vast majority of those marginal workforces (non-regular and small firm workers) in the latter segment do not receive union protection and other worker representation. Consequently, they have suffered low wages, insecure employment and exclusion from statutory welfare and legal standards. The union density of non-regular workforce was only 2.9% in 2017, which is much lower than 17.1% for the regular workforce. As shown in Table 12.2, while union density of large firms with 300 and more employees is 55.1%, it is only 0.2% and 3.5% in small firms, with less than 30 employees and 30–99 employees. Small firms with less than 30 employees are not legally obliged to form an LMC, and around 45% of firms

Table 12.2 Union Density by Establishment Size (as of 2016)

	Less Than 30 Employees	*30~99 Employees*	*100~299 Employees*	*300 and More Employees*
No. of wage workforce	11,434,000	3,750,000	1,993,000	2,458,000
No. of union members	19,290	130,805	299,531	1,353,698
Union density (%)	0.2	3.5	15.0	55.1

Source: MoEL (2017).

with 30–99 employees, which have a legal obligation to establish LMC at their workplace, do not form the LMC at all (Jang, 2016). It is criticised that unions, entrapped by the entrenched practice of enterprise unionism, have made little effort to represent the unorganised workers in non-regular employment and small firms, despite the stagnant union density of around 10%. Labour market polarisation, which has become more noticeable along with the widening wage gap by firm size and the proliferation of non-regular workforce, was to some extent attributed to the enterprise unionism, which excluded interest representation of those marginal workers (non-regular and small firm workers), since they were mostly located outside enterprise unions' organisational boundary. Hence, enterprise unionism was criticised for producing a 'solidarity crisis' within the labour movement as well as labour market polarisation (Lee, 2005).

Unions' strategic moves and achievements in response to challenges

Faced with a sustained decline in union density and a shrinkage in social influence, as well as growing labour market polarisation and proliferation of non-regular employment, since the late 1990s unions have various undertaken certain strategic actions to deal with those challenges and revitalise labour movements. The first significant action was the unions' strategic efforts to transform their organisational structure from enterprise unionism towards industry unionism. Many union leaders and activists, who had experienced employers' unilateral restructuring and union suppression during 1990s, particularly after the economic crisis 1997, felt that enterprise unionism was impotent to defend the existing membership in such unfavourable context and sought to recruit new members among the unorganised (non-regular and small firm workers) at the margins of segmented labour markets.[4]

Conscious efforts to transform organisational structures from enterprise unionism to industry unionism came to fore in early 1990s. In particular, a strategic move towards industry unionism was made public by the Korean

Trade Union Congress (KTUC), which was established as the second national centre of democratic unions (and was a precursor to the KCTU) in 1990. The KTUC, which was built on labour movement principles of social reform, declared that its strategic goal was to mobilise joint collective action at the industrial level and ultimately reorganise the existing union structure into industry unionism, in order to overcome the fragmented labour movement, rooted in enterprise unionism (Lim, 1998; Eun et al., 2008). The KTUC's strategic direction of industry unionisation was formulated with a dual aim: first, to build a powerful centralised union structure, differentiated with the loose association of enterprise unions under the FKTU, and second, to actively recruit unorganised workers and strengthen their bargaining power and sociopolitical leverage by its pursuit of social movement unionism.

Since the late 1990s, the strategic move has been made for transforming their organisational structure to industrial unionism, in order to tackle with the limitations of enterprise unionism. In 1998, the Korea Health and Medical Workers Union (KHMWU), comprised of nurses and other medical staff in hospitals, was formed as the first industry union. Subsequently, many unions in other sectors followed the example of the hospital union. These included the Korea Finance Industry Union (KFIU), the Korea Taxi Industry Workers Union (KTIWU) and the National Union of Media Workers (NUMU) in 2000; the Korea Metal Workers Union (KMWU) in 2001; the Korea Transport Workers Union (KTWU) in 2006; the Korea Construction Workers Union (KCWU) in 2007; and the National Public and Transport Workers Union (NPTWU) in 2011. Industry unionisation has been primarily led by the KCTU affiliates, although a couple of newly established industry unions (e.g., KFIU and KTIWU) are affiliated with the FKTU. This is because the KCTU, which was formed in 1995, has made a strenuous effort to transform its affiliates towards industry unionism. The KCTU made it clear in the founding doctrine that it would pursue the strategic goal of building industry unions and forging a unified movement of the working class, following the industry unionism policy of its precursor, the KTUC. At its annual general congress of 1999, the KCTU officially announced the roadmap to reorganise its affiliates into eight industry unions by 2007, as shown in Table 12.3. Although the KCTU has not yet achieved the entire transformation of its affiliates towards industry unions, as originally planned, it has made substantial progress in this organisational renewal, as demonstrated by the fact that 82.6% of its membership is affiliated with industry unions in 2016. By contrast, only 45.8% of FKTU affiliates belong to industry unions, as it has been less active at organisational restructuring. Although there exist some differences in the strategic emphasis on industry unionism between the KCTU and the FKTU, the total share of members, affiliated with industry unions within the two national centres grew from 10% (160,000) to 55% (1,088,000) of total union membership between 1996 and 2016.

Table 12.3 The KCTU's Roadmap for Industry Unionisation

	1999		*2007*
Industrial sector	Union Federation		Industry Union
Manufacturing	Metal Union Federation Chemical & Textile Union Federations		Metal Workers Union Chemical & Textile Workers Union
Construction	Construction Union Federations		Construction Workers Union
Medical	Hospital Union Federation	⇨	Public Service Union
Public Service	Public Service Union Federation		
Business Service	Facility Maintenance Union Federation		
Transportation	Taxi, Bus, Trucking Union Federations		
Finance	Financial Union Federation		Financial Workers Union
Education	Teachers Union, Faculty & College Union Federation		Teachers Union
Media	Media Union Federation		Media Workers Union
Service	Commercial & Hotel Union Federations		Commercial & Tourism Workers Union

Source: Lee and Yi (2012).

The formation of industry unions in Korea has posed a greater emphasis on centralised bargaining, in contrast to the decentralising trends in bargaining observed in most Western countries. In particular, three leading industrial unions, the KMWU, the KHMWU and the KFIU, made substantial progress achieving national agreements with their employers' associations. The KMWU has a three-level bargaining structure, comprising the national, regional and enterprise levels, while the KHMWU and the KFIU have two tiers: national and enterprise levels. These national agreements include some important clauses, including sectoral minimum wages and staffing policy, financial assistance and equal treatment to improve the employment conditions of non-regular workers and enhancement of working shift systems (Lee & Kim, 2013). In addition, some industry unions have been effective in recruiting new members (e.g., NPTWU), engaging in solidarity protest to assist non-regular workers' struggle (e.g., KMWU), and establishing their own research centres and developing policy recommendations to consult with the government (e.g., KFIU and NPTWU) by centralising organisational resource and operational structure (Lee, 2003; Lee & Kim, 2013).

At the same time, industry unions have been confronted with strong opposition from employers at large firms – particularly chaebols – and public institutions and become stagnant under the conservative governments (2008–2017) which were pursuing pro-business policies. Unions have faced employers' opposition to industry-level bargaining, especially from large firms, including chaebols, and public institutions (i.e., hospitals, universities and public enterprises), so that there has been little extension of industry-wide contracts to the unorganised or non-regular workforce (Lee, 2003). Under the conservative anti-union governments, the opposition of employers to the industrial unions' demand for centralised collective bargaining has become even stronger, thereby leading to their industry-wide bargaining suffering significant setbacks during the past ten years. Moreover, industrial unions have recorded not only very low organisational coverage, as evinced with their minimal union density of around 10%–20% in the relevant sectors, but also achieved the limited concentration of organisational resources (such as membership dues and union staff) and bargaining authority from their enterprise units (Lee & Kim, 2013). As such, while industry unionisation has to a certain extent been successful in organisational transformation from enterprise unionism, the new forms of unionism have been faced with crucial limitations in centralised bargaining and operations.

Another strategic move has been observed in the 'new union model' which aimed to organise the unorganised on the margin of labour markets (i.e., non-regular and small firm workers, and youth and the aged under the precarious employment or unemployment) since late 2000s. Non-regular workers, who suffered from disposable employment and discriminatory working conditions, attempted to organise their own unions at workplace from late 1990s. Most of those unions, however, failed to achieve organisational sustainability as well as their intended bargaining outcomes, due to employers' harsh suppression as well as regular workers unions' indifference or interference (Lee, 2005). Given the recurring failure to recruit non-regular workers at the enterprise level, new attempts to organise those precarious workers into the community-based general union were initiated in the late 2000s. The exemplar case of the community unionism is the Hope Solidarity Union (HSU), formed in 2009. During the 2010s, this union launched a series of active organising campaigns and was successful in unionising over 4,000 contracted workers in various work sites (including call centres, cable TV engineering shops and mobile phone service centres) in the Seoul Metropolitan area. The HSU has devised and operated a variety of community-based solidarity networking activities, such as cultural concerts, liberal arts and media study programmes, community gardening and international exchange for immigrant workers, to assist and involve non-regular workers in Seoul. These activities have extended beyond the boundary of the union's traditional organisational membership (Park et al., 2014).

In addition, there have been a series of attempts to form unions using a new organisational logic of age-cohort groupings during the 2010s. These new unions are exemplified by Youth Union, Alba Union and Senior Hope Union. The Youth Union was formed in 2009 as the first age-cohort union, which aims to organise and represent young precarious workers, aged between fifteen and thirty-five. This union has effectively launched a series of targeted campaigns to protest against the so-called black companies, which treat young workers in inhumane and illegal manners, in coffee shops and fast-food chains and pizza restaurants. The Youth Union reached a policy agreement with Seoul City in 2013 to undertake joint efforts to expand job opportunities for young workers and enhance their job quality. Owing to its successful activities to represent young workers by protest campaigns and policy consultation, the Youth Union's membership has increased sharply from 472 in 2012 to 1,270 in 2016, and the number of its non-member supporters has also grown from 244 to 604 during the same period. In 2013, the Alba Union was organised for representing young workers, employed in part-time jobs, called 'Alba' in Korean. The Alba Union has engaged in more militant protest action, targeting McDonalds franchises and major convenience store franchises, while initiating solidarity campaigns to raise the legal minimum hourly wage to 10,000 Korean won (approximately 9.34 US dollars in 2018). Along with its active campaigns, the Alba Union has drawn public attention and seen the sustained growth of its membership to around 400 in 2015. The Senior Hope Union was officially established in 2013 by activists and member who had retired from existing unions. This union has sought to represent senior workers and enhance their welfare and job opportunities by policy consultation with the central and local governments. However, the activities of the senior workers' union have not attracted as much public attention as the Youth Union and the Alba Union.

Moreover, a number of worker centres have been formed with the aims of representing non-regular workers' rights and carrying out various activities to protect those precarious workers. These worker centres have been formed nationwide since the Korean Contingent Workers' Centre was established in 2000. As local governments, including Seoul Metro City, began expressing their growing concern about precarious workers in local labour markets and offered financial assistance to the establishment and operation of local labour centres in 2010s, the number of worker centres, run by the local labour activists, has proliferated to thirty-seven in 2017 (Jung et al., 2017). In 2012, the Korean Non-regular Worker Centre Network was formed and has engaged in a variety of solidarity actions to mutually support non-regular workers' struggles across the country and put pressure the government to adopt policy solutions to improve precarious workers' employment conditions.

Conclusion: theoretical implications for VoU model

Since the 1998 economic crisis, the Korean political economy has been transformed from the state-led development model to the neo-liberal market-driven one, marginally equipped with the social dialogue scheme, which could be classified the LME in the VoC typology. Confronted with the polarisation of labour markets and proliferation of non-regular workers, which are key element of accompanied with the transformation towards the new political economy regime, two remarkable strategic initiatives have been remarkably undertaken by labour movements in Korea during the past thirty years. First, unions have made strategic efforts to move from the existing enterprise unionism towards industrial unionism. Second, a new approach of unionisation and worker representation is adopting the organisational logic of age-cohort grouping (e.g., the Youth Union, the Alba Union and the Senior Hope Union) and local community-building (e.g., the Hope Solidarity Union and local worker centres).

Industry unionisation in Korea is noteworthy in two ways: First, the strategic move of Korean unions towards a more centralised organisational and bargaining structure contrasts with many of Western countries, where industry unions have accepted decentralisation of bargaining systems, thereby weakening their bargaining leverage (Katz, 1993). Second, industry unionisation has been the main thrust of revitalisation strategies undertaken by Korean unions to cope with the fracturing of workers collectivism (Bacon & Storey, 1996) and a crisis of labour solidarity (Lee, 2005). According to the typology of union revitalisation strategies formulated by Frege and Kelly (2003), industry unionisation, launched by Korean unions, is basically targeted at 'organising organisational restructuring', including union amalgamation, in order to strengthen their sociopolitical influence and bargaining leverage. In addition, those unions which are attempting to transform their organisational structure towards industry unionism seek to improve their chance of their 'organising' the unorganised. They are also attempting to reshape the existing fragmented bargaining system into a centralised model in order to take organised labour out of market competition. However, it should also be noted that industry unionisation, which has been successful in relation to organisational restructuring, has not made significant progress towards centralised bargaining and organising of the unorganised. A major constraining factor has been large firms' determined opposition and negative policies of conservative governments to these reforms by industry unions.

The new approach to unionisation and worker representation, exemplified by age-cohort unions as well as local community-based union and worker centres, has made significant headway in organising precarious workers and protecting them by policy consultation and public protest campaigns. In this new organising model, unionisation by age-cohort groups appears to be distinct from organising strategies adopted by unions in some Western countries like the US and the UK (Frege & Kelly, 2003), while community-based unionisation having similarities. Those organising campaigns in Korea has been commonly led by various activist groups at the grass-roots level (e.g., youth activists, former student activists, local labour activists and retired union members), who are outside the mainstream of the union movement, rather than being driven by the existing unions' initiatives in the top-down manner.

Table 12.4 summarises union revitalisation strategies and their outcomes, adapting the comparative framework of varieties of unionism (VoU) by Frege and Kelly (2003). It is noteworthy that the other four union revitalisation

Table 12.4 Union Renewal Strategies and Their Outcomes in South Korea

Strategy	*Union action*	*Achievements*	*Constraints*
Reform of union structures	Organisational transformation from enterprise unionism to industry unionism	55% of union membership affiliated with industry unions Some achievements in organising campaigns and centralised bargaining	Stagnant industrial bargaining, due to employers' opposition and the conservative government's suppression
International solidarity	Affiliation to international union organisation	Little achievement	Union leaders' indifference to international solidarity action, except their petitions of domestic labour issues to the ILO.
Labour–management partnership	Little meaningful action (with unusual exceptions like LGE)	Little achievement	Confrontational labour-management relations persisted (e.g., employers' union-busting campaigns)
Organising	New union organising and worker representation, attempted by the age-cohort and community activism	Age-cohort and community unions (e.g., Youth Union, Alba Union, Senior Union, Hope Solidarity Union, Non-regular Workers Centres) succeeding in organising campaigns and exerting public voice/ impact for marginal workers groups	Limited organisational resources
Political action	Labor Party formed by the KCTU and Social Democratic Part by the FKTU	Labor Party gained a limited seats/leverage in the Congress; Social Democratic Party failed to obtain any seat at all	Rank-and-file's indifference to the national centres' political campaigns
Coalition-building	Union-Civil social movement (CSM) coalition often attempted	Some exceptional achievements, like candle-light demonstration, made, but many of union-CSM coalition campaigns made meaningful outcomes	Many coalition campaigns attempted in an ad hoc manner and a short-term time span, characterised as resistance solidarity against government and business

strategies of the VoU framework, such as social partnership, coalition-building, political action and international networking, have hardly made meaningful achievements in Korea, although some of these strategic initiatives were undertaken by unions. Those strategies have failed to produce noticeable outcomes, confronted by employers' entrenched anti-union attitudes, the government's neo-liberal policy stance, the rank-and-file's indifference and hollowed-out relationship with civil social movements.

Notes

1 The Act on the Establishment and Operation of Trade Unions for Teachers and the Act on the Establishment and Operation of Public Official's Trade Unions was, respectively, enacted in 1999 and 2005.
2 According to the changed survey, which has been conducted since 2008, the relative ratio of total wages small firms (with 10–29 employees), compared to large firms with 300 employees and more, has stayed around 60%–62% between 2008 and 2016.
3 While the share of non-regular workforce has decreased during 2010s owing to the government's strengthened regulation over the use of contingent and dispatched workers, the labour circle and NGOs have insisted that there have existed additional non-regular workers, amounting to 2.7 million (approximately 10% of the workforce) in such hidden forms as subcontracted and dependent self-employed labour (Jang, 2017).
4 In addition, the tripartite agreement to legislate the prohibition of company payment for union officers' wages, which was made in 1998 and finally implemented in 2010, encouraged union leaders, concerned about the reduced organisational resources of enterprise unions, to realign those resources in a centralised format by transforming union structure to industry unionism. Such changes in institutional arrangements of industrial relations strengthened unions' inclination towards industry unionisation (Visser & Waddington, 1996).

References

Bacon, J. & Storey, N. (1996). 'Individualism and collectivism and the changing role of trade unions'. in Ackers, P., Smith, C., & Smith, P. (eds.), *The New Workplace and Trade Unionism*, London: Routledge, pp. 41–76.
Eun, S., Jung, J., & Lee, J. (2008). *Is Industrial Labour Relations Realizable Future?* Seoul: KLI. (in Korean).
Frege, C. & Kelly, J. (2003). 'Union revitalization strategy in comparative perspective'. *European Journal of Industrial Relations*, 9(1): 7–24.
Hall, P. & Soskice, D. (2001). *Varieties of Capitalism*. Oxford: Oxford University Press.
Jang, H. (2016). 'Survey report on the operational state of labour-management council'. Research Report to the Ministry of Employment and Labour. (in Korean)
Jung, H., Rho, S., & Lee C. (2017). 'Past 10 years (2007–2017) and future prospect of local non-regular labour centers movement'. Paper Presented to the Seoul Labour Center Seminar. (in Korean)
Jang, J. (2017). 'Various employment types and labour market inequality'. *KLI Employment & Labour Brief*, No. 69 (2017–2). (in Korean)

Katz, H. (1993). 'The decentralization of collective bargaining: a literature review and comparative analysis'. *Industrial and Labour Relations Review*, 47(1): 3–22.

Kim, Y. (2015). 'Benefitiaries and under-paid workers of minimum wages', KLSI Issue Paper 2015-05. (in Korean)

KLI. (2017a). *2017 KLI Labour Statistics*. Seoul: Korean Labour Institute. (in Korean)

KLI. (2017b). *2017 KLI Non-regular Labour Statistics*. Seoul: Korean Labour Institute. (in Korean)

Lee, B. (2003). 'Industrial relations system'. in Kim, J. (ed.), *Employment and Industrial Relations in Korea*. Seoul: KOILAF, pp. 171–213.

Lee, B. (2005). 'Solidarity crisis of Korean labour movement'. *Korea Focus*, 13(1): 86–106.

Lee, B. & Kang, H. (2012). 'Hybridization of employment relations in the era of globalization? a comparative study case study of the automotive and banking industries in South Korea'. *International Journal of Human Resource Management*, 23(10): 2034–2050.

Lee, B. & Kim, J. (2013). *Revitalizing Strategies for Industry Union Movement*. Seoul: KCTU. (in Korean)

Lee, B. & Yi, S. (2012). 'Organisational transformation towards industry unionism in South Korea'. *Journal of Industrial Relations*, 54(4): 476–493.

Lee, J. (2002). 'Industrial unionization and change of bargaining structure'. Paper presented to the International Conference of International Labour Standards and Korean Industrial Relations, Seoul.

Lee, W. & Lee, B. (2003). 'Industrial relations and labour standards in Korea'. in Kwon, O. (ed.), *Korea's New Economy Strategy in the Globalization Era*. Cheltenham: Edward Elgar, pp. 173–191.

Lim, Y. (1998). 'Transformation of Korean labour regime and industrial relations: corporatism or re-radicalization?'. *Economy & Society*, 38: 102–124. (in Korean)

MoEL. (2017). *2016 Report on Organisational Status of Trade Unions*. Seoul: Ministry of Employment and Labour. (in Korean)

Park, M., Kwon, H., Yoo, H., & Jin, S. (2014). *Diversification of Worker Interest Representation and the Formation of New Industrial Relations*. Seoul: Korea Labour Institute. (in Korean)

Park, W. & Roh, Y. (2001). *Changes in Human Resource Management and Industrial Relations in the Period of Post-Crisis*. Seoul: KLI.

Visser, J. & Waddington, J. (1996). 'Industrialization and politics: a century of union structural development in three European countries'. *European Journal of Industrial Relations*, 2(1): 21–53.

13 Still trapped between the state and management

Unions and worker representation in Taiwan in an era of globalisation

Shih-wei Pan

Introduction

Taiwan's labour union movement has been confined between the legacy of a party-state and a management heavily dependent on the global supply chains. The legacy of the labour policy, established by the Kuomintang (KMT) after 1949, was a 'state-centred' employment relations system (Wu, 1999; Wang, 2010), in which the roles of labour and management were insignificant. Institutional change through the political liberalisation and democracy movement in the late 1980s did not alter the behaviour and mindset of Taiwanese society. Even though Taiwan still maintains rather strong purchasing power and a good quality of life, the economy is heavily dependent on the global supply chain as its manufacturers, which specialise in intermediary goods (Chen, 2016), are among the world's most flexible and efficient. But a high-quality workforce endures long working hours and stagnant wages.

In addition to labour unions at the workplace, labour advocacy groups (labour non-governmental organisations (NGOs)) have played a proactive role in representing workers' voices in Taiwan over the last three decades. The labour NGO is called 'lau-tuan' or workers' group (referred to as LTs hereafter). Statutory mechanisms on behalf of workers' interests in the employment relations system also exist. In the central government, various tripartite or quadripartite committees (labour, management, government and academics) are formed in the labour policymaking process. The corporate management also uses quality circle programmes and other similar schemes to increase productivity at the workplace.

While labour unions in Taiwan appeared to be gradually breaking away from the influence of political parties, following the political liberalisation movement of the late 1980s, their dependence on the government support seems to be even greater today. One major reason is that labour still lacks countervailing power to deal with management, and economic globalisation has given further leverage to management to render unions even more vulnerable. Another reason for the unions continued dependence on government may be attributed to the cultural and social tradition of the benevolent state as the rightful arbiter to determine the processes and outcomes of all social relations. A paradox has emerged, however, as the benevolent state, which is supposed to maintain a balance between labour and management, continues to weaken as it reconfigures to cope with the impact of globalisation. The result has been that the power of the state has shifted to the side of management. A labour union movement without a consolidated structure and economic strategy will weaken the framework set by both the state and management.

This chapter begins by introducing union and other worker representation structures in Taiwan. This is followed by an analysis of core challenges confronting unions and worker representation resulting from economic globalisation. Thereafter, strategies adopted by labour to deal with these challenges are examined. In the final section, consideration is given to factors which might be added to the existing 'varieties of capitalism' (VoC) and 'varieties of unionism' (VoU) theories in order to better understand employment relations in Taiwan as well as other economies which are based on traditional Chinese ethical principles.

The union movement in Taiwan

Taiwan's union movement can be traced to the Japanese occupation era (1895–1945). There were six unions in 1922, with only 827 members. In 1927, unions increased to fifty-seven and members grew to 8,175. By 1933, the unions had increased to 127, with 21,967 union members (Wu, 2002). Organised in 1928, the Federation of Taiwan Workers became the first union federation, and among its affiliations were machinery workers, carpenters, barbers, ship workers, metalworkers, printing workers, etc. These unions launched strikes to demand wage increases, improve working conditions, eliminate labour spies and other labour issues. Some unions won these strikes while others failed, and some union members were arrested. After the 1930s, the Japanese colonial government suppressed left-wing activities and the union movement in Taiwan gradually lost strength (Wu, 2002).

The Japanese colony of Taiwan was returned to the Republic of China (ROC) in 1945. In 1949, the civil war in Mainland China forced the then KMT central government to retreat to Taiwan. The KMT government introduced a system of labour laws according to legislations originated from China. Knowledge of labour policy and legislation originated from China before 1949 is important for understanding of how and why the union movement developed in Taiwan as well as ascertaining to what extent the union movement in Taiwan might be revitalised to become an effective partner in the relationship between workers and management.

Before 2011, unions in Taiwan were organised in two forms. First, the in-house enterprise or workplace-based unions were organised by industrial workers who were employed with a permanent employer; industrial workers were not allowed to organise or join a craft union. Second, self-employed workers (whether individual contractor or owner-operator), and workers with non-permanent employers, could organise or join a craft union at the city or county level. By joining the craft union, these workers were entitled to participate in the labour insurance scheme. However, industry or craft-wide unions across different workplaces or regions were not legally recognised. The in-house unions and regional craft unions could be affiliated with the craft or industry federation and to organise local labour councils. A single national union centre, the Chinese Federation of Labor, was organised through these industrial, craft federations and local councils, as well as by enterprise unions in state-owned companies.

In 2011, the Labour Union Act was revised to liberalise this structure. The new Act permitted the termination of monopoly unionism and allowed multiple unionism; teachers were also free to organise, and freedom of association was introduced in the public sector. Additional liberalisation occurred through the lifting of restrictions against organising industrial or craft-wide unions across different workplaces, although workers might continue to organise in-house unions based in the workplace or the firm.

Although the new labour legislation appeared to provide more choice for workers to organise, Taiwan remains a country in which the state is still expected to be the major decision maker in employment relations. Hence, unions still rely on government to intervene in the industrial relations. Moreover, the procedure to determine which union is authorised to bargain with an employer has not been clarified within a multiple unionism environment. Furthermore, in the absence of class consciousness, union leaders tended to form their own unions territorially, thus eliminating the opportunity to unite and share resources (Ho, 2008).

By 2015, overall union density in Taiwan was 33.2%. The unionisation rate for industrial workers, including enterprise and industrial unions, was only 7.3%. The membership density of craft unions was much higher at 42.9% (Ministry of Labor, 2017). The labour insurance scheme, which is in high demand by craft workers, stimulated the growth of craft unions (Kuruvilla, Das, Kwon, & Kwon, 2002, Chen, Ko, & Lawler, 2003). In 2015, total union membership stood at 3,348,702. Craft unions had 2,715,200 members, while industrial unions had only 633,502 members (Ministry of Labour (MOL), 2017).

The labour insurance scheme is one of the most important factors determining union density in Taiwan. The scheme was enacted in 1950, providing coverage for all workers. The scheme is only a social security system but also covers medical, maternity, workers compensation, old-aged benefits, etc. Craft workers, self-employed and those workers affiliated with no permanent employers, as well as workers employed in firms with less than five employees, are eligible for insurance coverage. As the number of workers in precarious employment has increased, craft unionism has grown, but craft unions provide only insurance and do not engage in collective bargaining.

Although industrial workers in Taiwan are organised at the workplace, they are nevertheless subject to management's prerogative for several reasons. First, industrial worker unions are normally organised in-house at small- and medium-sized firms and at the plant level in larger firms. The in-house union has an endogenous problem because it is very easy for management to intervene and control union activity. Furthermore, due to their small-scale and limited resources, in-house unions have very low monthly dues – on average, around between NT$30 and NT$300 (1–10 US dollars). Even though in-house unions can organise a federation, these are financially weak because the unions' income, collected in the form of dues, is generally kept in-house or at the local craft unions. The union federation is, therefore, unable to keep permanent staff to professionally manage the union to organise and bargain collectively. Although restrictions against union organising have been lifted since 2011, the unions' capacity to organise and bargain has improved very little because union leaders and workers have not changed their previous mindset.

Currently, there are ten national union central councils with more than 600 industrial- and craft-based national-affiliated federations. Many national councils are affiliated with duplex membership among those federations. At the county or city level, local labour councils likewise have duplex membership so that three to five local councils are normal. Within the firm or workplace, industrial workers may organise different unions, i.e., workers may organise in-house unions along different lines: by the entire firm, individual workplace, region, craft or industrial-wide union. For instance, at the biggest telecommunication firm in Taiwan, Chunghua Telecom, 12 unions represent 25,000 employees. Management has expressed its concern about the difficulty of dealing with political differences between different union leaders and problems related to the large number of unions (Pan, 2016b).

Other forms of labour representation

Various labour laws in Taiwan have been instituted to promote worker participation in management. For example, The Employee Welfare Fund Committee is stipulated in the Employee Welfare Fund Act, the Occupational Safety and Health committee is required by the Occupational Safety and Health Act, and the labour–management committee is part of in the Labor Standards Act, etc. The formation of these committees reflects the intentions of early policymakers, who adopted the conceptual foundation of the German industrial relations system, through which they expected to improve labour–management relations. However, the development of these systems failed owing to the overarching role of the state, which discourages a model of equal partnership between labour and management. For instance, the labour–management committee has a bipartite structure with labour and management representatives on each side. Labour representatives can be elected through an in-house union's convention or, if labour is not organised, through a general election among workers. The election is conducted by the firm, which also appoints management representatives. Experience has shown, however, that most firms falsify meeting records, pre-arrange appointees to be elected as workers' representatives and use the decisions of the labour–management committee to challenge unions' in-house proposals (Pan, 2001).

A labour director on the corporate board is required in state-owned enterprises. At least one fifth of the directors, and trustees of a state-run enterprise who represent state capital, are recommended by the relevant in-house labour union (Administrative Law of State-Owned Enterprise, ALSOE). The union may replace the recommended directors and trustees who are considered incompetent (ALSOE). These director(s) are elected by the in-house union. This system attempts to replicate the German co-determination system whereby the labour director on the company board oversees the firm's decision-making with regard to employees' interests (Wei, 2002). Compared to other participation mechanisms, this system is more successful because the management of the state-owned companies is also appointed by the government, so legal compliance is required.

Tripartite or quadripartite mechanisms have also been introduced at the national level in the decision-making process of the central government, especially at the MOL. Various functional committees are set up to serve as platforms to consult and inform labour and management with regard to labour and employment issues. These committees function to cover a wide range of concerns, including the minimum wage, migrant workers, labour insurance supervision, pension fund supervision, the overdue wages payment fund, etc. Both the union and management's national centres are invited to appoint representatives to attend these committees regularly. These platforms to consult on and inform regarding labour and employment issues have become more important in recent years for two key reasons. First, the government needs greater information to come to terms with the complexity of labour issues in an era of globalisation. Second, labour and management representatives are able to express their concerns and make suggestions regarding decisions related to policy and legislation. However, the platforms come at a cost because they can ignite political battles between labour and management, consequently making labour issues even more complicated.

Employers may activate private initiatives, such as quality circles, to ensure the voices of workers are heard. Quality circles are among the most common productivity-promoting institutions among Taiwanese firms, particularly in the manufacturing sector due to the close linkage in the supply chain involving Japanese manufacturers. This kind of mechanism, however, does not provide workers with autonomy because the leader and participants are arranged in accordance with management's agenda. While these arrangements may peripherally address workers' demands, priorities are generally set by management.

The labour advocacy groups – the Lau-Tuan

Over the last three decades, the most important voices on behalf of workers in Taiwan have been the labour advocacy groups, or Lau-Tuan (LTs), as they are called in Mandarin Chinese. LTs emerged during the late 1980s, as part of the political liberalisation and democracy movement. Due to the oil crisis and the enactment of the labour standards act, as well as political liberalisation, Taiwanese business was under both economic and political pressures in the late 1980s. Many firms rushed to move out of Taiwan or simply closed, while some even illegally retrenched their employees, refusing back pay. In response to inept official unions and deficient labour regulations, labour activists organised workers to form so-called self-rescue organisations to hold rallies and protests against the government to seek compensation for these workers. Some LTs aimed to challenge official union functions; some aimed to appeal to the public by giving voice to workers' situations and demands; others wanted to challenge government policies and legislation in order to bring change to regulations to improve worker protection. In general, LTs have proved to be very capable in raising attention to social issues, though in their attempt to best convey their stories to the media, they took somewhat atypical action to get attention. The LTs organised social and political campaigns to raise their concerns to the public, although these tactics were not used in the process of collective bargaining over economic terms and conditions.

The development of LTs reflects the powerlessness of unions in Taiwan's employment relations. This weakness may also be attributed to an imbalanced labour relations system, in which the state plays, as expected by society, the most important role. The existence of an employment relations system, in which the state takes the place of the union, stems from the idea of the benevolent state. In traditional Chinese society, the state is personified and given moral attributes so that people can judge its behaviour. The authority of the state is given by God but can be retracted if the state does not present good behaviour in response to the needs of the common people. The notion of moral essence embedded within the state has been embedded in Chinese society for at least 2500 years. In the Western political culture, the idea of state is different. Machiavelli enunciated the principle that realism rather than idealism should be the conceptual foundation of a modern state. The king's virtue served as only a tactic or strategy to maintain political power. Being virtuous is not the objective of the state. Indeed, a skilful monarch must balance good and evil behaviours to serve political ends. Without regard to virtue, Machiavelli even proposed the use of harsh power, as well as rewards, to maintain the strength of the state.

While the labour NGOs and unions work together to voice workers' rights and interests, the relationship between the two parties can be awkward. Both are in need of the other party to enhance labour solidarity yet both are also afraid of being surpassed by the other. On the one hand, political actions taken by unions and labour NGOs demonstrate workers' militancy. On the other hand, union leaders would rather to keep low profile and to co-operate with the management at the firm and workplace levels, to preserve enterprise-based unionism.

Core challenges confronting unions and worker representative bodies

More than 50% of the jobs in Taiwan are related to the global supply chain (Kizu, Kühn, & Vigeelahn, 2016: 8–9), and the economy depends heavily on the global market. Competition in global markets is not uncommon, but increased globalisation has caused many Taiwanese firms to struggle to alter their traditional strategies in order to stay competitive. Taiwanese firms are known for their flexibility and efficiency, features that derive from competition for marginal labour costs in the supply chain (Wang, 2001; ILO, 2016: 22). Pressure on management has made unions and workers in Taiwan even more vulnerable. Workers have to deal with three conspicuous challenges, namely: long working hours, stagnant pay and increasing non-standard employment.

A recent dispute concerning the revision of the labour standards legislation (LSA) shows how unions and LTs represented workers who were concerned about long working hours. In 2017, with an average of 2034 yearly total working hours, the Organisation for Economic Co-operation and Development (OECD) placed Taiwan fifth among countries with longest working hours in 2017 (Teng, 2017). Long working hours are common in Taiwan (Yang, 2016), and it is argued that they are responsible for many casualties (Sui, 2012). The MOL claims that Taiwan has fewer non-standard workers than other countries and that many Taiwanese workers choose not to take all the number of leave days to which they are entitled (Yu & Wu, 2016). The unions and LTs see things differently, arguing that because employers tend to maintain an insufficient workforce, overload workers with tasks. Consequently, employees must work overtime to cover the unfinished work.

The dispute over the LSA revision began in 2015. The MOL proposed the reduction of statutory working hours from eighty-four hours biweekly to forty hours weekly. During the negotiations, convened by the MOL, labour and management representatives agreed to a proposal of forty hours a week conditional upon the cancellation of seven national holidays to compensate for the loss of working hours. The MOL proposal met fierce resistance in the Congress by the then Opposition, the Democratic Progressive Party (DPP), which had launched a political campaign to attract working-class support in the 2016 presidential election. With the support of the Opposition party, an ideological battle between management and labour began, with some LTs close to the DPP strongly opposing the ruling KMT government's legislative proposal. The forty-hour week amendment was finally passed, but seven national holidays remained in place. Nevertheless, the promise made by the DPP only lasted briefly. After the DPP candidate Tsai Ing-wen was elected as President in May 2016, the new government announced revision of the law to cancel the seven national holidays to compensate for the loss of working hours. A tug of war between labour and management as well as between political parties was again ignited. The solution was the extension of statutory paid leave and a disputable 'one fixed day off and one flexible rest day' regulation in exchange for the cancellation of the seven holidays. However, the revision did not appease management, since the new rules made the working hour system more complex and overtime pay expensive which, in practice, made business operations cumbersome. Workers also were not satisfied, as the employers might eliminate possible overtime tasks and hence overtime pay would be reduced. The Minister of Labour was replaced and the legislation revised again in 2017 under considerable pressure from employers. Within a year, the LSA was revised twice to maintain flexible working hours, and a longer time period was provided so that employers could extend the working hours within a certain period, although total working hours could not exceed the statutory maximum.

Wage stagnation has long been an important issue in Taiwan. It began with the financial tsunami in 2009, when the KMT government instituted a NT$ 22,000 salary subsidy programme for young college graduates who either lost or were unable to find jobs because of the recession. To apply for the government subsidy, the programme requested employers to hire young workers at a starting salary of least NT$22,000 but which should be increased when business improved as the economy recovered. However, because this decision ignored market forces, young new entrants to the workforce started at NT$22,000 regardless of whether the business was able to offer better wages.

Wage stagnation is a major challenge to the labour market in Taiwan and a manifestation of the weakness of Taiwan's economic environment. In 2012, for instance, workers real monthly wages for the first seven months was NT$ 44,360 (US$1,513), down from NT$45,469 during the same period in 2003 (*The Wall Street Journal*, 2012). LTs and unions, as well as political parties, proposed an increase in the minimum wage. The minimum wage in Taiwan has been adjusted yearly between 2009 and 2017. However, many employers and liberal market economists argue that the rapid increase of the minimum wage will reduce the employment of marginal workers and that migrant workers will be the biggest beneficiaries. The real problem, however, concealed by the way Taiwan business operates in the global market.

For the last four decades, the competitive edge of Taiwanese businesses has been its flexibility and efficiency of operation, but this advantage comes at the expense of its workforce. Recently, however, the competitive margin from this traditional labour-cost saving strategy has been losing effectiveness because of globalisation, which allows employers to seek cheaper workforces in other developing countries. However, Taiwanese business has yet to transform its role in the supply chain (Chen, 2016).

From a labour and employment relations perspective, Taiwanese firms are disadvantaged by negligence by employers of workers' rights and interests, brought on by the logic of the global supply chain. Traditionally, Taiwanese firms have ignored employment and industrial relations because they have never been confronted by labour militancy. Departments that function to manage employment relations in Taiwanese firms generally do not exist. The neglect by management in Taiwanese firms of employment relations is embodied in their business structure vis-à-vis the global supply chain. Taiwanese manufacturers have played a key role in many global brands, such as producing components for the wafer fab producer, TSMC. These firms possess very flexible production capacity, including a large workforce, timely production, advanced technology and very competitive labour cost margin. The disregard of employment relations in Taiwanese firms can also be attributed to the management of the global brands' corporate social responsibility (CSR) policy (Pan, 2016a). Once these firms have observed codes of conduct and have been cleared from auditing, their business contracts are secured. The observance of CSR policy thus shelters firms, allowing them to disregard employment relations policies since these do not have strategic value to the company's profits. Furthermore, many global brands leave very little margin for their Taiwanese manufacturers to provide decent compensation and a satisfactory work environment as they do for their own employees (Pan, 2015).

In a nutshell, workers' wages have stagnated over the past two decades because the average Taiwanese worker has been forced to compete directly with much lower cost countries, including mainland China. The Chinese economy has affected business strategy in Taiwan. The focus of government policy has also shifted from labour to management. Taiwanese business owners who benefit from outsourcing typically do not transfer their income back to Taiwan or make additional investment. Thus, the real income gains of these firms are not fully reflected in workers' wages. The development of the service economy has yet to improve the situation because the sector comprises many low-wage food and beverage and retail services. While the Taiwan economy overall gained from outsourcing business operations abroad, business owners have been the most significant beneficiaries. Globalisation has not only made it easier for business to move capital to where it can obtain the best return but also enabled business owners to take advantage of off-shore banking and avoid paying taxation (Table 13.1).

Strategic actions taken by the unions and the labour movement

Unions in Taiwan have taken countermeasures such as launching industrial action on an individual basis to respond to management's illegal

Table 13.1 Challenges Confront Unions and Worker Representation in Taiwan

Internal Challenges	*External Challenges*
• About 80% of union members are from craft unions, mainly for labour insurance coverage, not for collective bargaining • Fragmented labour union structure existed at national, local and firm levels • Weakness of the confederations with duplicate affiliates among trade union centres (both national and local) • Compulsory membership for enterprise-based industrial union weakens workers' consciousness of solidarity • Weak funding base through dues, enterprise-based unions are over reliant on the support from the employer either physically or financially • Low manpower and capacity of labour union officials	• Global supply chain-based export economy: by long working hours, dispatch workforce and stagnated wage • Increasing levels of non-standard employment within the formal sector • Legacies of state benevolence with authoritarian period approaches to industrial relations • Trade union functions are replaced by government through legislations • Labour advocacy groups challenge trade union functions • Weakness of employer organisations

Source: Generated by the author.

behaviour. However, there is a lack of an overall strategy by unions and other forms of worker representation to cope with the impacts of globalisation. The problem lies in the fact that labour organisations are fragmented, relying too much on publicity generated through political campaigns instead of through economic bargaining. Since the overall strength of unions and other forms of labour representation is weak, they tend to tackle immediate issues through immediate action to raise the attention of the public and to expect the government and politicians to solve problems. Unions do not appear to have the capacity to develop a comprehensive and thoughtful strategy.

The case of the strike launched by the Taoyuan Flight Attendants Union (TFAU) against the China Airlines in 2017 illustrates how the unions in Taiwan become trapped in a 'politics-only' strategy. The dispute in the China Airlines case attracted President Tsai Ing-Wen's sympathy for the striking flight attendants and was eventually resolved through government intervention. Because the government is the largest shareholder of China Airlines, it replaced the President and Managing Director in order to resolve the strike. Although the dispute appeared to achieve an improvement in the workers' terms and conditions, this was not the result of bargaining between labour and management. Instead, it was a compromise by the government to demonstrate its concern for workers' well-being. Initially, the flight attendants' union appeared to win the case by concluding a deal with management. However, additional disputes between the parties continued after the end of the strike, including allegations that management had reneged on earlier promises. The TEAF had trouble mounting another strike because it had to face the challenge from the company-based in-house China Airlines Union, whose members has a more moderate attitude. The fragmented structure of the unions thus further weakened their advocacy of flight attendants' demands.

Labour union differentiation is the outcome of Party politics. In 2000, the newly elected DPP government implemented an open-door policy towards the liberalisation of monopoly trade unionism. Monopoly trade union system was a system implemented by the KMT government in the early twentieth century and was inherited from Bolshevik ideology. The DPP open-door policy was welcomed as a means of restoring the original economic function of trade unions. However, in practice, the open-door policy appeared to be an attempt by the DPP to attract the Taiwan Trade Unions Confederation as an ally (Kuruvilla, Das, Kwon, & Kwon, 2002: 32). Following the open-door policy, unions were further splintered. Thus, while the number of unions increased, their membership only grew slowly.

The problem has been whether unions could unite themselves without government intervention or the government would have to introduce statutory procedures to identify union representation in collective bargaining. The legislative strategy of the LUA revision was intended to promote freedom of association, and it was anticipated that the unions would take the initiative to consolidate. As it turned out, unless the procedure to identify union representation from among multiple unions was undertaken by the government, union fragmentation would still remain because union leaders tend to be territorial. The sense of entrepreneurship among union leaders may be traced to individualism in Chinese society. Union leaders compete with each other to form their own organisations, and individualism takes the place of class consciousness (Ho, 2008), discouraging the possibility of forming a coherent union movement.

In order to understand why the state is so involved in Taiwanese employment relations, one must look to the history of the political liberalisation and democracy movement of the late 1980s, which triggered union action to resist the labour relations structure established by the KMT government. The unions wished to get away from the KMT's benign state ideology and create an alternative to the monopoly unionism which was established by the KMT. The autonomous union movement during the late 1980s and 1990s shocked the KMT-backed unions and aroused worker consciousness. However, lacking solidarity, the unions remained very weak, relying on the government to resolve their problems. Coming to terms with the source of this weakness requires an understanding of the importance of the moral state in the Chinese society.

Unions actively participate in the policy decision-making process of the central government. This provides opportunities for labour and management, with the assistance of academia, to conduct a dialogue on particular issues which are of joint interest. Although the unions' participation of these discussions may not result in any substantial changes in government policy, the participation itself is meaningful because it may improve communication between labour, management, the government and union leaders. It may also result in gaining support from the rank and file workforce.

Labour's achievement and factors that have influenced outcomes

If we take a different view from the traditional perspective of a labour relations system as a balance between labour and capital, it may well be that a weak union movement is an appropriate fit for Taiwan's circumstances. In this environment, the state plays the most important role and management responds in a timely way to the needs of the market. Despite the unions' powerlessness in negotiating with management, they are still able to achieve elements of their agenda, among the most important of which is to raise workers' consciousness regarding their rights and interests. Organised labour has been successful in pressing the government to notice the effect of labour policy and regulations and helping it to amend regulations. To meet workers' expectations, both unions and the LTs have prevented major policy changes affecting workers' pensions. Management has also increasingly been willing to enter into dialogue with unions and workers to enhance communication and improve wages and working conditions.

As government increasingly loses its authority as a result of globalisation, the ideology of the benevolent state may eventually disappear. Hence, a reconfiguration of strategy the unions and worker representatives would seem inevitable. Whether unions are able to consolidate and strengthen their economic power to be commensurate with that of management is of vital importance to the livelihoods of Taiwanese workers (Table 13.2).

Key theoretical implications for the VoC and VoU perspectives

Global attention on the study of employment relations has raised the question of whether contemporary research frameworks developed in the West are relevant when analysing employment relations in China and other strong state-led economies, such as Taiwan and Singapore. This requires greater focus on the importance of the state and to what extent it must seek to achieve a balance in employment relations between the social partners. Recent theoretical approaches such as the VoC (Hall & Soskice, 2001) and VoU (Frege & Kelly, 2004) originated from studies of advanced economies are difficult to apply to employment relations in Asian economies like Taiwan.

Taiwan does not easily fit into the category of a liberal market economy or a coordinated market economy in terms of the VoC theory. Taiwan has a

Table 13.2 Strategies Adopted by Labour and Related Achievements in Taiwan

Strategy	*Actions*	*Achievements*	*Problems*
Political action	A strategy frequently taken to advocate workers' rights and interests by political rally, street protest and action drama, operating through the media and press to press state authorities.	Raised public attention and consciousness on workers' rights and interests, government and law-making body are under pressure to promote pro-worker policy.	Negative attention from the public, divisions within and between unions/ LTs over political strategy, diversion of resources from unions' industrial functions.
Social dialogue	Through quadripartite platforms in central government to advance the agenda of workers' interests during policymaking process.	Voice worker's needs; supervise the process of policymaking and labour administration.	Internal politics within and between different unions regarding representation status. Compromised with employer and government in policy decision-making process.
Labour–management partnerships	Through legal platforms to advance workers' benefits and interests at the corporate and workplace levels.	Increase firm-level workers' participation. Some unions may obtain key information for in-house daily negotiations.	Unions maybe under management co-optation because of the in-house structure.

Source: Generated by the author.

liberal economy but with strong presence of the state which frequently intervenes in employment relations. The Taiwanese employment relations system seems to follow the German model of coordination but only on the surface. Taiwan has a fragmented employment relations structure and a weak system of collective bargaining. Therefore, it is also difficult to classify Taiwan as a coordinated market economy.

As noted by Frege and Kelly (2004), union strategies in different countries are shaped by national industrial relations institutions, as well as by the interactions between union, employer and the state. Methods used to revitalise the union movement in advanced economies may not be relevant to Taiwan. Over the years, it has been the government in Taiwan which has enacted policies and legislation to transform and revitalise unionism in Taiwan, while unions and management have taken little part in the process of reforming employment relations.

In Taiwan, both labour and employers rely on the state to protect workers' rights and interests. This is a natural consequence of the 'moral' state since both labour and management tend to believe that it is ethical for the state to balance the interests of the parties. This also explains why unions and worker representatives in Taiwan take political action strategy to voice their demands to the state, instead of engaging in direct negotiations with management. The willingness and ability of unions to engage in organising or collective bargaining is also weakened by their 'mindset' of state dependence. The conditions and environment which incubates union movement in advanced economies, as outlined by Frege and Kelly, is different from what apply in Taiwan.

At societal level, Taiwan possesses strong spirit of entrepreneurship, individualism/selfishness which is reflected in small- and medium-sized firms, self-owned shops and road stands. Employment relations in Taiwan could have developed in a similar to a liberal market economy, except for the intervention of the state. This might be a legacy of autocratic state governance by the KMT rule before 1990s. But this explanation ignores that both labour and management share the belief that the government provides the best means for solving their problems. The idea of state control alone cannot explain the nature of employment relations in Taiwan. The end of martial law in the late 1980s did not lead to the revitalisation of unionism in Taiwan as it did in South Korea.

It has been argued that state corporatism could explain the nature and development of employment relations in Taiwan, at least before 1980s. (Hsu, 1987). Yet, the thesis is also flawed because never has Taiwan developed a strong labour or employers' organisation that constitute a corporatist framework in employment relations. Labour and employer organisations have never played major roles in the employment relations in Taiwan as they have in some other countries.

The essence of the 'moral state', as applied to employment relations in Taiwan, can be understood from two perspectives. First, the moral state in the Chinese value system (mainly Confucianism) was adopted by the emperor in the system of imperial governance. There was a structural and internalised cognition to behave in the system such as royalty, filial piety, benevolence, kindheartedness, etc. Second, ethics are embedded in the society and in the mindset of labour and management. The legitimacy of state governance or the 'power to rule' exists because the society also shares the same ethical values which are the basis of imperial rule. The state has to perform by these ethics in order to gain legitimacy from the citizens. Hence, it becomes a benevolent or moral state. The importance of the state is a key to understanding employment relations of Taiwan. However, the meaning of the state, based on the Chinese value system, may be different from that of the West. While there is often distrust of the state in many Western societies, in Taiwan, the society at large trusts the state to perform a benevolent role when determining the nature of employment relations.

However, the employment relations institutions and practices developed through either the corporatist or voluntary systems have not been functioning effectively in Taiwan because the behaviour of the parties in employment relations is deeply influenced by the idea of the moral state. Employment relations in Taiwan cannot be understood simply through the impact of institutional or market forces. The influence of the moral state, which has historically informed cultural and social life, has provided a shared understanding and identity based on Chinese value systems. This should be further studied to complement traditional research frameworks adopted by employment relations scholars.

State-led employment relations in Taiwan are likely to persist in the foreseeable future, creating not only economic inefficiency but also a continuing weak trade union movement. The issue, therefore, is not whether to adopt an employment relations system similar to the voluntary or corporatist model but to manage or reform the state-led employment relations system in order that labour and management can develop a more proactive role.

References

Administrative Law of State-Owned Enterprise, Government of the Republic of China (Taiwan) [Online]. Available at http://law.moj.gov.tw/Eng/LawClass/LawAll.aspx?PCode=J0120001

Chen SJ, Ko JR, and Lawler J (2003). 'Changing patterns of industrial relations in Taiwan'. *Industrial Relations*, 42(3): 315–340.

Chen TJ (2016). 'Supply chain positioning and innovation: Taiwan's challenge'. Think Piece for the Mega-Regionalism – New Challenges for Trade and Innovation Workshop, East-West Center, Honolulu, HI. Available at www.eastwestcenter.org/sites/default/files/filemanager/pubs/pdfs/7-3Chen.pdf

Frege C and Kelly J (2004). *Variety of Unionism: Strategies for Union Revitalization in a Globalizing Economy*. Oxford: Oxford University Press.

Hall P and Soskice D (eds) (2001). *Varieties of Capitalism: The Institutions of Comparative Advantage*. Oxford: Oxford University Press.

Ho MS (2008). 'A working-class movement without class identity: Taiwan's independent labor union movement and the limit of brotherhood'. *Taiwan: A Radical Quarterly in Social Studies*, 72: 49–91.

Hsu CK (1987) 'Taiwan labor under state corporatist policy'. *Proceedings of the 1st Conference of Labor-Management Relations: 192*. Association of Industrial Relations R.O.C. Taipei (in Chinese)

International Labour Organisation (2016). 'Decent work in global supply chains'. Report IV, International Labour Conference, 105th Session.

Kizu T, Kühn S, and Viegelahn C (2016) 'Linking jobs in global supply chain in demand'. ILO Research Paper No. 16. International Labour Organisation.

Kuruvilla S, Das S, Kwon H, and Kwon S (2002). 'Trade union growth and decline in Asia'. *British Journal of Industrial Relations*, 40(3): 431–461.

Lee YK (2011). *Militants or Partisans: Labor Unions and Democratic Politics in Korea and Taiwan*. Palo Alto, CA: Stanford University Press.

Ministry of Labor (2017). Statistics Report Yearly Bulletin [Online]. Available at http://statdb.mol.gov.tw/html/year/year05/i002000320e.htm

Pan SW (2001). 'Politics of workers' participation: a comparative analysis between Taiwan and Germany'. *Journal of Labor Research*, 1(2): 1–35.

Pan (2015). Discussions with the executives and managers at the Taiwanese shoemaker Yue yuan (Pou-chen)'s factory in Dongguan, Guangdong, PRC. May 25–27, I was invited to investigate the causes behind the strike.

Pan (2016a) 'Politics of Corporate Social Responsibility and Industrial Relations of Taiwanese Manufacturers in China: Trapped between Brands, NGOs and the State'. Conference of The Global Transformation of Work: Market Integration, China's Rise, and Labor Adaptation March 17–18, Rutgers University, New Brunswick, NJ.

Pan (2016b). 'The comments expressed by the top executive and managers of the Chunghua Telecom when I visited the Headquarter to discuss labor relations issue with the executives'. August 3.

Sui C (2012). 'Deaths spotlight Taiwan's 'overwork' culture'. *BBC News*. 20 March. Available at www.bbc.com/news/world-asia-16834258

Teng PJ (2017). 'Taiwanese employees worked 70 hours less in 2016'. *Taiwan News*. 01 October. Available at www.taiwannews.com.tw/en/news/3265470

The Wall Street Journal (2012). 'Solving Taiwan's wage stagnation mystery'. 03 October. Available at https://blogs.wsj.com/chinarealtime/2012/10/03/solving-the-mystery-of-taiwans-wage-stagnation/

Wang JH (2001). 'Contesting flexibility: the restructuring of Taiwan's labor relations and spatial Organisation'. *International Journal of Urban and Regional Research*, 25(2): 346–363.

Wang JWY (2010). 'The political economy of collective labour legislation in Taiwan'. *Journal of Current Chinese Affairs*, 39(3): 51–85.

Wei MM (2002). 'Analysis of the position of worker director in Taiwan: from German co-determination system'. *Bulletin of Labour Research*, 12: 219–255.

Wu SY (2002). Encyclopaedia of Taiwan. Ministry of Culture [Online]. Available at http://nrch.culture.tw/twpedia.aspx?id=100229 (in Chinese)

Wu YJ (1999). 'The contemporary context of Taiwanese industrial relations: the legacies of an authoritarian regime'. *Labour, Capital and Society*, 32(1): 6–33.

Yang S (2016) 'Gov't data shows 44`% of Taiwanese work overtime'. *Taiwan News*. 21 December. Available at www.taiwannews.com.tw/en/news/3056050

Yu HH and L Wu (2016) 'Taiwanese have 4th longest working hours: labor ministry'. *Focus Taiwan News Channel*. 16 October. Available at http://focustaiwan.tw/news/asoc/201610060016.aspx

14 Unions and labour representation in Thailand

Weakness continued

Thunyalak Weerasombat

This chapter analyses unions and labour representation in Thailand, tracing back historical development, addressing core challenges, sketching their strategic interactions, as well as providing theoretical implications.

Backgrounds

In 2017, there were approximately 56 million people eligible to be a part of the workforce in Thailand. The total number of employed people was 37.44 million. Of these, 15.34 million (41.2%) work in the formal sector, and a larger number of about 22.1 million (57.25%) work in the informal sector. Apart from Thai workers, Thailand has received a great number of migrant workers from neighbouring countries. As of November 2017, the number of registered migrant workers was 1,955,487. There has been a shift in the role of workers in Thailand. Data for the first three quarters of 2017 showed that agricultural products accounted for only 9.5% of the country's total exports, while 79.7% of exports were industrial products (Ministry of Commerce, 2017).

To understand the Thai labour movement, one needs to look through the process of Thailand's industrialisation, which can be traced back to the authoritarian regime of Field Marshall Sarit Thanarat inaugurated in 1958. Sarit was under the influence of the American government. The Americans offered support to Thailand during the Cold War. Because of this, Thailand adjusted its economic policy to be more liberal under the advice of the United States and the World Bank.

Accordingly, Thailand launched its First National Economic Development plan in 1961. Although more liberal in terms of foreign investment, the first plan still maintained the import substitution industrialisation (ISI) strategy, protecting domestically produced industries from imports and spurred production in labour-intensive industries. A number of legislations were introduced to support ISI. These included the Investment Promotion Act and an increase in tariffs (Linnemann, Dijck, and Verbruggen, 1987). Under the authoritarian regime, labour rights were not considered important, thus both labour organisations and wages were suppressed.

From the mid-1980s, following the success of newly industrialised economies (namely, Korea, Taiwan, Hong Kong and Singapore), Thailand shifted from the ISI to the export-oriented industrialisation (EOI) strategy. To promote the EOI by attracting foreign direct investment (FDI), several types of incentives were provided, for example, tax breaks and the exemption of import duties on machinery and parts required for assembling export products (Phongpaichit and Baker, 2002: 148–9). Labour policy was subservient to industrialisation with the aim of promoting the EOI. The government continued to keep wages low to attract investment (Manusphaiboon, 1993; Jantarawitoon, 2001). The emphasis on exports had continually been fuelled by an approach focused on taking away power from labour. Some scholars described the atmosphere for labour-intensive work during the EOI strategy as the 3Ls: low wages, low productivity (using low technology) and long working hours (Jareunreud, 2008: 2), all of which resulted in a low quality of work life.

The nature of Thai labour organisations: forms and origin

Not all workers in Thailand are represented in labour organisations. There are five categories of workers, but only two of them can set up a labour organisation. The first category is civil servants. Approximately 3.5 million people are working in government agencies, including the military. This group has neither the right to form labour organisations nor conduct collective bargaining. However, they are well taken care of by the state in terms of job security and abundant welfare.

The second category is public enterprises workers whose number before privatisation was about 240,000 people. They can set up unions but are not allowed to strike due to their responsibility to deliver public utilities and services. Though their status is legal, public enterprise unions have been separated from unions in the private sector. This fact is emphasised under the State Enterprise Labour Relations Act of 2000.

The third category is workers in the private sector. Approximately 14.4 million workers work in various companies, businesses and factories. They are legally covered under the Labour Relations Act of 1975, which allows them to assemble unions, voice their demands, strike and be involved in collective bargaining. However, not many workers in the private sector are members of a union. As of November 2017, there are only 442,665 employees in the private sector who are unionised (Department of Labour Protection and Welfare, 2017). This number is only 4.1% of employees, which is very little when compared to the 10.7 million formal employees who are covered under the social security system (Social Security Fund, 2017). This means that as many as 95.9% of employees have no access to trade unions and collective bargaining. Even worse is this amount is equivalent to only 1.15% of all workforces who work in the industrial sector (38.3 million).

The fourth category is informal workers. The 31.31 million informal workers are lacking either the rights to assemble unions or the space to voice and protect their rights as there is no labour relations act for this group of workers. Accordingly, they are facing unfair treatment, receiving a salary lower than the minimum wage, not receiving health insurance and have no access to social welfare like formal workers.

The last category is migrant workers whose number has kept increasing. In November 2017, Thailand had 1,955,487 legal migrant workers. This amount does not include approximately 2 million illegal migrant workers. Legal migrant workers can be union members but are not allowed to set up a union themselves.

Only employees in public enterprises and private companies have the right to set up and take part in labour organisations. Prior to 1991, employees in public enterprises and private companies could be unionised together in a form of a federation of unions. The coup government in 1991 removed state enterprise workers from the coverage provided under the 1975 Act and revoked the right to strike (Phongpaichit and Baker, 2002: 216–7). Such exclusion cut down about half the total of unionised workers.

State enterprise workers used to play a strong role in Thai labour movements. In the past, following the transformation from absolute monarchy to a democratic rule, many public enterprises were established. The state undertook consecutive investments in both public utilities and large-scale enterprises, which employed a large number of labour. Public enterprise workers have a long history of success and progress in their fight for labour rights, consistently playing an important role in Thai labour movements as a whole (Chatrakul na Ayudhya, 2010: 8). The removal of rights in 1991, in effect, reduced the power of labour as a whole. Currently, state enterprise labour organisations are under the State Enterprise Labour Relations Act of 2001. There are two levels of organisations: state enterprise unions and the Public Enterprise Labour Union Federation. At the level of state enterprise unions, the Act allows only one union in each state enterprise. At present, there are forty-seven state enterprise unions which have a large membership base. Approximately 72% (174,933 from 243,023) of workers are union members. There is one Public Enterprise Labour Union Federation, functioning as a national-level organisation of state enterprise workers.

For the private sector, there are three forms of labour organisations, including private enterprise labour unions (or trade unions), labour federations and labour union councils (or labour congresses). Labour organisations are organised vertically and are highly fragmented (Charoenloet, 2015). At present, there are 1,362 trade unions, 21 labour federations and 15 labour congresses (Department of Labour Protection and Welfare, 2017). However, only 212 trade unions are members of the federations and congresses. The rest do not register their membership, thus rendering the federation/congress members as a minority. Trade unions tend to bargain at the enterprise level, not augmenting their bargaining power through labour federations, resulting in less power to fight for labour issues at the national level.

Due to low membership, labour federations have fewer bargaining roles for trade unions. Accordingly, they tend to play supplementary and passive roles, such as providing education and giving advice upon union requests. The fees for federation membership are uneven and fail to provide a sizable resource. Lacking both members and financial resources, it is difficult for them to function effectively, particularly when negotiating with the government. Plural labour federations and councils do not help establish a solidarity of labour, especially with the one union one vote system.

According to the Labour Relations Act of 1975, a labour congress must consist of at least fifteen trade unions and/or labour federations. At present, there are as many as fifteen labour congresses. Too many labour congresses cannot create a unity of labour on policy decisions. This means they lack the power to negotiate with the government (Manusphaiboon, 1993: 247; Napathorn and Chanprateep, 2011a: 70). Labour congresses also share a similar problem with trade unions and labour federations and lack financial resources (Chatrakul na Ayudhya, 2010: 7).

Meanwhile, there are also three levels of employer representation, namely employer associations, federation of employer associations and employer councils. Currently, 316 employers are members of employer associations. Meanwhile, the federation of employer associations has two members and employer councils have fourteen members.

Historical development of Thai labour movements

As stated, worker representation has been limited. The historical background of Thai labour relations reveals such limitations. There were many attempts to dissolve unions since their inauguration. The first labour movement in Thailand emerged even prior to the change of political regime from absolute to constitutional monarchy. From the late 1880s until the mid-1930s, the first generation of hired workers in Thailand were Chinese. At that time, the majority of Thai labour was still either a part of the government or in the agricultural sector in rural areas. Therefore, as many as 600,000 Chinese were imported as workers (Hewison and Brown, 1994: 487; Phongpaichit and Baker, 2002: 189). They often resorted to strikes to protect their rights and welfare. Chinese workers in Thailand were not formally organised but were taken care of by several Chinese triads. They occasionally protested and launched violent strikes over unfair payment and work conditions, sometimes causing casualties and chaos in major cities. Viewing these outbreaks as a serious threat, the Thai government tried to limit Chinese workers' activities. For example, the government controlled these outbreaks by sending troops to intervene and deported any troublemakers back to China (Phongpaichit and Baker, 2002: 190–1). Strikes were strictly controlled, and the state enacted a Secret Society Act forcing associations to register members and outlawed any assembly of five people or more. Associations without registration under this law were considered illegal and were severely punished. However, no labour associations were allowed in practice.

Thailand transformed from an absolute monarchy to a constitutional monarchy in 1932. Throughout more than eighty years of democratic rule, Thai governments tended to suppress labour voices and delayed the development of labour relations. The first phase of governments (1932–70s) was mostly dominated by consecutive authoritarian regimes. Workers were granted some rights when a sympathetic government took charge, but these rights tended to be short-lived. Right after the regime change in 1932, the government allowed labour to register as an association. Accordingly, labour movements which used to work underground came to be able to do activities publicly. However, as many labour leaders had close ties to Pridi Bhaanomyong (the leftist leader), who was later accused of being an advocate of communism, authoritarian governments which took control afterwards came to block labour activities allegedly to prevent the spread of communism (Lamdee, Sae Tai, and Chatrakul na Ayudhya, 2008: 7–9). Accordingly, labour associations were put under strict control and later their roles were terminated as the government disallowed them to renew their registration (Chatrakul na Ayudhya, 2011: 41). Therefore, a reformation of labour laws was long delayed. The first Labour Relations Act was enacted in 1956. This law was partly a response to pressure from the International Labour Organisation (ILO) which criticised poor working conditions and limited labour rights prevalent in Thailand.

Unfortunately, this law lasted only two years. When the coup d'état took place in the middle of the cold war in 1958, the absolute autocratic government led by Field Marshal Sarit Thanarat abolished this law. The military-led government prohibited labour associations and outlawed strikes. Labour unions were banned for another fifteen years until 1975 when the Labour Relations Act was enacted. This act has remained in force until today. However, this law has several flaws. The most remarkable one is that there is no real protection for workers who initiate the setting up of a union as they may be fired when the employer discovers the initiative. The 1975 Act was possible in the aftermath of the 1973 student-led peoples' uprising which received considerable support from labour associations. At that time, the democratic space was enlarged, including that for labour movements. However, only one year after the law was launched, Thailand had another coup d'état in 1976. This time, many core labour leaders, who joined the student activists fighting for democracy, had to flee to the jungle with student activists, because both were targeted as communist agitators. Needless to say, the military governments until the late 1970s tended to marginalise labour. Whenever a coup d'état occurred, unions and labour activities were always among the first targets. As a rule, right after a coup d'état (especially, in 1947, 1958, 1976), unions were banned, strikes were made illegal and many unions leaders were imprisoned (Manusphaiboon, 1993: 244–5; Lamdee, Sae Tai, and Chatrakul na Ayudhya, 2008: 5–11).

The second phase of governance in Thailand is represented by the semi-democratic regime during the 1980s and the subsequent full democratic government after the Cold War at the start of the 1990s. Thanks to the

1975 Labour Relations Act, labour organisations and labour movements, including strikes, were legal. Labour rights were expanded. For example, a tripartite system was arranged and later laws addressing the social security system were launched in 1990. However, the pattern of labour movements changed from the national level to the company level because the 1975 law covers only workers in the private sector. The size of participation was also limited as workers in the informal sector and the self-employed were automatically left out of the labour movements (Chatrakul na Ayudhya, 2011: 43). This represents another limitation of labour power.

Though workers earned some rights during the 1980s and 1990s, such gains were compromised by the drive to attract foreign investment since the latter half of the 1980s. In 1991, another coup d'état occurred, and workers were oppressed again. By that time, the coup government removed state enterprise workers out of the 1975 Act coverage and revoked the right to strike (Phongpaichit and Baker, 2002: 216–17). As mentioned elsewhere, state enterprise used to hold a strong role in Thai labour movements.

The last phase started from the mid-1990s when Thailand enjoyed consecutive democratic governments until 2006 before another coup was launched. The coup this time targeted politicians, not the labour leaders. The country came back to democracy only a year later, though some street protests and state crack-downs shook the stability of the nation. Labour from the mid-1990s to the present has been consistently subjected to economic pressures, rather than political pressures.

The 1997 Asian Financial Crisis, in effect, reduced the power of labour. On the one hand, the economic crisis meant that it was imperative for the government to promote investment, so less rigid labour policies were applied. Importantly, the government delayed the amendment of the 1975 Act and still has not yet ratified the ILO Conventions No. 87 and 98 on Freedom of Association and the Right to Organise and Bargain Collectively. On the other hand, labour had less power to resist management due to the fear of being laid-off as the unemployment rate was as high as 5.3% in 1999 (Phongpaichit and Baker, 2002: 219). Firms, particularly multinational corporations (MNCs), expanded flexible employment by hiring more subcontractors and temporary workers whose rights are not protected properly. The coup in 2006 had an important impact on the workforce. Though not oppressing labour unlike traditional coups, the protracted political conflicts and polarisation split workers into two opposite camps (yellow shirts and red shirts). Labour groups became less harmonious and hesitant to work together (Chatrakul na Ayudhya, 2012: 117–9).

Apart from the institutional contexts of consecutive repressive regimes that mitigated the growth of labour, the cultural contexts have also slowed the development of labour organisations in Thailand. One is due to some of the concepts of Buddhism; another is the patronage system embedded in Thai society. Most Thai people, around 95%, are Buddhists (Lawler and Atmiyanandana, 2003). Key Buddhist concepts include the belief in '*karma*', which means that the actions in one's past life affect one's current life. If a person is not well to do and live in poor conditions, it is because he or she failed do good deeds in his or her past life. Thai people tend to accept what happens to them and passively cope with life events or challenges in life. Accordingly, they tend to be passive and submissive, not voicing their demands or fighting for their rights enough (Napathorn and Kuruvilla, 2017). The predominant patronage in the Thai culture, which is long-standing in Thai society, has created an ideology of submission and dependency, of acceptance of the stark vertical differences in status between employer and employee. In Thai, 'employer' is called '*nai-jang*' and employee is called '*luk jang*'. '*Nai*' refers to boss, while '*luk*' refers to children. The former holds a sense of higher status. Decisions on wages, working conditions and others are dependent on the employers' choices. Therefore, this traditional norm is averse to the acceptance of trade unions, organised labour and collective bargaining (Chatrakul na Ayudhya, 2010: 2). This cultural basis nurtures Thai workers to be less confrontational and more passive (Ibid., 2012: 111). Most Thai workers think about unions only when confronted with serious labour issues like being laid-off. If working conditions are acceptable, Thai workers will not think about the union (Napathorn and Chanprateep, 2011b: 116).

Globalisation and challenges confronting Thai labour

After the mid-1980s, the forces of globalisation have created massive changes to how production is organised, which unavoidably yield a considerable impact on the forms of employment. Due to the dramatic advancement of technology and deregulation policies, firms can fragment and relocate their production processes to many countries. Accordingly, globalisation is accelerating economic interdependence between countries encouraging a similar trend of deregulatory policies by governments. This includes the reduction of tariff barriers, the facilitation of the flows of capital and investment, as well as the oppression of labour and increased flexibility in working conditions (MacDonald, 1997: 5; Alex, Jiberto, and Riethof, 2002: 1, 17). Such trends are applied in many developing countries aiming to attract FDI (Archibugia and Pietrobellib, 2002: 877). According to Deyo (1997: 210), 'rapid industrialisation has nowhere spawned effective trade unionism or enhanced worker participation in the political or economic arena'. Labour movements especially in developing countries have mostly been weakened and marginalised for this reason. The most significant sources of FDI are MNCs (MacDonald, 1997: 5–7). In order to minimise costs, the production processes of MNCs tend to be fragmented or productive assets are produced in more than one country in particular developing countries where deregulations are applied (Frenkel and Royal, 1996: 7). MNCs usually apply flexible employment for the purpose of cost reduction.

MNCs prefer less trade unions and are generally not willing to bargain with them. They do so when it is required by labour laws in the host countries. Where MNCs appear to be inclined towards trade unions, it is based at the enterprise level (enterprises' trade unions), not at the national level. Accordingly, labour tends to be oppressed with low protection and poor labour organisation. Several East Asian countries are cited to prove this point. Frankel and Peetz (1998) found a convergent trend in China and Korea. Both employ more contingent workers who have low job security and weaker collective bargaining power. Similar effects are found in most Southeast Asian countries like Thailand where labour gets less support and fails to organise effectively.

Globalisation has had an impact on the forms of employment. To maximise efficiency, firms investing in Thailand utilise numeric flexibility in employment. Numeric flexibility, the utilisation of contracted workers, is crucial in saving costs, such as fringe benefits and hiring and training expenses. The economic crisis caused massive lay-offs. By the end of 1997, around 2 million workers were unemployed and a year after another 1 million workers were added to the toll. Even after the crisis, the lay-offs continued. Around 20,000–30,000 workers have been terminated from work every year. Many workers were pushed into flexible employment, including subcontracted workers and homeworkers. The current amount of subcontracted workers in Thailand has not yet been reported, but it is expected that the number must be high. For homeworkers, the most recent survey by Thailand's National Statistics Office (2015) reports the amount of homeworkers to be 440,251.

To recover from the economic crisis by welcoming FDI, the government promotes Thailand as a production base. Apart from allowing foreign capital to have the majority share in joint ventures, corporate tax is reduced during the early years of production, and labour protection is lax. For example, the 1998 Labour Protection Act has insufficient protection in particular for subcontracted and homeworkers, both of whom are not included in the definition of 'employee'. Accordingly, they are barred from organised labour and thus not covered by the Labour Relations Act. The Act was amended in 2007 to cover subcontracted workers as employees, stating they must receive similar wages, benefits and working treatments comparable to permanent workers. Yet, 'double standards' between permanent and subcontracted workers remain prevalent, particularly on bonuses and other welfare (Thailand Development Research Institute, 2012).

Homeworkers are covered under the Homeworkers Protection Act, enacted in 2010. This law specifies clearly that employers have a responsibility to serve homeworkers with fair and similar pay comparable to workers in the workplace. Still, unfair pay and long working hours remain as the norm (Nirathorn and Pattanasri, 2015). Wages, which can be quite uncertain depending on economic conditions, are often subject to an employers' arbitrary decision (Paitoonpong, 2016).

Such problems stem from the problematic definition of 'employee'. Only employees in that firm can be organised. However, the Labour Relations Law defines 'employee' as a person who works for an employer who pays them wages. This means that subcontract workers can only be the members of the union at their company who subcontracts them as it is that company that actually pays them, not the company they were originally employed by. Consequently, workers feel unmotivated to participate in the union at the subcontracted company because such a union cannot help improve working conditions in the company they are actually working.

For homeworkers, there is no specific labour relations law to protect their rights to organise. They are provided with only some social security, for example, skill training, special funds and low-interest loans (Charoenloet, 2015). However, they are often mistreated by employers. Homeworkers are often underpaid and work long hours. It is difficult for homeworkers to form a labour organisation to voice their demands and to protect their rights because they tend to have different work hours and work conditions (interview with a professor of labour and welfare management, 2017). Homeworkers are also spread out in various locations which makes it difficult for them to organise (Charoenloet, 2015).

Apart from numeric flexibility, there is functional flexibility. Workers are required to do a variety of work that has various responsibilities. This trims down their power, as more compliance to management is also required. Functional flexibility is a result of 'flexible production' aimed at optimum efficiency, such as Just-In-Time (JIT) and teamwork. Both put high demands on workers in terms of capability and responsibility. JIT requires workers to always ensure the smooth running of the production line and to reduce the amount of product defects to a negligible amount. Teamwork replaces job fragmentation as work interchangeability among team members is required. Workers are increasingly being asked to work overtime with short notice. Rather than standing against these high demands through unions and fighting for their rights, workers tend to comply with management's requests for fear of job security. Many companies in Thailand, particularly Japanese MNCs, apply these flexibility concepts to maximise worker utility.

Apart from globalisation, there are other challenges confronting Thai unions and worker representative bodies. A core challenge is shrinking number of unionised workers, owing to four factors. The first factor is demographic change. Since 2005, the total population has been slowly increasing at a mere 0.6% per year on average. Almost a 0% population growth (the birth rate is equal to or less than the death rate) is expected in 2022 (Wapattanapong and Prasartkul, 2006). Accordingly, Thai workforce will continue to decline. It is expected that the labour population in Thailand will account for only 60.5% of total population in 2035.

The second factor is the regression of employment and the increase in unemployment. In December 2017, the total employed workforce was 36.6 million, a decline of 2 million from 38.6 million in 2013 (Chalamwong, 2017a).

Table 14.1 External and Internal Challenges Confronting Thai Labour

External Challenges	*Internal Challenges*
Globalisation minimises the size of unionisation	*Shrinking number of unionised workers*
• Lay-offs resulting from the economic crisis and the aftermath reduced the number of formal labour who can be unionised • Increasing flexible employment, giving rise to massive informal labour, who are barred from organised labour • Functional flexibility renders labour less negotiation power, for fear of losing jobs.	• Declining number of Thai workforce due to demographic change (low birth rate) • Regression of employment and the increase in unemployment • Hiring more migrant labour who are unable to organise a union.

Meanwhile, unemployment in December 2016 (0.48 million) was higher than that in December 2013 (0.26 million) (Chalamwong, 2017a). The third factor is a massive use of informal labour, who are self-employed and neither covered under the Social Security Law nor the Labour Relations Act. In 2016, more than 58% of the Thai workforce was a part of informal labour. The percentage has continued to be at that level until recently. The fourth factor is migrant labour. As of November 2017, Thailand hosts approximately 2 million legal migrant workers. However, the total number of migrant labour, including the illegal ones, is estimated to be at least 3 million, equivalent to about 10% of the Thai workforce (Chalamwong, 2017b).

Migrant workers can only join the firms' union. There is no data on the number of unionised migrant workers. In reality, migrant workers are not motivated to join a union for fear of losing their jobs as well as lacking a sense of solidarity with the Thai workers in the same workplace who receive a different treatment and higher wages (interview with labour economic professor, 2017). All of these factors have weakened Thai unions and worker representative bodies as a whole both in terms of shrinking numbers and a decreasing willingness to participate in a union. To sum up, the above trends, which include both internal and external challenges, are expected to continue in the future (as shown in Table 14.1).

Labour's strategic actions

Actions that have been taken by the union and labour movements in Thailand seem unable to overcome the force of globalisation or manage the challenges presented. Evidently, there has been continuous attempts by Thai national trade unions to urge the government to ratify the fundamental ILO Conventions No. 87 and 98 on Freedom of Association and the Right to

Organise and Bargain Collectively. These attempts have repeatedly failed. The government is well aware that ratifying the ILO Conventions would give a strong signal to the international community that Thailand respects the fundamental labour rights. However, it has failed to do so, due to the concerns over cost competitiveness for Thai enterprises as well as concerns that the FDI would become less attractive. Accordingly, there has been an increase in labour disputes. During 2012–2016, the amount of submission for labour demands and disputes jumped from 462 in 2012 to 617 cases in 2016, with an average of 531 cases per year. In 2016 alone, around 400,000 workers were involved in disputes, mostly demanding fair bonuses, proper working conditions and sound termination packages (Tangtipongkul, Kulkonkarn, and Srisuchart, 2017: 9).

It is important to note the micro-focus character of most Thai labour unions. As most are company-based unions, they are only concerned about issues regarding wages and bonuses among members within the company. Accordingly, unions tend to be fragmented and fail to invest in the unity of labour movements as a whole (Napathorn, and Chanprateep, 2011b: 114–5).

However, there have been some strategic actions implemented to help strengthen labour movements in Thailand. Apart from labour organisations allowed by the labour law, Thai workers have formed and organised themselves in other bodies beyond the law's provisions, with the aim to strengthen their negotiating power. Such organisations include the Unions Area Group working groups for informal workers, Group of Migrant Workers and the Thai Labour Solidarity Committee (TLSC). The first three organisations have the same role as a union. Meanwhile, the TLSC functions like a labour federation. Interestingly, they seem to be more active, if not always effective, compared to labour organisations under the labour law.

The UAG is a combination of unions in the same geographical areas, namely industrial zones. They recruit members from different companies either in the same industry or the same area. Even without a strong legal underpinning, they nevertheless play a significant role in labour relations, thanks to the fact that they focus on the common well-being of workers in the same area who may also face similar issues. These industrial groupings have similar characteristics to a community-based organisation (CBO), which also engages in social activities with the community in which they are situated. The UAG has three main objectives. The first is to protect workers' rights and to attain fair treatment in the workplace. The second is to educate workers on their rights and important issues regarding their working life. The last is to promote democracy which is a significant base for the fair treatment of the workforce. Currently, there are eight UAGs in operation, consisting of seventy-six trade unions with 26,870 workers (Chatrakul na Ayudhya, 2010: 7–8). The strongest one is the UAG located in the condensed industrial area of the Eastern region.

These union groups are able to mobilise members to work together. In fact, the UAG's main strength is the ability to combine a large number of workers.

Though union establishment is allowed and protected by labour law, it is difficult to establish a union, as firms tend to perceive unions as obstacle to their productivity. Workers who aim to set up a union will often lose their jobs. With more members, the UAG has more power and can negotiate at both the company and industry levels as well as with the government. For example, in 2001 the UAG succeeded in fighting for the reemployment of union leaders, who were laid-off before setting up a union, at Ford-Mazda and TFO-Tech. At the national level, the UAG continuously pushes the government to correct labour problems. What the UAG has achieved includes pushing firms to strictly comply with the regulations, such as minimum wages and fringe benefits as stipulated by the labour law. So far, the UAG has succeeded in gaining more fringe benefits than is required by the law, particularly child care facilities at the company level in the industrial zones. The government has to listen to their demands as the Eastern region represents the key industrial area in Thailand. However, the UAG has a similar problem that is faced by typical labour organisations. Unfortunately, UAG effectiveness is hampered by a lack of financial resources due to low membership fee.

There is still no form of labour organisation for informal workers, such as homeworkers and the self-employed. There are difficulties in setting up a body to protect their rights as they are subject to different work conditions, work hours and wages. Yet, they are facing similar problems including unfair wages and work safety. As an example, taxi drivers often express concerns about car rental fee and loans when they purchase a taxi car.

Currently, there are two levels of organisations outside the scope of the labour law that try to take care of informal labour. There are two groups in the first-level Coordination Centre for National Informal Labour and the Foundation for Labour and Employment Promotion (known as 'Homenet Thailand'). The second level includes smaller groups for informal workers, such as the Association of Informal Labour, the Association of Motorcycle Taxi Drivers in Thailand and the Household Workers' Network in Thailand. Their focus is on three issues: fair income, skill improvement and employment stability. Some progress has been made as the Labour Law for Home Workers was enacted in 2010 and informal workers have also gained coverage under the social security system.

Migrant workers have not yet been permitted to set up their own unions or become committee members of trade union on the basis that they are non-Thais. They are only permitted to apply to become a member of an existing trade union. However, most migrant workers do not join for fear of antagonising their employer. As a result, migrant workers do not have any access to bargaining power (Chatrakul na Ayudhya, 2010: 5). However, there are two groups that help and provide some support for migrant workers. One is community-based organisations (CBOs) which are the communities of migrant ethnic groups, particularly Myanmarese labour. Another is the non-government organisations (NGOs) that help advocate their rights. An outstanding NGO is the Labour Rights Promotion Network Foundation

(LPN), which has set up a twenty-four-hour counselling centre for migrant workers to protect their fundamental rights and also aims to tackle human trafficking problem.

Another labour organisation working at the national level is the TLSC founded in 2001. Currently, the TLSC is the main organisation that lodges worker's demands as a whole to the government. It plays a major role in representing all groups of workers, informal and formal, unionised and non-unionised. TLSC members come from various labour groups. It operates within the committee structure consisting of representatives from twenty-nine organisations, including labour federations, other labour groups, NGOs and foundations (Chatrakul na Ayudhya, 2012: 117–19). They act as the leader of all Thai labour organisations. Since the economic crisis in 1997, Thailand has lacked a leading labour organisation because the unprecedented crisis resulted in mass lay-offs which ruined labour power as a whole. Many workers consequently became unemployed or were pushed into the informal sector. Labour movements in general lost the bargaining power they used to have. The TLSC aims to forge a unity between the labour movements and make them stronger using two major activities. First, at the firm level, the TLSC works as a mentor and advisor for unions. Second, at the national level, it demands new labour legislation and wage raises. So far, the TLSC has emphasised the needs of the whole labour force, such as calling for adjustments to the Labour Relations Act, asking to raise minimum wages in line with the increasing costs of living and, importantly, to accept the ILO Conventions No. 87 and 98. Though not authorised by the Labour Relations Act, the TLSC's strategic actions focus on cross-cutting labour issues that affect all workers. Consequently, the government came to accept its role by giving them a position in the tripartite system and tends to listen to their demands. Apart from advocating labour protection, the TLSC also pushes forward other social issues, particularly social inequality and social security. For instance, in 2018, the TLSC opposed the government policy on corporate tax reduction and on the discount of firms' contribution to social security funds. Considering the extensive roles it plays, the TLSC can be regarded as social movement unionism (SMU).

However, the TLSC is facing several obstacles. First of all, they are short of funding as income from member fees is low. Their organisational structure consists of a diverse set of committees, ranging from union federations, unions, area-based union groupings and NGOs that do not directly engage with union members in the enterprises. Therefore, in 2009, the TLSC changed its structure so that regular union members at the enterprise level could become members of the TLSC directly. This has opened up a direct link to workers. As a result, labour problems can now be directly communicated to the TLSC. The management committee of the TLSC now comprises of elected representatives from workers in both area- and industry-based unions. Now the TLSC is also open to informal-sector worker networks, taxi and motorcycle taxi networks as well as employee organisations in state enterprises.

Another positive strategic action is the networking between Thai labour NGOs and other NGOs both at the national and international levels. This networking has helped to strengthen negotiating power and advocate the rights of informal labour and migrant labour. Two predominant examples of Thai labour NGOs are the network of 'Homenet Thailand' and LPN. Homenet Thailand is an NGO taking care of the quality of working life for homeworkers and self-employed workers. Its network includes Homenet Southeast Asia and Women Informal Employment: Globalising and Organising (WIEGO). Meanwhile, LPN advocates and protects migrant workers' right and shares networks with many NGOs, such as the Action Network for Migrants (ANM), the Migrant Working Group (MWG), the Anti-Human Trafficking Network in Thailand (ATN) and the Cambodia and Thailand Anti-Human Trafficking organisation. Their key focus is to have the networks help them run proactive roles both combining fragmented groups of homeworkers, self-employed workers and migrant workers and to push their voice and demands to the government. Some examples of Homenet Thailand's achievements are their role in pushing policies expanding social protection for homeworker in the social security system. Meanwhile, the most recent example of the LPN's achievements is setting up guidelines for the Thai and Migrant Fisher Union Group (TMFUG) that will be enacted in the near future. It is expected that this union would focus on protecting the rights of fishing workers and provide them with legal assistance.

Over all, the key strategic actions being pursued by unions and labour movements in Thailand are to set up new forms of organised groups, which are not covered by the labour law (Table 14.2). These groups attempt to reunite

Table 14.2 Union Renewal Strategies and their Outcomes in Thailand

Strategy	*New Form of Organised Labour*	*Applicability*	*Benefits*	*Risks/Weaknesses*
Establishment of new forms of organised labour to strengthen labour as a whole	The Unions Area Group (UAG)	Combine unions in the same geographical areas, especially the same industrial zones	More negotiation power at both the company and industry levels as well as with the government.	Beyond the labour law's provisions
	Working groups representing informal workers (such as Homenet Thailand)	Voicing on behalf of informal workers.	Focusing on general key issues, such as fair incomes	Hard to harmonise demands of many informal workers because their employers and work conditions are different

Strategy	*New Form of Organised Labour*	*Applicability*	*Benefits*	*Risks/Weaknesses*
	Community-based organisations (CBOs) and the Labour Rights Promotion Network Foundation (LPN)	Present voices of migrant workers, as they are permitted to set up their own unions	Provide counselling and system for migrant workers to protect their fundamental rights	Migrant workers fear of antagonising their employer so they hardly participate in proactive activities, such as to voice beyond fundamental rights
	Thai Labour Solidarity Committee (TLSC)	Act as the leader of all labour groups, including formal, informal, unionised and non-unionised workers	Able to focus on the needs of the whole labour, such as the adjustments of the Labour Relations Act, asking to raise minimum wages	Beyond the labour law's provisions

the fragmented labour from different types of employment and provide them with a channel to voice their demands both at the enterprise and the national levels. To strengthen labour representation in Thailand, it is important that workers of all types are organised together (Charoenloet, 2015). Amid the increasing flexible employment, particularly subcontracted workers, self-employed workers and homeworkers, the negotiation power of labour tends to be qualified by a shrinking number of members. This is an inevitable impact of globalisation by which efficiency maximisation is the norms.

Theoretical implications

This chapter has presented the picture of unions and worker representation in Thailand as being weak and predicts that it will likely continue to be so owing to three factors. First, increasing flexible employment has resulted in a larger amount of informal labour, who are excluded from mainstream labour relations and are unable to join a union. Second, the government continues to focus on attracting FDI and not making the development of labour laws and rights a priority. Finally, a shrinking number of workers are expected because of demographic changes likely resulting in lower number of unionised labour.

The Thai case is in line with the *simple globalisation approach*, arguing that globalisation has dominated the convergent pressure through FDI in international economic activities across countries (Ohmae, 1990; Wade, 1996). Yet, it does not mean that globalisation has totally eroded national political autonomy. The *internal institutional approach* can correct the unlimited power of globalisation. The mediating role of internal institutions such as labour laws, monetary and fiscal policies and the national government are able to filter the power of globalisation (Evans, 1997; Garrett, 1998; Weiss, 1998). However, it also depends on the predominant character of the internal institutions, for example, the dual system of industrial relations in Germany helps its union to resist the pressures from globalisation (Turner, 1991; Thelen, 1993). For the Thai case, however, the inherent passive role of the Thai government on labour issues allows the forces of globalisation to exert itself more fully on labour.

Accepting that these two patterns describe labour relations in each country seems to lead us to two varied results: either that the globalisation forces will prevail or internal institutions are able to filter the power of globalisation. Alternatively, the *variety of capitalism model* (VOC) provides a more sophisticated explanation of the institutional effects in host countries.

According to the VOC thesis, market economies can be classified into two types based on their prevalent institutional characters – 'coordinated' and 'liberal' (Hall and Soskice, 2001). Institutions in 'liberal' market economies (LMEs) are designed to allow economic agents to work competitively through market mechanisms. Firms have attached themselves with short-term economic goals encouraging a radical development strategy to maximise short-term profits. Accordingly, LMEs prefer industrial relations that have only short-term commitments to workers. In contrast, the 'coordinated' market economies (CMEs) are opposed to competitive relationships. They rely on long-term institutionalised relationships across firms, businesses, trade associations and investors, allowing firms to embark on a more incremental development strategy, with a long-term perspective for profit making, rather than a short-term one. In CMEs, the industrial relations system tends to be based on bargaining and long-term commitments to employees.

The Thai case seems to fit more with the LME type, in which the state as well as the weak institutionalised relationships among relevant actors fail to shield the inadvertent impacts of globalisation on labour. Though Thai labour has been trying to exert some influence through new forms of organisations like the UAG and the TLSC, their impacts remain limited without institutionalised support from relevant institutions.

References

Alex E, Jiberto F, and Riethof M (2002) Labour relations in the era of globalisation and neo-liberal reforms. In Alex E, Jiberto F, and Riethof M (eds), *Labour Relations in Development*. London: Routledge, pp. 1–25.

Archibugia D and Pietrobellib C (2003) The globalisation of technology and its implications for developing countries windows of opportunity or further burden? *Technological Forecasting & Social Change* 70 (9): 861–883.

Chalamwong Y (2017a) Regression in employment and decreasing of unemployed rate in Thailand. Available at: https://tdri.or.th/2017/12/14-labour-market-2018/ (accessed 10 October 2017).

Chalamwong Y (2017b) Problem of migrant labour. *Prachachat*, 24 November, p. 12.

Charoenloet V (2015) Industrialisation, globalisation and labour force participation in Thailand. *Journal of the Asia Pacific Economy* 20 (1): 130–142.

Chatrakul na Ayudhya S (2010) The Thai labour movement: strength through unit. Available at: http://library.fes.de/pdf-files/bueros/thailand/07563.pdf (accessed 10 October 2017).

Chatrakul na Ayudhya, S (2011) Labour relations and labour movement in Thailand (in Thai). Report, Thammasat University, Bangkok.

Chatrakul na Ayudhya S (2012, April) Economic and labour inequality: problems and policy recommendation (in Thai). Report, Chulalongkorn University Social Research Institute and Thai Health Promotion Foundation, Bangkok.

Department of Labour Protection and Welfare (2017) Labour Organisation in Thailand. Available at: http://relation.labour.go.th/index.php/2017-08-25-04-50-47/238-2560-4 (accessed 10 October 2017).

Deyo, FC (1997) Labour and industrial restructuring in South-East Asia. In Garry R, Kevin H, and Richard R (eds), *The Political Economy of South-East Asia: An Introduction*. Melbourne: Oxford University Press, ch. 8.

Evans, P (1997) The eclipse of the state? Reflections on stateness in an era of globalisation. *World Politics* 50 (1): 62–87.

Frankel SJ and Peetz D (1998) Globalisation and industrial relations in East Asia: a three-country comparison. *Industrial Relations* 37 (3): 282–310.

Frenkel S and Royal C (1996) Globalisation and employment relations. Paper prepared for ILO/EASMAT in Bangkok, Paper No. 63, University of New South Wales, Sydney.

Garrett, G (1998) Global markets and national policies: collision course of virtuous circle? *International Organisation* 52 (4): 787–824.

Hall, PA and Soskice D (eds) (2001) *Varieties of Capitalism: The Institutional Foundations of Comparative Advantage*. New York: Oxford University Press.

Hewison K and Brown A (1994) Labour and unions in an industrializing Thailand. *Journal of Contemporary Asia* 24 (4): 483–514.

Jantarawitoon N (2001) *The History of Labour Movement in Thailand*. Bangkok: Addison Press Product.

Jareunreud W (2008, February) Impacts from economic crisis to Thai labour market. Report, International Labour Organisation, Bangkok.

Lamdee W, Sae Tai W, and Chatrakul na Ayudhya S (2008, April) The structure of the labour movement in Thailand. Report, The Thai Labour Solidarity Center, Bangkok.

Lawler, JJ and Atmiyanandana, V (2003) HRM in Thailand: a Post-1997 update. *Asia Pacific Business Review* 9 (4): 165–185.

Linnemann H, Dijck PV, and Verbruggen H (1987) *Export-oriented Industrialisation in Developing Countries*. Singapore: Singapore University Press.

MacDonald D (1997, May 5–13) Industrial relations and globalisation: challenges for employers and their organisations. In: *ILO Workshop on Employers' Organisations in Asia-Pacific in the Twenty-First Century*, Turin.

Manusphaiboon S (1993) Country studies: Thailand. In Stephen JD and Richard (eds), *Labour Law & Industrial Relations in Asia*. Melbourne: Longman House, pp. 241–269.

Ministry of Commerce (2017) Thailand Trading Report. Available at: www.ops3.moc.go.th/infor/db_sql/gp_web_export3.asp (accessed 7 December 2017).

Napathorn C and Chanprateep S (2011a) Recent labour relation and collective bargaining issues in Thailand. *Interdisciplinary Journal of Research in Business* 1 (6): 66–81.

Napathorn C and Chanprateep S (2011b) What types of factors can influence the strength of labour unions in companies and state enterprises in Thailand. *International Journal of Business and Management* 6 (2): 112–124.

Napathorn C and Kuruvilla S (2017) Human resource management in Indonesia, Malaysia, and Thailand. In: Fang LC and Sunghoon K (eds), *Handbook of HRM in Asia*. London: Routledge, pp. 333–354.

Nirathorn N and Pattanasri P (2015) Compensation design for home labour in Thailand (in Thai). Available at: http://research.mol.go.th/2013/rsdat/prg/eachview.php?okey=QEFPGW0&prg=viewlibdt.php&xkw=&Page=1 (accessed 4 December 2017).

Ohmae, K (1990) *The Borderless World: Power and Strategy in the Interlinked Economy*. New York: Harper Business.

Paitoonpong S (2016) Wage for homeworker (in Thai). Available at: www.matichon.co.th/news/344959 (accessed 12 November 2017).

Phongpaichit P and Baker C (2002) *Thailand: Economy and Politics*. New York: Oxford University Press.

Social Security Fund (2017) Number of Insured Persons (Article 33) 2008–2017 (in Thai). Available at: http://social.nesdb.go.th/SocialStat/StatReport_Final.aspx?reportid=172&template=1R2C&yeartype=M&subcatid=46 (accessed 12 November 2017).

Tangtipongkul K, Kulkonkarn K, and Srisuchart S (2017, September) Proper labour-management relations practices in Special Economic Zones (SEZs) in Thailand. Report for the Department of Labour Protection and Welfare, MOL, Bangkok.

Thailand Development Research Institute (TDRI) (2012) The implementation of Labour Protection Law 2007 and the inequity treatment of subcontracted and permanent Workers (in Thai). Available at: https://tdri.or.th/2013/05/subcontract-tdri/ (accessed 15 October 2017).

Thelen, KA (1993) Western European labour in transition: Sweden and German compared. *World Politics* 46 (1): 15–27.

Turner, L (1991) *Democracy at Work: Changing World Markets and the Future of Labour Unions*. Ithaca, NY: Cornell University Press.

Wade R (1996) Globalisation and its limits: reports of the death of the national economy are greatly exaggerated. In: Berger S and Dore R (eds), *National Diversity and Global Capitalism*. Ithaca, NY: Cornell University Press, pp. 60–88.

Wapattanapong P and Prasartkul P (2006) Population projections for Thailand 2005–2025 (in Thai). Available at: www.ipsr.mahidol.ac.th/ipsrbeta/FileUpload/PDF/Report-File-314.pdf (accessed 14 October 2017).

Weiss, L (1998) *The Myth of the Powerless State: Governing the Economy in a Global Era*. Cambridge: Polity Press.

15 The reform of Vietnam trade union and the government's role since *doi moi*

Ngan Collins

Introduction

As in other Communist societies, the trade union movement in Vietnam has a close relationship with the Vietnamese government through the Vietnam Communist Party (VCP) (Collins and Zhu 2003; Dang 2009). The Communist Party established the Red Workers' General Union (the predecessor of the Vietnamese General Confederation of Labour, VGCL) in 1929 with the aim of mobilising workers to liberate the country from foreign invaders. The leaders of the VGCL were members of the VCP and had contributed to the fight for the country's independence. This alliance assisted the 1954 defeat of the French at the battle of Dien Bien Phu and the establishment of the first Communist government in North Vietnam (Thayer 2010). During the subsequent war against the United States of America and its allies, the VGCL worked with the VCP to build the first stage of the socialist economy in the North and to support the national revolution in the South (VGCL 2014a).

After the war ended, the VGCL continued to act as a 'transmission belt', taking responsibility for government policies and assisting management of government enterprises to achieve economic targets. The VGCL supported the government in its efforts to implement its economic master plan, which aimed to improve workers' living standards, provide social welfare and assist managers to achieve production targets (VGCL 2014a). The VGCL's mission was to take action based on four premises: protecting the interests of workers in their working environment (by supervising the allocation of welfare benefits, visiting the sick and arranging parties for children); participating in managing the assets and property assigned to the state-owned enterprises (SOEs); encouraging and motivating workers to raise productivity; and educating members in socialist ideology and awareness through such measures as artistic and sporting competitions (The National Assembly 1990). The SOE boards included representatives from the VCP leadership, management, union representatives and youth, with union leaders of secondary importance to the Party secretary. Members of a management board were tasked with the common objective of achieving annual production and business and budget payment targets set by the state, and the role of unions was administrative rather than representative (Zhu et al. 2008). VGCL has been characterised by an unitarist approach in which the government has maintained tight control over all aspects of this institution and practices (Kerkvliet 2001; BTI 2018).

The Vietnam government established a programme of economic reform in 1986 (known as *doi moi*, or renovation). *Doi moi* was described by the VCP as the transformation process of the Socialist Central Planning Economy (*nen kinh te tap trung Xa Hoi Chu Nghia*) to a Socialist Market Economy (*nen kinh te thi truong dinh huong Xa Hoi Chu Nghia)*, directed and controlled by government policy and led by the leadership of Communist Party (Vu 2015). The key objectives of *doi moi* were to reduce the role of the state bureaucracy, liberalise the economic system, break down the monopoly of SOEs and cooperative-owned enterprises (COEs) by removing many of the constraints on the operation of private enterprise and establish a legal framework which would allow the economic system to respond freely to market forces (VCP 1987).

During recent years, in the context of a transition to a market economy, the government has faced the challenge of finding a balance between its tradition of maintaining strong control while allowing greater capacity for trade unions to bargain and represent interests in a market contract-based system (Collins 2018). While being by no means pluralist, this relationship must at least provide some limited scope for the negotiation of differing interests and for dispute resolution. Over time, tensions have arisen for the Vietnam government between the economic goals of its policy and the need to maintain legitimacy through the protection of labour from the negative power of competition based purely on market performance (Tran 2007a). In the previous centrally planned economy, government representatives controlled all aspects of workplace relations. Both management and labour were government employees and the government had a dual role as director of the economy and as an employer of each business unit. This arrangement changed dramatically after *doi moi*, which led to the widespread adoption of capitalist labour practices with profound effects on the industrial relations system and practice (Collins et al. 2011, 2013).

The rapid development of industrialised zones since *doi moi* has seen a rapid growth in the number of foreign-owned enterprises (FOEs) and domestic private enterprises (DPEs) in urban areas. This has resulted in significant migration of workers from rural areas, a large increase in employment by FOEs and DPEs and management driven by market performance (Arnold 2012). The new relationships between managers and workers in FOEs and DPEs are challenging the government whose legitimacy relies in part on being seen to maintain close relationships with trade unions in order to protect workers. Thus, while, on the one hand, the government needs to maintain social stability by protecting employees from exploitation in the workplace, on the other hand, its ability to increase accumulation (and create more job opportunities for a fast-growing young labour force) relies heavily on its capacity to attract foreign investment. This is most challenging for the Communist government in relation to the trade unions.

The research that underpins this chapter aims to examine key changes in the roles of trade unions and worker's representatives during the period of economic reform in Vietnam. This chapter also analyses tensions between state functions of *legitimation, accumulation* and *pacification* that was developed by Hyman (2008). It seeks to demonstrate how these tensions have impacted on the changes in relations between state and trade unions since *doi moi*.

Our research takes a qualitative approach that combines secondary analysis of the current empirical studies of Vietnamese trade unions in Vietnam with primary data analysis of forty-two in-depth interviews conducted between 2014 and 2017 with relevant stakeholders in Vietnam. At the policy-making level, interviews were conducted with a number of directly related government offices and international organisations such as the Department of Labour, Invalids and Social Affairs (DOLISA) in Ho Chi Minh City (HCMC), the Vietnam Chamber of Commerce and Industry (VCCI) in Ho Chi Minh City, the Labour Management Offices in the Dong Nai and Ho Chi Minh Industrial Zones, Trade Unions Officials in HCMC and Dong Nai and the International Labour Organisation (ILO) Vietnam office.

Interviews were also conducted with three key business ownership types including SOEs, DPEs and FOEs as well as union and worker representatives in twelve companies from three ownership types in two locations: HCMC, formerly Saigon, and Dong Nai province. These two main industrialised centres represent different aspects of Vietnam's industrial relations and economic development. These locations have been used as an experiment for a range of market-oriented policies and enterprise reforms, including the introduction of human resource management (HRM) (Collins and Zhu 2005). Different forms of ownership existed in the two locations, with DPEs were formed before 1975 under old southern regime, SOEs established after 1975 and FOEs were established right after the first Vietnam Foreign Investment Law (*Luật đầu tư nước ngoài*) was introduced in 1987 (Collins 2009).

Trade unions and industrial relations in a socialist market economy

Vietnam trade unions law states that every permanent employee is entitled to become a member of VGCL after being employed for six months, regardless of the sector in which they are employed. This has resulted in union density in the formal labour force being about 98% (Nguyen 2002).[1] The VGCL's purpose is described in terms of the Leninist principle of 'democratic centralism'. This principle requires that 'trade unions organise and operate democratically by opening attendance to all their members, with final decisions made according to the collective majority' (The National Assembly 2012a: 25). At the same time, there are various levels of the unions, with the lower levels having to follow the instructions of higher levels. All agencies of the VGCL are organised and operated in accordance with the leadership of the VCP. The charter of the VGCL also includes details of the unified organisational structure of trade unions. National industry unions bring together unions in state-owned corporations affiliated to the central government and unions in central state agencies and organisations. At the provincial level, trade unions are organised into National Industry Unions and the Provincial Federations of Labour. The latter administers four groups of unions, unions of SOEs affiliated to the provincial government, industrial-processing zone unions, provincial industry unions and the district federations of labour.

Implementation of *doi moi* has resulted in outstanding economic success. Vietnam is now one of Asia's fastest developing countries, with annual growth averaging 7.5% through the 1990s, rising to 8.5% in 2007 (Zhu et al. 2018). Even with the effects of the Global Financial Crisis, which resulted in a serious contraction in the foreign direct investment (FDI) in 2009 and threatened many businesses with bankruptcy (Trang 2008; Nguyen 2009), Vietnam has achieved an average gross domestic product (GDP) growth of above 5% since 2010 (ADB 2014). Through the reform process, the number of SOEs decreased sharply from about 12,000 in 1990 to about 2,700 in 2017. By 2000, COEs totally disappeared from the system. Similarly, the number of FOEs increased from about 1,000 to 14,600 enterprises, with an employment share of 2.7 million in 2017. From 2000, DPEs number increased from 30,000 to about 500,000 enterprises in 2017 with a growth in employment share of as many as six times to more than 6.5 million (GSO 2017; Nhan Dan 'People' Newspaper 2018).

Although new labour and trade union laws were promulgated in the early 1990s, for several years Vietnam's trade union continued to function as they had before *doi moi*. According to the Labour Code issued in 1994, the VGCL could act on behalf of their members to negotiate a Collective Working Agreement (CWA) (*Thoa uoc lao dong tap the*) with the employer in each organisation (The National Assembly 2012b). However, in reality, CWAs simply replicate the conditions prescribed in the Labour Code, as the Ministry of Labour, Invalids and Social Affairs (MOLISA) drew up a model agreement to be used as a guide for enterprise activities (Collins 2009). The CWA states the basic conditions on the rights of workers pertaining to labour contracts, work security, working hours and holidays and the use of company profits as well as wages, allowances and social insurance. It is officially signed at the Workers' Congress (*Doi hoi cong nhan vien chuc*) by the director and the union president before being sent to the MOLISA for ratification. It is valid for three years but can be modified every year according to the reality of company's performance. The updated version only needs to be signed by the company's union representatives and management board. The practices of CWA have shown its ineffective in most workplaces. According to an interview with an ILO official, almost 20% of factories failed to ensure their CWA was approved by more than 50% of workers covered. The most common reason was that they did not hold a worker vote to approve the agreement which is a legal requirement (interview with an ILO official, January 2016).

In practice, at the workplace level, collective bargaining, handling of grievances and settlement of labour disputes are formalities and have little actual impact on the labour–management relationship (Do 2011). Indeed, it is only since the mid-2000s that there have been any significant changes in response to increased FDI. Many new FOEs have exploited loopholes or inconsistencies in labour law and to take advantage of a lack of enforcement of labour legislation at the enterprise level (Tran 2007b; Siu and Chan 2015; Nguyen 2017). For example, Vietnamese law allows employers to dismiss workers if they have to scale down business operations. This loophole has been exploited by many FDI employers who replace their workers with new ones without suffering any legal consequences. To cut costs, for example, Honda Vietnam Co. has sacked thousands of workers annually and replaced them with newcomers (VNExpress 2016a).

As a consequence of exploitative employment practices, there has been a dramatic increase in the number of wildcat strikes since 2005, most of which have focused on demands for better wages and working conditions (Manning 2009; Cuong 2009; Kerkvliet 2011; Van Gramberg et al. 2013). For example, in December 2005, 18,000 workers employed at Freetrend Co. undertook a strike to demand a 21% wage increase. The day after its successful resolution, six more strikes occurred in the same industrial zone involving 11,900 workers (Clarke and Pringle 2007). In the first two months of 2006, 22 strikes occurred involving 58,000 workers (HCMC People's Committee 2006). In 2007, at least 541 strikes were held involving an estimated 350,000 workers (MOLISA internal report n.d.). This strike wave reached new heights in 2008, when 762 strikes were recorded. After briefly declining, the number increased to 981 in 2011, before declining dramatically in 2012 and 2015.

In 2017, number of labour strikes was reported to be rising again to 314 (VNExpress 2017). Instead of being concentrated in three southern provinces, namely Ho Chi Minh, Dong Nai and Binh Duong, as in the past years, the labour unrest has spread into northern and central regions. For example, in 2016, more than 2,500 workers at Matrix Vinh Ltd., a Chinese toy factory in the central province of Nghe An, held a four-day wildcat strike to protest against unreasonably heavy workloads and unfair working conditions (VNExpress 2016b). In 2017, 6,000 workers at the S-H Vina Co, Ltd, a Taiwanese garment factory in northern province, Thanh Hoa, struck for higher pay and changes to working condition rules (Reuter 2017). The protesters presented the company with a list of fourteen demands, including an increase to their basic salary, child benefits, seniority bonuses and allowances, adequate maternity leave, reasonable working hours and scrapping penalties for absence from work due to sickness or other emergencies

(VNExpress 2017). In the south, Binh Duong province had sixty-three collective labour disputes and strikes in fifty-seven enterprises involving 26,592 workers (Vietnam News 2018) (see Figure 15.1 for details). Almost 80% of these strikes were organised by employees in manufacturing FOEs located in industrial zones and provinces of Southern Vietnam (Schweisshelm 2014; Do 2017).

Not only have strikes become more frequent and involved larger cohorts of workers, they also tended to last longer. For example, in HCMC, in February 2008, a strike involving 10,000 workers continued for three days (Collins 2011). In March 2008, more than 15,000 workers at a Nike-contracted factory went on strike for nearly seven days (Economist Intelligence Unit 2008). In March 2015, the most significant strike in Vietnam's contemporary history involved about 85,000 workers in Pouyuen Vietnam in Tan Dao industrial zone, Ho Chi Minh City and lasted for five days (Quoc Thang and An Nhon 2015). Tensions were exacerbated by the Global Financial Crisis which led to job cuts of 15%, causing high unemployment in urban areas and a job shortage in rural areas (Collins 2011). In 2008, around 55,000 labourers were retrenched in HCMC and 80,000 workers lost their jobs in Dong Nai Industrial zone, owing to company closures. At the national level, about 400,000 workers were jobless in 2009 (Thanh and Nhu Quynh 2009). This is another key reason for an increasing number of labour disputes.

The explosion in the number of strikes is symptomatic of the emergence of a new, more confrontational pattern of labour–management relationships in the workplace (Slezak 2009), which are perceived as a potential threat to the credibility of the government. Those workers who go on strike are not able to negotiate with the employer through conventional forms of participation or union representation. They organise wildcat strikes partly as a way to push and mobilise the trade unions to bargain

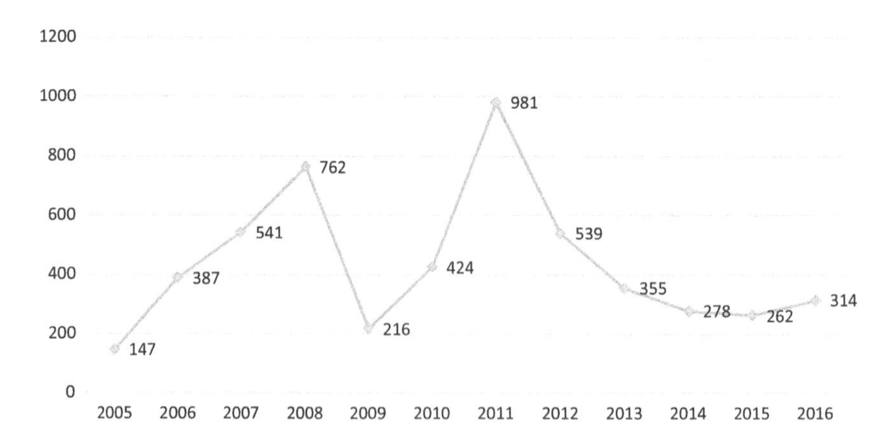

Figure 15.1 Number of Labour Strikes in Vietnam Since 2005.

or otherwise exercise leverage on their behalf. This can be seen as 'a new way of conceptualizing the role of unions in one-party, socialist states' (Anner and Liu 2016: 23). This has led the government to take further steps to curb labour unrest and respond to changes in firm-level labour relations by introducing a new form of tripartism, through the National Labour Relations Commission (NLRC), which was originally established in 2007. Chaired by the Minister, this body consists of the leaders of MOLISA, VGCL, VCCI and the Vietnam Cooperatives Alliance (VCA). The major objective of the NLRC is to advise the prime minister on industrial relations issues and labour policy. After three years of operation, in 2010, the NLRC was allowed to establish a tripartite labour relations committees at the provincial level (interview with Ho Chi Minh VCCI Office, January 2014).

The government also reduced its labour market role to creating and maintaining new institutions that act as employment agencies, providing vocational training, occupational guidance, social insurance and labour inspection. Furthermore, it required the trade union and MOLISA to cooperate with each other in the making and implementation of labour-related legislation and policies, compliance monitoring and grievance handling. Local union offices also received financial support from the national and provincial governments to conduct programmes on mediation and grievance handling for their members and raise awareness about the labour law in an attempt to avoid illegal strikes and maintain workplace harmony (interview with Dong Nai Union office, December 2015). The formal extension of tripartite institutions did not, however, address the question of the representativeness and independence of unions and, for this reason, worker activism at the firm level continues to present a challenge to the legitimacy of the VGCL. The chairperson of the VGCL must still be a member of the VCP Central Committee, and all representatives at regional and central levels need to have a position in the VCP (Clarke et al. 2007). These objectives were reinforced in the amended Trade Union Laws of 1990 and 2012 (The National Assembly 1990, 2012a).

In 2008, the Political Bureau of the VCP issued an official Resolution on the Working Class, which is focused on the protection of workers' rights, collective bargaining and workplace harmony. This guided the VGCL, which revised its statutes at the end of 2008 (Do 2011). The 2008 amendment to the Union Statute focused on key issues such as protection of workers' interests through collective bargaining, organisation of worker congresses, settlement of labour disputes and organisation of collective actions as the priority tasks of primary unions in non-public enterprises (Do and van der Broek 2013). The Amended Trade Union Law in 2012 gave some power to enterprise-level unions, such as allowing them to air workers' grievances in cases where these were aimed at private firms. However, it also stated that while employers are obliged to facilitate the formation of a trade union within their companies, they need to only do so if this is requested by their employees (The National Assembly 2012b). In other words, if management convinces workers to eschew trade unionism and negotiate directly with them, then they need not facilitate the formation of an enterprise union. Many FOEs have taken advantage of this loophole to deal directly with workers (interview with Dong Nai provincial unions, January 2015). As a consequence, while trade union membership density in SOEs and the civil service remains as high as 90%, union formation and organising in the DPEs and FOEs has been difficult. As of 2012, union density in DPEs was as low as 30%, while in FOEs, it was about 66%. Nonetheless, overall Vietnam's union membership has grown from about 2 million to 7.5 million during *doi moi* (VGCL 2012).

The combination of these factors reflects an increasing tension between the accumulation, legitimation and pacification functions of the Vietnam government. The government has sought to allow enterprises more freedom in their management and less strict supervision than before *doi moi* in order to promote the economic growth and development advantages needed for its political purposes (Collins et al. 2012). In other words, the state objective of accumulation/economic development is linked to the political legitimacy of the government. However, at the same time, it has to present itself as concerned for the welfare of workers and allowing a limited degree of autonomy for unions to represent workers. This creates a fundamental problem of legitimacy for a Communist regime that still officially proclaims itself as aligned with the working class while also seeking to maintain labour peace and attract foreign capital result. This tension results in a substantial difference between formal regulation and 'on the ground' practices. This also raises questions about the legitimacy and effectiveness of labour representation given the direct links between the VGCL and the VCP (Vo 2009).

Pressures for change

The prevalence of strikes has led both the government and the VGCL to pay increasing attention to industrial relations issues. If VGCL embraces government protection, it risks losing credibility as a representative organisation, but if it promotes reform by asserting its autonomy, it stands to lose its privileged political position. This has led, since *doi moi,* to increased tension between the state's pro-FDI policy, and the concern expressed by the trade unions. Further, despite attempts to empower the VGCL, its relevance to workers remains questionable. While employees in SOEs continue to regard the union as an organisation that provides support for their day-to-day activities, in the FOE and DPE sectors, workers often bypass unions. The outcome is that some 90% of labour strikes in Vietnam are organised without union involvement, reflecting workers' lack of belief in union capacity to represent them (interview with FOEs union officer in Dong Nai, December 2017) (Table 15.1).

Table 15.1 Internal and External Challenges Facing VGCL

Internal Challenges	*External Challenges*
• Dual union system (for public servants and for profit-making sector). • A lack of a clear vision for reforming union organisation dues to a dual-function tasks of union leaders (being party/management leaders as well as union leader) • Weakness of capacity building for leaderships to resolve labour conflicts at enterprise's levels. • Weakness of capacity to handle labour movements from both national and enterprise's union's leaders. • Unevenness in unionisation (union density) of various sectors capacity in the workplace • Low levels of member engagement in many unions • Poor processes for leadership renewal in many unions • Democratic governance of membership by constitution but little effectiveness in reality • Weak funding base through dues and in some cases an over-reliance on financial support from the government	• Strong government control to union organisation for both policy and practices • Trade unions considered irrelevant in labour movements at enterprises and been seen as a government's agency • New forms of business ownerships • Rapid growth of industrial zones to observe mass semi-skill labours • Internal migration of labour from rural to industrial areas • Low-wage (in DPEs and FDI manufacturing sectors) labour reliant but diversified • Many low-skill labours do not have enough knowledge of employment relations system • Increasing non-union leaders to lead labour movements at many workplaces • Size of the informal sector has been expanded • Weakness of employer organisations • Weakness of worker's consultation system • Increasing levels of precarious employment within the formal sector • Low capacity of labour officials, in part because of the lack of knowledge and skills to handle IRs issues in a free market system • Limited to freedom of associations • Weakness of effective mechanism to deal with labour disputes

In response, the VGCL has sought to develop new internal strategies to improve representation by workers. For example, in 2009, the VGCL's HCMC city office sent thirty independent union representatives to work in FOEs and DPEs in an attempt to promote trade unionism. As these union officials received their salary from trade union funds, it was hoped that they would have the power to act independently from management when negotiating on behalf of their members' interests. However, this innovative strategy was not successful due to management hostility and the fact that these external union representatives also did not understand the workplace setting (interview with SOEs union officer in Dong Nai, December 2017). This experience reflects a more general phenomenon, whereby grass-roots union representatives lack the knowledge and experience to deal with labour disputes, grievance and mediation processes in DPEs and FOEs. Recognising these problems, the government pushed the VGCL to provide training and appoint more professional union officers to industrial-processing zones and to coordinate with other agencies to settle collective labour disputes in enterprises, and especially in the FOEs (Do 2011).

The VGCL has also taken on the role of a quasi-independent industrial relations partner, pressuring the government to raise minimum wages and strengthen labour law enforcement. It is now more willing to disagree with the government on important issues, as was the case with the revision of the amended Labour Code in 2012. The inclusion of a principle removing payment to strikers and the right to strike in cases of rights disputes led the VGCL to argue that paying striking workers improves labour–management relations and that the removal of the right to strike in rights-based disputes would deprive workers of their most potent weapon in their representation of workers. The VGCL organised a number of consultative meetings at all levels of the union structure and invited key members of the National Assembly to union conferences where members strongly voiced their opposition to MOLISA's draft revisions (interview with Ho Chi Minh Union office, January 2015). The VGCL has developed a pro-labour press, which plays a strategic mediating role between the state, labour unions and employers. Two union newspapers, *Bao Nguoi Lao Dong* (The Workers Newspaper) and *Bao Lao Dong* (*Labours Newspaper*) use their forums to champion workers' rights and empower labour unions that negotiate with state bureaucracies and management on the workers' behalf (Tran 2007b). The newspapers ran a series of analytical articles against the MOLISA proposal. This resulted in MOLISA backing down, allowing workers engaged in rights-based disputes to temporarily stop work and limiting the scope of non-payment to workers actively participating in an interest-based strike (interview with Dong Nai union office, January 2015). Similarly, the absence of two-way dialogue with workers in the process of development of the Amended Social Security Law 2014 led to strong criticism of MOLISA by many stakeholders including the VGCL (interview with Ho Chi Minh DOLISA, January 2016). Table 15.2 was adopted from Frege and Kelly (2003) to summarise key strategies adopted by the VGCL in order to deal with the current challenges.

Union concerns about the proposed amendments to the Social Security Law were amplified by worker mobilisation and strike action. This was exemplified by a strike that began in Pouyuan Vietnam (a Taiwanese-owned garment manufacturer) which soon spread to a larger cohort of workers in the Tan Dao industry zone. For five days, all work stopped at Pouyuan Vietnam, and there were disruptions to work in many other factories in the zone. The protests attracted widespread coverage in the media and support from non-governmental organisations (NGOs) and various professional associations. The pressure on the government to settle the dispute was evident in the

Table 15.2 VGCL Strategies and Their Outcomes

Strategy	*Applicability*	*Benefits*	*Risks*
Reform of union structures	Reform of union organisation to be quasi-independent from government	Improved enterprises union; maintained members in public sector; responded more to member's interests; increased member engagement	Splits from government leadership team effect on role of union in labour policymaking process at the national level; restructuring process has not had a clear vision for union organisation.
International solidarity	Engage with international unions and NGOs to learn about international trade union organisations and international IRs systems	Provided new knowledge for reforming the union organisation and resolving labour disputes; strengthen leadership skills and competencies; helped to increase collaboration between VGCL and other international unions	Might brought confusing to VGCL unclear-reform direction; also a risk of accusations from governments and employers of external control
Labour–management partnerships	Primary strategy for VGCL	Maintained union decisive roles in IR decision process; handle effectively IR issues at enterprise level; prevented poorly managed IR matters at enterprises	Can be reverted back to be 'the government transmission's bell' or management's tools against member's interests
Organising	Generated mobilisational power to establish VGCL's goal and vision	Stronger bargaining power; increased member engagement and trust; may have support from NGOs and international unions	May increase the risk of losing support from government and management; expensive and difficult to connect to non-union workers
Political action	Successfully involved to reform IR policy at the national level; organised campaign to voice union roles in negotiations of IR issues at enterprise level	Improved VGCL statue to be a real worker's representative and increased independences for union organisation from political system; formation for member's voice at enterprises	Increased a risk of losing leadership role in political system; competed with other informal labour's actions organised by 'black leaders'
Coalition-building	Has underpinned successful policy campaigns at the national level on increasing the minimum wage and other IR policies	Has provided greater voice on the national and regional levels underpins capacity to achieve substantive policy changes	Hardly to break through the old union Leninist principle that jeopardises the reform of VGCL organisation; vulnerable to differences in members' strategic approaches and capacity

direct involvement of the Ho Chi Minh DOLISA and the Deputy Minister of MOLISA in negotiations with worker representatives at Pouyuan Vietnam. The Vietnam National Assembly organised emergency meetings to discuss the matter, with the government subsequently agreeing to further amend the law to provide employees with a choice on access to their contributions to the social security fund (Phuong 2015).

There have been other informal or unofficial strike actions that are indicative in recent years (Chuang 2018). In each industrial zone, there are informal workers' organisations that are led by so-called black leaders that make it possible to communicate between factories and even between sectors. Frequent wildcat strikes occur within enterprises located within industrial zones. Once a strike takes place, workers at other factories in the same zone quickly communicate with other workers in the surrounding neighbourhoods and worker dormitories who have similarly concerned about low wages and poor working conditions (Anner and Liu 2016).

Since the 2000s, there have been wildcat strikes and collective activity organised outside the VGCL (interview with HCMC Industry Zone Labour Office, December 2015). The solution to these disputes often involves the VGCL as a representative of government but not of the workers' interests. In most cases, the VGCL has had to deal directly with 'black leaders' to resolve the disputes, which again challenges the union's legitimacy as workers' representatives (interview with Dong Nai Industry Zone Labour Office, December 2016). Despite the obvious need for the VGCL and labour offices to develop effective dialogue with these leaders, there is no uniform method for this as the current industrial relations system makes no reference to them and allows them no formal role (interview with HCMC Industry Zone Labour Office, December 2015).[2]

Another challenge in recent years is the rapid growth of the informal sector of the economy. According to World Bank data, there were an estimated 22.5 million smallholder farmers (43%) and 11 million non-agricultural labourers (21%) among 52.6 million people in the labour force in 2014. There were another 7.4 million wage workers without labour contracts (14%). These compared with 11.3 million wage workers with contract (22%), of whom 1.4 million were employed in SOEs (2.6%), 2 million in FOEs (3.8%), and 3.9 million in domestic private sector (7.5%). Since 2016, the government has made many statements about improving conditions for doing business, but this movement is still an uncertainty (BTI 2018).

The final factor that has contributed to pressures for change in the trade union movement comes from international influence. Notably, there appears to be greater government tolerance for, and even facilitation of, international influence and engagement in industrial relations, including through the VGCL. Vietnam suffered a US economic embargo between 1975 and 1994, and the US government only established a formal diplomatic relationship with Vietnam in 2001. Even after Vietnam joined with

World Trade Organisation (WTO) in 2007, there have been ongoing tensions over some critical political issues of human rights, religious freedom and freedom of association. This history led many leaders within the VCP to distrust outside influences that might damage the Socialist ideology of the state. As a consequence, the ILO is one of few external ILOs allowed to establish an office in the country. Its Vietnam office assisted the government to develop its first Industrial Relations Institute under MOLISA but had few opportunities to work directly with the VGCL until the late 2000s (interview with ILO Vietnam office, January 2016). Since that time, it has worked with the government and others to improve various labour issues such as assessing the application of international labour standards in garment factories; involvement in the process of amending the trade unions law in 2012; and advice to the government on amendments to the Labour Code, where it suggested the need for reforms in collective bargaining institutions and their independence (MacIntosh 2013). More recently, the government has also demonstrated much greater openness to international unions and other associations, and has encouraged the VGCL to seek new knowledge from these organisations, including the Solidarity Centre (the international wing of the American Federation of Labour-Congress of Industrial Organisations) and APHEDA (the international union aid organisation of the Australian Council of Trade Unions).

As the result of ongoing pressure for real reform, and the requirement for further democracy in the area of labour relations, the government realised the urgent needs for establishing labour organisations outside VGCL. In November 2016, the Conclusion No. 96/KL-TW was issued regarding to permission of establishment of independent trade unions or labour organisations which are not affiliated to VGCL. Article 2.10 of this important legal piece stated 'continuing reform of the trade union organisation and its operation and well manage the establishment and operation of new organisations of labourers at enterprises' (Lao Dong Newspaper, 18 May 2017). This was the first time that the government has acknowledged the existence of independent unions and formally recognised these organisations operating outside VGCL. This is the result of both grassroots movement and the economic pressure has brought by international integration process.

The Trans-Pacific Partnership (TPP) proposed by the Obama administration was the most significant attempt to reform labour relations since *doi moi* began thirty years ago. The TPP proposal challenged the role of the state in managing labour issues and also the leadership statute governing the role of the VGCL. It revealed the tension faced by the Vietnam state between *accumulation* (encouraging of economic performance and competitiveness in TPP agreement), *pacification* (maintaining of social order, defusing conflict at workplace to keep its leadership in place) and *legitimation* (pursuing social equity and foster voice at work as responses to the reality of pluralist workplace).

Discussion and conclusion

In the period since the global recession of 2008–2009, the Vietnam government has acknowledged that the process of international economic integration has not been well coordinated or effectively integrated with other changes. This has resulted in the process of implementing *doi moi* in the country's institutional system being poorly synchronised. Many policies, in general, and labour policies, in particular, have not been closely linked to the process of enhancing competitiveness, meeting the requirements of defence, protection of political security, social order and safety. Responses by the government to changes and addressing the impacts from the regional and international environment have been confused and incomplete. The government has a broad vision of what it wants for trade unions as it makes the transition from a command economy to a market-based system built on contractual employment relationships.

Vietnam's institutions lack the necessary tools to negotiate and resolve disputes in the market-based contract system. The government claims that it wants to establish bipartite relations between employers and labour and to engage in tripartism as promoted by the ILO, up to a point. But it is not willing to step back and give up its control over trade unions. As a consequence, although the VGCL has gained a certain degree of autonomy from the government, it continues to operate largely as it did before *doi moi,* focusing more on the provision of welfare and education of workers than on representing its members' interests. In brief, while the VGCL has attempted to assert some independence, its continuing subordination to the government constitutes a barrier to the success of its efforts to reform. As a consequence, the trade union movement remains fundamentally dependent on management in the workplace and subordinate to the VCP at the national level.

The failure of institutions to adjust to the realities of the market system mean that there is ongoing pressure for change. Currently, the VGCL is facing the internal pressure to improve representativeness and membership in the private sector which still is much lower than in public sector, despite VGCL's continuous efforts. At the national level, the roles of union representatives in collective bargaining, grievance handling and dealing with wildcat strikes (and how they are settled) have been widely criticised.

From the government perspective, further reform of the industrial relations system is necessary for two reasons. First, labour unrest has been most visible in DPEs and FOEs operating in the manufacturing sector, which is one of the key engines of Vietnam's economy. Labour conflicts have reduced the competitiveness of the sector which, in turn, has had a negative impact on national economic growth. This situation has compelled the government to undertake action to reduce workplace conflict or, in other words, to link accumulation to pacification. At the same time, the legitimation objective remains important. The VCP's ideological ties to the working class mean that it cannot simply ignore the demands of labour, a factor made more relevant by the increase in independent worker mobilisations outside the formal system. While the latter has begun to have an effect on government intervention and policy, including on issues such as social security, these independent workers' actions lack the means to convert industrial conflict into a system of independent enterprise-based unions.

The role of unions at enterprise level has made VGCL different from its neighbouring country China. Even though two countries have similar political and economic systems, the VGCL's charter recognised its right to strike as well as granting enterprise unions more autonomy and collective voice, compared with their Chinese counterparts.

As this discussion has shown, escalating divisions between workers and management at the enterprise level has led to open conflict and the demand for more effective representation of workers' interests, with the latter linked to greater openness of Vietnam to international influences. However, multi-unionism, or true freedom of association, implies a political pluralism that would deeply threaten the one-party regime. This complex situation has left the government with no choice but to employ a restricted strategy of 'managed trade union reform' in an attempt to shore up its leadership position in a 'market economy with a socialist orientation' (Thayer 2010: 439) This is despite the obvious limitations of addressing the challenges facing trade unions operating in a new social-economic system.

The context of economic reform and changes in the global environment has created different pressure on government to shift from controlling to managing the role of unions in the economy. The challenges to the government leadership have both political and economic aspects. For example, in the late 1900s, as result of the Asian Financial Crisis, the economy had been slowed by declining FDI, most of which was from Asia at that time, as well as declining domestic business performance. In response, the government issued many 'business friendly' policies such as reform FDI Law in 2002 and the Enterprise Law in 2003, in order to strengthen economic performance and competitiveness (*Accumulation*). These policies helped to establishing a wave of new businesses as well as the development of new industrial zones. However, this fast growth of businesses, especially around HCMC and Dong Nai areas, was not accompanied with suitable industrial relations policies suitable and led to waves of labour unrest in the mid-2000s. The government reacted was strengthening its leadership in order to maintain social order to reduce conflict at workplace (*Pacification*). In the late 2000s, it began its consultation process for reform of trade unions organisation and other aspects of industrial relations.

There followed negotiations between VGCL and MOLISA on a number of industrial relations matters. VGCL was granted greater operational autonomy. Even though this was only a first step towards more independence from government control, the VGCL took the opportunity to learn how to manage the labour movement in a more pluralist market economy. However, the government still needs to pursue social equity and foster voice at work in response to the reality of pluralist workplace (*Legitimation*) to be able to fulfil.

In a context of an emerging economy such as Vietnam, it is important to note that labour, management and government have complex interactions with each other. These interactions are determined by many factors, such as political parties being aligned with the labour movement (Katz et al. 2015). Furthermore, in the Vietnam political system, the government, through the leadership of the VCP, is built on the principle of protecting the working class from exploitation of capitalism. This principle controls both the parliament and court systems. In other words, the Vietnam government is a singular institution that issues economic policy as well as leading the political system.

The greatest challenge for the Vietnam communist government is joining a pluralist economic world where rules and principles have been designed on democratic principles which mostly do not fit in with the policies of the Vietnamese government. This chapter has demonstrated that the Socialist market economy in Vietnam does not fit with either liberal market economy (LME) or coordinated market economy (CME) that was developed by Hall and Soskice (2001). The variety of capitalisms (VoC) framework addressed the relationship between different institutions in advanced capitalist economies including industrial relations. Vietnam's political and economic contexts are totally different from the environment on which the VoC theory was based. Hence, there is a need for a new framework that can be applied to an emerging economy with single-party control, such as Vietnam, where the government's political purpose is the driving force for all of its economic actions. In time, the one-party system is likely to be challenged to change its control mechanism over trade unions. While Vietnam's trade union movement has been liberalising since *doi moi*, it is still far away from a genuine democratic system.

Notes

1 A parallel labour market did exist in which workers had either oral contracts or no contracts at all, leading to a predominance of unstable and casual jobs; however, there are no studies or official statistics reporting on this large informal labour force, which accounts for approximately 85% of employment and contributes about 20% of the country's GDP (Arnold 2012). However, this chapter focuses only on the formal labour force.

2 Many of these leaders are senior workers who have earned great respect from their members who truly believe they represent workers' interests, although some are simply opportunistic. For example, in the late 2014, in Linh Xuan Industry Zone, there were 20–30 factories where workers demanded bonuses for the New Year (Tet). Allegedly, the 'black leaders' in this zone took that information to bosses and threatened to strike unless they were paid off (interview with Dong Nai Industry Zone Labour Office, January 2015).

References

Anner M and Liu X (2016) Harmonious unions and rebellious workers: A study of wildcat strikes in Vietnam. *ILR Review* 69(1): 3–28.

Arnold D (2012) Social margins and precarious work in Vietnam. *American Behavioural Scientist* 57(4): 468–487.

Asian Development Bank –ADB (2014) Key indicators for Asia and the Pacific: Special chapter poverty in Asia- A deeper look. Available at: www.adb.org/sites/default/files/publication/43030/ki2014_0.pdf.

BTI (2018) Country Report 2018 Vietnam. Available at: www.bti-project.org/fileadmin/files/BTI/Downloads/Reports/2018/pdf/BTI_2018_Vietnam.pdf.

Clarke S, Lee C-H, and Do QD (2007) From rights to interests: The challenge of industrial relations in Vietnam. *Journal of Industrial Relations* 49(4): 545–568.

Clarke S and Pringle T (2007) Labour activism and the reform of trade unions in Russia, China and Vietnam. Paper presented at the NGPA Labour Workshop, 10 December.

Collins N (2009) *Economic Reform and Employment Relations in Vietnam*. London: Routledge.

Collins N (2011) Vietnam's labour relations and global financial crisis. *Research and Practice Human Resource Management* 19(2): 60–70.

Collins N (2018) Vietnam's state-owned enterprises reform. In J Wilson (ed.), *Vietnam in the Indo-Pacific: Challenges and opportunities in a new regional landscape* (pp. 20–30). Perth: Perth USAsia Centre.

Collins N, Nankervis A, Sitalaksmi S, and Warner M (2011) Labour-management relationships in transitional economies: Convergence or divergence in Vietnam and Indonesia? *Asia Pacific Business Review* 17(3): 316–377.

Collins N, Sitalaksmi S, and Lansbury R (2013) Transforming employment relations in Vietnam and Indonesia: Case studies of state – owned enterprises. *Asian Pacific Journal of Human Resource Management* 51(2): 131–151.

Collins N and Zhu Y (2003) Vietnam's labour policies reform. In S Frost, O George, and E Shepherd (eds.) *Asia Pacific Labour Law Review: Workers Rights for the New Century* (pp. 375–385). Hong Kong: Asia Monitor Resource Centre.

Collins N and Zhu Y (2005) The transformation of HRM in transitional economies: The case of Vietnam. *Journal of Comparative Asian Development* 4(1): 161–178.

Collins N, Zhu Y, and Warner, M (2012) HRM and Asian economies in transition: China Vietnam and North Korea. In C Brewster and M Wolfgang (eds.), *Handbook of Research in Comparative Human Resource Management* (pp. 577–598). Vienna: Edward Elgar Publishing.

Chuang (2018) Đình công tự phát (wildcat strikes in post-socialist Vietnam). Available at: http://chuangcn.org/2017/05/dinh-cong-tu-phat-wildcat-strikes-in-post-socialist-vietnam/.

Cuong T (2009) Ho Chi Minh City workers decreased in 2009. Available at: www3.tuoitre.com.vn/ViecLam/Index.aspx?ArticleID=294064&ChannelID=269.

Dang NT (2009) Vietnamese trade union: The eighty years of construction and evolution (Chang duong tam muoi nam xay dung va phat trien cua cong doan Viet nam). *The Communist Journal (Tap Chi Cong San)* 801: 03–07.

Do QC (2011) Understanding industrial relations transformation in Vietnam: A multi-dimension analysis. PhD thesis, Sydney: The University of Sydney.

Do QC (2017) The regional coordination of strikes and the challenge for union reform in Vietnam. *Development and Change* 48(5): 1052–1068.

Do QC and Van den Broek D (2013) Wildcat strikes: A catalyst for union reform in Vietnam? *Journal of Industrial Relations* 55(5): 783–799.

Economist Intelligence Unit (2008) The political cost of inflation. Available at: www.economist.com/displayStory.cfm?story_id=10987640.

Frege C and Kelly J (2003) Union revitalization strategy in comparative perspective. *European Journal of Industrial Relations* 9: 7–24.

General Statistic Office – GSO (2017) Structure of gross domestic product at current prices by types of ownership and kinds of economic activity. Available at: www.gso.gov.vn/default_en.aspx?tabid=775GSO.

Hall P and Soskice D (2001) *Varieties of capitalism: The institutional foundations of comparative advantage.* Oxford: Oxford University Press.

Ho Chi Minh City (HCMC) People's Committee (2006) Report: Ho Chi Minh City labour strikes in three years 2003–2005 and early 2006 (Bao cao ve tinh hinh dinh cong tai cac doanh nghiep thanh pho Ho Chi Minh trong ba nam 2003–2005 va dau nam 2006). Ho Chi Minh City: Internal Document, 28 February.

Hyman R (2008) The state in industrial relations. In P Blyton, N Bacon, J Fioroto, and E Heery (eds.), *Handbook of Industrial Relations* (pp. 258–283). London: SAGE.

Katz H, Kochan T, and Alexander J. S. Colvin (2015) *Labour Relations in a Globalizing World.* Ithaca, NY: Cornell University Press/ILR Press.

Kerkvliet B (2001) An approach for analysing state-society relations in Vietnam. *Sojourn* 16(2): 238–278.

Kerkvliet B (2011) Workers' protests in contemporary Vietnam. In A Chan (ed.), *Labour in Vietnam* (pp. 160–210). Singapore: Institute of Southeast Asian Studies.

Lao Dong Newspaper (2017) Whole document of Conclusion No. 06NQ/TW Central Committee Congress 4-XII (Toàn văn Nghị quyết số 06-NQ/TW Hội nghị Trung ương 4 khóa XII). *Lao Dong Newspaper*, 18 May. Available at: http://laodong.com.vn/chinh-tri/toan-van-nghi-quyet-so-06nqtw-hoi-nghi-trung-uong-4-khoa-xii-608410.bld.

MacIntosh M (2013) Institutional influences on firm level HRM: Some evidence from the Vietnamese garment and footwear sectors. *Asia Pacific Journal of Human Resources* 51: 228–247.

Manning C (2009) Globalisation and labour markets in boom and crisis: The case of Vietnam. Working Papers in Trade and Development. Canberra: The Australian National University.

Nguyen TLH (ed.). (2002) Vietnam's labour market: Orientation and development (Thi truong lao dong Viet nam dinh huong va phat trien). Hanoi: Labour and Social Affairs Publishing House.

Nguyen TP (2017) Workers' strikes in Vietnam from a regulatory perspective. *Asian Studies Review* 41(2): 263–280.

Nguyen VD (2009) Vietnam economy in front of global financial crisis. Available at: www.tcptkt.ueh.edu.vn/.

Nhan dan 'People' Newspaper (2018) Vietnam sees decline in number of State-owned enterprises. Available at: http://en.nhandan.com.vn/business/economy/item/5785902-vietnam-sees-decline-in-number-of-state-owned-enterprises.html.

Phuong H (2015) Government agreed for workers to choose their contribution options to Social Security Scheme (Chinh phu dong y de lao dong chon hinh thuc huong bao hiem xa hoi), Available at: http://vnexpress.net/tin-tuc/thoi-su/chinh-phu-dong-y-de-lao-dong-chon-hinh-thuc-huong-bao-hiem-xa-hoi-3176359.html.

Quoc Thang and An Nhon (2015) Pouyuen Vietnam's workers disagreed with the amended social security law (Cong nhan Pouyuen Viet nam khong đong tinh quy đinh bao hiem moi). Available at: http://vnexpress.net/tin-tuc/thoi-su/cong-nhan-pouyuen-viet-nam-khong-dong-tinh-quy-dinh-bao-hiem-moi-3175291.html.

Reuter (2017) Around 6,000 workers strike at Vietnam garment factory. Available at: www.reuters.com/article/us-vietnam-strike/around-6000-workers-strike-at-vietnam-garment-factory-media-idUSKCN1BI2CC.

Schweisshelm E (2014) Trade unions in transition- Changing industrial relations in Vietnam. Briefing Paper. Hanoi: Friedrich Ebert Stiftung Vietnam Office. Available at: www.fes.de/gewerkschaften/common/pdf/2014_09Vietnamese_TU_in_Transition.pdf.

Siu K and Chan A (2015) Strike wave in Vietnam, 2006–2011. *Journal of Contemporary Asia* 45(1): 71–91.

Slezak J (2009) *Conflicting Loyalties: Changing Roles and Relations of Labour Unions in Vietnam*. School for international training. Armidale: University of New England.

Thanh and Nhu Quynh (2009) Supporting unemployed caused by global financial crisis. Available at: http://dantri.com.vn/c133/s133–310541/ho-tro-nguoi-lao-dong-mat-viec-lam-do-suy-giam-kinh-te.htm.

Thayer CA (2010) Political legitimacy in Vietnam: Challenge and response. *Politics & Policy* 38(3): 423–444.

The National Assembly (1990) Law on the Trade Unions. Hanoi: Truth Publishing House.

The National Assembly (2012a) Law 12/2012/QH13. In Law on Trade Union. Hanoi: Truth Publishing House.

The National Assembly (2012b) XIII session 3 Announcement 20. In Labour Code. Hanoi: Truth Publishing House.

Tran AN (2007a) Alternatives to the "Race to the Bottom" in Vietnam minimum wage strikes and their aftermath. *Labour Studies Journal* 32(4): 430–451.

Tran AN (2007b) The third sleeve: Emerging labour newspapers and the response of the labour unions and the state to workers' resistance in Vietnam. *Labour Studies Journal* 32(3): 257–279.

Trang T (2008) Slates for export time of crisis. Available at: www.vneconomy.vn/20081112100341491P0C10/go-kho-cho-xuat-khau-thoi-khung-hoang.htm.

Van Gramberg B, Teicher J, and Nguyen T (2013) Industrial disputes in Vietnam: The tale of the wildcat. *Asia Pacific Journal of Human Resources* 51(2): 248–268.

Vietnam Communist Party – VCP (Dang Cong San Viet Nam) (1987) *Document of fourth national communist party congress (Van kien dai hoi dang toan quoc lan thu IV)*. Hanoi: Truth Publishing House.

Vietnam General Confederation of Labour – VGCL (2012) Pushing for developing of new memberships (Đay manh cong tac phat trien doan vien). Available at: www.congdoanvn.org.vn/.../congtactochuccanbo.doc.

Vietnam General Confederation of Labour -VGCL (2014a) The historical development of Vietnamese trade union. Available at: www.congdoanvn.org.vn/details.asp?l=1&c=23&c2=23&m=577.

Vietnam News (2018) Binh Dương to settle collective labour disputes, strikes. Available at: http://vietnamnews.vn/society/421469/binh-duong-to-settle-collective-labour-disputes-strikes.html#ajajsCo2DwYTMBVP.97.

VNexpress (2016a) Labor ministry orders probe into Honda Vietnam's alleged massive layoff. Available at: https://e.vnexpress.net/news/business/labor-ministry-orders-probe-into-honda-vietnam-s-alleged-massive-layoff-3473296.html.

VNExpress (2016b) 2,500 Vietnamese workers strike at Chinese toy factory. Available at: https://e.vnexpress.net/news/news/2–500-vietnamese-workers-strike-at-chinese-toy-factory-3479149.html.

VNExpress (2017) Thousands of Vietnamese workers take to highway to protest wage cuts. Available at: https://e.vnexpress.net/news/news/thousands-of-vietnamese-workers-take-to-highway-to-protest-wage-cuts-3727370.html.

Vo A (2009) *The transformation of human resource management and industrial relations in Vietnam*. Oxford: Chandos.

Vu VP (2015) Best solutions for relationship between economic reform and political reform (Giai quyet tot moi quan he giua đoi moi kinh te va đoi moi chinh tri). *The Communist Review* (Tap Chi Cong San). Available at: www.tapchicongsan.org.vn/Home/Quan-triet-thuc-hien-nghi-quyet-dai-hoi-dang-XI/Noi-dung-co-ban-van-kien/2011/977/Giai-quyet-tot-moi-quan-he-giua-doi-moi-kinh-te-va.aspx.

Zhu Y, Collins N, Webber M, and Benson J (2008) New forms of ownership and human resource practices in Vietnam. *Human Resource Management* 47(1): 157–175.

Part 3

Conclusion

16 Reflections on varieties of union movements and worker representation in the Asia-Pacific region

Byoung-Hoon Lee, Russell D. Lansbury and Sek-Hong Ng

This volume delineates varieties of labour unionism and worker representation in thirteen countries of the Asia-Pacific region, in accordance with an analytical framework devised for cross-country comparison. Labour movements in the Asia-Pacific countries have been confronted with diverse challenges, derived from external constraints and internal weakness, which sometimes interact. The structural power of unions has been hampered by external constraints such as the state-dominated labour politics and fragmented and/or informal labour markets. The associational power of unions has been limited by a set of persistent internal weaknesses, including low union density, decentralised bargaining structures and organisational division. Confronted with external constraints and internal weaknesses, labour movements in the Asia-Pacific countries have made various attempts to strengthen union power and expand worker representation under their specific contextual conditions. Major strategic repertoire of labour movement revitalisation in the Asia-Pacific region is comparable with those adopted by European unions. In the Asia-Pacific countries, unions' partnership is rarely reported in policymaking and corporate governance, while non-union organisations, such as labour advocacy non-governmental organisations (NGOs) and worker centres are very active in representing and organising precarious workers who fall outside the scope of union protection.

Variegated settings for union movements and worker representation

This volume delineates varieties of labour unionism and worker representation in thirteen countries of the Asia-Pacific region, in accordance with an analytical framework devised for cross-country comparison and outlined in the introductory chapter. The framework used five common research questions to comparatively diagnose the current state of union movements and labour activism in each country by examining their historical evolution, major challenges confronting them, their strategic moves to produce meaningful outcomes for revitalisation and theoretical implications for the labour movement literature. A comparative perspective, across time and space, elucidates both similarities and diversities. While intra-regional variations are apparent among labour movements in Asia, they also share elements in common. Our contributing authors have each painstakingly surveyed and documented the nature and evolution of labour movements in their jurisdictions.

The thirteen countries, covered in this volume, are diverse in many respects. Above all, the size of population and markets varies across these countries, which ranges from the mega-states of China and India, to the small city states of Singapore and Hong Kong. According to the World Bank list of economies in 2018, the countries in our book may be classified by their level of economic development into three groups: high-income developed economies: Japan, Australia, Singapore, Hong Kong, South Korea and Taiwan; middle income developing economies: Malaysia, Thailand, Indonesia and the Philippines; and middle income transitional economies: China, India and Vietnam (World Bank, 2017). The historical trajectory of industrialisation and the current state of industrial configurations in these countries are also quite diverse.

The thirteen countries in the Asia-Pacific region which we have examined may also be categorised as a variegated collection of heterogeneous political economies, representing uneven and polymorphic development of market regimes, such as hierarchical market economies and city capitalism (Gomez & De Micheaux, 2017), network market economies (Schneider, 2007), socialist market economies (Sigley, 2006) as well as variants of liberal and coordinated market economies. The classification of these countries as economic variegation goes far beyond the simplified 'varieties of capitalism' scheme, formulated by Hall and Soskice (2001), who clustered Western advanced economies into the dichotomised typology of liberal and coordinated market economies. In addition, historical legacy of late modernisation (including colonisation-cum-decolonisation) and cultural backgrounds had a profound impact on the distinct shaping of state-union relationship and employment relations across these countries. This is exemplified by different levels of maturity of political democracy and the persistent influence of diverse religious traditions such as Confucianism, Islam, Hinduism, Buddhism and Christianity.

As such, the countries covered in this volume provide a diversity of national settings for labour movements which are distinct from those of Western advanced economies. In the concluding chapter, we attempt to compare union movements and worker representation across the thirteen countries and sum up their key characteristics contrasting with those in Western advanced countries. We also address theoretical implications arising from these comparisons.

Major challenges to union movements and worker representation

As discussed by the country chapters in this volume, labour movements in the Asia-Pacific countries have been confronted with diverse challenges, derived from external constraints and internal weakness, which sometimes interact. Some challenges to the labour movements of the Asia-Pacific region are comparable with those of Western advanced countries in Europe and North America, while the other challenges are specific to the labour situation of the Asia-Pacific countries. It is noteworthy that some new challenges are emerging along with mega-trends of socio-economic transformation, such as globalisation, industrial restructuring and the digital revolution. There are also many preexisting challenges which have imposed persistent constraints on union movements and worker representation.

A major external challenge, which is frequently observed in the Asia-Pacific countries, is derived from economic and labour policies adopted by the state in order to constrain union movements in various ways. In many Asia-Pacific countries, unions have been controlled and even suppressed by the state in the process of economic development. Unions in many developing Southeast Asian countries have been constrained from exercising their labour rights to organise by the state's interventionist policy priority to induce foreign investment and promote late industrialisation, including export zones. Unions in the socialist market economies have fallen within the ambit of state control and, as part of the Communist Party apparatus, must represent and administer its labour policy. It is often reported in these country chapters that the state has intervened to prevent unions and workers from protesting against employers' illegal employment practices and forceful union-busting, rather than punishing those employers' misdeeds. Even though some of these countries have been transformed from an authoritarian state regime to political democratisation, employers' anti-union behaviours have continued. Furthermore, the public perception of worker representation, including unionisation, as key human right remains underdeveloped within the entrenched bulwark of paternalistic sociocultural norms, in contrast with some advanced Western economies such as the Nordic countries.

Since the late 1990s, it has been commonly observed that in most Asia-Pacific countries neoliberal economic reforms were driven by the state, including privatisation of the public sector, deregulation of labour markets and liberation of financial markets. These factors led to unions losing their bargaining power and experiencing their organisational coverage stagnating or shrinking. This trend is comparable to what has occurred in many Western advanced countries during the recent decades of neoliberal reforms. Chew and Ryan Tan note, in their country chapter, that the government in Singapore has treated unions as key social partners during the period of economic development and in the recent phase of industrial restructuring. At the same time, the Singapore unions are also viewed by their critics as being too much under the control of the state.

Another important external challenge, which has hindered labour movements in the Asia-Pacific region, is the fragmentation of labour markets and extensive informal sectors. Labour markets in the Asia-Pacific countries are 'balkanised' by various fracture lines, including different ethnic groups and class/caste status (Malaysia and India), employment status and firm size (South Korea, Taiwan and Japan), informality (India, Indonesia, Philippines and Vietnam) and lack of citizenship rights of temporary migrant workers from overseas or domestic rural regions (Australia, China, Singapore and Thailand). Labour market polarisation in most Asia-Pacific countries has been deepening along with the proliferation of precarious workers. These developments have been exacerbated by the expansion of service jobs, digital platform-mediated work interface and the state's labour market flexbilisation policies in many countries of the region. In addition, the majority of the workforce in several countries is employed in the informal sectors, which are excluded from the protection of labour laws and social insurance. This is demonstrated by the relevant International Labour Organisation (ILO) statistics indicating that India (84.7%), Indonesia (72.5%), Philippines (70.1%), Vietnam (68.2%) and Thailand (37.7%) are the countries with largest proportion of workers in the informal labour market. Even in the developed and transitional economies, such as South Korea, Japan, China and Taiwan, precarious and migrant workers are often reported to suffer social exclusion. The increasing fragmentation and persistent informality of labour markets have hindered unions from organising and representing vulnerable workers, who are located outside the primary and formal sectors.

Union movements in the Asia-Pacific countries have several internal weaknesses, when representing the working class, compared with those in advanced Western economies. As revealed in Table 16.1, union density is below 20% in most Asia-Pacific countries and, in particular, below 10% in four Southeast Asian countries (Indonesia 7.0%, Malaysia 8.8%, Philippines 8.7% and Thailand 3.5%). The exceptions are China (44.9%) and two city states (Hong Kong 25.3% and Singapore 21.2%). By contrast with those in

Table 16.1 Union Representation in Asia-Pacific Countries (%)

Country	*Union Density (2015)*	*Collective Bargaining Coverage (2016)*
Australia	15.0	47.1
China	44.9	40.6[3]
Hong Kong	25.3	N/A
India	12.8[5]	N/A
Indonesia	7.0[4]	10.0[7]
Japan	17.4	16.7
South Korea	10.1	11.8[1]
Malaysia	8.8	1.3
Philippines	8.7[2]	1.6
Singapore	21.2	18.1[4]
Taiwan	14.6[6]	N/A
Thailand	3.5	3.1
Vietnam	14.6[5]	N/A

Source: ILOSTAT DB (https://www.ilo.org/ilostat/faces/ilostat-home/home?_adf.ctrl-state=133csinddr_4&_afrLoop=395698269531932#!)
Notes: 1 – 2015 data; 2 – 2014 data; 3 – 2013 data; 4 – 2012 data; 5 – 2011 data; 6 – 2011 data; 7 – 2008 data.

a number of European countries, which have sector-wide bargaining mechanisms, unions in most Asia-Pacific countries have developed within a decentralised enterprise bargaining framework. Even Australia, which used to have a largely centralised industrial relations system, has become increasingly decentralised (Andersen et al., 2017). Hence, as shown in Table 15.1, collective bargaining in Asian countries generally covers only the insiders (union members), or a small proportion of them (in Malaysia and Philippines), within the enterprise. Furthermore, unions in many Asia-Pacific countries are weakened by organisational division and rivalry, derived from political party affiliation, ethnic tensions and contesting identity of unionism. Unified union movements, with a single national centre, are present in several countries, like China, Vietnam, Australia and Japan, but most of them have experienced the loss of political leverage and organisational power over policymaking and collective bargaining. Factors influencing these trends include discontent among rank-and-file membership with bureaucratic unionism in the socialist market economies or state-led neoliberal reforms in the developed market economies.

Building on theoretical concepts of working-class power, derived from Wright (2000), the power of union movements in the Asia-Pacific countries has been constrained in various ways. The structural power of unions has been hampered by external constraints such as the state-dominated labour politics as well as by fragmented and/or informal labour markets. The associational power of unions has been limited by a set of persistent internal weaknesses, including low union density, decentralised bargaining structures and organisational division within the unions. Under these circumstances, union movements in Asia-Pacific countries have experienced much harder times than what Gumbrell-McCormick and Hyman (2013) describe as the current state of trade unions in Western Europe.

Strategic repertoires for labour movement revitalisation

Confronted with external constraints and internal weaknesses, labour movements in the Asia-Pacific countries have made various attempts to strengthen union power and expand worker representation under their specific contextual conditions, as addressed in the country chapters. Table 16.2 illustrates examples of strategic repertoire which has assisted labour movements to gain meaningful outcomes from their attempts at revitalisation. Major elements of strategic repertoire adopted for revitalising labour movements in the Asia-Pacific region appear to be comparable with those adopted by European unions, outlined by Frege and Kelly (2003) in their 'varieties of unions' analysis.

In many Asia-Pacific countries, unions have launched organising campaigns targeting unorganised workers, particularly those who are in non-regular and informal employment. While the campaigns in some countries (such as Australia, China, Singapore and India) have been driven by a central union federation at the national level, organising campaigns in some

Table 16.2 Examples of Labour Movement Revitalisation in Asia-Pacific Countries

Country	*Renewal Action by Union Movement and Other Worker Representative Organisations*
Australia	• Nation-wide organising campaigns since the adoption of formal ACTU policy in 1999 • Union mergers since late 1980s (reducing the number of unions from 299 to 52) • 'Your Rights at Work' campaigns in 2005–2007, by the ACTU, contributed to the shift of political power and election of a labour government in 2007
China	• The ACFTU campaign for unionising Fortune 500 companies increased union density in major FDI companies to over 80% by 2008 • Democratic election of worker representatives has been driven by wildcat strikes
Hong Kong	• Unions have used social campaigning to promote non-bargaining activities (e.g., mutual aid, skill formation networking, cultural projects) and the enforcement of minimum wage law for precarious workers
India	• The central union's organising campaigns for informal workers resulted in increases in union membership from 12.3 million in 1989 to 24.6 million in 2002 • Joint efforts with Global Union Federations (e.g., IndustriALL, IUF) for pressured MNCs to recognise local unions and to negotiate collective agreements • Unorganised worker organisations (UWO) and transgressive protest repertoires were used to represent workers in platform-mediated employment
Indonesia	• Industrial unions used a centralised organisational structure as well as gaining resources from enterprise units • Mobilisation of 'factory-raids' tactics and local minimum wage negotiations • Unions' active involvement in political campaigns and agitation for social security reforms by forming a joint national council of the three confederations and building union-NGO alliances • International unions (including ITUC) and NGOs engaged in the organising independent unions
Japan	• Targeted union organising of non-regular workers at enterprise and community levels • Merger of enterprise unions to respond to corporate restructuring • Pressure placed on Japanese MNCs to adopt OECD guideline and sign a global framework agreement
Malaysia	• Formation of multi-state industry unions (from the existing enterprise unionism in 2010)
Philippines	• Unions collaborated with progressive academics and CSOs to organise non-regular and informal workers in pursuit of social movement unionism • Solidarity economy movement led by labour NGOs and people's organisations in order to gain representation for domestic/home-based workers and the tribal rural poor
Singapore	• General branch membership gained non-bargaining benefits, thereby producing a sustained increase in NTUC membership • Tripartite partnership for worker empowerment of life-long learning and fair employment practices
South Korea	• Organisational transformation from enterprise unionism to industry unionism (industry unions' membership grew from 10% in 1996 to 55% in 2016) • Alternative organising of precarious workers (i.e., age-cohort unionism & community worker centres)

Country	*Renewal Action by Union Movement and Other Worker Representative Organisations*
Taiwan	• Self-rescue organisations of redundant workers initiated by labour advocacy groups (Lau-Tuan)
Thailand	• Labour solidarity committees comprised 29 organisations of unions and NGOs and provided a voice in labour policy making • Union area groups formed to jointly organise and represent workers in industrial zones • Civil labour advocacy network (i.e., Homenet Thailand) representing informal/self-employed and migrant workers
Vietnam	• Grassroots movement placed pressure on the socialist government to grant legal recognition of independent unions • VGCL's involvement in supporting 'black leaders' of wildcat strikes

other countries (such as Japan, South Korea and Thailand) have been mobilised by grass-roots activism at the community level. Some strategic approaches adopted by the organising campaigns are innovative and produce meaningful achievements, such as Fortune 500 unionisation (in China), age-cohort union movements (in South Korea), general branch membership with non-bargaining benefits (in Singapore) and multi-union collaborations, called union area groups, in industrial zones (in Thailand).

Unions in several countries have undertaken transformations of their organisational structures in various ways. These are exemplified by union mergers in Australia; centralised industry unionisation in South Korea, Malaysia and Indonesia; and corporate group unionisation in Japan. In the two socialist market economies, China and Vietnam, as grass-roots activism and wildcat strikes have proliferated during the recent decade, prompting meaningful changes to the state-dominated union movement. In Vietnam, independent unions, not affiliated with the official national centre, were granted legal recognition, while democratic elections of worker representative at some disputed workplaces were permitted in China.

In some Asia-Pacific countries, unions have made strategic moves towards the coalition-building with civil society organisations (CSOs) for organising and representing precarious workers. Positive examples of unions' coalition-building with NGOs include union-CSO networking with social movement unionism in the Philippines and labour solidarity committees in Thailand. In India and Indonesia, solidarity networking with global union federations and international NGOs has occurred to promote the organising of unions and pressuring of multinational corporations to recognise these unions. Another interesting case of international solidarity is in Japan where unions have succeeded in persuading some Japanese global companies to adopt Organisation for Economic Co-operation and Development (OECD) guidelines and global framework agreements.

Unions in some countries have launched successful campaigns for socio-political action, either by themselves or in alliance with NGOs. The 'Your Rights at Work' campaigns by Australian unions, for example, were influential in the defeat of the conservative government in the 2007 national elections. Unions in Indonesia became actively involved in political campaigns to promote pro-labour social security reforms by forming a joint union council as well as union-NGO alliances. Unions in Hong Kong initiated social campaigns to enforce minimum wages and promote non-bargaining activities (such as mutual aid, skill formation networking and cultural events) for precarious workers.

Partnership is treated as a strategic repertoire for union movement revitalisation in Western 'varieties of unionism' literature, but it is rarely reported in the Asia-Pacific countries, where the state and employers have tended to exclude unions from influencing policymaking and corporate governance. The only exception is Singapore, where tripartite partnership has been developed for empowering workforce by life-long learning and fair employment practices, but with close government involvement. Unions in Indonesia and South Korea have often employed militant tactics, such as factory raids and sit-down strikes, rather than seeking labour-management partnership, which they insist is difficult to achieve in a climate of anti-unionism.

Non-union organisations, such as labour advocacy NGOs and worker centres in several Asia-Pacific countries (such as India, the Philippines, South Korea, Taiwan and Thailand) are very active in representing and organising precarious workers who fall outside the scope of union protection. The solidarity economy movement led by labour NGOs and peoples' organisations in the Philippines, 'self-rescue' organisations of redundant workers initiated by labour advocacy groups (Lau-Tau) in Taiwan and non-regular labour centres in South Korea are notable examples of non-union worker representation. The active presence of non-union labour activism to represent unorganised workers in many Asia-Pacific countries might be associated with the limited coverage of organisational protection by enterprise-based unionism.

The five strategies of union movement revitalisation in Frege and Kelly's VoU framework – organising, organisational transformation, sociopolitical campaigns, coalition-building and international solidarity – are often observed in the Asia-Pacific countries. The specific forms of these strategies adopted by labour movements of the Asia-Pacific region, however, are somehow distinct from their Western counterparts. Moreover, it is apparent that labour-management partnership is rarely utilised, while non-union labour activism to achieve a form of worker representation is prevalent in the Asia-Pacific region. This finding may be explained by the vulnerable state of union movements in the Asia-Pacific countries, which have not obtained sufficient democratic influence in the institutional settings of political economy and labour-management relations, compared with unions in many Western advanced economies.

Some theoretical reflections on variegated labour movements in Asia-Pacific countries

What theoretical implications can be drawn from this comparative review of labour movements in the thirteen Asia-Pacific countries? Given the heterogeneity of national political economies and cultural-cum-historical backgrounds in these countries, it is not feasible to simply classify them into variants of the 'variety of capitalism' typology. Rather, these countries should be viewed as a collection of variegated national regimes, distinct from the Western advanced economies. This supports the critique by Peck and Theodore (2007) concerning the theoretical limitation of the 'variety of capitalism' perspective. In this vein, a comparative review of diverse labour movements in the Asia-Pacific region may help broaden and refine the analytical lens through which to view the 'varieties of unionism' framework, which has focused mainly on Western economies. The analyses of unions and labour movements in thirteen countries of the Asia-Pacific region, undertaken in this book, demonstrates the need to expand academic research into unions and labour movements beyond the geographical boundary of Western advanced countries.

As noted in chapters by Ng, the late Keith Thurley provided the insightful concept of 'Asian unionism', based on his decoding the unique character of unions in some Asia countries, including Hong Kong. Thurley described Asian unionism as being parochial and malleable in its ability to represent workers' interests. He also argued that unions in many Asian countries utilised 'patriotic sentiments' to collaborate with the state and capital for advancing the national economy, rather than being oriented towards class consciousness (Thurley, 1988; and cited by Ng). Thurley's conception of Asia unionism is an intriguing attempt to capture the distinct orientation of Asian unions, which is contrasted with Western counterparts. However, Thurley's concept of Asia unionism is based mainly on East Asia countries, which historically share the culture-bound contexts of Chinese Confucian tradition. Hence, it is debatable whether his theoretical model can be validly applied to Southeast and South Asian countries, which have quite different cultural backgrounds and industrial relations settings to countries in East Asia. Furthermore, even in some East Asia countries, such as South Korea, Taiwan and Hong Kong, the union movements are divided and some newer unions have displayed a confrontational or recalcitrant attitude towards both the state and employers, which deviates from Thurley's conception of Asian unionism.

There appear to be many varieties of labour movements in the Asia-Pacific region. These include state-dominated unionism, political unionism, business unionism, social partnership unionism, militant unionism and NGO-style advocacy activism. Hence, it is not possible to 'force' labour movements in the Asia-Pacific region into a specific cluster within the 'varieties of unionism' framework. However, the six categories of revitalisation strategies cited by Frege and Kelly (2003) are useful for examining comparable strategic moves by labour movements in these countries. It is also difficult to specify a theoretical model, based on some of Asia-Pacific countries, and generalise it to the other countries. Given the co-existence of diverse labour movements in the Asia-Pacific region, it is necessary to adopt a more 'nuanced' approach to comparative analysis by considering contextual factors (such as history and culture, political economy and industrial relations institutions) in a holistic manner rather than attempting to build a mega-theory of Asia-Pacific unionism, as suggested by Cooke in her China chapter.

In a nuanced comparative perspective, three factors which constrain labour movements in the Asia-Pacific region, to a large extent, are the state, market forces and religious traditions. First, the state continues to be the key actor in the Asia-Pacific region as it shapes the regulatory setting of employment relations and labour associations. It does this by pursuing multi-policy objectives of accumulation, pacification and legitimation in the process of economic development and social stabilisation, as emphasised by Ford and Gillan (2016) as well as by Collins in the Vietnam chapter. Second, the growing dominance of market forces, not only prompted by the globalisation but also driven by the government's deregulation policy, is commonly observed in many Asia-Pacific countries. These factors influence the convergence of industrial relations towards a neoliberal direction and drive labour movements to the margin. This is comparable to the argument made by Baccaro and Howell (2011) in their recent comparative research of Western European countries. Third, it is often reported in many Asian countries that the oriental religions, such as Confucianism, Buddhism, Islam and Hinduism, have a persistent effect of internalising hierarchical collectivism among workers and encouraging their psychological dependence on paternalistic company management (as noted in the Hong Kong and Thailand chapters) and the moral state (as noted in the Taiwan chapter), thereby inhibiting the growth of independent union movements and undermining workers' labour rights consciousness. This may be contrasted to the impact of the Protestantism on capitalistic work ethics in Western countries, as addressed by a classical work of Max Weber (2001).

Finally, two more points may be noted for future research. First, Bechter and her colleagues (2012) indicate that 'methodological nationalism' used to compare labour movements across countries often ignores cross-sector/segment differences within a specific country. In light of segmented labour markets and the extensive presence of unorganised workforce in many Asia-Pacific countries, such within-the country comparison is of particular significance. Second, the Asia-Pacific region is one of the most dynamic geographical areas on the globe. Labour movements in this region are not exceptional, as exemplified by the remarkable rise of Indonesian union movements and the sudden fall of Filipino unionism. Thus, it is necessary to examine the transformative dynamics of how political economy regimes and labour movements across the Asia-Pacific countries interact to create changes by going beyond 'snap-shot' style comparisons, as underlined by Wad in his Malaysia chapter.

Our comparative analysis of the national case studies of unions and worker representation in the thirteen countries of the Asia-Pacific region can be viewed as a refined application of the 'variety of unionism' schema, in that it denotes a spectrum similar to the varied forms of Western unionism. However, such a schema is still inadequate insofar that it fails to explain the peculiar characteristics of labour movements in the Oriental region as well as cross-national variations in non-Western workers' organisations. As noted in Chapter 2, the next step in the study of trade unions and labour movements in Asia could be to develop a theoretical framework to identify and explain the commonalities of non-Western worker movements, as well as classifying varieties of the Asian labour movements in a taxonomic form. We hope that our volume may stimulate future research on unions and labour movements in the Asia-Pacific region.

References

Andersen, S.K., S. Kaine, and R. Lansbury (2017), "Decentralised Bargaining in Denmark and Australia: Voluntarism versus Legal Regulation", *Australian Bulletin of Labour* 43(1): 45–70.

Baccaro, L. and C. Howell (2011), "A Common Neoliberal Trajectory: The Transformation of Industrial Relations in Advanced Capitalism", *Politics & Society* 39(4): 521–563.

Brechter, B., B. Brandi, and G. Meardi (2012), "Sectors or Countries? Typologies and Levels of Analysis in Comparative Industrial Relations", *European Journal of Industrial Relations* 18(3): 185–202.

Ford, M. and M. Gillan (2016), "Employment Relations and the State in Southeast Asia", *Journal of Industrial Relations* 58(2): 167–182.

Frege, C. and J. Kelly (2003), "Union Revitalization Strategy in Comparative Perspective", *European Journal of Industrial Relations* 9(1): 7–24.

Gomez, E. and E. De Micheaux (2017), "Diversity of Southeast Asian Capitalisms: Evolving State-Business Relations in Malaysia", *Journal of Contemporary Asia* 47(5): 792–814.

Hall, P. and D. Soskice (2001), Varieties of Capitalism: The Institutional Foundations of Competitive Advantage, Oxford: Oxford University Press.

Gumbrell-McCormick, R. and R. Hyman (2013), *Trade Unions in Western Europe: Hard Times, Hard Choices*, Oxford: Oxford University Press.

Hall, P. and D. Soskice (2001), *Varieties of Capitalism: The Institutional Foundations of Competitive Advantage*, Oxford: Oxford University Press.

Peck, J. and N. Theodore (2007), "Variegated Capitalism", *Progress in Human Geography* 31(6): 731–772.

Schneider, B. (2007), "Comparing Capitalisms: Liberal, Coordinated, Network, and Hierarchical Varieties", (mimeo).

Sigley, G. (2006). "Chinese Governmentalities: Government, Governance and the Socialist Market Economy", *Economy and Society* 35(4): 487–508.

Thurley, K. (1988), "Trade Unionism in Asian Countries", In Jao, Y.C., Levin, D., Ng, S., and Sinn, E. (eds.), *Labour Movement in a Changing Society: The*

Experiences of Hong Kong, Hong Kong: Centre of Asian Studies, University of Hong Kong, 24–31.

Weber, M. (2001), *The Protestant Ethics and the Spirit of Capitalism*, New York: Routledge.

World Bank (2017), *World Development Indicators 2017*, Washington, DC. https://openknowledge.worldbank.org/handle/10986/26447

Wright, E. (2000), "Working-class Power, Capitalist-class Interests, and Class Compromise", *American Journal of Sociology* 105(4): 957–1002.

Index

Note: **Bold** page numbers refer to tables; *italic* page numbers refer to figures and page numbers followed by "n" denote endnotes.